PROF. A.J. STRATHERN

The Dynamics
of Changing Rituals

Toronto Studies in Religion

Donald Wiebe
General Editor

Vol. 29

PETER LANG
New York • Washington, D.C./Baltimore • Bern
Frankfurt am Main • Berlin • Brussels • Vienna • Oxford

The Dynamics
of Changing Rituals

The Transformation of Religious Rituals
within Their Social and Cultural Context

Jens Kreinath, Constance Hartung,
& Annette Deschner, Editors

PETER LANG
New York • Washington, D.C./Baltimore • Bern
Frankfurt am Main • Berlin • Brussels • Vienna • Oxford

Library of Congress Cataloging-in-Publication Data

The dynamics of changing rituals : the transformation of religious
rituals within their social and cultural context / edited by Jens Kreinath,
Constance Hartung, Annette Deschner.
p. cm. — (Toronto studies in religion; v. 29)
Includes bibliographical references.
1. Ritual. 2. Rites and ceremonies. 3. Religion and sociology.
I. Kreinath, Jens. II. Hartung, Constance. III. Deschner, Annette.
IV. Series.
BL600.D96   390—dc21   2003011715
ISBN 0-8204-6826-6
ISSN 8756-7385

Bibliographic information published by **Die Deutsche Bibliothek.**
Die Deutsche Bibliothek lists this publication in the "Deutsche
Nationalbibliografie"; detailed bibliographic data is available
on the Internet at http://dnb.ddb.de/.

The paper in this book meets the guidelines for permanence and durability
of the Committee on Production Guidelines for Book Longevity
of the Council of Library Resources.

© 2004 Peter Lang Publishing, Inc., New York
275 Seventh Avenue, 28th Floor, New York, NY 10001
www.peterlangusa.com

Printed in Germany

Table of Contents

Acknowledgments

Back in 1998, when we as a group of graduate students began organizing an international symposium on the dynamics of changing rituals for the *Graduiertenkolleg 'Religion und Normativität*,' we did not expect that the symposium and its key concept 'dynamics' would have the impact on the formation and institutional establishment of a whole new field of ritual studies it has had. In considering the various requirements in organizing an international symposium, we tried to compose an exposé that could bring together the various interests of our fellow graduate students, our professors, and a number of renowned scholars from different fields of research while focusing on a very specific issue that promised to result in new empirical and theoretical insights. As it turned out, we succeeded in hitting on an issue that met with such a resonance that extended far beyond the *Graduiertenkolleg* and the symposium we organized.

It goes without saying that the publication of this volume with contributions by scholars from a wide range of disciplines would not have been possible without the support and critique of many individuals who passionately launched and improved the outcome of this present book. For the most part, the contributions to this book stem from an international symposium held at the *Internationales Wissenschaftsforum Heidelberg*, October 28–31, 1999. The symposium was organized by a number of graduate and post-graduate students from the *Graduiertenkolleg 'Religion und Normativität'* under the supervision of its academic board of professors and lecturers, which at that time was headed by Gregor Ahn from the *Institut für Religionswissenschaft*, each of whom we would like to thank here. For their collaboration and their contribution, we would also like to thank the interdisciplinary working-group *'Ritualdynamik*,' which was founded shortly after we had invited quite a number of scholars to the symposium.

For the realization of this symposium, our thanks go first and foremost to the *Deutsche Forschungsgemeinschaft* and the *Stiftung Universität Heidelberg* for their generous financial support, which made it possible for us to invite a good number of well-known specialists on a broad range of topics bearing on the 'dynamics of changing rituals.' We also extend our thanks in particular to the *Internationales Wissenschaftsforum Heidelberg*, especially to its directors, Michael Welker and Theresa Reiter, and their student assistants, for providing logistical support and hospitality during the symposium.

For coordinating the symposium, our special thanks go to Silja Joneleit-Oesch. Moreover, we also would like to thank all the participants in this symposium for their inspiring enthusiasm, which helped us to make this event an overwhelming success.

The publication of this volume would not have been possible without the financial assistance of the *Deutsche Forschungsgemeinschaft*. We also extend our thanks to Theo Sundermeier and Jan Assmann for their support, as well as to Marion Steinicke for coordinating the first steps of our editorial process. We also would like to thank Elaine Griffiths for translating the introduction and for proofreading most of the non-native contributions. We would like to extend our special thanks to Jan Snoek, who put his editorial competence at our disposal and assisted us with passionate commitment, which included establishing contact with Donald Wiebe. Moreover, our thanks go to Marcus Brainard for his editorial advice and helpful comments during the final stages of this project. For covering postal costs, we would like to thank the *Institut for Religionswissenschaft*.

We also would like to thank the staff of Peter Lang for their tireless and accommodating support during the various stages of the production process and their helpful advice on editorial issues. Finally, we would like to express our gratitude to Donald Wiebe not only for accepting this volume in his series, but also for carefully reading the final manuscript and giving us his encouraging comments.

Introduction

Jens Kreinath, Constance Hartung,
Annette Deschner

During the last few decades, rituals have received much attention from a large number of disciplines not restricted to the humanities and social sciences. Recent research in ritual studies has shown that rituals are not at all static, but, on the contrary, more often subject to dynamic changes, even if their participants continue to claim that they have been the same since time immemorial. When do rituals change? When do they change accidentally and when are they changed intentionally? Are there particular kinds of rituals that are more stable or unstable than others? Which elements of rituals are liable to change and which are relatively stable? Who has the power or agency to change rituals intentionally? Who decides whether or not to accept a change? With the contributions to this volume, these questions have opened up a new dimension in the field of ritual studies: the dynamics of changing rituals.

The present studies, which explore this new subject of ritual studies as it has been developed thus far, can be ordered according to four thematic constellations: (1) General Theoretical Approaches, (2) Transfer and Transformation of Ritual Contexts, (3) Recursivity and Innovation, and (4) Performance, Media, Script, and Representation. Scholars were invited to address various aspects of these categories in their lectures at the symposium, and it is these lectures that formed the basis for this volume.

An introduction and initial look at the emerging focus on the dynamics of changing rituals is given in the contributions by Don Handelman and Jan G. Platvoet, who present *general theoretical approaches* to the analysis of changing rituals.

A further group of papers, which address the theme of *transfer and transformation of ritual contexts,* deals with whether, and how, a change of context entails or results in a change of rituals. This issue is taken up in the papers by Susanne Schröter, Anette Rein, Alexander Henn, Peter Weber, William D. Furley, and Michael Stausberg. Their articles cover a broad geographic range and give a complex analysis of transfer and transformation processes that can arise not only through cultural interaction but also through different group interests within their various social and political contexts.

The dimension of *recursivity and innovation* is addressed in the contributions by James W. Fernandez, Achsah Guibbory, Patricia B. Ebrey, Martin Gaenszle, Tzvi Abusch, Andreas Odenthal, and Matthias Jung. They analyze changes in rituals arising through the modification of ritual practices. With the innovation of rituals, the group performing the ritual relates itself to its tradition by explicitly responding to the emergence of current demands. Existing traditions—not necessarily part of a ritual—can be taken up when a ritual is innovated. Recursivity, by contrast, is intended not to introduce a new ritual practice but to be a strategic attempt to return to the tradition of a practice no longer used but remembered as an older, more original. The recursive change of ritual is achieved through a modernization of an existing ritual practice which aims to re-contextualize older, revived ritual traditions.

Another aspect of the academic study of changing rituals is the analysis of the thematic constellation of *performance, media, script,* and *representation.* The script is made up of the rules followed by a ritual. The performance is the carrying out of a ritual on a given occasion, which largely but never fully follows or embodies the rules of the script. For this reason no performance is like any other. If the modification of a ritual is attributed to the fact that a performance changes through its repetition, one is justified in speaking of a variation in ritual (James W. Fernandez, Alexander Henn, and Martin Gaenszle). But the ritual performance can also impact on and transform the script of a ritual (Patricia B. Ebrey and Peter Weber). Conditions for such changes in the script are often cultural contacts or migration processes (Anette Rein, Alexander Henn, and Michael Stausberg). In the interaction between script and performance, however, the change of ritual performance may be attributed to a change in the script (Martin Gaenszle, Matthias Jung, and Andreas Odenthal). The media in which rituals are communicated and perceived can play an important role in the connection between ritual performance and representation. The media by which rituals are framed not only change the forms of perception and communication in rituals (Günter Thomas); they also transform the meta-communicative frame of the interaction between actors and spectators (Klaus-Peter Köpping). Thus, by means of the analysis of the interplay between actors and spectators, it becomes possible to question, for example, the distinction between ritual and theatrical performances (Dietrich Harth and Anette Rein).

Through the introduction of the dynamics of changing rituals, the selection of the present articles attempts to place new accents on the research in ritual studies. Former research—at least in the history of religions and social and cultural anthropology—has mainly emphasized the description and analysis of religious worldviews and historical motifs or symbols and social relations within the context of the respective ritual traditions. The approach to the dynamics of changing rituals, however, seeks to encourage an inquiry into the social and cultural facets and consequences of ritual performances. The basis of a ritual should not be sought only in its roots in religious traditions or social relations; one should also inquire into its actual shifts and negotiations as they appear in the practice and performance of rituals. Consequently, this new approach to the dynamics of changing rituals can challenge the established pattern of research in ritual studies, which arose from academic reflection on the static and enduring aspects of rituals. This new focus in the research on rituals is intended to raise questions about the multifarious modalities for the emergence of change in rituals. In this context, there are indications of dynamic features in ritual changes, as well as in their respective social and cultural contexts, that may be responsible for the modifications and transformations of ritual practice.

A change affecting the whole area of ritual practice can therefore—as shown by the categories introduced above—lie in the ritual itself and also in its social and cultural contexts. On the other hand, change can also induce persistence by guaranteeing the survival of a ritual tradition through a change in practice. Despite the great variety of the case studies, the view generally shared by the authors in this volume is that while the 'framing' of a ritual—which is formed through its performance, media, script, and representation—constitutes the ritual's identity, it is not static at all but constantly undergoes change.

Contributions

A general theoretical starting-point is provided by Don Handelman's article "Re-Framing Ritual." Handelman transfers the scientific concept of the 'double helix' of the moebius ring, in which the inner and outer sides intertwine dynamically, to the description of rituals. This allows one to recognize that they can change in every performance. The idea that rituals are determined or influenced by an outside world that is clearly set apart from the ritual's dynamic is replaced by the concept of a 'dynamic framing' or interweaving in which the content and elements of ritual constantly interact with the various socio-cultural environments involved.

On the one hand, rituals can change in their performance and thereby react to changes in the respective social and cultural contexts. On the other hand, new rituals can arise as a consequence of rapid social changes. The fact that both the frame and the content of rituals can be constantly renewed during the performance is clarified by James W. Fernandez in his contribution on "Contemporary Carnival (*carnaval*) in Asturias: Visual Figuration as a 'Ritual' of Parodic Release and Democratic Revitalization." Fernandez considers one of the preconditions for renegotiating the meaning of carnival in its playfulness by which the actors may allude to the globalization process and the corresponding opportunities for cultural pluralism. It is this playfulness that, according to Fernandez, may lead to the revitalization of local traditions in Asturias.

In "Rituals of Rebellion – Rebellion as a Ritual: A Theory Reconsidered," Susanne Schröter takes up the classical approach of Gluckman's theory of ritual rebellion and considers the interpretation of conflict management in African societies from a new theoretical perspective. Whereas 'rituals of rebellion' are commonly seen as oriented to the content of social order in that they sometimes reverse the social order in ritual practice, Schröter, by contrast, takes new case studies into account that inquire about an articulation of resistance and rebellion that was originally not intended as a ritual but was ultimately performed as such.

Rituals are not just changed by their performance; they also change by being written down and given a literary form. In the article "Communion, National Community, and the Challenge of Radical Religion in Seventeenth-Century England," Achsah Guibbory makes a case for how an imaginary national community was evoked through the literary handling of the Eucharist in post-Reformation England.

In "Artaud's Holy Theater: A Case for Questioning the Relations between Ritual and Stage Performance," Dietrich Harth starts from the impact Artaud had on the practical and theoretical notions of 'theater aesthetics' and traces the line from Artaud's attraction to fragmentary and double-thinking to his notion of 'ritual theater.' After summarizing Artaud's notion of theater, Harth arrives at the conclusion that ritual and theatrical performance do not differ in form. The differentiation is determined more by viewers' expectations and their estimation of the performative event.

On the example of a Balinese temple dance, Anette Rein demonstrates in her "Balinese Temple Dances and Ritual Transformations in the Process of Modernization" the extent to which a ritual can be adjusted to the expectations of spectators—in this case, tourists—without thereby losing its ritual functions for the performers. Rein illustrates how transfer processes can affect the interpretation of a ritual and ultimately lead to such variations that one is compelled to raise questions about whether the performance of Balinese dance is to be regarded as a ritual or as having been transformed into a theatrical performance.

The question of ritual transformation is also essential to Klaus-Peter Köpping's essay "Failure of Performance or Passage to the Acting Self? Mishima's Suicide between Ritual and Theater." Yet this transformation does not occur as a result of cultural interaction but as a result of a clash of different group interests and expectations. The dramatic staging of the Seppuku-rituals by the Japanese writer Mishima fails, since the spectators do not consider this to be a ritual. Mishima instrumentalizes the ceremonial killing in order to point up the moral decadence of Japanese society, but in so doing, the frame of the ritual performance dissolves: it is felt by those present to be a farce because in their eyes the main actor no longer is able to personify authentically the traditional values connected with the ritual act of suicide.

While in the case of Mishima's suicide a ritual community does not feel itself to be such, Günter Thomas enlarges in his essay, "Changing Media – Changing Rituals: Media Rituals and the Transformation of Physical Presence," on how a disembodied ritual community constitutes itself through ritualized television behavior, following its own liturgical order determined by the media programming. Thomas therefore focuses his analysis on the transformation of the relationship between presence and representation, as well as between perception and communication.

"Changing Media – Changing Rituals": under different conditions this title could also have been used for Patricia B. Ebrey's paper, "The Incorporation of Portraits into Chinese Ancestral Rites." She shows how the reception of Buddhist art has affected Chinese ancestor-cult and the presence of ancestors has concentrated more and more on embodying them as portraits due to a shift in the modes of visual perception. Yet it is not just a matter of changing the media in rituals: this leads generally to a new version of the script for performing the ancestral rites by transforming the ritual through the introduction of new media for representation.

Besides changes in aesthetic customs, rituals can also be varied through linguistic modifications. As Martin Gaenszle demonstrates in his "Transgenerational Changes: The Social Process of Transmitting Oral Ritual Texts among the Rai in East Nepal" on the example of the oral transmission of ritual competence, however, there are limits to these variations. While a certain degree of modification is considered a guarantee of ritual competence and authority, far-reaching changes in ritual among the Rai have to be negotiated with the ancestors and to be legitimized by them.

Fundamental shifts in meaning within a ritual are discussed by Alexander Henn in "Politics of Acculturation: The Dynamics of Hindu-Christian Ritual in Goa, India" in view of the Hindu New Year festival *zāgor*. He argues that rituals can have a different meaning for the actors than the spectators are led to believe. On the example of the censorship of the Catholic Church and its influence on the Hindu rituals during colonialism, Henn illustrates how the Catholic ritual practice was adopted, yet coded in a complex way with other meanings and combined with other performative genres so as to undermine the strategy of ritual acculturation by the Catholic Church in a lasting way.

In the ritual of the New Year festival the change of meaning and its coding takes place progressively by a shift in the communicative situation of the ritual performances and not through the direct intervention in the script by transforming the ritual's function. The latter, by contrast, is the cause of the dynamic processes in the rituals described by Peter Weber in "Shifts in Place and Meaning: The History of Two Cult Centers in Pre-Colonial Tanzania." Weber emphasizes the identity-giving function of cultic centers and their importance for the origin of ritual networks and the establishment of political power.

Along similar lines, William D. Furley describes in his article on "Athens and Delos in the Fifth Century B.C.E.: Ritual in a World of Shifting Allegiances" how the instrumentalization of a ritual for political interests and strategies transforms its meaning and function and how the participation in a ritual may have become a political statement.

On the example of ancient sorcery, Tzvi Abusch discusses the process of implementing ritual practices in "Considerations when Killing a Witch: Developments in Exorcistic Attitudes to Witchcraft in Mesopotamia." Sorcery, which originally belonged to popular Mesopotamian culture and had no negative connotation, was transformed on a symbolic level through its adaptation in the temple cult, which was accompanied by a process of demonizing witches.

The change in socio-cultural conditions may entail modifications of ritual practice on an institutional level and be supported by strategies of ritual integration. As Andreas Odenthal shows in "Ritual between Tradition and Change: The Paradigm Shift of the Second Vatican Council's Liturgical Reform," the latter can be considered as a paradigm shift in the history of the Catholic Church insofar as it takes into account the social and theological changes. The reinterpretation of religious rituals initiated by the church precedes a change in attitude towards rituals on the part of actors and participants. The liturgical reform can therefore be seen as the attempt to integrate the antinomian tendencies of society into the ritual practice of the church.

From a different perspective, Matthias Jung also takes up the issue of liturgical reform after Vatican II. In "Expressive Appropriateness and Pluralism: The Example of Catholic Liturgy after Vatican II" he sees such reform as resulting from an interaction of the Catholic Church with the conditions of religious pluralism in democratic societies. Jung regards the life world in modern societies as a 'form of expressive appropriateness' where in ritual the modern identity of congregational members is to be merged with traditional views. The newfound ritual identity is reflected in the reorganization of church rituals.

Besides examples of institutional changes of a ritual tradition, there is a number of organizational and contextual changes that can be discerned in ritual practice. In "Patterns of Ritual Change among Parsi-Zoroastrians in Recent Times" Michael Stausberg describes the forms of changes that can be found in the performance of older Zoroastrians rituals. Due to the socio-economic contexts of the Zoroastrian community, rituals have to be restructured also on the organizational level. He argues that if in a religious community the need for a religious profile emerges, new rituals may be introduced.

In view of the variety of ritual forms and their academic interpretations, one may ask whether the traditional view of ritual as repetitive religious behavior is not primarily due to the cultural self-identity of the researchers. In his theoretical article "Ritual as War: On the Need to De-Westernize the Concept," Jan G. Platvoet illustrates the extent to which research categories in the history of religions are contextual. Moreover, he argues for an ethological approach in ritual theory in order to describe more appropriately the dynamic inherent in rituals. In more recent ritual theory he discerns three shifts: first, from an exclusively religious to an inclusively ethological definition; second, from the thesis of an integrative function of rituals for society towards a theory of 'redemptive hegemony'; and, third, from the proposition of covert violence in rituals to the assumption that even in Western societies rituals can also appear to have a violent, aggressive, and destructive social impact.

The comparison of different dynamics of changing rituals in different cultures—which pervades all the essays in this collection—makes clear how important it will be for ritual studies in the future to form a more complex descriptive matrix for the theoretical issues involved. As Jens Kreinath argues in his "Theoretical Afterthoughts," timelessness, immutability, and stasis cannot do justice to the analysis of the dynamics of changing rituals. Rather, he claims that research must broaden its scope to include such issues as change and variation, modification and transformation with regard to the aspects of change in function, form, meaning, and performance. As he sums up, the authors of this collection, who—with their differing approaches and disciplines—succeed in offering a broad range of perspectives showing the diverse ways in which the dynamics of changing rituals can inspire further scholarly inquiry.

Re-Framing Ritual

Don Handelman

Framing is a central problem in understanding how rituals are organized within themselves and how they relate to the realities outside themselves. In Batesonian terms, the framing of ritual is meta-communicative. The frame enables the shift from one reality to another, from the profane or mundane to that of ritual. The frame of a ritual communicates how that ritual is to be perceived and assimilated by those who enter into it. Ritual frames are constituted by meta-communication—indeed, they are meta-communication. In Batesonian terms, meta-communication is both the separation and the linkage between the world within ritual and the world outside this. The meta-message of a ritual frame shifts us into another mode of perception, cognition, and feeling with regard to whatever is within the frame. The frame may communicate a meta-message, like that of *This is ritual*, thereby shifting modes of perception with regard to what is within the frame; and, too, the meta-message, *Let us believe*, to orientate participants to that which will occur within ritual. Because the frame itself constitutes a meta-level of communication, the relationship between the frame and the 'content' it encloses is hierarchical and lineal—it is the frame that communicates how its content should be experienced and processed by participants.

In my terms, ritual frames are constituted by the epistemological intent of the meta-level towards that which it encloses and contains. Since the existence of framing is a problem in epistemology, the frame is often *asking*, as it were, how its meta-messages should be applied to whatever is inside it. Framing, then, is neither automatic nor mechanistic. If this is so, then (unlike the Batesonian template) frames vary in their rigidity and self-containment; and even an imperative meta-message, like that of *This is ritual*, is not seamlessly self-referential, but may be negotiated.

The above suggests that the conceptualization of framing needs to be loosened. Framing continues to be a useful idea through which to discuss whether, and in which ways, ritual is separated from and is linked to other cultural realities. Yet this can be actualized only if we rethink, in analytical terms, how rituals are organized within themselves, rather than assuming either that ritual is necessarily an utterly different reality from the mundane, or that it is not. My argument is intended as a small step in this direction.

Beginning with a critique of lineal framing, I continue by suggesting that framing may be thought of as much fuzzier. In closing, I discuss one alternative formulation—that of moebius framing.

A Critique of Lineal Framing

In his pioneering article, "A Theory of Play and Fantasy," first published in 1955, Gregory Bateson made the incisive argument for cognitive framing constituted by meta-communication. The idea of frame was no longer to be invoked just as a metaphor for how the contents of a phenomenon were organized and ordered. The cognitive frame did the organizing. Using Whitehead's and Russell's Theory of Logical Types, Bateson (1972) argued that frames are exclusive and inclusive. His major illustration was that of a picture frame, hanging on the wall that reorientates our perception to its interior once our gaze encounters its lineal form. By including certain messages (and meaningful actions), the frame necessarily excludes others; and by excluding messages (and actions), it necessarily includes others. This approach to framing does not permit frames (that is, meta-communications) on the same level of abstraction to intersect or to overlap with one another. Were this the case, jumbled perceptions would result, since where the outside of the frame ended and where the inside began (and vice versa) would become fuzzy.

The lineal approach to framing is especially germane to the study of ritual, since in making such a clear-cut epistemological distinction between inside and outside, it draws our attention to two issues. First, to the structure and character of the frame itself; and, second, to the logic of ritual within the frame. This gives urgency and agency to acts of framing as mediating between exterior realities and the interiors of ritual; and so, to how framing organizes its own interior. The borders, the frames of ritual, become crucial to comprehending ritual practice.

Yet, in terms of the study of ritual, what are the problems with the Batesonian approach to framing? I identify six problem areas here. *First*, lineal framing is essentially hierarchical. In keeping with the Theory of Logical Types, levels and meta-levels are organized in a clear hierarchy of abstraction and encompassment. Therefore the cognitive meta-message that brings the ritual frame into existence does not allow, as noted earlier, for overlapping or competing meta-messages that are lodged at the same level of abstraction as is it itself.

Second, lineal framing is exclusive and inclusive. Bateson's depiction of lineal framing strongly encourages a clean-lined logic of exclusion and inclusion, of either/or, witness his exemplar of the picture frame. The content of the frame is either inside or there is no content.

Third, lineal framing turns ritual into the passive recipient of change that must originate outside the ritual frame. The degree and the ways to which ritual is understood to be effected by the world outside itself depend to no small extent on how ritual is framed. The lineal ritual-frame delineates its content more as space that is relatively static, in relation to the world outside itself. The metaphor of the picture frame hanging on the wall, unmoving, as we approach, pass through, enter its framing and then leave, evokes ritual as lineally defined and hierarchically framed. This kind of frame is a cultural province of meaning that is encountered and entered by our shifting perceptions. The frame affects our perception by existing, yet not by actively doing something to us. The lineal frame is shallow and rigidly contained; there is little recursivity or inflection, little movement for that matter between the outerness and the innerness of the frame. The lineal frame seems to have little dynamism of its own. To move from one (ritual) frame to another (within a single ritual, or among rituals), we shift frames, shuffling them about, merely replacing one with another, so that each frame resembles a hard and fixed set-piece, inserted mechanistically into social life.

Fourth, lineal framing is unidirectional. Its flow is one way, from the meta-level of organization to whatever the meta-level subsumes. Lineal framing separates cleanly between the frame of ritual and the practice of ritual within the frame, and then limits or eliminates interaction between the two. Ritual is made akin to a container, giving form to whatever is within it (see, for example, Myerhoff 1977). The relationship between the perception and definition of ritual and the practice of ritual is also made static. Practice within ritual is turned into a derivative of the meta-message of the ritual frame. Explicitly and implicitly, lineal framing contributes to the scholarly understanding of ritual as unchanging; as changing only in response to stimuli (political, economic, historical) external to itself; as unquestioned truth (Rappaport 1971); and as constituted through repetition (Moore and Myerhoff 1977, 7) and order. Should spontaneity occur, this happens in prescribed times and places (see Turner 1969). This conception (explicit or implicit) of framing also contributes to the ease with which the study of ritual is turned into that of ritualization (Bell 1992).

Fifth, the content of the lineal frame does not generate change within itself. If there is any negotiation over the character of the frame, this will focus on the epistemological intent of the frame, since its contents are keyed inevitably to its meta-message. Therefore ritual is perceived in so much scholarly work not to change from within itself, through innovations in ritual practice while ritual is being practiced. Instead, change is understood to impact on ritual from its outside, from the other side of the frame and through the power of the broader social and moral orders in which the ritual is itself embedded. Negotiation outside the frame, over the conditions of existence of the ritual frame, is understood to determine the form, practice, and experience of ritual. When the power to change ritual is located only or mainly outside the ritual frame, then, ironically, ritual is analyzed as highly sensitive to political shifts in the broader society, and therefore as highly politicized. This turns ritual into just one more gauge or index of whatever is happening in the wider moral and social orders.[1]

Sixth, since ritual is so commonly framed in lineal terms, frames *within* ritual also tend to be conceptualized in this way. In accordance with lineal framing, frames within ritual *nest* within one another. The idea of nested frames may appear to complexify lineal framing, yet this probably is not the case. Nested framing more likely continues the logic of hierarchical organization and of exclusion/inclusion that are hallmarks of lineal framing. In any case in which we think there are frames within frames—for example, a play frame defined by the meta-message, *Let us make-believe*, within a ritual frame defined by the meta-message, *Let us believe*,—we must ask whether these frames nest cleanly and neatly within one another. Such nesting may be thought of spatially, in horizontal terms, for example, a shift from the more exterior to the more interior, or from a dominant ritual frame to a subordinate play frame. Or, nesting may be conceived of spatially in vertical

---

[1]   These epistemological problems are exacerbated if no distinctions are made in order to differentiate rituals from one another in terms of their internal logics of organization. I argued in *Models and Mirrors* (Handelman 1998) that certain kinds of ritual are relatively more resistant to external (political and other) pressures. Rituals that I call *models* are organized to make change take place through the logics of their own systemic organization. Models are more resistant to external pressures than are rituals that I call *mirrors*, which are organized to reflect social order. However, the model depends implicitly on premises of lineal framing. Because lineal framing demands the clear-cut division between the interior and the exterior of framing, it is this framing which, in the first instance, enables the concept of ritual as model to exist. This is so, because the concept of model summarizes rituals, which are composed of causal relationships, organized systemically as a relatively closed system, and intended teleologically to predict and to create outcomes that effect realities external to the ritual frame. These systemic aspects of the model likely will not work without the clear-cut division between the interior and exterior of the frame, which lineal framing demands. I think this is so, even if one works with a conception of system that is more 'open' than it is 'closed.'

terms, for example, a cosmic, metaphysical frame that encompasses framing on the level of human action. The same criticisms made against the relationship between the master frame and its 'content' holds for relationships among frames nested within one another.

If we assume that frames are nested, then this strongly implies that ritual is composed of clear-cut sequences of ritual action. This indeed is often the case, yet it is hardly a universal feature of phenomena we would classify as ritual. The principle of exclusion/inclusion continues to operate in nested framing. If we think that a frame is constituted by a meta-message, like *Let us believe*, then passage into the realities of ritual is defined first and foremost by belief in the normative strength of horizons, rather than by their possible lability. Then, if we think there is a play frame nesting within this ritual frame, the certainty of ritual belief is said to contain, channel, and restrain any subversive, playful capacity to disorder or to dissolve the phenomenal bedrock of ritual reality.

The logic of nested frames strongly implies that ritual cannot be threatened from within itself; that ritual cannot alter itself from within itself during its practice. Thus, the aesthetic creativity of participants has no role in their very practice of ritual. As a prelude to discussing moebius framing, let me point out for the moment that framing may be much more *fuzzy* and flexible than it is lineal. This puts into question the universality of lineal approaches to ritual framing.

Bateson himself argued, with respect to psychotherapeutic sessions, that frames changed. He commented: "the process of psychotherapy is a framed interaction between two persons, in which the rules are implicit but subject to change. Such change can only be proposed by *experimental* action, but every such experimental action, in which a proposal to change the rules is implicit, is itself part of the ongoing game" (Bateson 1972, 192, my emphasis). Therefore, added Bateson, the character of therapy is not that of a rigid game, but that of an evolving system of interaction, which changes the rules for framing. Though not couched in these terms, Bateson raised an interesting problem that I can only mention here—whether it is possible to design rituals that are programmed, as it were, to change themselves as they are practiced. For example, Helena Wulff (1998, 113–114) discusses a ballet in which the choreographer, William Forsythe, creates dance frames that are made to evolve onstage during the performance itself. Forsythe, who does not distinguish between rehearsal and performance, ensures that the dancers alter their steps during performance, embedding improvisation into this usually highly structured dance form.

Any serious alternatives to lineal framing should open the frame to alteration and perhaps to change, both from its inside (its 'content,' as it were) and from its outside. This criterion puts into question the lineal criteria of exclusion/inclusion and of hierarchical organization. A recent study by Galina Lindquist (1997; see also Handelman 1999) on neo-shamanic ritual in Sweden shows how ritual may be constituted in terms of fuzzier rather than nested, lineal framing. Neo-shamanic ritual is constructed deliberately as playful, in the sense that such ritual plays with framing itself. This playful attitude (Sutton-Smith 1997) to ritual, to practicing the experience of ritual, opens ritual to itself, putting its framing into question and thereby going beyond the received meta-communicative wisdom of any frame. The playful attitude to experience obviates the idea of snug, restful frames, comfortably nesting within one another, an attitude that is so prevalent in anthropological thinking that constrains and mutes play phenomena within ritual frames. In Swedish neo-shamanic ritual it is more the overlapping, the interpenetration, the very messiness of cognitive framing that encourages openness to the subjective experiencing of ritual. The epistemological intent of these rituals is to make cognition itself fuzzy, loose, and less certain. Therefore the very practice of such ritual is ritual-reflexive, in that participants seem to be perceiving and acting simultaneously within more than one frame.

Entry into and exit from many of these neo-shamanic rituals is dramatistic, extravagant, entertaining, self-referential, and full of humor and fun. These framings—these entries and exits—seem to be playful elaborations of the very existence of horizons of possibility that might be explored through the subjective, inner times of ritual experience. Such entries are the practice of sheer potentiality, the practice of a sense of wonder that creates possible worlds through their enactment. Intensely ludic, the rituals practice experimental, improvised, uncertain preludes and postludes to the experiences of directionless, durationless, inner subjective time.

The performance of ritual that is reflexive to its own performance of ritual (*during* its performance) is a hallmark of the recursivity that is integral to many of these neo-shamanic rites. The participants are both artists and critics of their own imaginaries as they perform their inventions—and to some degree, through their own deep recursivity, these rituals are made to alter themselves while they are being performed. It may well be that this particular condition of the emergence of change is possible only when frames of cognition do *not* nest neatly, inclusively, hierarchically, within one another, but instead are more jumbled together. Then each frame seductively offers both an inside view and an outside view of itself to itself, and so, too, in relation to another frame that is providing similar optics to itself and to its counter-frame. This fuzziness among frames, or their jumbling together, leads towards an alternative to lineal framing—that of moebius framing—which I discuss now.

Moebius Framing

The idea of moebius framing argues for a single frame that speaks to the problem of being inside and outside the frame with virtual simultaneity, thereby opening the ritual frame to the outside world while enabling the ritual to be practiced as relatively closed. Through such framing, the outside is taken inside, through the frame, and integrated with the ritual. No less, the inside is taken outside of itself, and thereby is made part of the ritual frame. Therefore the frame is in process within itself, and in a near simultaneous relationship to its inside (its 'content') and to its outside (social order).[2]

The moebius surface or the moebius ring exists through an ongoing condition of 'becoming'—in other words, it is dynamic within itself. The paradoxical geometry of the moebius surface is well known (Rosen 1994; Handelman 1998, xxii–xxiii). This deceptively simple topological conundrum is constituted by a single surface which is both external and internal, outside and inside to itself (Rosen 1994, 7–12). The moebius surface is twisted on itself so that the inside of the surface continually and continuously turns into its own outside, its outside into its own inside. If we perceive the moebius ring as a frame, then this framing is inherently dynamic, continuously relating exterior to interior, interior to exterior. There is no longer any hard-and-fast lineal separation between 'frame' and 'content' on the one hand, and between realities external to and internal to ritual, on the other. The moebius surface seems to reach beyond itself, towards becoming something else within itself. The moebius surface is changing and recursive, perhaps even monitoring how it is altering itself.

The moebius surface attends less to the hierarchical relationship between 'frame' and 'content,' and between master and subordinate frames, because the frame is *polymorphic* within itself. As such, the epistemological status of the moebius surface is more that of a mover, a shifter, a transformer between

---

[2]   Elsewhere (Handelman 1992) I have argued that if the framing of play is conceptualized as lineal, then this lineality of the frame conceals the processuality of paradox within itself. Nonetheless, because this processuality within the play frame is paradoxical, it seals the frame into its own lineality, rather than opening the interior of the frame (its 'content') to its exterior (social order), and vice versa.

inside and outside and back, than it is a static, rigid frame that always maintains its selfsame status so long as it exists. In this regard the response of the
quantum physicist, David Bohm, on seeing Rouault's painting, *The Clown*, is
apposite. Bohm emphasizes how the 'objective' qualities of the constitution
of the painting transform his 'subjective' perception, making both integral to
a single system of experience that is outside, yet inside itself.

Bohm (correspondence of Bohm with Rosen, in Rosen 1994, 247) writes
that: "In this painting, a clown was depicted by means of a complex set of
color patches, within his own outward form. But [at] the outset, to each
patch, there was a corresponding, but larger and inverted patch in a complementary color. As I watched the painting, I noticed my eyes beginning to os-
cillate between corresponding patches. Suddenly, the whole mode of seeing
and experiencing shifted. The patches were still there, but they did not ob-
trude themselves on my vision. Instead, I sensed a vast flow of energy in
which the 'clown' poured out his whole being toward the world. This went
out in a circulatory stream that twined around behind me and entered my
own being. I literally experienced what it was like to be that clown. I *was*
that clown, and the energy flowed in through me back to him, to go on circu-
lating. ... Here was a symbol that was able to transform my consciousness,
so that I was no longer separate from the clown that was being 'observed.'"
The frame here is moebius-like as it comes into being, including within itself
both Bohm and the clown, as the latter (his own lineal framing dissolving)
enters Bohm who feels that he is within the clown. Bohm and the clown are
both outside and inside one another, integral to, in Bohm's terms, a single
stream of energy that here shifts framing towards the polymorphous.

In moebius framing the epistemological status of the distinction between
the outside of ritual and its inside is put into question. It is not that the outside—say, the political and the economic—intrudes more into ritual; but
rather that the moebiusness of framing, in its ongoing movement between
inside and outside and back, brings them into and through one another, perhaps transforming in both directions as it opens in both directions. This may
be so, as well, for frames within ritual that resist the hierarchy and lineality
of nesting, and that generate new phenomena that are unplanned, yet that are
a potentiality of the ritual frame. This seems to be the case in Sundar Kaali's
(n.d.) discussion of a Tamil ritual-drama, *Hiranya Natakam*.

This ritual-drama enacts the well-known Hindu story of the demon-king,
Hiranya, and his son, Prahlada, who is deeply devoted to the god, Vishnu.
Hiranya is seemingly invulnerable, having received a boon from the god
Brahma that he will not be killed in the interior or in the exterior of a place;

neither in the air nor on the ground; neither by day nor by night, and so forth. Angered by Prahlada's love for Vishnu, the demonic king challenges his son to ask the god to appear immediately. Vishnu emerges from within a solid pillar on the threshold in the form of his *avatar*, the man-lion, Narasimha, and disembowels the demon-king, recreating the proper order of the god's cosmos. With the exception of Vishnu/Narasimha, most of the characters in this ritual-drama are simultaneously doubled onstage, each double seemingly a copy of its other. Vishnu is the singular cosmic ruler, the master frame within the ritual-drama that contains and defines all the other characters.

One may speculate as to how these characters came to perform in two's, but this seems to be an emergent development that appeared only in some of the villages of the region in which this ritual-drama is enacted. The phenomenon of doubling characters onstage emerged through the history of the practice of enactment. The creation of doubling had the effect of, as it were, opening up or expanding a character. Though doubling looks like *mimesis*, neither double is the original. Doubling adds layers and creates depths, implying possibility that is hidden from view.

Doubling creates a deeply recursive space within the doubled character, one that is full of indeterminate, polymorphic possibilities. This suggests, though we cannot see this, that the doubles are interacting with one another onstage and that their interaction is generative, containing the possibility of bringing something new into being from within the ritual-drama. Put otherwise, onstage there are *two* ritual-dramas going on simultaneously, in tandem; and the two are articulated at a single cosmic apex by the encompassing frame of the singular god, Narasimha. Yet, from within the emerging embryonic space between them, these parallel mimetic performances are on their way to generating a variant of this ritual-drama in which each play, each set of performers, may diverge substantially from the other, creating a new story-line. Within the master frame the two performances are joined moebius-like with one another, such that it is difficult to perceive where one ends and the other begins. Unlike Forsythe's ballet, into which improvisation is programmed, in this version of *Hiranya Natakam* change is an emergent function of similitude itself, first of the similarity of the single solidary ritual-drama in relation to itself, and then of the similarity of its two ritual-dramas split mimetically in relation to one another yet related moebiusly.

Especially interesting here is what indeed did happen during one performance. The defeat of the demon-king is marked usually by removing his crown and giving it to the god, Narasimha. On this occasion, however, a performer of high status removed Narasimha's mask at the climactic moment and brought it to the demon-king, Hiranya (apparently without knowing consciously why he did so). This performer thereby brought into being the triumph of the demon-king over the god. Subordinate framing braided suddenly with master framing. At this moment their relationship became less nested and more moebius-like, changed from within by the emerging 'content,' the new story-line in which the demonic defeats the divine. Though this ending (and, so too, the relationship between the frames) was corrected, the emergent ending seemed a possible outcome, emotionally and logically. Moreover, given Narasimha's encompassment of the cosmos, this was an outcome with profound implications.

To take the moebius argument one step further, I suggest that the frame it creates may be itself composed of different strands, in relation to a particular ritual setup. Each strand may index, say, an aspect of cosmology, of symbolism, of ritual practice, of ritual practitioners, and so forth. These strands are braided together to constitute the ritual; yet they also constitute the ritual frame. As the strands braid with one another they turn inside-out, outside-in, appearing (and disappearing) together in different combinations, in different rhythms. The braided strands that are appearing then constitute the ritual frame (perhaps during a particular ritual moment or phase). As these braided strands disappear, other aspects of their braiding appear, becoming the moebius-like ritual frame, and so forth. The frame is simultaneously inside and outside, appearing and disappearing from view, always in movement, always becoming. There is no clear-cut distinction between that which is inside and that which is outside.

This perspective suggests that the ritual—indeed, ritual practice—recursively generates its own framing which frames ritual practice. The ritual frame, then, is not an *a priori*—the frame does not exist until the frame comes into existence through the doing, the practice of framing. Yet in order to practice framing the frame must exist, which it does not. This is the paradoxicality of the existence of something that does not exist until it exists, but which must exist in order to come into existence. Such paradox is problematic for the framing of ritual only when the logic of ritual practice is understood to be lineal, so that the distinction between non-ritual and ritual is grasped as quite clear-cut, quite unambiguous. Thus the conception of ritual frame as a kind of linear topology should not be applied blindly. Instead, more scholarly attention should be given to the self-organizing complexity of framing.[3]

---

[3]   I have tried to indicate how this might be done in a discussion of the City Dionysia of fifth-century Athens (Handelman n.d.). Though I do not discuss framing *per se* there, I do use the idea of braiding.

Conceptualizing framing in terms of moebius-like properties of ongoing processuality makes the frame *context-sensitive*, rather than context-dependent. As it turns outwards, the moebius frame can include new elements and outside pressures into itself as it turns inwards, depending on how these external features braid together with the existing strands of the ritual. So too, the frame can take into itself emergent features that are created through ritual practice, and that then appear, becoming part of the frame as a strand in a particular braiding of ritual practice. This is what may be happening in the example of *Hiranya Natakam*.

Moebius framing enables ritual to act on the world without being constituted as a system of teleological causality. Moebius framing produces a high degree of intercalation of ritual reality and of life outside of ritual. Both act on one another continuously, braiding each into the other. Because such ritual can make use of new elements from outside itself—indeed, as the ritual itself is performed—the ritual can change itself as it is performed, without destroying its capacities to act on the world outside itself. In the senses used throughout this exposition, rituals characterized by moebius framing are always changing in and through practice—no matter how small the changes—even as these rituals are reproducing themselves in their gross features.

To explore the framing of ritual is to question the universal validity of the Durkheimian separation of the sacred from the profane. The Durkheimian distinction, which is essential to the modern study of ritual in anthropology and in religious studies, has been overburdened, conceptually. To an important degree, the distinction likely issues from premises of monotheistic theologies. This distinction has flourished in contexts through which monotheisms have set the intellectual tone for scholarship, and have pervaded thinking on the subject. Lineal framing, premised on criteria of hierarchical ordering and of the clean-cut separation between outside and inside, fits much too neatly and cleanly within monotheistic ideas of ritual organization. The formulation of lineality limits and skews our capacities to comprehend how change in ritual emerges from ritual practice, as well as the complexities of relationships between the interior and the exterior of ritual, between ritual and social order. Theorizing ritual framing as fuzzier and as more moebius-like may begin to exfoliate these and other issues, making them more accessible to further analysis.

References

Bateson, Gregory. 1972: A Theory of Play and Fantasy (1955). In: *Steps to an Ecology of Mind: Collected Essays in Anthropology, Psychiatry, Evolution, and Epistemology*. New York: Ballantine. 177–193.

Bell, Catherine. 1992: *Ritual Theory, Ritual Practice*. New York and London: Oxford University Press.

Handelman, Don. 1992: Passages to Play: Paradox and Process. In: *Play and Culture* 5:1–19.

———. 1998: *Models and Mirrors: Towards an Anthropology of Public Events*. 2d ed. New York and Oxford: Berghahn Books.

———. 1999: The Playful Seductions of Neo-Shamanic Ritual. In: *History of Religions* 39: 65–72.

———. n.d.: Designs of Ritual: The City Dionysia of Fifth-Century Athens. In: *Celebrations: Sanctuaries and the Vestiges of Cult Activity*. Athens: Norwegian Institute at Athens, in press.

Kaali, Sundar. n.d.: Masquerading Death: Aspects of Ritual Masking in the Community Theaters of Thanjavur. In: *Behind the Mask: Dance, Healing, and Possession in South India*, ed. David Shulman and Deborah Thiagarajan. (South Asian Series). Ann Arbor: University of Michigan Press, in press.

Lindquist, Galina. 1997: *Shamanic Performances on the Urban Scene: Neo-Shamanism in Contemporary Sweden*. (Stockholm Studies in Social Anthropology 39). Stockholm: Almquist & Wiksell International.

Moore, Sally F. and Barbara G. Myerhoff. 1977: Introduction: Secular Ritual. In: *Secular Ritual*, ed. Sally F. Moore and Barbara G. Myerhoff. Assen: Van Gorcum. 3–24.

Myerhoff, Barbara G. 1977: We Don't Wrap Herring in a Printed Page: Fusion, Fictions and Continuity in Secular Ritual. In: *Secular Ritual*, ed. Sally F. Moore and Barbara G. Myerhoff. Assen: Van Gorcum. 199–224.

Rappaport, Roy A. 1971: Ritual, Sanctity, and Cybernetics. In: *American Anthropologist* 73: 59–76.

Rosen, Steven M. 1994: *Science, Paradox, and the Moebius Principle: The Evolution of a 'Transcultural' Approach to Wholeness*. (Series in Science, Technology, and Society). Albany, N.Y.: State University of New York Press.

Sutton-Smith, Brian. 1997: *The Ambiguity of Play*. Cambridge, Mass.: Harvard University Press.

Turner, Victor W. 1969: *The Ritual Process: Structure and Anti-Structure*. (Lewis Henry Morgan Lectures 1966). Chicago: Aldine.

Wulff, Helena. 1998: Perspectives Towards Ballet Performance: Exploring, Repairing, and Maintaining Frames. In *Ritual, Performance, Media*, ed. Felicia Hughes-Freeland. London: Routledge. 104–120.

Contemporary Carnival (*carnaval*) in Asturias: Visual Figuration as a 'Ritual' of Parodic Release and Democratic Revitalization[*]

James W. Fernandez

Documentados desde muy lejos las farsas y carnevaladas de la epoca invernal ... todos con caracter lúdico y subversivo ... el sistema Cristiano no ha conseguido erradicar ese hálito renovador de los rituales farsecos peculiar de este tiempo festivo privilegiado, por más que haya colocado en su transcurso fiestas litúrgicas tan importantes como la Navidád y la Epifanía. (Javier Fernández Conde 1981, 119)

Hoy comamos y bebamos, y catemos y holguemos, que mañana ayunaremos. Por honra de Sant Antruejo, parémonos hoy bien anchos. Embutamos estos panchos, recalquemos el pellejos: que costumbres es de consejo, que todos hoy nos hartemos, que mañana ayuneremos. (Juan del Encina [1468–1529] 1975)

Playfulness and Planfulness: On Method amidst Madness

Carnival in Catholic Europe has generally been understood as a time of playfulness in which things are done and said that cannot be as easily done or said at other times of the year. Carnival celebration and its playfulness, the hilarity, extravagance and ribaldry characteristic of it—'the world turned upside down' as it is said—is usually contrasted with the sobrieties, the practicalities the seriousness of engagement—the planfulness of normal everyday life.

Because of the ribaldry, mockery, parody, and burlesque found in carnival, its atmosphere of general impiety and profanity in short, it is sometimes difficult to see it as a ritual. It seems to confound the enduring Durkheimian

[*] I am indebted for generous advice, observations and commentary on Los Barcos to various members of that group but particularly to their *primus inter pares*, Celso Fernandez, Cangas de Onis. For valuable general discussions of Quevedo in relation to carnival I thank María Jesús Pando Canteli! As always I have learned from the commentary and ever-nurturing criticism of Renate Lellep.

categories of the sacred and the profane, which assign ritual to the sacred world and studies the way that as sacred action ritual evokes and confirms the sacred condition and its power to order and assuage the human condition. And yet carnival play can be a highly repetitive and ritualized representation of life. And in its very profanity it attains that kind of time out of time that is the characteristic of ritual action. Its farcical and derisory quality may seem to bring low what is high, disorder what is orderly but it also has persuasive powers of assuagement to those afflicted with the discontents of social order. And, of course, it is not born in full bloom or as whole cloth but takes considerable planning. There is planfulness in this playfulness; there is method in this madness, and meaning in this method. And it is this that we wish to consider over time, which is to say, in evolutionary perspective. For the rituals of carnival in the various parts of Spain have been in dynamic evolution over the last century.

Before turning to the materials at hand let me also say a word about the tropological method employed here, a method, which is attuned first of all to meaning as the figuration and re-figuration of popular associations (or collective representations). Hence it focuses on local analogic thinking rather than professional analogic thinking of the anthropological analyst. In this paper, I want to think about carnival in Spain as a changing ritual dynamic and I want to think about the 'meaningful methods' (Fernandez and Herzfeld 1998) and the 'context sensitive' explanation by which we might approach this wintry madness. These are methods which approach without undue imposition and undue dichotomization the conjoint playfulness and planfulness of the human condition in this particular province of the human condition (see Fernandez 1994). The theory and method I and others would and have proposed is tropological theory which has its roots in Sophistic and Aristotelian Rhetoric and Poetic and in recent work on the central cognitive functions of metaphor. This theory addresses the inescapable epistemological necessity in our figuring out, to state it most challengingly, who, what and why we are and what the human life situation means. It evokes the inescapable necessity of the tropes in enabling us, in other words, to manage our inchoate condition! Carnival, in short, is one kind of very interesting and challenging way of figuring out the inchoate, of figuring out what oppresses us and of making that oppression less burdensome.

Theories of Carnival: Interpretations of Carnival in Andalusia

For a very long time now in social science, carnival, like ritual, despite its time out of time impractical ludic if not frivolous features, has been taken quite seriously. There have been, of course, different theoretical emphases. For structural functionalists human life in culture, where the normatively obligatory must be made the desirable or at least the acceptable, carnival like ritual functions to provide a time (out of practical time) of structural re-adjustment. It is part of the re-balancing of society and the re-solidifying of social bonds. It is, despite the ritual violations of normal custom, a re-commitment to cultural norms. But, beyond that generally accepted perspective, studies have differed, and they have differed particularly as to the psychological component. Some have emphasized the social safety valve acts of carnival seeing it as an expressive opportunity for psychological re-adjustment to both the excessive constraints of orderly life in society or as a expressive reaction to certain unacceptable, hence felt to be unreasonable or repressive, orderlinesses of that life. Since no human behavior is without its politics, nor is any interpretation of human behavior, students have differed as to how seriously to take the rebelliousness almost always present—if only implicitly—in carnival. While some students have focused on carnival as rituals of release or safety valves with functional consequences other have focused on carnival and carnivals where the rebelliousness is much more evident and where the consequences of carnival can be interpreted as forms of real world resistance to repressive authority—resistance which seeks, in the end, to effect real political changes in the social order. It must be kept in mind, however, that everywhere in Europe where carnival is practiced it flourishes as anti-establishment expressivity. It is followed immediately thereafter the church-imposed sobrieties, privations and forfeitures of Lent. It exists in vital relationship to the looming authority structure and strictures of the religious establishment.

There is, thus, both a politics and a psychology to the interpretation of carnival events, as there is to all ritual events. To position ourselves and the associative method of anthropological tropology as regards this theoretical tradition let me briefly examine its relevance to two important monographs on Andalusian carnival that have recently been published: Jerome Mintz's *Carnival Song and Society: Gossip, Sexuality and Creativity in Andalusia* (1997) and David Gilmore's *Carnival and Culture: Sex, Symbol and Status in Spain* (1998). These two books are the fruit of more than three decades of research in and on Andalusian Spain by each author (1965–1995 for Mintz and 1971–present for Gilmore). Both books provide substantial and valuable ethnographic material, particular carnival songs and comments upon them. Both books are mainly interested in the carnival as celebrated by the lower classes, *campesinos* (countrymen) and rural agricultural and craft workers of the small Andalusian towns. They are less interested in the more elaborate displays of conspicuous consumption invested in carnival by the middle and upper classes of the larger cities. It is the lower classes who compose and sing the carnival songs whose revelatory and critical social and psychological content have been most interesting to most anthropologists it ought to be said.

The two monographs are energized by different analytic preoccupations and hence differ significantly in their interpretive stance. For Mintz the 'essential property of carnival' upon which all can agree is its expression of a yearning for freedom from the unfair restraint and repression of life in society. Carnival is energized by a belief in the possibility of social justice and of comity and courtesy in community relations, and by approval of their presence and indignation at their absence. There is in carnival a 'moral compass' that steers the composition of the songs and acts, which Mintz analyzes (Mintz 1997, chap. 13, Epilogue, 250–252, and passim). Carnival says what cannot otherwise be so well said given the constraints of normal social life, or under such repressive political regimes as Spain has seen over the years.

Gilmore is energized by more probing psychological interests and finds 'Spanish society' projected into carnival, where it "yield(s) up some of its darkest secrets ... those secrets which affect people deeply and shape their social relations ... secrets about sex, gender and status" (Gilmore 1998, 1). We see that while Mintz only very hesitatingly speaks of Spain in his interpretations guiding himself by local sense of differences in carnival from one part of Andalusia to another not to mention one part of Spain to another, Gilmore does not hesitate to make that generalization, though most usually for all of Andalusia rather than for all of Spanish society. It is the thesis of this book that Andalusian ideas about sex, gender and status are best and most accessibly expressed in the rituals of the February carnival or the *locura de febrero* (the February Madness) (Gilmore 1998, 3).

The driving paradigm in Gilmore is an interestingly rethought set of neo-Freudian ideas about the deep structure of carnival, a structure that Mintz does not attempt to access if, indeed, he believes at all in its value as an analytic device for directly accessing local meaning. Thus while Mintz sees carnival as the expression of moral sentiments and senses of freedom violated as observed and experienced by the carnival singers in community life, Gilmore mainly understands it as 'collective therapy,' the expression of deep psychological conflicts in the individual and the society about sex, gender, and status relations. Mintz sticks much closer to the anthropologist's ethnographic last. And the ratio of field data to interpretive effort is very high in comparison with Gilmore.

But there is more than a neo-Freudian paradigm driving Gilmore's analysis. He also employs tropological, topological, political, and economical analyzes to round out his interpretations. These latter deserve comment for they come closer to the associative analysis characteristic of the figurational approach adopted here. In several chapters on "The Geometry of Sex" (Up and Down) "The Geography of Sex" (Here and There), "The Mayete as Carnival Caricature," and "Ideology and Counterpoint" (Copla Politics) Gilmore explores not the conformity of the carnival behavior of the townspeople to psychoanalytic categories and a general theory of male and female identity formation neo-Freudian in conception, but considers that behavior in terms of primordial vectorial expressivity,[1] putting up and putting down, putting out and putting in, being able to exert power over people and having power exerted over oneself or one's group. Here he follows closely, employing local terminology and local figurations, the ways that these primordial experiences are articulated in carnival song and action. In absorbing descriptions and listenings, he allows, as does Mintz, the people to speak for themselves as they confront in their carnival fabulations the contradictions and paradoxes of their lives. These primordial vectors of social life are described convincingly in the intense industry of the olive harvest with the men above in the trees and the women below gathering up the olives. Or take his discussion of the inside/outside dynamics of bar life, a male inner *sanctum* where women are excluded and kept outside except during carnival when they turn inside and outside, upside down and inside out! Whatever virtue may lie in the use of neo-Freudian categories and psychoanalytic interpretations these late chapter descriptions are lodged in the basic vectors of local life and bring us close to the active associational dynamics of life and memory as contained, as we have said, in *The Interpretation of Dreams*.

An underlying irony, in respect to political vectors of acceptance or rejection of the established order, which is present in both the Gilmore and Mintz analysis is the paradoxical support which these carnival mockeries and enacted murmurings about self and others, together with the more active protests and repudiations, give to the norms of individual comportment and the

---

[1] What the cognitive tropologists George Lakoff and Mark Johnson refer to as the primordial *gestalts*, that is to say irreducible vectors of life (see Lakoff and Johnson 1980).

actions of the social-political order against whose failings they are directed. Both authors mildly ironize about the romantic or radical interpretations of carnival who grant more real-world historical, revolutionary effect to carnival protests than is justified by what Mintz calls these, in the final analysis, 'shadow plays' (Mintz 1997, 251).

It is pertinent to remark the impact of contemporary states of affairs *vis-à-vis* political economy on the overall understanding of what one studies. These books were published a year apart and in fairly prosperous democratic times (the late 1990s) in Spain and Europe, in which affluence had tempered the earlier radical resentments about the mal-distribution of surplus value and undemocratic government. Analyses published during late Franco times or early in the democracy where there was much more active resentment of persisting mal-distributions and political oppressions were often quite naturally attentive to the radical energy and radical implications of carnival. In any event both authors take what might be called a Bahktinian-Freudian perspective on carnival, which is to say a perspective fully aware of the 'uncomfortable contradictions' of social and political life with which carnival struggles, acceptance and rejection, adhesion and repudiation, and the ambivalences that it manifests in that struggle. Both authors ironically come to the conclusion that the disorder of carnival—that is, the political parody, social satire, and mainstream mockery (as well as carnival laudation of certain key figures and events)—actually contributes to social order. Mintz after a long study of carnival came to the conclusion that, "social controls in rural Andalusia were achieved not through government regulation and police surveillance but rather through social sanctions that were enforced by gossip, and by various forms of criticism and public censure" such as carnival (Mintz 1997, 251).[2] Mintz more tellingly observes, as a consequence of his knowledge of Andalusian radicalism, brought out in his classic study *The Anarchists of Casas Viejas* (1982):

> In the past the true radical children of Andalusia, the anarchists and anarchosyndicalists, thought carnival to be a foolish distraction from the education and action necessary for social revolution. The Great Day for which they waited was not carnival but the general strike and the eradication of government. (Mintz 1982, 251)

---

[2]   Mintz quotes both the historian Natalie Z. Davis on Carnival in early modern France (1975) and Max Gluckman on 'rituals of rebellion' among the Zulu and their congeners in Southeast Africa (1963) to support the thesis of carnival's overall support of social integration and social continuity (Mintz 1997, 256, n. 5).

Carnival in a Global-Local World

Before turning to contemporary carnival in Asturias let me make some further observations on the evolution of carnival in Spain, by which I mean in southern Andalusia as portrayed in Mintz and Gilmore and in northern Asturias as evidenced in our research. Both regions have been influenced by globalization processes and multinational awareness. And both authors make clear the impact of television and the mass media on carnival costuming and carnival themes in the last twenty years. What used to be a community confined event energized by the desire to comment through song or skit approvingly or (mainly) disapprovingly on individual or class actions that impinged on the local moral community and its sense of itself, has now become a *fiesta* reaching out to include presentations of self, of social group and of community which are much influenced by national or international events. This does not mean a focusing away from local community events entirely but, rather, a kind of 'glocalism,' as it is called, in carnival presentations. Indeed the carnival skits and floats of the present provide an apt body of data through which to address 'glocalism.'

It might be further remarked, in respect to the world-turned-upside-down feature of carnival that in the small relatively closed rural communities of former days where everyone knows everyone else, to have made oneself unrecognizable in carnival was to truly turn things upside down. Just the opposite is true of the relatively impersonal relationships of modern day towns and cities. To really reverse the order of things nowadays is to reveal one's persona, to claim or reveal identity in an increasingly impersonal yet publicity saturated world where one is made anxious about becoming known for at least just one's '15 minutes of street fame!' The change from *concealing* to *revealing*—because one is competing for prizes in a relatively impersonalized sociality—is for many Asturians what most distinguishes present from past carnival traditions.

Carnival (*carnaval*) and 'Street Theater' in Asturias

In Andalusian studies a major feature of small town carnival are the songs with social content (*coplas*), which have been extensively analyzed in the literature of that region. A central feature of Asturian *carnaval* in the view of its observers and participants are the masks and masking. Indeed, the mask (*careta*) is so important that often the preferred name for *carnaval* is *mas-*

carada. In the *Enciclopedia Asturiana*, *carnaval* is primarily defined as "las fiestas en las que se usan desfraces y máscaras" (fiestas in which desguises and masks are used) (Nuevo Zarracina 1970, 98). One of the most important of Asturian painters of the early to mid-twentieth century, Evaristo Valle, is as well known for his *carnavaladas* as any other part of his work. His particular attention to the carnival masks and costumes in action is reminiscent of Goya's *Grotesques*. Solana like Goya is an artist also particularly skillful at rendering the human figure in action, and an artist attracted by carnival coloration. The attention that Valle gave repeatedly to various aspects of carnival has become a well-recognized part of its historical tradition in Asturias. What seemed to particularly appeal to this painter was the transformation from the uniformities of the dress and manners of everyday life into this picturesque if not grotesque presentation of self.[3] Indeed the grotesqueries were particularly attractive to Valle—a painter otherwise given to caricaturing in his *Notables series* the substantial people of his home city Gijon. One of his most telling *carnavaladas* in this sense shows three grotesques accosting and ragging upright and portly town burgers in the town square, the Baile de Carnaval, in which the contrast between the well dressed burgers and the raggedly dressed carnival figures is strikingly presented (Carantoña 1986, 175).

More frequently in Asturias and particularly in former days, carnival was referred to as *antroxu* (Castillian: *antruejo, entruejo*) the romance form of the Latin *introitulus* or *introitus*, the entering into Lent (*cuaresma*). It was expected to take place on one of the last three days before the beginning of Lent (*ceniza*, Ash Wednesday). In accordance with its Latin roots, with frequency in the Asturian literature *carnaval* is assigned classical origins in the Lupercalian and Saturnalian celebrations of the Romans,[4] particularly the

---

[3]   Francisco Carantoña in his book *Evaristo Valle* (1986) includes a newspaper commentary on a 1918 exhibition of the painter in which there were a number of *carnavaladas*: "nada es 'tan de Valle' como sus 'carnavaladas,' según unánima opinión. El carnaval es un tiempo de sinceridad y de libertad; cada cual se muestra como es. Se expresa, se gesticula, se hacen muescas y ademanes, se rie, se baila sin trabas ni respetos. Para un artista como Valle, enamorado del gesto, del movimiento, de la expresión, el carnival es el tiempo de recoger visiones. En elk Carnaval se deshace la uniformidad de nuestro vestir, se llega a lo pintoresco, a lo grotesco en el traje y a lo bellamente decorativo .... Pero las 'carnavaladas' de Valle no se quedan en la simple descripción de tipos y actitudes. Tipos y actitudes son para el medios materiales—tan materiales comomlas pinturas y los pinceles— para la expresión del espiritu grosero y plebeyo, que coga al ofrecerse en espectaculo a la ciudad durante esos dias y canta su vistoria en voz taberneria sobre lo delicado y lo excelente" (Carantoña 1986, 34).

[4]   "Sus origenes claros son las fiestas lupercales y las bacchanals romanas, en las que las bacantes—sacerdotisas de Baco—recorrian las calles, cubierta en parte su desnudez por

frequency with which animal masks of various kinds were employed in turn of the century *carnaval* gave reason to recalling Lupercalian ceremonies with their celebration of the wolf-man (*homo lupus*) transformations of the spirits of the dead.[5]

Of importance also is the etymology of the word *carnaval* understood (Moliner 1988, 529) to derive from the Italian *carnelevare*—to carry away or remove (*levare*) the meat (*carne*) in preparation for the fasting of Lent. A good deal of attention is paid in Asturias to the good eating, even to satiety, that should accompany *antroxu* and precede the deprivations of Lent. Fat Tuesday or *Mardi Gras* notions in other languages express this emphasis. Since pork meat, mostly in various kinds of sausages (*chorizo*) has been the main meat in the Asturian diet and was a food often prohibited during Lent, the contemporary American phrase 'to pig out' would not be too extravagant a phrasing for the meanings involved. And this etymology would also help explain the curious phrasing of the final phase of the more elaborate celebrations of carnival: the burial of the sardine (*entierro de la sardina*) which very few in Asturias are able to explain adequately, even those celebrants from coastal cities like Gijon who suppose it is employed because their fishing fleets depend on sardine fishing which brings in wealth and good eating. Mintz and his informants in Cadiz may be right here that the word *sardina* is a deformation of the word *cerdito* meaning either little pig or the entrails and other inedible parts of the pig which are left after the 'pig out' of carnival and which at the end of the celebrations must be appropriately buried in preparation for Lent (Mintz 1997, xxxiii, n. 27 in consultation with Alberto Ramos Santana)! In the inland town in Asturias, whose *carnaval* we consider here, they have reworked—in the same spirit—this mysterious usage, "since we don't live by the sea but rather by a river" with the burial of the salmon fry (*esguitu*).

---

una piel de tigre al tiempo que eran perseguidas por grupos de sátiros en estado de embriaguez" (Nuevo Zarracina 1970, 98). There was a kind of sacred secularity in these Roman rites, which one might argue, because of its proximity to Lent, is also characteristic of *carnaval*. Not only was the sacred turned upside down into the secular but in the Roman social order as well, underlings including slaves might even pretend to rule over and beat their masters!

[5]   See in this connection the well-known painting of Evaristo Valle, *Carnavalada de los Osos*, picturing carnival celebrants in animal dress in the mountains. Though called 'bears' in the title of the picture they appear more like wolves or foxes in the painting, perhaps even moles or *javali* (wild pigs) (Carantoña 1986, 206). Not as well known but more accurately named is Valle's *Carnavalada de los Lobos* (see Carantoña and Casariego 1984, 72).

Whatever the ancient origins and etymologies of these pre-Lenten days of play and their relationship to excesses even orgies of eating, the contemporary carnival of the last decade in Asturias, whose ethnography we present here, is, at once, a significantly different carnival than formerly while at the same time it preserves, in respect to 'street theater' more traditional elements. Whereas formerly carnival frivolities were accompanied by masked groups roaming the streets and ragging and harassing bystanders (by mock 'beating' and poking), in recent years these groups have become much more organized and present elaborate carnival floats and marching bands. The harassment and mock beating of spectators and passers by with inflated pig bladders and sticks still occur however.

We can make both these changes as well as differences between provinces, clearer by comparing Andalusian carnival by related efforts made over this last decade by persisting groups of celebrants in one Asturian town, Cangas de Onis on the Sella River in the East of Asturias. One says groups of celebrants because as in Andalusia the truly interesting carnival presentations are the creative productions of groups although one or two members of these groups may, as a matter of course, be the principle creators of the carnival songs (*coplas* in Andalusia), costumes, and floats (*carrozas* in Asturias).[6] In Andalusia these groups are variously called *murgas* (strolling bands of singers), *chirigotas* (strolling bands of wisecrackers and insulters), *comparsas* (strolling bands in masquerade), *coros* (choruses), or *charangas* (bands of costumed music makers) depending on their dominant mode of presentation. Carnival, although always graced with the presence of individual self-inspired merry makers, is centrally the playful presentation of the work and previous planning of groups. We see this in the *coplas* of Andalusia, in the hammering out and group memorization of the songs laden with piquant and sometimes downright derogatory social content. We see it in the more traditional street *comedias* of pre-civil war Spain, which was 'street theater' put on by a well-practiced neighborhood group. We see it in the elaborate floats (*carrozas*) of contemporary Asturias impossible to mount without group effort. This work and planning and meaning we will now consider.

We should not move on, however, without saying something more about the nineteenth- and early twentieth-century 'street theater' in small town Asturias of the nineteenth century and the pre-civil war twentieth century. This 'street theater' took the form of masked figures (*sidros o guirrios)* dan-

---

[6]   Both Mintz and Gilmore identify these principal composers of the *coplas* as we will here for the *carrozas*.

cing in and around a troop of performers of locally written, though relatively traditional or folkloric, 'comedies' in the *Commedia del Arte* tradition (Asturian: *les comedies de quirrios*). This Christmas and New Year (lasting until Lent) tradition was suppressed by the Nationalist regime because of its marked comical and politically critical spirit.[7] It has largely disappeared in Asturias because of that suppression and for other reasons, particularly the challenge of the media. But one can argue that elements of it survive and particularly its critical spirit in the contemporary street theater of these carnival floats. In the town on which we focus, Cangas de Onis, in the eastern part of the province, a town of some 6,000 inhabitants, there are two main carnival groups or *cofradias* (brotherhoods) who compete, *Sociedad Festiva Vazquez de Mella* (a local and regional conservative thinker and politician of the turn of the century) and the *Sociedad Festiva de los Barcos* (of the Boats) also known simply as *Los Barcos*! We will take the last ten years as indicative of their carnival activities.

The first group, *Vazquez de Mella*, generally offers traditional scenes, a float, for example, in which a cow of local breed (*casina*) gives repeated birth to a variety of outlandish objects. The other group, *Los Barcos* on whom we concentrate our attention makes playful, ironic commentary on provincial national and international events and personalities. The themes of the first group tend to the more folkloric (*costumbrista*) and the second tend to be more manifestly political, although locals readily recognize and assign a differing political orientation to both groups, leftist, on the one hand, and rightist, on the other. There are, thus, several carnival sub-cultures and also a clear politics of carnival culture, as between local *costumbrista* and provincial, national-international focus. These differences are also at play in the competitions. Where juries tend to be composed of members of the other political persuasion, and that fact is known beforehand, there is hesitancy to try and enter the competition. Thus *Los Barcos* after several years spent presenting their floats without success in an adjacent town (Arriondas)—floats, which had consistently won prizes elsewhere—decided that the jury was

---

[7] The students of this popular genre and rescuers of forgotten attic texts, Victor Rodriguez Hevia and Luis M. Iglesias Cueva find in it little moralizing intent but rather critical (ironic) comment on the two great themes, both the foibles of family life and the failings of national projects and the intentions of national politics in Spain. The presentation of the former is intended to provoke laughter and of the latter ironic reflection: "Encontramos en ella una doble intención, critica y cómica. La critica a los gobiernos, a los militares, a las guerras, al servicio militar obligatorio, a las contribuciones...." The comic they point out is developed more in portrayal of family relations (Rodriguez Hevia and Iglesias Cueva: 1981, 269-286).

politically unfriendly (too many right wing members in 'pin striped suits' [*trajes de vira*] and withdrew their participation and competition for the prizes offered).[8] We will treat here only a sampling of these floats of one group (*Los Barcos*) of the last decade trying to capture the ironic meanings involved and leave for more lengthy presentation elsewhere the full panoply of presentations over the ten year period.

Ten Years of Carnival Floats

In 1991 the first year we will consider this succession of floats the subject was the Gulf War and a float representing the Spanish contribution to the Allied Effort, the destroyer, Numancia, constructed out of white sheets draped around a white delivery truck decked with cardboard canons, and driven by two 'officers.' Men and women of the *cofradia*, dressed in extravagant sailor suits, the women often false bearded, held the structure up as, peeping over the gunwales, they walked forward, ahead around and behind the truck dancing to the sound of military marches played over the loudspeaker. It was a very merry military vessel that made its way down the street. The truck was accompanied by the leader and main creative force in the *cofradia*, a bar owner, Celso Fernandez, dressed in a mock military-business suit, an extravagant beard and carrying a briefcase plastered with the name of the then Catalan Minister of Defense, Narcis Serra. He also carried a mock computer keyboard, which he punched to 'give directions to and change of directions to the boat.' This float was a wry comment upon what was popularly appraised in Spain as a rather insignificant Spanish contribution to the Gulf War, although much trumpeted by the government and the press. It was also a comment upon the government's political manipulation, at a safe distance, of this military 'trick' (*baza*) in the international card game of war. The boat and its crew was accompanied by three 'camp, or

---

[8]   There are in present day democratic Spain, with the exception of Catalonia and the Basque Country which have special politics, essentially two competing parties, the Socialists (PSOE) who held power for 14 years from consolidation in 1982 to 1996 and the Conservatives (PP) who are presently in power. Both are Centrist Parties. But there is still enough presence of the more extremist politics of twentieth-century Spain to produce many undercurrent antagonisms in carnival. One quick observation on Prize Committees is that they are either composed of *Fachas* (Fascists) or *Progres* (Progressives) and hence inimical to a particular carnival groups politics. The National Socialist *Schimpfwort*, Reds, has completely disappeared as too reminiscent of Fascism and the Franco years with which no group wants to be associated.

better, boat followers,' three male members of the *cofradia* dressed as imposing 'vamps' in seductive and shapely black thigh length mini skirts. As one of our collaborators remarked this transvestitism is so widespread in Spanish carnival that one would think that Spanish men wanted to be women. But, of course, this is the case not only in carnival in Spain as any spectator of New Orleans or Brazilian or Brittany carnival will recognize.[9]

The following year, 1992, the five hundred year celebration of the Discovery of America the *cofradia* built a more elaborate vessel, a Columbian caravel (*carabela*), the Santa Maria, with large bed sheet sails and a motley crew including six women dressed as Indians, and several bearishly dressed missionaries in sack cloth (*arpillera*). This time the group's leader, Cristóbal Celsín, while standing 'amidships' and gesturing grandly towards the horizon also carried a telephone which he occasionally used to call the President of the United States informing him that the ship would soon arrive to 'discover' him. It was said that: "In this new imperial American world [the *Planeta Americano* as it has come to be called in Spain][10] the Presidents of the United States need all the discovery or uncovering [*quitando de su cubierto*] by the world that is possible." From time to time the Indians would march forward ahead of the caravel and kneel so that they could be *discovere* by the ship and especially by the missionaries who had come to 'raise them to their feet and enable them to walk as full men and women.' This was a play on traditional missionary rhetoric. As usual there were playful details not easily picked up by spectators but part of the pleasure of the group. For example: so that all three ships of the Columbus expedition should be present one group member dressed as a street walker (*La Pinta*, the painted one) and another as a young girl (*La Niña*).

Sometimes the group has a difficult time discovering a theme, which they can playfully develop and they take a more obvious theatrical topic whose playful possibilities may reveal themselves later. This was the case the fol-

---

[9]   For a psychoanalytic interpretation of transvestitism in Andalusian Carnaval particularly and Carnival in Spain generally see Chapter 6 on "Macho Man and Matriarch" in Gilmore 1998, 74-90. But transvestitism is so widespread in Carnival generally in my experience, in New Orleans and Brazil for example, that it would be difficult to make the case for Spain alone. For a recent and widely praised film about womanly feelings and cross sex identifications in men (also about cross dressing) see Pedro Almodovar's *Todo sobre mi madre*.

[10]   After the popular book, *El Planeta Americano* by Vicente Verdú (1996), explaining the character and presumptions of the American people and their political economy, the dominant culture in the present world. This makes America, and the Americans, therefore, a good object of carnival mockery.

lowing two years. After mulling the issue over during several group suppers in 1993 the group decided to pick up on the Minstrel Show theme and play and sing in Black Face. They constructed one of the most elaborate floats in their experience, a Mississippi River Boat, a stern-wheeler. It was large enough to contain a dancing platform concealed by the boat's sides. But this could be suddenly opened up revealing three of the town's largest and brawniest bearded men dressed as can-can girls twisting and flouncing their skirts. The unexpected irony emerged in the decision to name the boat with its motley 'multi-racial' crew, *The Mayflower*. Alexis de Tocqueville would have been delighted. It was he after all who, in his *Democracy in America*, forecast that the character of America and its future would arise not from its Puritan founders, the actual passengers and crew of *The Mayflower*, but rather from the challenges of its multi-racial composition!

In 1994 once again the group was challenged with finding an inspiring theme and at last, after much debate and several rawkish dinners, settled rather obviously on the Beatles and "The Yellow Submarine." It solved the boat problem but otherwise seemed rather alien. It took great effort to build a plausible submarine more than 40 feet long with a conning tower. It took close attention to manoeuver it through the streets. It was difficult for the submarine sailors hidden in the awkward structure, for example, to learn maritime directions shouted at them from the conning tower: to port, to starboard (*a babor, a estribor*) frequently recast by the novice crew, in perilous and urgent moments in their progress through the streets, in a landlubberly idiom, "to the left" or "to the right."

But the irony asserted itself in the last few days when the group leader decided to dress as a combination of the Mexican Clown Manuel Moreno (*Cantinflas*) and the recently bankrupt, indicted and convicted banker Mario Conde, one of the financial and conglomerate 'wizards' of the Spain of the 1980s whose bank, BANESTO one of Spain's largest, was discovered to be insolvent and the victim of pillaging by its President and board. So as Mario *'Que S'esconde'* ('Mario Who Hides Himself'), a play on words, the leader of the group strode along in a combination business/clown suit beside the submarine giving it directions and attempting to bring it to the surface and refloat it. It was an apt metaphor. The reference, of course, was to the foundered bank, a golden submarine indeed, but also to the submarine financial operations that characterized the eighties and the activities of such once highly respected, even adulated bankers as 'Mario Who Hides Himself.' There were, as usual, various associated by-plays of rich meaning. There was a cyclist in a yellow biker's shirt—the sign, as is well known, of the leading cyclist in a multi day race such as the Tour de France. He was riding a 1920s bike and was periodically whipped along by 'Mario Who Hides Himself.' The reference was to the famous Spanish (Basque) cycle champion of the 1990s, five times winner of the Tour de France, Miguel Indurain, who rode (was then actually still riding) for the BANESTO bike team and was reputed to have been spurred on in the Tour de France and to have profited handsomely from Conde's ill-gotten generosity. Nothing is sacred in carnival.[11]

We have said enough to indicate at once all the thought and hard work that goes into these floats, their planfulness and the parodic pleasures that the groups involved (and spectators) derive from their presentation and their playfulness. There are, of course, monetary stimulants. Because of the competitions reward structure in the half dozen or so towns where this 'street theater' is presented a successful float group can make as much as five or six thousand dollars. But it is not the money, the groups argue, which in any case is usually spent in paying for group dinners, but rather both the *camaraderie* of the hard work that goes into planning and building of the float and the joy (*alegria*) of putting it out on the street with all its parodic power. They feel they achieve—we can say this for them—a compelling combination of planfulness and playfulness, a combination that we might also say must surely characterizes the pleasure of human life at its best, the pleasure of a creature capable of both powerful projects and also sardonically aware of their ephemerality in time!

Conclusion

In this essay I briefly focus on a very widespread human institution of release and revitalization known in the European, and especially the Catholic tradition of Lenten fasting as carnival. Small towns and villages in Spain are the locus of our interest in this phenomena rather than large cities where the wealthy and aristocratic classes have frequently taken up and used carnival for their own class confirming interests and where as is the case of *Mardi Gras* in New Orleans, carnival is a mix of the carnivalesque representations of various class-based associations, fellowships, fraternities and clubs. In these small town carnivals, though class interests and political antagonisms

---

[11] One refers to the virtually godlike status which Indurain's cycling feats, five times champion of the Tour de France, obtained for him as sportsman in Spain.

are also present, the upper classes are not as 'upper' and do not influence the panoply of *carnaval* to such an extent.

In the interests of the revelatory contrast of changing carnival in Spain we have made a comparison between the *carnaval* of southern Spain (Andalusia) in which piquant and pungent carnival song play a major role and the *carnaval* of northern Spain, where masking and the construction of floats, not without their parodic political and social commentary, are featured much more than song.

Carnival poses a problem for anthropological understanding, indeed for any social science understanding of organized social life and particularly of the highly organized life known as ritual. For it turns normal social life on its head in a mocking and insouciant manner. To play a bit with the distinction between the sacred and the profane, where ritual is understood to be the instrument of the sacred, carnival is a set of profane rituals whose profanity nonetheless have been so 'sacred' to popular culture as to effectively resist, as one of our epigraphs indicates, the church's attempts to bring more piety and sobriety into the sacred transitions of the winter season!

We have also wanted to take account of dynamic change in ritual. For the carnival in Asturias of the last decade or more has been much impacted by increases in the scale of awareness of the world, by globalization. The *carnaval* of today is in many ways much different from the carnival of the past, which was much more confined to the concerns of local place and at best provincial place. It sought to provide release to local place just before the tightening down of the Lenten season. Secularization has now loosened the constraints of the Lenten season to the extent that occasionally this street theater trespasses over into the first weeks of Lent. For above all the carnival discussed here has been impacted by the town's and the province's new sense of their place, and lack of place in the emerging world order of commercialization and tourist promotions, and multinational corporations.

But just here in this notion of 'place and lack of place' we come upon one source of the irony and parody of the powers that be: despite the awareness of the world shown in these carnival floats there is a continuing sense of peripherality felt by their creators. We might even argue that parody and irony is always energized by the sense of peripherality. In the parodic *coplas* of Andalusia it is the peripheral classes, the workers and *campesinos*, who mainly energize the mockery.

The ironic energy that can be found in peripherality is only one of many possible accounts to be rendered of something as over-determined as carnival. There are many meanings to be ferreted out by ethnographic inquiry.

The conundrum of carnival has been examined as we have seen from many perspectives: from an ethical perspective as a manifestation or reassertion of the claims of moral community; from the psychoanalytic perspective as a way of dealing with the deep contradictions of identity formation in society; from the political perspective as a rebellious response to the hegemonic and paternalistic practices of dominant classes and institutions. Here we have wanted to practice the tropological approach based as much as possible on elicitation of the associations at work in the planning and performing of carnival as representational street theater—associations brought forth and refigured in ironic register. And this trope is not just our figuration. We have actually time and again found that irony, often in the stronger form of parody, on the lips of our correspondents and collaborators.

The trope of irony and of the double and undercutting vision, the world reversed (*al reves*) has considerable precedence in the Spanish Great Tradition. It is the dominant trope in the Quijote, that parody of knightly power and misadventure. It is present in the *Vida es Sueño* tradition of the Golden Age, of Quevedo and Calderon (see de Quevedo 1965), if not also in *The Dream of Reason* in Goya's *Caprichos*. There may well be some linkage between the world-turned-upside-down theme in the Spanish Great Tradition and the world turned upside down of carnival although we would be at risk in seeing carnival as only a trickle down effect of the Great Tradition. It would be more accurate, perhaps, to see in carnival the more primordial sentiment, the popular engagement with the recurrent abuse of the 'will to power' and with the enduring and contrary puzzlements of the human condition (see Vico 1978 [1744]). The refinements and accentuations of the Great Tradition come later, the carnivalesque working its way upwards to begin with, although the subsequent interrelation enabled the privileged imaginations of the Great Tradition to subsequently work their way down.

But our interest here is not so much in the dialectics of the Great and the Popular Traditions, though this must be a recurrent theme for any anthropology's study of carnival, but rather with understanding that particular combination of planfulness and playfulness and that sense of parodic possibility that inspires the carnivalesque as we know it in Asturias, that motivates its planning and its playing out. So let me end by suggesting one strong motive. We recall once again the fact that carnival was suppressed and prohibited during the authoritarian Francoist years. This recalls the discomfort of authoritarian regimes generally with carnival. Many reasons have been advanced for this authoritarian suppression and prohibition. Prominent among these is the fear of such regimes that masking will be used to conceal perpetrators of public violence in their settling of old scores or their carrying out of subversions. This explanation surely accords with the intense interest of authoritarian regimes in law and order and with the fact that the suppressions they practice result in many resentments to be expressed and many scores to be settled. But I think also important is a frequent enough observation of Asturian interlocutors. Very simply authoritarian personages do not like to be mocked and their actions parodied. And since parody of just these personages and actions lies at the heart of carnival it is intuitively inimical to authoritarianism. We might even go so far as to say, in the search for more general principles, that whatever else democracy means and whatever institutional guarantees it requires, and there is much debate about that in post-authoritarian Spain, it means the right and the freedom to parody the pretensions of power! Democracy supposes a right to the planful/playful, publicly enacted ironies of street theater![12] For forty years in Spain that right did not exist. Now it flourishes. I am reminded of that bumper sticker that appeared on low end and second hand cars in the United States during the Vietnam War when the Official Story of successful military engagement was a very dominant narrative: "Question authority!" That seems to me is one thing that carnival has always been about!

References

Carantoña, Francisco and Jesús E. Casariego. 1984: *Las mascaradas de Evaristo Valle.* Oviedo: Instituto de Estudios Asturianos.

Carantoña, Francisco. 1986: *Evaristo Valle (1873–1951).* 2d ed. Gijón: Fundación Museo Evarsto Valle.

Conde, Javier Fernández. 1981: Religiosidád populár Asturiana. In: *Enciclopedia temática de Asturias.* Vol. 9: *Etnografía y Folklore.* II. (Folklore), ed. José Gómez Álvarez. Gijón: Silverio Cañada. 98–119.

Davis, Natalie Z. 1975: *Society and Culture in Early Modern France.* Stanford: Stanford University Press.

Encina, Juan del. 1975: *Cancionero de 1496.* Madrid: Ediciones ISTMO.

---

[12] Of course, there is plenty of parody and irony going on in authoritarian times about the authorities but necessarily at a very private level. Indeed some authoritarian argue that the ironies of the pub, the bar and the coffee house, the ironies of the *tertulia* as it were, constitute a kind of authentic ground level democracy (see Carantoña and Casariego 1984, 88). The point is democracy requires the right to public displays of ironic commentary about authority!

Fernandez, James W. 1994: Spielerisch und planvoll: Zur Theorie der Tropen in der Anthropologie. In: *Historische Anthropologie* 2:1–19.

Fernandez, James W. and Michael Herzfeld. 1998: On Meaningful Methods. In: *Handbook of Methods in Cultural Anthropology*, ed. H. Russell Bernard. Thousand Oaks, Calif.: Sage. 89–129.

Freud, Sigmund. 1955: *The Interpretation of Dreams*, transl. from the German and ed. James Strachey. New York: Basic Books.

Gilmore, David D. 1998: *Carnival and Culture: Sex, Symbol and Status in Spain*. New Haven: Yale University Press.

Gluckman, Max. 1963: *Rituals of Rebellion in Southeast Africa*. Glencoe: Free Press.

Lakoff, George and Mark Johnson. 1980: *Metaphors We Live By*. Chicago: University of Chicago Press.

Mintz, Jerome R. 1982: *The Anarchists of Casas Viejas*. Chicago: University of Chicago Press.

Mintz, Jerome R. 1997: *Carnival Song and Society: Gossip, Sexuality and Creativity in Andalusia*. (Explorations in Anthropology). Oxford and New York: Berg.

Moliner, María. 1988: *Diccionario del uso del español*. (Bibliotheca románica hispánica 5). Madrid: Gredos.

Nuevo Zarracina, D.G. 1970: Carnalval. In: *Gran Enciclopdia Asturiana*. Vol. 2, ed. Silverio Cañada. Gijón: Silverio Cañada. 98.

Quevedo, Francisco de. 1965: *Los sueños*. (Clásicos Castellanos). Madrid: Espasa Calpe.

Rodriguez Hevia, Victor and Luis M. Iglesias Cueva. 1981: Una Muestra de Teatro Popular: *Les Comedies de los Guirrios*. In: *Enciclopedia Temática de Asturias* Vol. 9: *Etnografia y Folklore* I. (Etnografia), ed. José Gómez Álvarez. Gijón: Silverio Cañada. 269–286.

Verdú, Vicente. 1996: *El Planeta Americano*. Barcelona: Editorial Anagrama.

Vico, Giambattista. 1948: *Scienza Nuova: The New Science of Giambattista Vico*, transl. from the 3d ed. (1744) by Thomas G. Bergin and Max H. Fisch. Ithaca: Cornell University Press.

Rituals of Rebellion – Rebellion as Ritual: A Theory Reconsidered

Susanne Schröter

This essay revisits a famous anthropological theory, the rituals of rebellion, which was developed by Max Gluckman in order to explain African ways of conflict management. It traces the treatment of this model in anthropological theory, especially in the work of the late Victor W. Turner and finally discusses its applicability to the wider setting of modern rebellions.[1]

Rituals of Rebellion as Conservative Phenomena

Gluckman first presented his idea of the 'rituals of rebellion' in 1952 when he delivered the Frazer lecture at the University of Glasgow. He was obviously inspired by James Frazer's account of the priest-king of the Italian grove of Nemi in his famous book *The Golden Bough*. According to the myth, the king was killed by his successor, who, like himself, had to become a murderer before becoming a king. In Frazer's opinion, the Italian scenario was more than a singular artefact—it was a rite that could be found in many agrarian cultures where it was integrated into the annual cycle. He compared this custom with various myths of male heroes, Adonis, Tammuz, Osiris, and Dionysos, who represented the growth and decay of vegetation and, like the plants, which died annually only to rise again. While Frazer's theory quickly became very popular he had little evidence for the existence of the phenomena. So he must have been very pleased, in 1911, to receive a letter from the anthropologist Charles Seligman reporting on a practice similar to the Italian myth—the killing of a divine king among the Shilluk, a people living in the southern Sudan.[2] The Shilluk king, Seligman pointed out, was so much associated with fertility and new life, that he was immured alive or strangled when he became weak, unsuccessful or unable to fulfill all his sexual obliga-

---

[1] My thanks go to Anna-Maria Brandstetter, James W. Fernandez and Harold Scheffler for critical questions and comments on the manuscript.
[2] Seligman's letter to Frazer is cited in Ackermann (1987, 244–245).

tions. Apart from this it was considered legitimate for each of his sons to contest his power by attacking him and attempting to overthrow him by force.

The phenomenon of the ritual regicide of the Shilluk did not only impress Frazer. Years after the appearance of *The Golden Bough*, it inspired many other anthropologists to do further research, among them W.P.G. Thomson (1948), Edward E. Evans-Pritchard (1948; 1951), Paul Philip Howell (1944; 1952; 1953), William Arens (1979) and Burkhardt Schnepel (1988; 1990). I will not discuss the question of whether the killing of the king should be understood as fiction or as reality, but rather turn to the context within which the Shilluk conceive of the idea of regicide as being meaningful to the increase or restoration of the community's well being.

The king (*reth*) is seen as one who incorporates Nyikang, the primordial hero responsible for diverse natural processes, especially the weather. The task of his human representative is to bring a favorable influence to bear on these processes. Famine, droughts and illnesses are recognized as the king's failures and the more often he fails the more he has to be concerned about his declining popularity, which could finally lead to his death. Schnepel mentioned the case of a king who reigned from 1918 to 1943 and had to justify two phases of famine (Schnepel 1990, 199ff.). During the first, in the early 1930s, one of his potential successors attempted to overthrow him and could only be stopped by the intervention of the army. During the second drought he himself elected to die.

What is interesting for the topic under discussion here is not so much the circumstance of his death, which was surrounded by speculations, but the fact that one of his princes was involved in the revolt. In challenging a king who had turned out to be weak, he was acting in correspondence with the Shilluk worldview, where military success is interpreted as indicating that a prince is strong enough to take over the position of a king. Consequently, times of *interregnum* were often times of bloody feuds and civil wars until the British government enforced *pax britannia*. These violent processes were part of the installation ceremonies because the Shilluk did not just want a king, they wanted the right one. He was to be selected by Nyikang, and one prerequisite was military success.

Shortly after Evans-Pritchard's monograph on the Shilluk appeared, Gluckman compared the data presented by Frazer with his own findings in Southeast African societies. However, he did not restrict himself to the phenomenon of regicide, expanding the model to include a wider frame of ritual rebellions. To him the most striking feature of all the rites he observed was

the fact that they openly expressed social tensions. He thus shifted his analytical perspective from the spiritual meaning within the agricultural year,
which had been stressed by Frazer, to social conflicts within particular societies. In his article "Rituals of Rebellion in South-East Africa,"[3] he described
two major conflict lines among the South African Zulu: one between men
and women and the other between the king and his subjects.

The first was enacted within a fertility rite which was related to the Zulu
Princess of Heaven, Nomkubulwana, and required a series of transgression
of gender boundaries by women and girls. The girls wore men's clothes, and
herded and milked the cattle, which was an exclusive male activity and
strictly taboo for them. At various stages of the ritual women and girls went
naked, and sang obscene songs while men and boys hid in their homes.
These rites of female transgression, Gluckman discovered, were not unique
among the Zulu but could be found among several other people. In his article
he mentioned the Tsonga of Mozambique where women even attacked men,
and also the Swazi and the Transkeian Thembu; who practiced rites of female rebellion, which he designated as 'bacchantic.' All these rites, he argued, must be understood as an expression of gender inequality in South
African societies and the subordination of women in daily life. Women were
symbolically associated with evil powers, were excluded from political
power, were exchanged for cattle to the benefit of their brothers and were in
general, treated as a 'second sex,' to borrow the term introduced by Simone
de Beauvoir in 1949.[4] Within the bacchantic rites they adapted the dominant
role, behaved as if they were their brothers who stayed at home as if they
were women. They humiliated men and acted in a lewd and provocative
manner. While breaking the fundamental taboos of society they thus revealed the tensions between men and women and released them. According
to Gluckman this is the deeper meaning of the ceremonies, insofar as the
rituals served as a means of integrating centrifugal powers in society. In
Gluckman's opinion the women's intention was not to change the gender order but to continue their lives as mothers, sisters and wives after the ceremonies. Zulu women, he pointed out, while suffering from the patriarchal
system "became temporarily lewd viragoes, and their daughters martial
herdsmen; but they accepted the social order and did not form a party of
suffragettes" (Gluckman 1963, 127).

---

[3]   The article was first published in 1954 and again in 1963 in a volume entitled *Order and
      Rebellion in Tribal Africa*. The latter is cited here.
[4]   Gluckman never used this term, which he probably didn't know, but his descriptions fit
      exactly in de Beauvoir's schema.

This approach was also taken to explain the second kind of rituals of rebellion, the ones directed against the king. Gluckman mentioned the Swazi *incwala* ceremony, which was described in detail by Hilda Kuper (1947). It consisted of a public humiliation of the king, songs of hatred and a ritual threatening of the king who had to flee into a sacred enclosure. Because the ones who were mostly engaged in this ceremonial rebellion were members of the royal clan, Gluckman interpreted this relationship as one of the core conflicts of Swazi society, which was politically organized into a unification of several territorial segments. Each of these segments was economically independent and only under precarious control of the center. The segments often behaved competitively and their rulers strove to extend their power. Each of them had the possibility of being the next king and thus hostility and fights were not unusual. Although Gluckman did not observe a rite comparable to the one Kuper had described, he found the general political situation among the Zulu very similar to the Swazi. Murder within the royal line was a frequent occurrence.

Gluckman drew a distinction between these assassinations and revolutions, because they were never directed against the institution of the kingdom but just against a particular person. On the contrary, he defined "every rebellion therefore (as) a fight in defense of royalty and kingship" (Gluckman 1963, 130). Here Gluckman argued that every king had to cope with the values of kingship and try to be a good king. Whenever he failed he showed his deficiencies in fulfilling his duties to the country and was consequently in danger of being overthrown by one of his royal relatives.

Generally, Gluckman stressed the difference between revolution and rebellion. According to him the latter "proceed within an established and sacred traditional system, in which there is dispute about particular distributions of power, and not about the structure of the system itself" (Gluckman 1963, 112). To him neither the women nor the rebelling princes were interested in a radical change of society. On the contrary, the final goal of all these rituals was a social blessing and the strengthening and renewing of the established order. Gluckman used Aristotle's concept of *catharsis* to analyze the effects of rituals of rebellion. The performance of hostility, the revelation of social tensions and the possibility of a temporary taking over of the position of the ruling party produced purifying effects that would lead to a diminishing of tensions and a stabilization of society.

It is obvious that Gluckman argued from an institutionalist's point of view and that his idea of societies was quite static.[5] In "Rituals of Rebellion in South-East Africa" Gluckman designated African societies as 'relatively stationary' and 'repetitive' systems (Gluckman 1963, 127), a thesis which he revised in his introduction to the volume on *Order and Rebellion in Tribal Africa* that appeared nine years after publication of the article. He there responded to an earlier critique of Isaak Schapera who had argued that, far from always strengthening the state, African rebellions led to the opposite, namely the splitting of a segment or the migration of the rebellious group (Schapera 1956, 175). Gluckman corrected his former theory which he himself described as "colored by the fact that I studied ... two states where the cycle of rebellions without fission was dominant" (Gluckman 1963, 33) and recognized these as exceptions within a wider framework of African societies where rebellion more often led to separation. Despite these considerations Gluckman was criticized, as Toine van Teeffelen pointed out, for not differentiating between 'non-antagonistic contradictions' and those which could lead to revolution (Teeffelen 1978, 78f.).

Rebellions and Communitas

One of Gluckman's students, Victor W. Turner, who did his fieldwork among the Ndembu of Zambia, later went beyond the framework of his teacher's model and thus extended it. Turner combined Gluckman's approach with the ritual theory of Arnold van Gennep who had largely worked on transitional rites. According to him rites of transition contain three phases: separation, margin and aggregation (see van Gennep 1960). Turner was primarily interested in the second phase, which he calls the liminal period. Liminality is characterized by certain attributes from which the experience of egalitarianism is the most striking one. During this phase society appears as "unstructured or rudimentary structured and relatively undifferentiated communitas" (Turner 1969, 96). With an example from his own research on Ndembu installation rites he shows the usefulness of this approach, which gives Gluckman's explanation of *catharsis* an additional depth.

---

[5]   Bruce Lincoln criticized Gluckman that he did not recognize historical conditions (1987). Lincoln also pointed out that Swazi *incwala* as described by Kuper (1947) had undergone a dramatic change of meaning which resulted in a fundamental stripping the king of his power.

Among the Ndembu the incoming new chief had to show up dressed in a ragged loincloth. Parading through the rows of his future subjects he had to endure affronts and humiliation with a bowed head and was not allowed to retaliate. The leader of those who opposed him was the head of an autochthonous group, which had been subjugated in the past after long battles. He had an important role in the installation process, advised the chief to use the mighty witch medicine and was ritually called 'mother.' During the installation he delivered a long speech to the king where he accused him of being an adulterer, a thief and a sorcerer. He admonished him to stop this behavior and become a responsible ruler. After finishing his speech he gave a signal to another member of the community thus authorizing everybody to criticize the chief. What ever he had done could now be revealed and no one who accused him publicly had to fear any reprisal.

What was mainly enacted in this ritual was "the power of the weak" (Turner 1969, 108) and a temporary travesty of the ruling order. Thus, Turner did not only stress the purification effect of the ceremony but took into consideration the fact that oppressed groups are often associated with a special amount of magical powers.

Turner was convinced that the weak could not only become strong in a ritualized context but also in secular life. In his books, *The Ritual Process* and *From Ritual to Theatre*, both inspired by the students' revolt, which undoubtedly influenced these ideas, Turner analyzed certain movements, some of them religiously motivated like the early Franciscans, others, like the Beatniks, more secularly orientated. All practiced communitas or were at least strongly concerned about developing communitarianism in daily life. The behavior, which was recognized as a means of expressing ritual liminality, was in these cases reformulated as a principle. Unlike the Shilluk, Ndembu and Zulu who, according to their anthropologists, never intended to engage in a revolution, the movements cited by Turner were mainly interested in changing the society. Communitas was considered to be more than a ritual stage; it became the final goal of all political and spiritual efforts. Here the members of such a movement created a model of society which was necessarily opposed to the ruling order. However, studying these movements Turner recognized that, despite all their intentions, after a while structure appeared within the so-called anti-structure, hierarchy emerged and the community of equals changed into a stratified organization. Thus, according to Turner, every attempt to endure and prolong the liminal phase is doomed to fail: the rebellion reveals itself to be just a ritual.

It is to Turner's credit to have opened up Gluckman's ideas of rituals of rebellion and put it into a wider frame of ritual theory. His knowledge is impressive and his unorthodox intercultural comparisons have not lost their fascinating power. However, to a certain degree his approach seems to be eclectic. In his writings he groups diverse rituals and rebellions, social movements and unusual circumstances under various aspects using them as examples for his thoughts on social drama, liminality and play. Undoubtedly this is evocative, but it is not an encompassing theory, which is able to put the diverse metaphors and tropes into a coherent relationship. Even his concept of 'liminality' is vapid since he extends it to modern leisure genres like sports, home entertainment and attending a concert. To characterize these activities he uses the term 'liminoid phenomena,' which, in my opinion, is a category that has less than tenuous connection to ritual.

Despite my critique of Gluckman's functionalistic approach and Turner's unsystematic approach I consider their theories can provide useful insight into the phenomenon of rebellion in general.

In the following I examine three different kinds of rebellion of which at least two have only been analyzed from economic, social and political points of view: Melanesian cargo cults, a case of recent headhunting in Indonesia, and Western youth subcultures. All these rebellions have a common pattern that distinguishes them from Gluckman's feuds and the other examples of rituals of rebellion in that their activists intended to trigger fundamental changes in society. Despite this, they developed elaborate ritual spheres, which were inseparably related to the rebellious project as such.

Cargo Cults in Melanesia

Cargo cults are prophetic movements, which emerged towards the end of the nineteenth century in New Guinea and some Melanesian islands, especially the New Hebrides, the Solomon islands and Fiji. Cargo, the white colonialists' commodities, which had reached Melanesia by air or by sea, symbolized a strange power and was the central metaphor of the cults. The members of a cult expected their ancestors to return soon and to bring with them all the desired goods: steel axes, weapons, money and canned food. This event would be the beginning of a new happy era.

The particular movements were founded by prophets who told their followers they had been in contact with spiritual beings who had given them exact instructions on the required ritual practice. Often this included a prohibition of work in the fields, the responsibility for constructing landing-places for the ancestors and the duty to participate in ceremonies. Until the middle of the twentieth century these movements were recognized as collective hysteria or possessions by ghosts. This changed after World War II, when anthropologists began to interpret them as reactions to the dramatic social changes triggered by colonialism and the technological and economic power of the whites. Anthropologists like Peter Worsley (1957), Wilhelm E. Mühlmann (1961) and Ton Otto (1992) defined cargo cults as anti-colonial rebellions and put them into the context of a universal religion of the oppressed. Worsley saw their primarily positive effect in the unifying results for the Melanesian people, which contributed to the overcoming of segmentation within Melanesian society. Worsley and others have additionally defined them as direct precursors of Melanesian nationalism. They thus did not characterize them as traditional rites and expressions of a pre-modern consciousness but as classical modernizing movements. Consequently, Worsley, whose most important study was published in 1957, expected a successive transformation of the cults into secular organizations like unions and political parties. An oft-cited cult, the Paliau movement, seemed to prove this theory. It began as a millenarian movement and then, after a phase of disappointment, which followed the failure of the prophecy, continued with political and social activities within the villages. Under a strict set of rules Paliau's followers, who had came from different ethnic groups, lived peacefully together within the villages. According to Holger Jebens and Karl-Heinz Kohl, Paliau initiated "the import of western organization models long before the colonial government itself introduced them" (1999, 14; translated by the author).

Cargo movements were different from Zulu or Shilluk feuds. Their members never intended to maintain the ruling order but attempted to change it radically. No longer would the whites be the only possessors of wealth—their goods and the power related to them would become the property of Melanesians. The leaders developed new social, political and religious models and strove to put them into practice. The colonial government reacted promptly. The cults were forbidden, the army was mobilized, and the leaders were arrested and banned. In some cases fantastic alternate models were created to redirect the anti-colonial feelings in a different direction. In Fiji, for example, the colonial administration tried to deactivate the Fiji Luweniwai movement by the founding of cricket clubs (see Mückler 1996). For this purpose they invented an encompassing ritual inventory including ritual titles like High Lord Admiral or Major General. At the beginning this strategy seemed to be successful but in time the members of the cricket clubs derived political attributes from these titles. The colonial government recognized that the harmless clubs had become places of political anti-colonial agitation and suppressed them.

Addressing the question of communitas I would argue that cargo cults tried to develop a sense of equal distribution of wealth and as such reinstall the pre-colonial situation on a modern level. As anthropologists like Kenelm Burridge (1960) and Peter Lawrence (1964) have pointed out, indigenous Melanesian communities had kept a certain balance of power through the exchange of goods and the competition between 'big men' in order to increase the amount of supplies in circulation. This mechanism of maintaining egalitarianism between men was deeply disrupted by the colonial encounter. Through their belief that the white people's wealth had been stolen from their ancestors, who would bring it back and restore equality again, Melanesian people responded to this imbalance and found a way of reorganizing their lives in anticipation of a traditional utopia.[6]

Cargo cults were obviously rebellions and their members obviously used ritual means. Unlike Gluckman's idea it was not the ritual but the rebellion against the ruling order that was the activists' main goal. Choosing the ritual form of resistance they tied their present to their pre-colonial past. This included reinterpretations of their myth and a general revitalization of their culture. Thus, Jebens and Kohl analyzed rituals with reference to Fritz Kramer as the "attempt to cope with threatening influences from the outside through the use of mimesis" (Jebens and Kohl 1999, 17; translated by the author).

Headhunting as Ritualized Rebellion

The next rebellion I want to mention began in December 1996 as an incident between a group of indigenous people on the island of Kalimantan, the Dayak and migrants from the island of Madura. As a result of the relatively minor conflict a great number of Dayak gathered and started rampaging through the Madurese villages. They burnt the houses, chased the inhabitants, beheaded many of them[7] and finally placed their victims' heads on

---

[6] According to Harold Scheffler, cargo cults emerged primarily in areas with a rather egalitarian social system (personal communication).

[7] Official sources reported that 2000 people were killed, 5170 made refugees and more than 1000 houses destroyed (see Sukma 1998, 106).

sticks along the roads. Commenting on that incident, a German newspaper[8] quoted a Christian missionary: members of his community had told him that although they continued to be good Christians they would now temporarily become Dayak again and fight for their interests as Dayak would.

The reason for the conflict was not very different from those occurring in other parts of Indonesia at that time, and although there also were some local aspects, it was primarily a result of Indonesia's policy of *transmigrasi* (see Fulcher 1980; 1981), that is, the policy of sending peasants from the overpopulated islands of Java and Madura to some of the outer island while offering them land and an amount of money for the expenses of the first year. In many places this led to conflicts between these settlers and the autochthonous population who often became minorities in their own region. A different way of living, of farming and trading, the competition for resources and access to jobs and an ethnocentric attitude on both sides increased the difficulties.[9] Within the Indonesian scale of upheaval this outburst of violence was not considered surprising but just seen as a further area of conflict. What is more important to our topic is the fact that the Dayak resorted to headhunting for their purpose. Headhunting was widespread in pre-colonial Indonesia and it belonged to a set of customs that was strongly related not only to an indigenous mode of warfare but also to the realm of fertility and procreation (Hoskins 1996). As such, it was the focus of a group of ceremonies. On colonizing Indonesia the Dutch banned headhunting. It disappeared almost completely and was just performed symbolically.

By beheading the Madurese the Dayak were not just intervening in a local rebellion, they were acting in a highly symbolic manner. Additionally they used the beheading to demonstrate their ethnicity and thus reconstructed their ethnic affiliation. In older ethnographic accounts headhunting was used as a kind of ethnic marker[10] and even today headhunting is seen as "the Dayak's particular form of interethnic relations" (Drake 1989, 277). Visible to the whole world—the pictures were printed by both the regional and the international press—they presented themselves as Dayak, a group with special fierce war tactics and rituals and related themselves to their glorious past

---

[8] *Frankfurter Rundschau* of March 20, 1998.
[9] In the Kalimantan case this was not only a conflict between autochthonous people and migrants but between two migrants groups: the Malay and the Madurese, which let to a coalition between Dayak and Malay.
[10] This had led to titles like *The Head-Hunters of Borneo* (Bloch 1881).

of resistance to Dutch colonialism and Malay hegemony.[11] They also revived the image of themselves as wild people, barbarians—an image, which is widespread within the Indonesian context.[12]

Choosing headhunting as a means of political protest they also acted within a highly sensitive sphere of talking about violence. According to Anna Tsing (1996), the lines between headhunters and their victims have now become blurred, so that some Dayak groups feel themselves to be victims of unknown raiders while at the same time using verbal violence as a means of creating identity. Rumors of headhunting occur regularly in Indonesia, and recently indigenous people have often described themselves as victims. They especially suspected the state, the police, international companies and missionaries of initiating such violent actions in order to get human sacrifices for construction projects or to wipe out a certain people. In some cases they might even have used Dayak groups for political purposes.

So, when the Dayak of West Kalimantan decided to become temporary headhunters they engaged in this ambivalent discourse of power and turned their role from that of a victim to that of a perpetrator.

Western Youth Subculture

The last example, the organization of post-adolescent young people in diverse subcultures, is neither a phenomenon of non-Western countries, nor a response to colonialism or an expression of ethnic tensions in a multicultural state. Actually, it is an international phenomenon, not just a Western one, since we find very developed subcultures all over the world in the urban sector. However, as a cultural phenomenon it originated in the West and is deeply related to a certain stage of economic and social development, mainly the dissolution of kinship ties and the eradication of ritual life.

Although youth has always been the main force of any rebellion, the phenomenon of youth subculture emerged as mass phenomenon after World War II. While the war generation enjoyed their newly achieved wealth and comfort, their children gathered in the streets, smoked in public and listened to a music that was seen as the "niggers' revenge for … slavery" (Farin 1997, 14, translated by the author). Rock 'n' roll was born and with it the

---

[11] Garang (1974) mentioned several rebellions in 1870, 1887 and 1901. Also the banning of the Ngasi-Njuli cult 1905 led to oppositional movements in 1920 and 1922.

[12] Rumor that groups of Dayak rove around looking for heads occurred from time to time among the Chinese and Muslim population of Kalimantan (see Bhar 1980).

culture of the Teds. Teds recruited themselves mostly from working-class youth but dressed as dandies, imitating the style of King Edward, the black sheep of the British royal clan. The Teds were followed by the Mods, who distinguished themselves carefully from the first. Like the Teds they seemed, at first sight, to be elegant and, on closer inspection, rather odd. They carried umbrellas in the sun and did not mind wallowing in mud in their new clothes. According to Farin, it was not easy to classify them properly. They seemed to be both conformist and provocative "behind the friendly façade subversion was sneering" (Farin 1997, 15, translated by the author). The Mods were followed by Rockers with their motor-cycles and crude cult of masculinity, and another working-class phenomenon, the skinheads. Finally, at the end of the 1960s youth subculture exploded into a great variety of forms: hippies, beatniks, urban guerillas, punks, heavy metals, Ancient Goths and many others. Since this time a growing number of sociologists, politicians, educationists, psychologists, social workers and members of the church have been occupied with explaining and classifying them, with find-ing solutions for problems they have caused and considering preventive measures.

Although there are numerous scientific approaches to explaining urban youth culture only a handful of researchers (see Inhetveen 1997; Turner 1969; 1982) have taken account of the ritualistic aspect. This, however, is obvious. Members of Western youth cultures form ritual communities. They develop a special dress code which functions as a marker to outsiders, create their own values, their own mode of behavior, their own music, literature, art and—last but not least—a set of rituals which keep the group together, shape their relationship, and present them to the outside. Some of the groups have professed religious or occult affiliation but the majority conceive themselves as atheists and attacks on the church and the Christian belief system are of-ten part of their public behavior. Their rebellion is not only directed towards authorities or representatives of the state but also to society as a whole. Miller has called this "the ethics of cultural opposition" (Miller 1991). This makes youth subcultures unique among the wide range of rebellions: they are rebels against their own society, against parents, teachers, and the older gen-eration in general and also against most of their age mates. Consequently, their behavior is an active refusal of current customs, values and rules. Some, like the leftwing autonomous groups, stress their opposition to the state's power monopoly and perform regular highly ritualized fights with the police (see Manrique 1992), others like the skinheads constitute their group identity while provoking ordinary people with racist slogans and violence.

Often members of youth cultures reject middle class carriers and practice a self-chosen poverty: they rely on welfare systems or work in a low paid, alternative sector. Mostly they have a developed sense of equality and constitute a radical communitas within the groups. This seemed even valid for the majority of right wing skinheads.[13]

Youth subcultures, especially those assumed to be a threat to the public, were explained as results of failed youth policy (Boniter-Dörr and Weinknecht 1993; Heitmeyer 1989), as effects of the ongoing individualization of society (Beck 1986; Furlong and Cartmel 1997) and the alienation of its members or as an effect of class conflicts and social instability (Hall and Jefferson 1976; Heitmeyer 1988; Osgerby 1998). All these analytical approaches, although they serve quite well as an explanation of the particular form of youth cultures, give no answer to some reasonable questions. Why is their protest so highly ritualized and why is it temporarily limited to the phase of late adolescence? Most of those alienated, disorientated and forlorn young people who revolt so fiercely turn into ordinary citizens when they reach a certain age. The latter is a relatively hidden process when the protagonists belong to the working class or do not get into influential positions. In the case of young leftists, however, the break becomes obvious. Many activists of the former students' rebellion belong now to the societies' elite, and recently we have witnessed the change from rebels to established politicians within the Green parties. Such developments are not always positively recognized. This is shown by the very polarized debates over the rebellious of the German minister for foreign affairs, Joseph Fischer, in his youth.

By considering all these circumstances we can point out several constitutive elements for Western youth cultures: (1) they create a group, (2) they establish communitas within the group,[14] (3) they elaborate their own rituals, (4) they live in a liminal state, (5) they use the means of rebellion to define their extraordinary situation, and (6) they reintegrate into society when they have become 'real' adults. Thus my argument is that since traditional rites of transition have disappeared in industrial societies young people have created their own rites. The transformation from non-adult to adult creates needs rituals which fit perfectly into the scheme of *rites de passage* described by van Gennep and Turner. Together with Gluckman's thesis that ritual rebellions finally do not lead to a revolution—as expected by, at least, the young leftwing—these theories offer useful models for analysis.

---

[13]   These are the findings of Klaus Farin's famous studies (Farin 1996; 1997), which correct the common notion of skin heads as leader-oriented, authoritarian characters.

[14]   Some, like the hippies, did this explicitly (Miller 1991), others did so more implicitly.

Rituals of Rebellion: A Powerful Answer to Social Change

When we have a look at the similarities of the cases discussed above we see that all these movements occurred in situations of rapid social change. The Melanesians were faced with colonialism, the Dayak feared being marginalized and threatened by the state, and members of Western youth subcultures suffered from ongoing changes in modern industrial societies. They all belong to groups who lacked access to power and wealth and thus were unable to participate as equals in society. By creating a cult, a subculture or by engaging in a revolt people solved the problem of belonging to an oppressed group in several ways:

First, they empowered themselves while creating a counter-world with its own rules and values that gave meaning to their existence. Doing this they also demonstrated that they did not accept either the prevailing order or their own inferior status.

Second, they improved their role in society. When people of oppressed groups organized themselves they did not only develop strength and self-confidence but also developed a powerful position in society. This happened especially when people used violence. In the case of autonomous groups this was a clearly expressed strategy, in other cases it might have been more a psychological activity.

Comparing this to Gluckman's model of rituals of rebellion one can recognize a significant difference. Neither the Melanesians nor the Dayak or Western youth intended to practice a ritual. According to their self-image, they were rebels, and their goal was to bring about a noticeable change of the social order. They were probably unaware of the fact that they were also ritualists. This is especially true for members of leftwing organizations who planned not only a rebellion but also a revolution. Thus, to apply the African model to the cited cases one has to turn it upside down. Generally, it is a dialectical relationship. Political rebellions can drift to mere rituals and ritual rebellions can reveal themselves to be more political than ceremonial. Although ritual rebellion was practiced in African divine kingships there was also real political rebellion which, when it failed, resulted in bloody revenge and violent oppression for the rebelling group, as Lincoln (1987) showed for the Swazi. Thus, the princes were both rebels and practitioners of reversal rituals and one might speculate about their personal intentions. The participants of rebellions, which were defined as social or political ones did not only engage in political action, they also used the means of ritual. The result in both cases was necessarily uncertain: a divine king could be killed on the occasion of an event, which was thought to be a ritual and the political rebel could end up as a ritualist.

However, for analytical purposes it would seem to make sense to use the means of ritual analysis in order to understand social and political rebellion. This would provide additional insights into processes, which until now have just been analyzed from the angles of political science and sociology.

References

Ackerman, Robert. 1987: *J.G. Frazer. His Life and Work*. Cambridge: Cambridge University Press.

Arens, William. 1979: Divine Kingship of the Shilluk: A Contemporary Re-Evaluation. In: *Ethnos* 44:167–181.

Beauvoir, Simone de. 1949: *Le deuxième sexe*. Paris: Gallimard.

Bhar, Supriya. 1980: A Headhunter Scar in a Simunul Bajau Village in Sandakan, 1979. In: *Borneo Research Bulletin* 12:26–29.

Beck, Ulrich. 1986: *Risikogesellschaft: Auf dem Weg in eine andere Moderne*. Frankfurt a.M.: Suhrkamp.

Bloch, Carl. 1881: *The Head-Hunters of Borneo*. London: Oxford University Press.

Bonifer-Dörr, Gerhard and Günter Weinknecht. 1993: *Hakenkreuze, Türkenwitze... rechtsextreme Jugendliche eine pädagogische Herausforderung*. Lübeck: Heidelberger Institut für Beruf und Arbeit.

Burridge, Kenelm. 1960: *Mambu: A Melanesian Millenium*. London: Methuen & Co.

Drake, Richard A. 1989: Construction Sacrifice and Kidnapping Rumor Panics in Borneo. In: *Oceania* 59:269–279.

Evans-Pritchard, Edward E. 1948: *The Divine Kingship of the Shilluk of the Nilotic Sudan*. Cambridge: Cambridge University Press.

———. 1951: The Shilluk King-Killing. In: *Man* 51:116.

Farin, Klaus. 1996: *Skinhead – A Way of Life: Eine Jugendbewegung stellt sich vor*. Cologne: Bund-Verlag.

Farin, Klaus. 1997: *Die Skins: Mythos und Realitaet*. Berlin: Ch. Liks Verlag.

Frazer, James G. 1900: *The Golden Bough: A Study in Magic and Religion* (1890). 2d ed. London: Macmillan.

Fulcher, Mary B. 1980: Dayak and Transmigrant Communities in East Kalimantan. In: *Borneo Research Bulletin* 14:14–24.

———. 1981: Avoidance and Ambiguity in Interethnic Relations: Population Resettlement in East Kalimantan. In: *Borneo Research Bulletin* 15:108–113.

Furlong, Andy and Fred Cartmel. 1997: *Young People and Social Change: Individualization and Risk in Late Modernity*. Buckingham: Open University Press.

Garang, Johannes E. 1974: *Adat und Gesellschaft: Eine sozio-ethnologische Untersuchung zur Darstellung des Geistes- und Kulturlebens der Dajak von Kalimantan*. Wiesbaden: Franz Steiner Verlag.

Gennep, Arnold van. 1960: *The Rites of Passage* (1909), transl. from the French Monika B. Vizedom and Gabrielle L. Caffee. London: Routledge & Kegan Paul.

Gluckman, Max. 1954: *Rituals of Rebellion in South-East Africa.* Cambridge: Cambridge University Press.

————. 1963: *Order and Rebellion in Tribal Africa.* New York: Free Press.

Hall, Stuart and Tony Jefferson (eds.). 1976: *Resistance Through Rituals: Youth Subcultures in Post-War Britain.* London: Hutchinson.

Heitmeyer, Wilhelm. 1988: Ökonomisch-soziale Alltagserfahrungen und rechtsextremistische Orientierungen bei Jugendlichen. In: *Risiko Jugend: Leben, Arbeit und politische Kultur,* ed. Frank Benseler, Wilhelm Heitmeyer, Dietrich Hoffmann, Dietmar K. Pfeiffer, and Dieter Sengling. Münster: Votum Verlag. 219–232.

————. 1989: Jugend, Staat und Gewalt in der politischen Risikogesellschaft. In: *Jugend – Gewalt – Politik. Sozialisation von Jugendlichen und politische Bildung,* ed. Wilhelm Heitmeyer, Kurt Möller, and Heinz Sünker. Munich: Juventa Verlag. 11–46.

Hoskins, Janet (ed.). 1996: *Headhunting and the Social Imagination in Southeast Asia.* Stanford: Stanford University Press.

Howell, Paul Philip. 1944: The Installation of the Shilluk King. In: *Man* 44:146–147.

————. 1952: The Death and Reburial of the Reth Dak Wad Fadiet of the Shilluk. In: *Sudan Notes and Records* 33:156–164.

————. 1953: The Election and Installation of Reth Kur Wad Fafiti of the Shilluk. In: *Sudan Notes and Records* 34:189–204.

Jebens, Holger and Karl-Heinz Kohl. 1999: Konstruktionen von „Cargo": Zur Dialektik von Fremd- und Selbstwahrnehmung in der Interpretation melanesischer Kultbewegungen. In: *Anthropos* 94:3–20.

Inhetveen, Katharina. 1997: Gesellige Gewalt: Ritual, Spiel und Vergemeinschaftung bei Hardcoremusikern. In: *Soziologie der Gewalt,* ed. Trutz Trotta. Opladen: Westdeutscher Verlag. 235–260.

Kuper, Hilda. 1947: *An African Aristocracy: Rank among the Swazi.* London: Oxford University Press.

Lawrence, Peter. 1964: *Road Belong Cargo: A Study of the Cargo Movement in the Southern Madang District, New Guinea.* Manchester: Manchester University Press.

Lincoln, Bruce. 1987: Ritual, Rebellion, Resistance: Once More the Swazi Ncwala. In: *Man* (n.s.) 22:132–156.

Manrique, Matthias. 1992: *Marginalisierung und Militanz: Jugendliche Bewegungsmilieus im Aufruhr.* Frankfurt a.M.: Campus.

Miller, Timothy. 1991: *The Hippies and American Values.* Knoxville: The University of Tennessee Press.

Mühlmann, Wilhelm E. 1961: *Chilianismus und Nativismus: Studien zur Psychologie, Soziologie und historischen Kasuistik der Umsturzbewegungen.* Mit Beiträgen von Alfons M. Dauer [et al.]. (Studien zur Soziologie der Revolution 1). Berlin: Dietrich Reimer Verlag.

Mückler, Hermann. 1996: *Fidschi: Zwischen Tradition und Transformation. Koloniales Erbe, Häuptlingstum und ethnische Heterogenität als Herausforderung an die Zukunft.* Frankfurt a.M.: IKO – Verlag für Interkulturelle Kommunikation.

Osgerby, Bill. 1998: *Youth in Britain Since 1945.* Oxford: Blackwell.

Otto, Ton. 1992: The Paliau Movement in Manus and the Objectification of Tradition. In: *History and Anthropology* 5:427–454.

Schapera, Isaak. 1956: *Government and Politics in Tribal Societies*. London: Watts.

Schnepel, Burckhard. 1988: Shilluk Royal Ceremonies of Death and Installation. In: *Anthropos* 83:433–453.

———. 1990: Shilluk Kinship: Power Struggles and the Question of Succession. In: *Anthropos* 85:105–124.

Sukma, Rizal. 1996: A Year of Politics and Sadness. In: *Institute of Southeast Asian Studies: A Commemorative History*. Singapore: Institute of Southeast Asian Studies.

Teeffelen, Toine van. 1978: The Manchester School in Africa and Israel: A Critique. In: *Dialectical Anthropology* 3:67–83.

Thomson, W.P.G. 1948: Further Notes on the Death of a Reth of the Shilluk. In: *Sudan Notes and Records* 29:151–60.

Tsing, Anna L. 1996: Telling Violence in the Meratus Mountains. In: *Headhunting and the Social Imagination in Southeast Asia*, ed. Janet Hoskins. Stanford: Stanford University Press. 184–215.

Turner, Victor W. 1969: *The Ritual Process: Structure and Anti-Structure*. (Lewis Henry Morgan Lectures 1966). Chicago: Aldine Publishing Company.

———. 1982: *From Ritual to Theatre: The Human Seriousness of Play*. New York: Performing Arts Journal Publication.

Worsley, Peter. 1957: *The Trumpet Shall Sound: A Study of "Cargo" Cults in Melanesia*. London: MacGibbon & Kee.

Communion, National Community, and the Challenge of Radical Religion in Seventeenth-Century England

Achsah Guibbory

Seventeenth-century England offers rich ground for exploring the dynamics of changing ritual. It was a period of intense religious conflict and witnessed a civil war fought in part over religion. At the center of religious conflict lay the ritual of Communion—one of the two Sacraments retained by Protestant churches after the Reformation. Arguments over the practice of Communion in the early seventeenth century revealed the absence of a shared consensus about the nature and meaning of the ritual. Once war broke out (in 1642) and the structures of religious authority were weakened, the ritual became further destabilized and contested.

Communion was deeply bound up with notions of 'community,' and thus 'transformations' of the ritual entailed changed notions of 'community.' In post-Reformation England, the rite of Communion had social and political as well as spiritual significance. It functioned to construct community beyond the walls of the church. To alter or to reject the rite of Communion established by the Church and Parliamentary law was to propose a change in the structure and organization of society—and for this reason (and not solely for spiritual reasons) was immensely threatening.

Communion and National Identity

Though Henry VIII broke from Rome, it was under Edward VI and especially Elizabeth I that the Church of England as a distinctive Protestant church was officially formed. The *Book of Common Prayer* was published in 1559, and Parliament passed legislation for Uniformity in worship. All clergy had to use the *Prayer Book*. Recusants who refused to attend the English Church services were fined, and Catholics persecuted. The aim of these measures was to construct the identity of English Christianity and the community of the English nation, defined against Rome in the wake of the Reformation.

Benedict Anderson has argued that the modern 'nation' dates from the end of the eighteenth century, and grew out of and replaced two older forms of community—the political community of the dynasty and the religious community of Christianity (Anderson 1995, 9–36). Though Anderson argues that the sovereign nation emerged only at the end of the eighteenth century, I would argue that early post-Reformation England was a transitional period when an incipient idea of nation came into being that had a strong religious dimension. In the wake of the Reformation, there was a self-conscious attempt to define a specifically English Protestant religious community imagined to be coterminous with the nation's borders.

After the Protestant Reformation, there was no longer a single Christian religious community, united by shared language (Latin), ritual, and papal authority. Though a number of Christians hoped for re-unification of Christendom and there was a shared Protestant identity, the effects of the Reformation worked against the sense of a unified transnational Christian community. Insisting that the Bible be printed in the vernacular so that all Christians could have direct access to God's Word, the Reformation fostered a diversity of Christian communities, each having its own translation of the Bible and worshipping in its own language. In England, separation from the authority of Rome in religion produced a separate sovereign state, in which both religious and political authority lay with the monarch.

The process of formalizing and legalizing the liturgy and ritual worship of England was a way of defining an English communal, national identity. Though it is often said that Protestantism separated church and state, that was not true in late sixteenth- and seventeenth-century England, where membership in the established Church of England was mandated and Catholicism was defined through Parliamentary law as treason. This conjunction in post-Reformation England of religious and national identity fostered a special sense of nationhood, in which religious worship played a crucial role. Shared liturgy and religious rituals would encourage a sense of shared communal bonds that were not just generally Reformed but specifically English. England would have an inclusive, national church, sharing a single Communion. The ritual meal thus had a socio-political as well as spiritual function: it cemented bonds among English people even as it connected each believer with Christ in an affirmation of eternal salvation.

There were challenges to this ideal of community. Some Catholics refused Communion while 'Church papists' outwardly conformed but remained secretly Catholic. Some puritan ministers, too, disrupted the idealized English Protestant unity: they objected to wearing the surplice during Communion and to having communicants kneel at receiving the bread and wine. James I contained the friction in the church, in part by not insisting rigorously on conformity to the ceremonies (see Fincham 1993, 11; Fincham and Lake 1993; Tyacke 1987).

The Rise of Laudian Worship

The situation changed after 1625, with the ascension of Charles I, himself a lover of ritual and married to a Catholic queen (see Sharpe 1992, chap. 1 and 2; Davies 1992). As the ritual of Communion was bound up with the construction of a political as well as religious community, the changes in Communion that characterized Charles's reign inevitably had sharp political significance.

Charles promoted clergy who favored a highly ceremonial worship and emphasized the Sacrament of Communion rather than preaching (see Sharpe 1992; Davies 1992; Fincham 1993; Lake 1993; Tyacke 1987; Milton 1995; Guibbory 1998). William Laud rose to power through the 1620s and was appointed Archbishop of Canterbury in 1633. These years saw the development of 'Laudian' worship, which emphasized ritual and uniformity. With its attention to ceremonies surrounding the ritual of Holy Communion, Laudianism tried to revive what Eamon Duffy has described as the corporate Christianity of pre-Reformation England, though it infuriated 'hotter Protestants,' who saw the ceremonies as a return to Catholicism (Duffy 1992). But there was also a strong sociopolitical aspect to Laudian religious worship. Just as the legally formalized Communion under Elizabeth worked to construct the imagined community of the English nation, so the Laudian changes to the ritual of Communion were supposed to shape the English community, though to a different end.

The performance of bodily gestures such as kneeling were to integrate body and soul in worship; the re-enactment of traditional forms connected the worshipper with an ancient, pre-Reformation tradition of worship. Bodily forms of reverence would also express the people's humble 'reverence,' and acknowledge the priests' power and God's 'majesty.' Charles and the Laudians imagined such a Communion as the bedrock of a well-ordered, hierarchical society, for it enacted communal integration and submission to higher authorities—a submission transferable to earthly powers. Though these ritual changes were highly divisive, their proponents believed a properly ceremonial Communion would unify the people and teach a reverence and submission that was politically useful to Charles I, whose absolutist ideology taught that the king was God's representative, answerable only to God.

We see the Laudian valuation of a highly ritualized Communion in the writings of John Cosin. Cosin erected an expensive altar at Durham Cathedral and made it the center of an elaborate Communion service. He thought he was continuing a venerable tradition that extended back to the ancient Jews (Cosin 1855, 35–36, 88). Cosin insisted the priest formally "consecrate" the "sacrifice" of the Eucharist (109), wearing the "appointed" vestments (305). Once the elements are consecrated, they must be received "with reverence" (101). "Our kneeling, and the outward gesture of humility and reverence in our bodies, is ordained only to testify and express the inward reverence and devotion of our souls towards our Blessed Saviour" (345). Just as outward behavior mirrors inner, so church behavior mirrors political behavior. The people must exhibit due reverence in approaching God's "inner chamber" (the Chancel) and partaking of the feast, much as they would in approaching a king (319–320). In Cosin's analogy, the function of Communion to confirm a particular sociopolitical order becomes clear. Bowing and kneeling in the presence of God in the church teaches communicants the transferable reverence and obedience appropriate to Charles's increasingly absolute monarchy during the 1630s.

The English poet, George Herbert, was no Laudian, yet his volume of poetry *The Temple* expresses a similar sense that an inclusive Communion is essential to the health and peace of the nation. His poem "The British Church" celebrates the national church as the beautiful, sole bride of Christ. Constructing his volume of poetry on the basis of an analogy with the English Church, Herbert emphasizes the centrality of Communion, focusing on the experience of the Eucharist from the first poem ("The Altar") to the last ("Love III"). Condemning the "wranglers" who are destroying the "Peace" of the Church by objecting to ceremonial "set forms" ("The Familie," ll. 7, 9, 11), he insists "all" ("The Invitation," ll. 1, 7, 13, 19, 25, 31) are invited to "The Banquet" of God, as if an inclusive national Communion would be the solution to sociopolitical as well as religious disorder.

Puritan Reactions

To puritans, however, clergy like Cosin were reviving a highly ceremonial Communion that was the first step to bringing back the Catholic Mass and submission to Rome. With its attention to the Altar and bodily gestures, Laudian ceremonialism provoked people who believed that a commemorative or spiritual ritual was being transformed into something outward and 'carnal,' and that the prelates were arrogating to themselves a power that violated the more egalitarian implications of the gospel and the Reformation. Cosin's Communion service at Durham Cathedral prompted an outraged sermon by Peter Smart on July 7, 1628. Smart brought charges against Cosin and five others at Durham Cathedral a few years later (Smart 1869). Where Cosin valued continuity with the past (even the Jewish past), Smart insisted that Cosin's introduction of an altar and his innovations at Durham Cathedral were "sacrilegious" and "Antichristian," a revival of "Jewish types" and Catholic practices (Smart 1628, 7, 9). By replacing tables with altars, the "innovating" clergy were transforming the ritual of Communion into something at once material and mysterious. They were replacing a simple communal, commemorative meal, partaken at a "table" placed "in the midst of the quire" (33), with a hierarchical, mystified service, in which a "priest" (not minister) attended a beautified altar whose elevation and fixity turned it into an object of reverence, an "Idol" (26). Objecting to Cosin's practice of bowing and using "ceremonies" not "fit for the holy Communion" (24–25), Smart complained that "the altar is every day worshipped with ducking to it" (13–14). Such a ritual not only seemed to be idolatry; it also made a sharp distinction between the priestly class and the others who were kept at a distance. Where Cosin and the Laudians saw clerical authority as linked with and supporting the king, puritan critics objected that the new ritualism exalted the power and authority of the clergy, and made the church the locus of wealth and splendor. The Laudian attempt to change Communion into a more formal, hierarchical, and mystified rite thus implied threatening changes in the social and political structure.

Laudian Innovations

William Laud was most closely identified with the new ceremonial Communion, particularly after he was appointed Archbishop of Canterbury. But even as Bishop of St. David's, Laud made innovations. In his *Visitation Arti-*

cles for 1622, he insisted the Communion table be placed in the Chancel
rather than the quire (see Laud 1853, 381), reinforcing the sense that the
Chancel was the "holiest" part of the church, that there were "degrees" of
holiness homologous to the degrees of status in the sociopolitical order. The
sacrament of Communion was of supreme importance to Laud because he
believed the altar was "the greatest *place* of God's *Residence* upon earth"
(Laud 1637, 47). Countering the Protestant sense that God is not specially
present in particular places and persons, Laud emphasized distinctions: consecrated churches are sacred, and the altar and the Sacrament of Communion
are the special site of God's presence—a site to which the priest alone has
full access.

One of Laud's most controversial innovations was the railing of the altars. To receive Communion, a person had to come up to the rail and kneel—
the gesture marking submission to the priest as well as God, the rail materi-
ally effecting and symbolically figuring their separation from the holy. The
distance between communicants and the clergy paralleled the distance between humans and God, and between subjects and monarch. Antipathy
aroused by the railed altars in the later 1630s was strong. Laud's accounts to
the king in 1638 and 1639 mention that an increasing number of people were
refusing to receive communion at the railed altars (see Laud 1853, 360, 362).
Bishop Richard Montagu, a supporter of Laudian practice, admitted in his
1638 account for Norwich that it was "cumbersome" and confusing: people
in large parishes had to receive communion in shifts, creating traffic problems (quoted in Prynne 1646, 98–100).

Laud defended the rails as necessary for protecting the altars from misuse. He recounted to the king an accident in Tadlow on Christmas day 1638
that made clear why rails were needed:

> ... in sermon time a dog came to the table, and took the loaf of bread prepared for the holy
> sacrament, in his mouth, and ran away with it. Some of the parishioners took the same
> from the dog, and set it again upon the table. After sermon, the minister could not think fit
> to consecrate this bread.... (Laud 1853, 367)

Rails could protect the altar not only from a dog's appetite but also from its
other natural activities. Bishop Richard Montagu in his Visitation Articles
for Chicester in 1635 insisted that the altar be enclosed "with a raile ... close
enough to keepe out dogges from going in and prophaning that holy place,
from pissing against it or worse" (quoted after Prynne 1646, 94). But the
rails were not just to keep animals away. Laud's 1640 *Canons* insisted that
all communion tables be "decently severed with rails to preserve them" from

the "profanations" of "irreverent" people—"some leaning, others casting their hats, and some sitting upon, some standing, and others sitting under the communion tables in time of divine service" (Laud 1853, 625). Laud saw the railing of the altars as necessary decency, protecting holy objects from 'profanation,' but his outraged critics saw his innovations as reducing the people to the level of animals whose touch was polluting—a violation of the idea that the believer is the Temple of God, and that all believers are God's priests.

Thus the puritan minister Henry Burton complained that in "these dayes of Apostacy" men "erect Altar-worship" and persecute God's "faithful ministers and people" (Burton 1636, 25). Many "godly Ministers" have been "suspended, excommunicated," "outed of their livings"—"used, as if they were dogs, and not men" (27). The prelates, "stopping the mouths of the living God" in persecuting preaching, have set up a lavish "table, that bodes the [Popish] banquet to come" (105), the Masse.

Laudians wanted a uniform ceremonial Communion to unite and shape an obedient nation. The 1640 Canons, produced by Laud and endorsed by King Charles, insisted that participation in the prescribed worship of the established Church of England, and particularly Holy Communion, was essential to the political as well as religious health of the English community. There have "sprung up ... a sort of factious people" who despise the *Book of Common Prayer* and who refuse to "join in the public ... worship," "contenting themselves with the hearing of sermons only" (Laud 1853, 622). From now on, Protestant "delinquents" would be subject to the same penalties as Catholic recusants. This move infuriated Laud's opponents, who believed he had created an idolatrous Communion that deprived the godly of nourishment rather than feeding them (Burton 1636, 27).

When Laud was tried by Parliament in 1644, he was charged by his prosecutor, William Prynne, with having "defiled" the cathedrals, chapels, and parish churches in England with "Popish" altars and ritual (Prynne 1646, 59–60). What comes out vividly in Prynne's account of the trial is Laud's rigor in enforcing a uniform practice of Communion. Prynne recounted cases of ministers suspended for their objections to the rail and kneeling and forced to make public recantations of their "errors," and cases of churchwardens "excommunicated" for not railing in the tables (93–105).

While Laud was being detained, tried, and executed, Parliament was busy reforming religion. It officially dissolved the Church of England and outlawed the use of the *Book of Common Prayer* including its service for Communion. But though the Presbyterian Parliament wanted to get rid of Laud's 'popish' ritual, it believed a shared worship and Communion was important. Though Parliament never agreed on how to reconstitute a national church, in 1645 it published a *Directory for the Publique Worship of God* replacing the *Book of Common Prayer*. All references to "priests" and "altars" were gone; the "Table" was to be placed so "Communicants may orderly sit about it, or at it" (50–51). Where the established Church of England had insisted that "all" must partake, constructing a community at once inclusive and repressive, the *Directory* reflected puritan concerns that Communion be limited to the godly: "the Ignorant and the Scandalous are not fit to receive this Sacrament of the Lord's Supper" (48). The community formed by this Communion would necessarily be smaller than the whole of England. Yet it would still be a national community, a nation of the 'godly.'

The Threat of Radical Religion

The *Directory for the Publique Worship* was not widely used. Some Anglicans continued to use the Prayer Book ceremony secretly, but religious radicalism, which proliferated during the late 1640s and 1650s, presented a greater challenge. Seeing in the religious radicals the threat of sociopolitical as well as religious anarchy, Parliament passed a Blasphemy Ordinance (1650) and tried to control and punish 'blasphemers' and heretics. The threat that radical religion posed was represented by its challenges to the ritual of Communion that had for so long been important in constructing the community of the nation. If there were no shared national ritual of Communion, what would happen to the English social order the ritual affirmed?

The sects and 'heretical' individuals threatened England's community with their re-definitions, and, in some cases, outright rejection of Communion. We know about these radicals in part through the pamphlets of conservative Protestants outraged by the burgeoning heterodoxy. In 1646 Thomas Edwards' *Gangraena* catalogued the errors, heresies, and "strange Opinions of the Sectaries of these times" (Edwards 1646b, title page) which included sectarian re-interpretations of Communion. Edwards complained that some people, taking the puritan objection to clerical 'consecration' of the elements to an extreme, assert "That our common food, ordinary eating and drinking is a Sacrament of Christ's death, and a remembrance of his death till his coming againe" (Edwards 1646b, 4). Such a heterodox belief erased the distinction between holy and profane, church and home, between religious ritual and ordinary life-hinting at a society without distinctions sharply at odds with the hierarchically ordered, stratified society of seventeenth-century England. At the other extreme were those godly people who believed "That none are to be admitted to the Lords Supper, though believers and Saints, nor their children, to be baptized, but only they who are members in a Church-way" (Edwards 1646a, 29). Such a position also threatened the social fabric of the country by dividing England into numerous, self-contained communities that spurned kinship with the larger English Protestant community.

Ephraim Pagitt's *Heresiography, or a Description of the Hereticks and Sectaries of these latter times*, which went through six editions between 1646 and 1661, mapped the sects in England, which he saw as threatening civil as well as religious order. Pagitt complained that "men [are] refusing to receive the holy Communion," but he also complained about the manner in which certain sects performed Communion. The Anabaptists "receive the holy Communion most unreverently, sitting with their hats upon their heads" (Pagitt 1646, 33). If reverent posture during Communion figured submission and reverence towards one's earthly superiors, the egalitarian, leveling implications of receiving "with hats on" spelt socially disruptive attitudes, confirmed by the Anabaptists preaching "community of goods, every man to be a-like" (35). Sects that refused to have Communion with anyone who was not of their own church took to the extreme the puritan position that Communion be restricted to the 'godly.' Pagitt complained that the Independents "participate with none of the Reformed Churches in the Lords Supper," and cited Milton as an example (Pagitt 1661, 102).

If Communion was understood by the dominant groups (whether Laudian or Presbyterian) as necessary to social order, deviations from Communion were seen as socially and politically dangerous as well as spiritually deficient. Ranters and Quakers, who rejected all ritual forms of Communion, were the groups most vigorously and fiercely persecuted in England.

Quakers rejected all 'outward' worship, stressing the personal, spiritual connection of the individual believer to God and denying all need for ministers and Communion. Believing that God teaches by the Spirit, the inner light, Quakers took the Protestant emphasis on inwardness and the spirit to a further extreme than men like Henry Burton could have imagined. Pagitt noted in shock, "They deny the Sacrament of the Body and Blood" (Pagitt 1661, 254). The Quaker leader George Fox, attacking traditional Protestant-ism as if it were as misguided as Catholicism, insisted that Communion is a mere "carnal" and "mediate means," unnecessary for those who possess the "light" of Christ within (Fox 1654, 7).

The Quakers as a sect survived their persecution and grew, but the Ranters were successfully beaten down. Though the Ranters have been accused of not being a 'Religion' (Pagitt, 1661, 259), of simply being a collection of people devoted to drinking, swearing, and group sex, they embraced beliefs that must be understood within the context of religious history. Their shocking, socially disruptive practices constituted both a rejection and a transformation of the ritual of Communion (Smith 1983; Hill 1972, chap. 9 and 10).

Like the Quakers, Ranters believed that God is within "the Creatures," and thus that churches and rituals like Communion are unnecessary. But they went still further, for they insisted there is no sin; "all is pure, nothing unclean," as Laurence Clarkson put it (1650, 9). While rejecting the Sacrament of Communion, their transgressive behavior actually constituted a radical revision of the ritual. Pamphlets like *The Routing of the Ranters* (1650) described the Ranters' eating, drinking, and dancing in taverns as a perversion of church ritual. They have "bread and beer and ale, sing bawdy songs to the tune of David's Psalms," and enjoy promiscuous sex in a licentious communion that enacts their belief that there is no distinction between holy and unholy, sacred and profane, pure and impure (*The Routing of the Ranters* 1650, 2, 4).

Abiezzer Coppe, the most infamous Ranter, proclaimed in *A Fiery Flying Roll* (1649) the socially and politically radical implications of his transformation of Communion. Announcing the imminent Day of Judgment, Coppe offers a *"last warning to the Great Ones of the Earth"* (heading chap. II, first *Fiery Flying Roll*; Coppe [1649a] 1983a, 89): *"Each Begger that you meet Fall down before him, kisse him in the street"*; "Deale thy bread to the hungry" who cry, "Bread, bread, bread for the Lords sake" (chap. II; Coppe [1649a] 1983a, 90). Coppe rails against churches and their ordinances as "base nasty stinking" (*A Second Fiery Flying Roule*, chap. V; Coppe [1649b] 1983b, 107), flaunting instead his "hugging of Gipsies" and others whom the proper world condemns as "BASE" (chap. V, 106–107). Distinguishing himself both from presbyterian or Anglican churches and from sects who would restrict Communion to the 'godly,' Coppe denies all formal rites of Communion in favor of a lower-case communion that typographically enacts his levelling theology. "I know there's no Communion to the Communion of Saints, to the inward communion, to communion with the spirits of just men made perfect, and with God the Judge of all. No other Communion of Saints do I know. And this is Blood-life-spirit-communion" *(A Second Fiery Flying Roule*, chap. VII; Coppe [1649b] 1983b, 112). Believing that he is "fed" by God, Coppe feels a connection with all humanity, particularly the base and low. If true communion is inward and spiritual, it also takes an outward form of sharing one's food and body with the poor, even with "Harlots" (chap. VII; 112). "Why should I turne away mine eyes from mine own flesh? Why should I not break my bread to the hungry, whoever they be?" (chap. VII; 112). Coppe's revisionist Communion stands at the extreme from Laudian Communion, with its symbolic enactment of hierarchy and degree, but also from the Communion of conservative puritans who wished to preserve social, economic, and political distinctions. The radical, leveling position of Coppe's tract becomes clear as he identifies the church's Sacrament of Communion with people who "own" things, who believe their "horses and ... cows are [their] own" (chap. VIII; 114). Angrily exposing the hypocrisy of Christians having a Sacrament of Communion while endorsing private property, Coppe insists that "true Communion amongst men, is to have all things in common, and to call nothing one hath, ones own. And the true external breaking of bread, is to eat bread together in singlenesse of heart, and to break thy bread to the hungry, and tell them its their own bread, &c. els your Religion is in vain" (chap. VIII; 114).

Coppe defines his communion against the ritual practiced in churches. "The true breaking of bread—is ... saying if I have any bread, &c. it's thine, I will not call it mine own, it's common. These are true Communicants, and this is the true breaking of bread among men" (chap. VIII; 115). This transformation of the ritual of holy Communion overturns the entire hierarchical and socioeconomic structure of English society in the seventeenth century. True Communion is having everything 'in common,' no "MEUM" or 'teum' which at God's coming will be "confounded ... into community and universality" (chap. VI; 109). No wonder the Ranters provoked fears of anarchy. They were rejecting the very structure of community that the authorized church ritual (whether that of the Church of England or of the presbyterian Parliament) had worked so hard to construct.

The Restoration

Given the widespread belief that a broadly shared experience of Communion is the foundation of a stable, orderly society, it is no surprise that the Restoration of monarchy in 1660 was accompanied by the return of the banished Prayer Book, with its rites and liturgy. Parliament's 1662 Act of Uniformity once again compelled ministers to use the Prayer Book, and subsequent acts clamped down on dissenters. The Prayer Book with its rite of Communion was seen by many as insurance against a recurrence of the social and political instability of the Civil War period.

The arch-royalist John Gauden well expresses this sense of connection between religious ritual and social order, between Communion and national community. In his *Considerations Touching the Liturgy of the Church of England*, Gauden insisted that public worship and "*Sacramental* celebrations" are "the confirmation of true Christian communion with God ... and ... with one another"(Gauden 1661, 1–2). The restoration of a uniform national Communion will make the English a well knit nation of loyal subjects. Gauden emphasizes the "sweet communion of all Christians" (10) in England, not so much with God as with each other: through ritual, people are "*united* as to each other" and "to their *King* or *Prince*" (28).

A uniform Communion uniting Protestant England was, however, an impractical dream. Though a national Communion was again enforced, England's Protestant religious community had been permanently ruptured. Nonconformists defied the new laws and risked prison and fines (Keeble 1987, 48–49; Davies 1975, 444–448, 490–495). Not until 1687 would the penal laws against nonconformity be repealed-and then through the Catholic king James II's Declaration of Indulgence.

Milton's Paradise Regained

I want to conclude with one of the most famous nonconformists—John Milton, who refused to receive Communion within the restored English Church but opposed any toleration act that would allow Roman Catholic worship. As far as we know, Milton never attended any church after the Restoration. We see Milton's radical alienation in *Paradise Regained* (1671), which features a scene that demands to be read within the religious history I have been sketching.

Milton's reworking of the Biblical account of the temptation of Jesus highlights the Son's vigorous, disdainful rejection of Satan's offer first to feed the people by turning stones to bread, and then to partake of a lavish banquet Satan has prepared—a temptation which Milton added to the gospel accounts. We might hear an echo of the Quakers' spiritualized interpretation of Communion as the Son interprets his mission spiritually, insisting that "Man lives not by Bread only" (*Paradise Regained* 1.349), though the Son puts himself at a distance from the social conscience of Abiezzer Coppe, as he disdains to take care of the material needs of the poor.

But it is the Son's rejection of Satan's "Table richly spread, in regal mode" (2.340) that is crucial. Milton's poem carries a dangerous valence as the Son's words voice Milton's own refusal to conform:

> Thy pompous Delicacies I contemn,
> And count thy specious gifts no gifts but guiles. (2.390–391)

The only "Delicacies" the nonconformist Son will eat are those provided by God. After he's resisted all Satan's temptations, including the temptation to liberate the nation of the Jews, the Angels:

> … set him down
> On a green bank, and set before him spread.
> A table of Celestial Food, Divine…. (4.586–588)

Content to be "refresht" (4.637) by God, the quietly defiant Son provides both a model and reassurance for human beings faced with the pressure to conform to what Milton saw as the Satanic Communion of the English Church and the mistaken community of the English nation.

References

Anderson, Benedict R. 1995: *Imagined Communities: Reflections on the Origin and Spread of Nationalism*. Rev. ed. London: Verso.

Book of Common Prayer. London 1559.

Burton, Henry. 1636: *For God, and the King*. London.

Clarkson, Laurence. 1650: *A Single Eye: All Light, no Darkness; or Light and Darkness One*. London.

Coppe, Abiezzer. [1649a] 1983a: A Fiery Flying Roll. In: *A Collection of Ranter Writings from the Seventeenth Century*, ed. Nigel Smith. London: Junction Books. 80-97.

Coppe, Abiezzer. [1649b] 1983b: A Second Fiery Flying Roule. In: *A Collection of Ranter Writings from the Seventeenth Century*, ed. Nigel Smith. London: Junction Books. 98-116.

Cosin, John. 1855: *The Works*. Vol. 5: *Notes and Collections on the Book of Common Prayer*. Oxford: John Henry and James Parker.

Davies, Horton. 1975: *Worship and Theology in England*. Vol. 2: *From Andrewes to Baxter and Fox, 1603–1690*. Princeton: Princeton University Press.

Davies, Julian. 1992: *The Caroline Captivity of the Church: Charles I and the Remoulding of Anglicanism, 1625–1641*. Oxford: Clarendon Press.

Duffy, Eamon. 1992: *The Stripping of the Altars: Traditional Religion in England 1400–1580*. New Haven: Yale University Press.

A Directory for the Publique Worship of God. London, 1645.

Edwards, Thomas. 1646a: *Gangraena*. London.

Edwards, Thomas. 1646b: *The Third Part of Gangraena*. London.

Fincham, Kenneth. 1993: Introduction. In: *The Early Stuart Church, 1625–1642*, ed. Kenneth Fincham. Stanford: Stanford University Press. 1–22.

Fincham, Kenneth and Peter Lake. 1993: The Ecclesiastical Policies of James I and Charles I. In: *The Early Stuart Church, 1625–1642*, ed. Kenneth Fincham. Stanford: Stanford University Press. 23–49.

Fox, George. 1654: *A Declaration against all Profession and Professors ... from ... Quakers*. London.

Gauden, John. 1661: *Considerations Touching the Liturgy of the Church of England*. London.

Guibbory, Achsah. 1998: *Ceremony and Community from Herbert to Milton: Literature, Religion, and Cultural Conflict in Seventeenth-century England*. Cambridge: Cambridge University Press.

Herbert, George. 1974: *The English Poems of George Herbert*, ed. Constantinos A. Patrides. London: Dent; Totowa, N.J.: Rowman & Littlefield.

Hill, Christopher. 1972: *The World Turned Upside Down: Radical Ideas During the English Revolution*. London: Penguin.

Keeble, Neil H. 1987: *The Literary Culture of Nonconformity in Later Seventeenth-Century England*. Athens, G.A.: University of Georgia Press.

Lake, Peter 1993: The Laudian Style: Order, Uniformity and the Pursuit of the Beauty of Holiness in the 1630s. In: *The Early Stuart Church, 1625–1642*, ed. Kenneth Fincham. Stanford: Stanford University Press. 161–185.

Laud, William. 1853: *The Works of the Most Reverend Father in God, William Laud. D.D.* Vol. 5, part 2. Oxford: John Henry Parker.

Laud, William. 1637: *A Speech Delivered in the Starr-Chamber*. London.

Milton, Anthony. 1995: *Catholic and Reformed: The Roman and Protestant Churches in English Protestant Thought 1600–1640*. Cambridge: Cambridge University Press.

Milton, John. [1671] 1957: Paradise Regained. In: John Milton: Complete *Poems and Major Prose*, ed. Merritt Y. Hughes. Upper Saddle River, N.J.: Prentice Hall.

Pagitt, Ephraim. 1646: *Heresiography, or a Description of the Hereticks and Sectaries of these latter times*. 3d ed. London.

Pagitt, Ephraim. 1661: *Heresiography, or a Description of the Hereticks and Sectaries of these latter Times*. 6th ed. London.

Prynne, William. 1646: *Canterburies Doome*. London.

The Routing of the Ranters. London. 1650.

Sharpe, Kevin. 1992: *The Personal Rule of Charles I*. New Haven: Yale University Press.

Smart, Peter. 1628: *A Sermon Preached in the Cathedral Church of Durham July 7, 1628*. London.

Smart, Peter. 1869: Articles, or Instructions for Articles to be Exhibited by his Majesties High Commissioners. In: *The Correspondence of John Cosin, D.D., Lord Bishop of Durham*. (Publications of the Surtees Society 52). Durham: Andrews & Co. 169–199.

Smith, Nigel. 1983: Introduction. In: *A Collection of Ranter Writings from the Seventeenth Century*, ed. Nigel Smith. London: Junction Books.

Tyacke, Nicholas. 1987: Anti-Calvinists: The Rise of English Arminianism c. 1590–1640. Oxford: Clarendon.

Artaud's Holy Theater:
A Case for Questioning the Relations
between Ritual and Stage Performance[*]

Dietrich Harth

Artaud's Afterlife and Life

Today, the name of Antonin Artaud, who died in 1948 at the age of 51 after years in asylums and psychiatric clinics, is a landmark in both the practical and theoretical fields of theater aesthetics. The now famous leading figures of post-war neo-avantgarde revolt against the theater as a place for the routine worshipping of the classics—Jerzy Grotowski, Peter Brook, Richard Schechner, Julian Beck, Eugenio Barba, and Ariane Mnouchkine—all pointed to the landmark Artaud as if to say: behold the Holy Icon of the new order that we are going to establish on the ruins of an outworn bourgeois convention. This testifies to Artaud's influence on stage practice. In aesthetic theory, as far as this thinking to the second degree is concerned with critically investigating the boundaries between philosophy and the arts, the French author's writings are going through a process of canonization, especially since he was made famous by the homage paid to him in the work of Michel Foucault, Jacques Derrida, and Susan Sontag.

Let us also not forget the copyright for the neo-avantgarde Happenings bestowed on the playwright by Jean-Paul Sartre, who argued that the Happening should follow Artaud's belief that only theatrical actions are apt to release the violence latent within the spectators (see Hayman 1977, 158). Surprisingly, Sartre's speculation is backed up by some strange evidence. In 1952, at Black Mountain College in the United States, a so-called 'Untitled Event' was put on, which fulfilled all the—to use a paradox—'anarchic rules' we expect when attending a Happening. The composer John Cage, the poet Charles Olson, the painter Robert Rauschenberg, and the dancer Merce Cunningham were the protagonists in this peculiar mixed-media event, the thorough description of which would perhaps give some clues to the dialec-

[*]   I am very grateful to Jonathan Long for his kind help in improving my English.

tics of ritual and anti-ritual. The performance of the Event entailed a radical destruction of the conventions we are accustomed to when attending the opening of an exhibition, a musical premiere or a performance by a modern ballet troupe. Admittedly, it might be the retrospective canonizing view of the historian which gives the anti-ritualistic Event the meaning of a new ritual called the Happening, whose intention was to set free the energies kept under anesthesia by the sublimating force of conventional cultural performances and artistic forms. But precisely this intention can be detected as one of Artaud's most powerful inclinations.

One part of the Black Mountain Event consisted in reading aloud passages from the first English translation of Artaud's *Le Théâtre de la Cruauté* while Robert Rauschenberg simultaneously fixed his *White Paintings* to the ceiling and the musician David Tudor rigorously 'played' a prepared piano. While this was going on, the initiator of the Untitled Event, John Cage, who had been prompted to read Artaud by Pierre Boulez, shocked the audience with one of his famous compositions with a radio. To sum up: the 1952 Untitled Event did not present a given plot or world vision, nor did it tell a story furnished with dramatic adventures and individual characters, it just happened in order to demonstrate nothing but the very act of performing, and it left—quite literally, and fully in accordance with one of Artaud's central claims—a void at the center, signifying the absence of the work of art. It is, I think, quite appropriate in this context to quote a relevant remark by Michel Foucault, which might give the void a little bit of a shape: "Madness," he writes in *Madness and Civilization: A History of Insanity in the Age of Reason*, "is precisely the absence of the work of art, the reiterated presence of that absence, its central void experienced and measured in all its endless dimensions. ... The world," Foucault continues, in his defense of the subversive powers of artistic madness, "the world that thought to measure and justify madness through psychology must justify itself before madness, since in its struggles and agonies it measures itself by the excess of works like those of Nietzsche, of van Gogh, of Artaud" (Foucault 1973, 287, 289). Before we follow Foucault, let us look once more at the Untitled Event from the angle of a theater historian. From this angle—I oversimplify—the whole thing looks very much like a parody of Artaud's blueprint, because a parody—as we may recall—is something that is *meant* to be that thing which it actually *is not*. Moreover, the technique of outperforming the performance reminds us of the carnivalesque actions propagated and made manifest by the Italian Futurists—see Federico Tommaso Marinetti's *Teatro di Varietà* (1913)—and of the ugly performances of the German Dadaists.

If, then, we follow Foucault, we have to state a paradox, since no 'art works' by Artaud exist, at least not in the traditional sense of the word. Instead there is absence and—if we take a close look at his writings—there is a wild longing for a new art, or better, for what he himself calls "renouveler la culture" (Artaud 1978, 218). Artaud is convinced that there is a gap between art and culture, which cannot be closed by art alone because art is not mimetic, hence does not imitate life—in his own words: "L'Art n'est pas l'imitation de la vie," yet, he continues, art—that is, the art of performance—could re-establish the lost links with the transcendent principle of life: "principe transcendant avec lequel l'art nous remet en communication" (Artaud 1978, 242). My point is that Artaud, who apparently knew Oswald Spengler's *Untergang des Abendlandes* (1923) very well and hated like him the modern "éclatement des valeurs" (the shattering of values) (Artaud 1971, 69) sought the foundations of a new beginning by diving deep into the sacred ocean of an imagined pre-modern communal culture, at the very heart of which ritual gestures and totemic signs speak for themselves. And yet he did not trust his own intentions and in one of his late writings even talked about ritual as a fraudulent trick (see Artaud 1979, 63).

To find out if this can be called a contradiction and, if so, how it could be made comprehensible, I first will recapitulate very quickly a few biographical facts and then go explore some theoretical arguments, without wishing to get swamped by detail. Finally, my last step will lead to Artaud's peculiar view of the Balinese theater. This will provide a platform for addressing, on a more general level, some of the specific problems concerning the explanation of repetition and change, of similarities and differences between theater and ritual, and so on.

All of Artaud's ideas and convictions that I have mentioned so far are deeply rooted in a subjective state of mind with a strong affinity to what the author himself liked to call Alchemy: the art of transition, transmutation or metamorphosis. And if we take this seriously, which I have decided to do, we should not expect a standardized or evenly balanced discourse. The fascination of Artaud's writings has its own poetic logic, and this logic to some degree echoes the author's personal experience. This is particularly the case if one considers all those circumstances which have to do with the pain and anguish an author has to endure when he is pushed by a creative urge to go beyond all known linguistic expressions. Artaud's poetic beginnings as a member of André Breton's surrealist group seemed to be a failure, but in a very characteristic way eventually turned out to be a success: Jacques Rivière, in the early 1920s editor of the *Nouvelle Revue Française* rejected the poems of the young writer. The very same Jacques Rivière, however, subsequently published his correspondence with the newcomer in which Artaud explained the difficulties he had to go through while trying to transform his vivid visions into written language: "As a poet," he later wrote when experimenting with something like a private language, "I hear voices which are no longer part of the world of ideas" (Artaud 1983, 9, my translation, D.H.). This seems to me an adequate expression for what he experienced when feeling that he could not close the gap between an exploding imagination and the impoverished tool of traditional language; an experience to which, in the opening essay of *Le théâtre et son double*, he gave the weight of a programmatic sentence: "Briser le langage pour toucher la vie" (Shatter language in order to get in touch with life) (Artaud 1978, 14).

I will leave the meaning of 'life' to further comments and for the moment assert that to get in touch with life apparently meant: to get in touch with the stage. In 1927 Artaud, together with Robert Aron and the playwright Roger Vitrac, opened his own theater, the Théâtre Alfred Jarry. In the years before this—having lost his surrealist membership—Artaud acted in several Paris productions staged by Charles Dullin (1885–1949) and by Georges Pitoëff (1884–1939), both directors with a remarkable sense for the new and—we may recall—for meta-theatrical actions including the study of Japanese stage productions. Artaud did not make a real career as a successful and notable actor-director either on the stage or screen where he could be seen from time to time during subsequent years as a bit-part actor. Neither did he gain the sympathy of the audience with his own theater productions. If we want to find out why there is so much magic and charisma in Artaud's name, we therefore have to consult his writings, notwithstanding the fact that he himself often enough blamed literacy for the deplorable *éclatement des valeurs* that he, along with so many contemporaries, considered the stigma of modern culture.

The Attraction of Fragmentary and Double Thinking

To get a better grasp of Artaud's writings, let me briefly address the genesis, the scope, and the particular tone of Artaud's writings. The bulk of the texts printed in the 16 volumes of the Paris edition of his complete works were published posthumously. Artaud himself was—as we have seen—a critic of literate culture and preferred oral articulation and direct communication of thought. A lot of his texts meant for publication were not written down by himself, but dictated. And as a—probably intended—outcome of this procedure the reader is confronted again and again with a lively, often fickle, or rather porous text-surface and with a fragmentary deep structure of discourse. A striking example is *Le théâtre et son double*, a small book he published in 1938 in a print-run of four hundred copies in the Gallimard collection *Métamorphoses* without any public resonance worth mentioning. Today this book is regarded as Artaud's masterpiece, despite or because of the fact that its structure and contents are far removed from the expectations of a reader who looks for unity, for coherence, and neatly composed terminology. *Le théâtre et son double* contains a diversity of reports, notes, aphoristic fragments, extracts, letters, essays, lectures and manifestos, the first draft written down in 1932, the last one revised in 1936 during the author's stay in Mexico. But the particular attraction of the author's scattered thoughts for the neo-avantgarde theater practitioners obviously lies in his sometimes descriptive, sometimes confused, and quite often normative discourse about the organic structure of his new theater and the impact of its attraction on the sensibility of both actors and spectators. Dealing with the techniques of acting, staging, stage design (especially lighting) and with particular forms of verbal and nonverbal expression, Artaud's writings still offer a neat, easy-to-handle building kit for the devotee of an alternative theater culture.

Perhaps one can say that there is a double orientation, or even better, double thinking in Artaud's claim to give French and European theater, or Western culture in general, a powerful and formative place in social life. This double orientation is very clearly alluded to by the title of his book *Le théâtre et son double*, though this title was recommended to him by a close friend (Jean Paulhan). It says that there is a specific form of institutionalized performance art with all its technical accoutrements built around a something, which, although it cannot be represented, cries out for representation. This mysterious something—called *le double*—is none other than life itself. So it is not by chance that Artaud uses the notion 'energy' when speaking about the effecting power his theater, which—as we will see later—is both new and old at the same time, should exert on the spectator. "Le théâtre lieu de la magie, de l'appel des notions et des energies" (Artaud 1978, 245), reads a note in *Dossier du théâtre et son double*, and Artaud continues that it is time (my translation, D.H.): "to rediscover those energies within ourselves which create order and give rise again to the stock of life (*et font remonter le taux de la vie*)." This energy, being the tension, which is, built up trough the antagonistic motion of two opposing forces—Eugenio Barba's formula is 'balance in action' (see Barba 1995, 16ff.)—this energy in Artaud's conception has its offspring in the thrilling and never ending interchange between chaos and order. If I am not mistaken, this is the meaning of what the author himself sometimes calls 'metaphysics'; and 'cruelty' seems to be nothing else but the organic, the life-centered substance of the abstract philosophical term.

To show the mind-boggling and challenging *Sprachspiel* (linguistic play) the interpreter of Artaud's writings has to cope with, let me quote a central passage from the author's *Second Letter on Cruelty*, first published in 1932:

> La cruauté n'est pas surajoutée à ma pensée; elle y a toujours vécu: mais il me fait en prendre conscience. J'emploie le mot de cruauté dans le sens d'appétit de vie, de rigueur cosmique et de nécessité implacable, dans le sens gnostique de tourbillon de vie qui dévore les ténèbres, dans le sens de cette douleur hors de la nécessité inéluctable de laquelle la vie ne saurait s'exercer; le bien est voulu, il est le résultat d'un acte, le mal est permanent. Le dieu caché quand il crée obéit à la nécessité cruelle de la création qui lui est imposée à lui—même, et il ne peut pas ne pas créer, donc ne pas admettre au centre du tourbillon volontaire du bien un noyau de mal de plus en plus réduit, de plus en plus mangé. Et le théâtre dans le sens de création continue, d'action magique entière obéit à cette nécessité. Une pièce où il n'y aurait pas cette volonté, cet appétit de vie aveugle, et capable de passer sur tout, visible dans chaque geste et dans chaque acte, et dans le côté transcendant de l'action, serait une pièce inutile et manquée. (Artaud 1978, 98)

The English translation by Victor Corti reads as follows:

> Cruelty is not an adjunct to my thoughts, it has always been there, but I had to become conscious of it. I use the word cruelty in the sense of hungering after life, cosmic strictness, relentless necessity, in the Gnostic sense of a living vortex engulfing darkness, in the sense of the inescapably necessary pain without which life could not continue. Good has to be desired, it is the result of an act of willpower, while evil is continuous. When the hidden god creates, he obeys a cruel need for creation imposed on him, yet he cannot avoid creating, thus permitting an ever more condensed, ever more consumed nucleus of evil to enter the eye of the willed vortex of good. Theatre in the sense of constant creation, a wholly magic act, obeys this necessity. A play without this desire, this blind zest for life, capable of surpassing everything seen in every gesture or every act, in the transcendent aspect of the plot, would be useless and a failure as theatre. (Artaud 1995, 80)

This passage, I think, reveals some of the basic aspects of Artaud's conception. I will try to give a very condensed account of my own, rather idiosyncratic reading: the text tells us something about a Gnostic, that is, a dualistic view of life. It is a view which attempts to think Good and Evil, Life and Death at the same time, like a pair of absolute powers chained to each other and dancing in a whirl (this is the meaning of the French *tourbillon*): on the one hand life is creation, is *appétit de vie* or *tourbillon de vie*—I prefer the German *Lebenstrieb* and *Lebensstrudel* to Victor Corti's slightly incorrect translation—on the other hand it is *Todestrieb* (the death-drive), consummation, devouring or—to quote another of Artaud's difficult combinations— "un massacre qui est une transfiguration" (both massacre and transfiguration) (Artaud 1978, 100). To make this invisible whirl of antagonistic powers not only visible, but also perceptible to all senses, is the idea behind all of Artaud's endeavors. There is, however, one powerful handicap he is challenged to cope with, and this is the predominance of the written text and of the dramatic author, contemporary French theater being highly dependant upon literature and a type of performance which, in Artaud's eyes, is dominated by an old fashioned style quaintly affiliated with a corrupt moralistic and psychological world view.

In a letter to André Gide (August 7, 1932) Artaud applied the aesthetic idea of constant creation to his personal vocation as a future theater director, calling himself a "creator or inventor of a theatrical reality which is absolute and self-sufficient" (Hayman 1977, 83). The absolute or, as he sometimes called it, the virtual reality of the theatrical performance is not dependant upon a traditional stage, though the space where it should unfold its energetic powers and the relevant technical support are a central object of Artaud's ruminations. This has a lot to do with his claim to do away with the written dramatic text, in order to develop 'another language': "langage dans l'espace," "langage visuel des objets, des mouvements, des attitudes, des gestes," "langage de sons, de cris, de lumières, d'onomatopées" (spatial language—the visual language of things, of movements, attitudes, gestures—the language of sounds, cries, of lights and onomatopoeia) (Artaud 1978, 86). The other language or language of otherness described here is not just confined to what we usually call body-language. Artaud gives it a mediating place between body and mind: "à mi-chemin entre le geste et la penseé" (Artaud 1978, 86), and frequently alludes to a ritual background. "Le théâtre," he notes in the *First Manifesto* for the *Theatre of Cruelty*, "n'est qu'un reflet ... de la magie et des rites" (Artaud 1978, 88). It is, therefore, not surprising to find out that Artaud uses terms such as *théâtre alchimique* and *théâtre sacré* in order to express his zest for cultural change which is not content with criticizing the status quo. Rather, he wanted to overthrow long-term traditions in order to establish a type of performance, which can be acted and understood by all humans, regardless of their origin and background, because the expressive means of this performance are timeless, universal and yet energetic in the sense of a transforming power. The pragmatic performativity of a coinage like 'holy theater' is no mystery: it is thought to keep the issue safe from outside critical interventions.

Experiencing the Orient in Paris

Speaking of another language, which—in my view—has to be understood as
a language of otherness, is justified if we take seriously Artaud's view of the
cultural difference between the Orient and the Occident. Our author here is
quite in accord with those eurocentric prejudices Edward Said has detected
as the driving force behind an imagined Orient and the resultant Orientalism
(see Said 1979). In several texts, Artaud confronts the literary culture of the
Occident with a culture of magical gestures and rhythms, which—he
claims—is the genuine oriental language, a language of signs that could only
be perceived on the stage of the Oriental, that is, the Asian theater.

During the 1922 Colonial Exhibition at Marseille he had seen a Cambo-
dian dance group. In 1931 he saw in Paris—there was again a Colonial
Exhibition—the performance of a Balinese group and immediately wrote
down what he had seen and which aspects had made the deepest impression
on him. It was a most remarkable occasion: the Balinese group from Peliatan
performed a collage of classical religious and secular dances conducted by
its German-born curator Walter Spies. Artaud was not the only admirer of
the Balinese performance in Paris. Beryl de Zoete, a British theater critic,
and Miguel Covarrubias, an anthropologist and painter, who, in 1937, was to
put Bali on the map with a popular book, joined in (see Covarrubias 1973).
De Zoete and Spies had studied Eurythmics in Hellerau (near Dresden) with
Jacques Dalcroze, an important theater reformer. After extensive research in
the late 1930s, they published the still useful classic *Dance and Drama in
Bali* (see De Zoete and Spies 1982). Spies was also a painter who had attended the classes of the Berlin-based poet-painter Oskar Kokoschka,
another famous representative of a progressive modern art and theater culture. The influence of Spies on Balinese dance and painting during the years
before the Paris exhibition is a well-known and well-documented fact. All
this I mention here because it makes evident that Artaud did not see what he
believed to be pure Oriental theater. He witnessed, as it were, the drama of
the rapid cultural change that took place in Bali under the rule of the Dutch
colonial power, the cultural change being forced upon the islanders as 'Bal-
isering,' a Dutch slogan, the correct reading of which is *Balinisation of the
Balinese* (see Hitchcock & Norris 1995). I'm not sure if Artaud had the right
intuition when he said, in a lecture he delivered in 1936 to an audience in
Mexico: "Les extraordinaires représentations du Théâtre Balinais à
l'Exposition coloniale ... font, pour moi, partie du mouvement théâtral en
France" (Artaud 1971, 68).

Artaud's descriptions of the sign-language he perceived in Balinese dance and drama are striking because of their imaginative and fascinating verbal inspirations. He himself admitted that he could not decipher the signs but frequently made comparisons with ritual gestures. The most striking features for Artaud, however, were the bodily distortions and asymmetrical robes of the dancers, which he liked to compare with the pictographic, in this case strangely animated, characters of Egyptian hieroglyphs and Chinese ideograms. If you ever have seen a Hip Hop or Rave show with its entire vibes, its energetic and technical seductions, you probably will be able to follow Artaud's descriptions of the animated images he hallucinated immediately after his visit to the Exposition Coloniale:

> syncopated modulations at the back of the throat, brutal jerks, angular postures, rustling branches, the musical angle formed by arm and forearm, a rarefied aviary where the actors themselves are the fluttering, machines creaking, animated puppets, musical phrases cut short, hollow sounds, insect flights, etc. (Hayman 1977, 77)

This is not a descriptive report; it is the *invention* of an event.

In Artaud's comparison with animated hieroglyphs and ideograms I see an important clue to the double coding he projected into the Oriental theater by observing the figures in motion from a point of view, which encompasses both the pictorial or aesthetic appearance and a hidden semiotic energy. The fact that Artaud could not decipher the message, increased, so it seems, his enthusiasm and intense delight. In the stylized amalgamations of gestures, rhythms, music and voice, the depersonalized human body appeared to him as a symbol in which physical and metaphysical aspects fused into something that was beyond all social or psychological actuality and beyond the narrative contents of classical Western drama. So it is, on the one hand, surprising that in some passages of his book Artaud advocates, "le retour aux vieux Mythes primitifs" (Artaud 1978, 119). On the other hand, however, this is perhaps nothing but another example of his love for ambiguities and double thinking.

Re-Enchanting Modern Theater

Artaud summarizes his aesthetic experience thus: the enchanting 'revelations' of the Balinese theater travel via 'physical' rather than 'verbal' ideas or imaginations (Artaud 1978, 66). He saw more than an exotic play, he saw what he reported to be "une alchemie mentale" (Artaud 1978, 64) and declared:

Dans les réalisations du Théâtre Balinais l'esprit a bien le sentiment que la concep-
tion s'est d'abord heurtée à des gestes, a pris pied au milieu de toute une fermentation
d'images visuelles ou sonores, pensées comme à l'état pure. (In the Balinese theater
productions the mind certainly has the feeling that the capability of conception met
with gestures first and that this capability has taken place right in the middle of a fermentation of visual or acoustic images, imagined as it were in a pure state.) (Artaud
1978, 60, my translation, D.H.)

And yet one cannot deny that Artaud's conception of a modernized *théâtre*
sacré was inspired by some sort of abstract religious idea which—at least in
his writings about the Theater of Cruelty—had nothing to do with orthodoxy
or a confessional creed. But Artaud's frequent use of notions like 'metaphysics' and 'transcendence' obviously points to something behind all phenomena, even if we call this something 'life itself' and interpret it in a rather
distancing way as the transcendental condition of all being. I prefer to read
those transcendental traces as signs, which point to a hidden but unifying
meaning beyond the monotonous and uniform logic of a picture of reality
that is both conceptually petrified and weird at the same time. Artaud's
dream is the dream of a poet who wants to break up the immobility he himself fears and wants to fill the void left by the scientific disenchantment of
life with a principle whose very substance is deeply immersed in and permanently transformed by that particular plasma floating between creation and
decay. The key to communicating with this poetic pulsation—'poetic' in the
sense of a creative energy—the key is hidden in that nonverbal 'language'
that exists between bodily gesture and mind and that Artaud compares with
the 'language' of ritual. This sign-language is thought to stimulate the sensibility of both the actors as well as the spectators in order to enhance their
ability to approximate by *analogy* the ever-changing order of life. In fact,
this does not conform to Aristotle's *Poetics,* since for the Greek the spoken
and written word was the master-key to culture and to knowledge. We must
not forget that in Aristotle's view the paradigm for all literary genres, trag-
edy, was a case for *philosophical* and not for religious or theological
speculations (see *Poetics* 1453b, 1451b). But I think Artaud's Theater of
Cruelty is not so far from this view as it is often represented as being. There
is no question that Artaud has to be seen as belonging to a series of anti-
Aristotelian dramatists, many of them his precursors in the business of enthusiastically liberating the scope of theatricality from traditions, habits and
rusty dogmas: the Swiss stage-designer Adolphe Appia, the English director
Edward Gordon Craig, the Italian supra-modernist Federico Tommaso Marinetti, the Russian playwrights and actor-directors Vyacheslav Ivanov and
Vsevolod Meyerhold, the German Bauhaus-artist Oskar Schlemmer, etc.—

There is also, of course, no question that Artaud was against the authority of the text and against its dull recitation on stage, which showed nothing but the features of an extravagant but inanimate style.

All this taken for granted, I still insist that Artaud—not unlike Aristotle—saw in theater a means to gain knowledge through a free interplay between sensibility and reason or, to borrow the title of Jon Elster's recent study about rationality and emotions, knowledge through the 'alchemy of the mind' (Elster 1999). Perhaps this can explain Artaud's seemingly ambiguous description of the Balinese theater performance as *architecture spirituelle* (spiritual architecture) and as *pouvoir évocateur* (evocative power) (Artaud 1978, 53), the latter referring to rhythm and physical movement. There is no evidence that Artaud was familiar with Ferdinand de Saussure's conception of the evocative power of speech (Saussure's term is *pouvoir evocatrice*). The affinity, however, is striking. Knowledge—Artaud is convinced—can be obtained while being involved in a play melding the spiritual with the evocative. And this kind of knowledge obviously means self-knowledge, an immediate awareness of one's own existence. As Artaud himself puts it in an aphoristic sentence in his famous *Théâtre de Séraphin*: "Quand je vis je ne me sens pas vivre. Mais quand je joue c'est là que me sens exister" (Artaud 1978, 145).

But that is not all. In his *First Manifesto* on the Theater of Cruelty, the author presents in a rather systematic way an inventory of the techniques, methods, and strategies that the directors, actors, and spectators of the new theater are obliged to follow. Of special interest is what Artaud says about the use of the so-called 'concrete stage-language.' This 'language' comprises verbal as well as musical signs and—last but not least—the transformations of physiognomic expression. And here he discusses the methods, which could be of use for a registration and labeling of all these signs, including even the 'thousand and one' changes of the actor's face (Artaud 1978, 91). So it seems that Artaud not only aims for a new, a concrete, objective and immediately understandable 'language,' but that—like any ethnographer—he is seeking a sound and effective method of description and registration which make it easy to teach the new 'language' in drama school.

We thus see that there is not only a wild rebellion against the old gods, but that there is also a rationale behind Artaud's practical endeavors and challenging writings which should make us wary of classifying his holy theater as an attempt to revive on the modern stage the ritualistic obligations of a religious community. Irritation, of course, is a feeling one cannot avoid when reading Artaud's sometimes programmatic, sometimes ambiguous and sometimes paradoxical writings. But whatever the results of such irritated readings might be, there is no doubt that Artaud consciously wanted to energize his texts with a *pouvoir evocateur* similar to that evocative power he believed to be the soul of the so called 'oriental language.'

Indefinite Conclusions

Keeping all this in mind, it will not be easy to come to definitive conclusions. Nevertheless, the attempt may be made:

To look at an event and call it a *ritual* or a *theatrical* performance is a question of attitude and of expediency, that is, there is no essential opposition between the two. One and the same performance, be it secular or religious, can be experienced either as ritual or as theater.

Formal features alone are inadequate as explanation; repetitions, to mention this much-debated example, may occur on stage as well as on temple-grounds, but they are not even useful as a measurement of change because there is no repetition without change. And so the intense and ambitious search for change in human actions—customs and habits and rituals—will be entangled in self-contradictions if it does not take into account historicity or at least a theory of temporal dynamics.

Therefore, if we—the disengaged students of different, distant, or even long-extinct cultures—ask for certainty, we tacitly make decisions on the basis of a rationality which not only belongs to our cultural background but is *the* powerful energy dominating and shaping all those operations that we associate with ideas of control and self-control in research.

Artaud, being an artist, had no reason to follow the rationality code of the researcher. And yet his attempt to rejuvenate something like a holy theater, which speaks to the masses with an emotionally stirring but not destructive 'language' of peculiar gestures, movements, rhythms, vibrations, etc., does not in the least preclude the search for a third way by reconciling rationality with sensation. And what is equally important, this search once again made use of the old, stereotyped Orient-Occident comparison, imagining the East as a holistic cosmos with the features of vital ritualism rather than estranged religiosity, and an authentic unity of artistic performance and supernatural communication.

Rituals and liturgies, like all other patterns of religious cult can, of course, form part of those actions we perceive as theater performances even if all the ingredients that we consider specific for the performance of a drama are lacking. Theatricality signifies a specific way of looking at actions comprising the need to interpret not only these actions but also the sensations and intellectual impressions they cause in the spectator's mind. This need to interpret sets free the impulse to gain knowledge or self-knowledge. In my view, it is bound to that type of aesthetically mediated rationality that I have tried to demonstrate by unraveling Artaud's double thinking.

References

Artaud, Antonin. 1971: *Messages révolutionnaires*. (Collection idées 411). Paris: Gallimard.

―――. 1978: *Œuvres complètes*. Nouv. ed. revue et augm. Vol. 4. Paris: Gallimard.

―――. 1979: *Van Gogh, der Selbstmörder durch die Gesellschaft*, transl. from the French by Franz Loechler. Munich: Matthes & Seitz.

―――. 1983: *Frühe Schriften*, transl. from the French by Bernd Mattheus. Munich: Matthes & Seitz.

―――. 1995: *The Theatre and its Double*, transl. from the French by Victor Corti. Montreal: Calder.

Barba, Eugenio. 1995: *The Paper Canoe: A Guide to Theatre Anthropology*. London and New York: Routledge.

Covarrubias, Miguel. 1973: *Island of Bali* (1937). Singapore: Periplus.

De Zoete, Beryl and Walter Spies. 1982: *Dance and Drama in Bali* (1938). Singapore: Oxford University Press.

Elster, Jon. 1999: *Alchemies of the Mind: Rationality and the Emotions*. Cambridge: Cambridge University Press.

Foucault, Michel. 1973: *Madness and Civilization: A History of Insanity in the Age of Reason*, transl. Richard Howard. New York, Vintage.

Hayman, Ronald. 1977: *Artaud and After*. Oxford: Oxford University Press.

Hitchcock, Michael and Lucy Norris. 1995: *Bali – The Imaginary Museum: The Photographs of Walter Spies and Bery de Zoete*. Kuala Lumpur: Oxford University Press.

Marinetti, Federico Tommaso. 1913: *Il teatro di Varietà: manifesto futurista publicato dal "Daily-mail" 21 novembre 1913*. (Manifesto del movimento futurista 18). Milano.

Said, Edward W. 1979: *Orientalism*. New York: Vintage.

Spengler, Oswald. 1923: *Der Untergang des Abendlandes: Umrisse einer Morphologie der Weltgeschichte*. 2 vols. Munich: C.H. Beck'sche Verlagsbuchhandlung.

Balinese Temple Dances
and Ritual Transformations
in the Process of Modernization

Anette Rein

In autumn 1999, the members of the Indonesian Society for the Performing Arts met for a five-day international conference on the occasion of their organization's tenth anniversary. The facilities of the former princely spa Tirta Gangga in East Bali provided a splendid backdrop. During the day there were theoretical discussions concerning the performing arts of Indonesia and their relationship to tradition, on the one hand, and the processes of modernization and globalization on the other. In the evening there were performances from Bali, Java, Sulawesi and Irian Jaya, which sometimes lasted well into the night.

On the final day an excursion was organized to two neighboring villages, Bungaya and Asak. These villages were chosen because they belong to the *bali aga* (the so called old or original Balinese) villages. According to the official image, the *bali aga* cultivate an original Balinese tradition, which still contains a trace of a Pre-Hinduistic tradition. Corresponding to the subject of the conference: "Milleniart: The Celebration of the Origins" the visitors were supposed to gain insight into authentic Balinese tradition. *Wisata Budaya* (Cultural Heritage) was the title of the event, and in three oversized touristbuses the 90 participants drove to the villages.

As a conference participant, I was very anxious to see what would happen in these villages. Fourteen years ago I started my research on the temple dance *rejang* during the big annual village rituals in Bungaya and Asak (see Rein 1994). Now I would have the opportunity to participate in an indigenous presentation by the villagers—while being a member of a group composed of mainly Indonesian conference-tourists. It was also announced that *rejang* would be danced. This was decisive for my participation in the tour—and I could hardly wait to see what would happen.

The three big buses, which nearly blocked the small village streets, stopped first in front of the *pura balé agung* (the village temple) of Bungaya.

Standing on a *balé*, a group of young girls welcomed the guests. Their traditional costumes identified them as members of the group of *daa* (the unmarried girls of a village). Groups of female and male elders were sitting or standing on another *balé*. Together they form the *kerama désa* (the council of elders of the village).

After the conference-tourists had taken their seats on *balé* (platforms) opposite the elders, a dance was performed to welcome the guests. After a short break a voice resounded through a megaphone, giving information about the social organization of the village, the different rituals of the year, and the varying performances within the rituals. At the same time, members of the tourist group walked around in the temple and climbed the *balé* in order to talk with the elders—and to take photos.

In the meantime the group of young unmarried women and men had lined up in the middle of the temple court. This provided another opportunity for the visitors to take photos. In spite of pleading by the tourists, the girls refused to dance the *rejang*. Using a megaphone someone announced that the dance would be performed during a ritual in another five days. A gift and a donation to the head of the village marked the end of this presentation already the next presentation in the neighboring village of Asak in view.

Here, the setting was different. The village had declined to invite the 90 guests into their village temple. There was no dance performed. The village elders were already sitting on the *balé masyarakat*, a secular meeting point for the villagers. The guests were invited to take a seat on the floor opposite the elders. Different traditional elements were chosen by the villagers to present aspects of the ritual life of the village like: a woman was sitting in the background at her loom (showing the production of a ritual cloth), a special orchestra, usually playing during temple rituals—*gamelan gambang*—and the elders sang a ritual melody as a welcome song. The guests were served with traditional cookies and beverages (aqua)—to the accompaniment of announcements over a megaphone about the organization of the village.

Two young couples were standing at the entrance of the *balé*, dressed in their splendid ritual costume. The presence of the very famous Indonesian poet Rendra gave the opportunity to take a photo featuring a modern Indonesian celebrity together with representatives of an Old Balinese community. Everybody played the game without any protest.

In the context of my topic the analysis of this confrontation between modern scientists and artists with traditional village life the following questions arose:

How can one explain or classify the events just described?
Had I participated in a theater performance, in a ritual or in something else?

I will start with the question: Why did one group of girls refuse to dance whereas another group performed without any problems? The name of the dance with which the guests from home and abroad were greeted in Bungaya is *panyembrama*. However, the head of the dancing group announced the performance under the name of *péndét*. When I asked him if this was not a performance of the so-called *panyembrama*, he conceded this point. But, in his further comments he insisted on referring to the dance as *péndét*.

The dance *panyembrama* is derived from a sacred dance *péndét*, which is still an important part of many rituals in Bali. During a Hindu ritual, groups of men or woman dance in the temple courtyard. In their hands they carry offering bowls filled with flowers, rice, and burning joss sticks. Using relatively simple dance steps, they approach the shrines where they deposit their offerings.

After the independence of Indonesia in 1949 the central government in Jakarta instrumentalized the temple dance for their own purposes. Dance groups made up of young girls were ordered to welcome the guests at the airport, and later they danced at the Bali Beach Hotel during official banquets (see Picard 1996). It was still the temple dance *péndét*, which was now performed in a profane context. The reaction of religious leaders to this apparent equation of political leaders with gods was so outraged that the Balinese conservatory was ordered to create an official welcoming dance. This new dance was choreographed at the end of the 1960s under the name *panyembrama*.

Why did the leader of the dance group in Bungaya insist on calling this dance *péndét* and not *panyembrama*?

This has to be explained in the context of the event *Wisata Budaya*. The village had been directed to present something representative of their life, which could be used as a demonstration of the antiquity and the authenticity of their village culture. This directive, which seemed to be a straightforward one, created a dilemma, which the village resolved in a very creative way. When told to arrange for a tourist event, the villagers knew immediately what they were in for. But all of the 'typical activities' which, according to the official Indonesian cultural policy, provide evidence of authenticity and a special ethnic identity—for example, rituals, dances, music and songs—are usually connected with ritual times and are not allowed to be performed in a profane context (see Rein 1996). Since the 1970s, in connection with the steadily growing tourist industry, exceptions to this rule have been allowed in some South Balinese villages specializing in regular performances, which are traditionally connected with temple rituals.

The East Balinese village of Bungaya is not yet (1999) part of the tourism industry. The lack of professionality on the part of the organizers became obvious at the moment when the leader of the dance group, insisted, against his better judgment, on calling the *panyembrama* dance *péndét*.

The environment, in which the dance was performed, was the village temple of Bungaya. This is a ritually important place, where secular performances—such as the *panyembrama* dance—had never been performed before. The dance was especially ordered for the tourist event. The need of the organizer to satisfy the search for originality was apparently fulfilled by giving the dance a new name. Through the use of the name of the ritual model for the secular dance, the secular dance could be used as an emblem of an authentic *bali-aga* tradition.

Ritual dances are part of all large-scale Balinese religious life. The spectrum ranges from danced processions to performances of different masked dances. Each village commands a fixed repertoire of ritual performances, which are also mentioned in the *awig-awig* (the village chronicles). This does not mean that the choreographies are described in detail. The names of the different dances are merely mentioned in the chronicles, and, in some cases, they are linked to the names of rituals. In the context of tourism and the standardized program of *Parisada Hindu Dharma* (the official religious organization) (see Bakker 1993, 2f.), many villages have extended their ritual program in the last years. The new dances are usually well-known ones, which are adapted to intra-village norms of aesthetics and choreography. Popular extension of this sort are *baris* (the war dance), *rejang* (the fertility dance) and *péndét* (the offering dance) danced by the members of a community.

Usually the dancers do not have any dance training. Correspondingly, the movements have to be simple. The dancers perform in rows one behind the other, so that they can imitate each other's movements. In comparison, the movements of the *péndét* of Bungaya are characterized by complicated dynamics and changes in direction. Amateurs carrying heavy offering bowls cannot dance these.

Likewise, the Balinese does not regard complicated, skillful movements as representative of spiritual forces. They cannot be used to establish contact with the alternate reality. Through the untrained, imitating movements the gods present themselves within a ritual. Only through raw, seemingly spontaneous movements can one come into contact with spiritual beings. Dance movements in the profane dances are regarded as being owned by human beings. They can be choreographed, trained and varied any time without restrictions. This is expressed by individual names of the movements performed. Unlike the profane movements, the sacred ones are characterized as *polos*. This word has several connotations. It is used for things as well as for human beings in order to signal special qualities such as 'being pure,' and 'being empty without any design.' In the context of the dance movements, *polos* means that the movement are not 'filled' with human intention or creativity but that they can be used by spiritual beings or filled with their energy. These dances are understood as activities for performing a ritual. Furthermore, it is not said that the participants in the ritual are actually dancing; rather the name of the performance is transformed by a prefix into a verb designating the action performed. In this manner, the word *rejang* denotes both a sacred girl's dance and the costumed girl herself. *Merejang* or *ngerejang* designates the execution of the ritual movements.

In Bali in the 1970s, in response to the growing tourism industry, profane and sacred dances were distinguished from one another and categorized. Balinese intellectuals said that if tourism were planned from the capital city in Java, Balinese culture would be sold out completely. A commercialization of all parts of Balinese life should not be uncritically accepted, they argued. In a seminar conducted in 1971 the categorization of the Balinese praxis of arts in sacred and profane was decided. Whereas the profane parts were released for the commercialization, it remained taboo to perform ritual acts upon request.

Although the leader of the group called the welcoming dance *péndét*, it was a performance of a profane dance, which could have occurred anytime and anywhere. The environment in which the dance was performed, was the village temple of Bungaya, a ritually important place. Even though the influence of the tourism industry has eroded the borderline between the sacred and the profane, the refusal of the *daa* makes it obvious that in Bungaya these boundaries still have value. This group of nine young women presented themselves in their traditional ritual dance dress. They welcomed the guests at the entrance of the temple and, by popular request, they agreed to line up in the middle of the temple in the burning sunshine, to give the tourist another chance to take their photos.

Their refusal to dance can be explained as follows: The dance *rejang* is connected to fixed times and places of performance. The *daa* dance during the important temple rituals to honor the rice goddess Dèwi Sri and the god of material wealth Rambut Sedana. Their participation in the dance is their duty as members of a temple group. Because of their descent from the village's founding families, their sex, and their social status as virgins, the girls have a duty to dance. This serves to display the social position and power of leading dynasties in public.

The meeting of the conference-tourists, the religious as well as political office holders of Bungaya was, in the estimation the girls, not an acceptable ritual frame which would have made it possible for them to dance the *rejang*. As Humphrey and Laidlaw might say, the girls did not and could not have the right 'ritual commitment' needed for a ritual performance (see Humprhey and Laidlaw 1994, 88–110).

Their refusal to give a demonstration of the dance does not mean that there is no *rejang* outside of ritual contexts. In spite of the prohibition of commercializing ritual dances, and of taking ritual dances out of their context, a dance called *rejang* was performed as early as 1986 during the annual Art Festival in the capital city Denpasar. This dance was a *kreasi baru* (a new creation), which only had the name in common with the East Balinese dance. Announced as a temple dance, the Denpasar *rejang* could be distinguished by the costumes of the dancers and the complicated movements, which illustrated a whole story on the stage.

The costumes of *rejang* dancers are used as signs of tradition and cultural values within different context. In recent years, *rejang* dancers have participated in the parades at the beginning of the Art Festival as representatives of their villages. One consequence is that in the East Balinese village Tenganan, where at the same time the biggest annual ritual is celebrated, the groups of unmarried girls and boys are divided in two parts. One part of each group dances the ritual dance in Tenganan, whereas the other part participates in the parade as part of the opening ceremony for the Art Festival (see Français Simburger 1998, 312).

What concepts are behind these developments, and who are the decision-makers?

To answer this question, four different yet interrelated levels should be differentiated: (1) the international or global arena, including international tourism, (2) the national arena, including the production of national identity together with the corresponding cultural policies, (3) the local level, and (4) in the case of Bali, the regional level with its own cultural standards for a distinct Hindu identity with the statistically dominant Islamic culture.

Proponents of Balinese Hinduism struggled to have their form of Hinduism recognized by the government in Jakarta as an official religion. This recognition came, finally in 1962. In order to escape the apparent stigma of the lack of a holy book and a high god, the organization *Parisada Hindu Dharma* was founded and went to work. The result was a fundamentalization and a standardization of Balinese religious life. Religion is now taught in school by authorized textbooks; ways of praying were adapted to an Islamic standard. There are new regulations for costumes and the colors associated with particular rituals have been standardized (for example, black costumes, not colorful costumes, for funerals). Old Balinese temples were rebuilt in the new Bali style following the South Balinese architectural style of the Gianyar area. That means that an open ritual space became surrounded with a high wall of concrete, and the former open place for many activities was closed for daily purposes.

In order to be able to present themselves to national audiences, especially the Old Balinese villages are required to participate in the annual festival with their ethnic specialties. However, the villages are free to decide to what degree they want to use ritual elements to promote their public image.

The local right of self-determination depends, among other things, on the categorization of religious activities. It is important to 'distinguish' between *agama* (the civil religion of Balinese Hinduism, the bureaucratic system of national and regional religious institutions) and the *adat* (the local area tradition or custom). For the latter the Balinese proverb is still valid: *Iain désa— Iain adat* (other villages—different customs). And this counts especially for the Old Balinese village with their own rituals.

Let me take the temple dance *rejang* as an example to illustrate the heterogeneity and simultaneity of developments. Being part of a hybrid contemporary theater-dance scene, the new *rejang* has little in common with the traditional dance *rejang*, which happens during village rituals in East Bali. The use of the noun 'traditional' does not mean that this dance can be regarded as a timeless static phenomenon. In this context, tradition means that *rejang* belongs to the expressed concept of the identity of a single village. But there is no standard *rejang*. If a village has the ritual dance, the choreography will be different in many details from a *rejang* danced in other villages in Bali. *Rejang* is a dance genre that exists in many different forms. There are no two villages, which perform the same *rejang* in their ritual program. And each *rejang* is subject to a steady process of change. Changes can happen because of individual preferences, fashions or because of practical reasons, which are evident in details of the costumes (for example, plastic instead of natural material; the replacement of *bunga kamboja* for flowers made of woolen threads five years ago). The composition of the dancing group can be changed because of a village chief who decides that previously exempt families from now on have to send their daughters to the dancing place. Such changes are closely connected with changes in the choreography. The daughter of one of the formerly exempt families insisted on dancing in the first position of a row—without knowing the dance movements. The replacement of biological criteria with school class levels as a criterion for participation in the dance, may be seen as an expression of modernization processes.

Within one village there are no generally valid criteria concerning the participation in the *rejang*. In many cases, non-local school education or vocational training lead to an individual lifestyle for girls and women of marriageable age. While some women refuse to participate in village rituals, village chiefs are often interested in the reconstruction of old priestly functions and old ritual forms.

These inventions of tradition, which I could observe in one East Balinese village, are welcomed by some parts of the village population. In their opinion, the village has become much more independent of Brahman high priests because they now have their own traditional priests with the same ritual power. Others regard these changes more or less critically. Because of the reconstruction of ritual schedules, the participation in the ritual is much more exhausting than some years ago for the *rejang* dancers. In former times they could go home after performance in the same night (see Rein 1998). In August 1999 they had to be in the temple area without interruption from 10 p.m. until 1 a.m. During that time the girls participated in a procession, conducted libation, sang ritual songs, and had to stand around a *balé* where other priests were offering and praying. After a short break of one hour, in which the girls went home and put on other costumes, their next dance performance started at 2 a.m. and lasted until 5 a.m. in the morning.

In the reconstructed old traditions, these time schedules are strictly followed compared to the past, when they were treated in an easy way. In 1997 there were still lengthy interruptions, and the dance *rejang* was already finished at 2 a.m.

The new rules are beyond the physical capacity of many dancers, who are not used to a strict, ascetic way of life. And furthermore, they are not committed to this lifestyle. Consequently, separately or in small groups, they disappeared in the darkness of the night to the background where several *warung* offered drinks, food and sweeties. Remaining seated, they could have refreshments while relaxing before their next ritual duty.

This reconstruction of ritual designs, the recovery of the roots of their own culture, has to be seen as a consequence of the process of modernization, globalization and the construction of a national culture. As Robertson proved, localism is not a reaction to the process of globalization but an inherent condition of it (see Robertson 1993). In the 1990s, on the motto 'diversity sells,' the Indonesian government started to accept ethnic differences in the context of catering to an international tourism market. Yet this was followed by "'inventions and tradition' and 'imagination' of tradition and locality (e.g., ethnic tourism), and partially politically motivated as minority groups assert their voices and claims within global and transnational arenas (e.g., various UN sponsored, international conferences)" (Français Simburger 1998, 253f.).

It is in this sense that the performances of the two East Balinese villages for the conference "Milleniart: The Celebration of the Origins" have to be understood. Although there are severe prescriptions for spheres of activities, people told me that the presentation of the ritual elements outside of a ritual time was possible in order to give guests insight into the cultural life of the villages. The villagers presented nationally accepted emblems of their special ethnic quality as a promotion session with the hope that, in the future, they will also receive the label of an official tourist village: Desa Wisata connected with an economic development.

In conclusion, I would like to state that I did not systematically interview all the participants in the events described above. During that day of travel through the villages, I documented the events and recorded the comments of several participants. Following my initial question as to whether I had participated in a theater performance, a ritual, or something else, the girls' spontaneous refusal in Bungaya to dance gave the answer. My initial question as to whether I had participated in a theater performance, a ritual, or something else, was answered by the girls' refusal to dance in Bungaya. This was not a theater performance, but an event somewhere between modernity (read: economic interests) and traditional religious village life, whose religious practice was in part still imbued with vivid mysteries. Although the official tourist industry is fond of slogans such as "Religion sells," village officials still respect the right of individual members of the community to refuse to participate in such events in order to maintain their religious identity.

However, in the aftermath of the terror attack in 2002 in the main tourist center in Bali (Kuta), which had disastrous consequences not only for tourism on Bali, the whole discussion about modernity and tradition must be reframed.

References

Bakker, Frederik L. 1993: *The Struggle of the Hindu Balinese Intellectuals: Developments in Modern Hindu Thinking in Independent Indonesia.* Amsterdam: VU University Press.

Francais-Sumburger, Angela. 1998: 'Politics of the Center' in Bali's Cultural Periphery: Transformations of Power in an Old-Balinese 'Village Mandala'. Ph.D. diss., Graduate Faculty in Anthropology at The City University of New York.

Hooker, Virginia M. (ed.). 1993: *Culture and Society in New Order Indonesia.* Kuala Lumpur: Oxford University Press.

Humphrey, Caroline and James A. Laidlaw. 1994: *The Archetypal Actions of Ritual: A Theory of Ritual Illustrated by the Jain Rite of Worship.* (Oxford Studies in Social and Cultural Anthropology). Oxford: Clarendon Press.

Kipp, Rita S. and Sudan Rodgers (eds.). 1987: *Indonesian Religions in Transition.* Tuscon: University of Arizona Press.

Nuryanti, Windu (ed.). 1997: *Tourism and Heritage Management.* Yogyakarta: Gadjahmada University Press.

Picard, Michel. 1996: *Bali: Cultural Tourism and Touristic Culture*, transl. by Diana Darling. Singapore: Archipelago Press.

Rein, Anette. 1994: *Tempeltanz auf Bali: Rejang – der Tanz der Reisseelen.* (Frauenkulturen – Männerkulturen 2). Münster: LIT.

———. 1996: TanZeiten auf Bali. In: *Tanzkunst, Ritual und Bühne: Begegnungen zwischen den Kulturen*, ed. Marianne Nürnberger and Stephanie Schiderer. Frankfurt a.M.: IKO-Verlag. 67–102.

———. 1998: Dancing Rejang and Being Maju? Aspects of Female Temple Dance in East Bali and Concepts of National Culture in Indonesia. In: *Canberra Anthropology* 21:63–83.

Robertson, Roland. 1995: Globalization: Time-Space and Homogeneity-Heterogeneity. In: *Global Modernities*, ed. Mike Featherstone, Scott Lash, and Roland Robertson. London and Thousand Oaks, Calif.: Sage Publications. 25–44.

Failure of Performance or Passage to the Acting Self? Mishima's Suicide between Ritual and Theater

Klaus-Peter Köpping

On November 25, 1970, Yukio Mishima, the famous Japanese author and playwright—actor in gangster-movies, in many modernized Noh plays and on the classical Kabuki stage as female impersonator (*onna-gata*)—performed his final *coup de theatre* by committing suicide in public on the balcony of a general's quarters in front of the audience of many hundred officers and soldiers of the Japanese Self-Defense Force at their Tokyo Headquarters: he was 45. Mishima chose the age-old form of *seppuku* (in common parlance also labeled *hara-kiri*), of suicide as a ritual act by disembowelment, in which the head is cut off by an attendant with a sword after the belly has been slit toward the heart with a short dagger. Nobody watching some of these events, some preserved on film as documentary, some re-enacted, can avoid being moved by these harrowing scenes. One scene in particular remains etched in the memory of the viewer: when Mishima, his face distorted in fanatic exultation, tries to rouse the interest of the assembled military to his self-proclaimed impending and meticulously planned suicide before them, derisory laughter meets his harangue about the declining morals of the Japanese nation, the need to restore martial virtues and to re-institute the imperial power of the Japanese Tenno.

Considering the response of the audience, and taking into account our knowledge of Mishima as consummate actor who had performed such ritual suicide in several famous movie-sequences before, one cannot but feel for the futility of Mishima's enterprise, yet at the same time having the uncomfortable feeling one is attending a badly acted drama. The awe-inspiring magnificence of this horrific form of self-annihilation is almost offset by the overdramatized, painfully obvious histrionics, framed by Mishima's speech, his voice breaking in high-pitched fanaticism. The meticulous planning before the deed contrasts starkly with the performance on the balcony, and one begins to wonder whether it was not so much the deed of suicide which inspired the derision of the audience but the very histrionics of its announcement and the haranguing of soldiers about past glories to be restored. It may have sounded and felt just too embarrassing, not only in the context of the time and the position of the military in a democratic environment, but the very form of its delivery which—taking the Japanese imagery and the reporting of historical occasions of suicide which Mishima tried to replay—is at odds with the mood, which should prevail during such occasions. It is here that Mishima's miscalculation about the ritual shows itself. Such misjudgment appears paradoxical, given that in his acting career and role-playing he was fully familiar with the etiquette attending such extraordinary events which are either conducted in utter privacy—as was the case, a few years later, with the older colleague, friend, and 'teacher' of Mishima, the noble laureate Yasunari Kawabata—or a solemn public ritual, always attended by the hushed atmosphere of the impending sacred act of sacrifice of life: it was never seen as a religious ritual in the narrow sense, no divinities being invoked or appeased.

Mishima's failure lies in the performative action itself; he failed to rouse an interest among the military in reviving what he considered the 'authentic' Japanese spirit of the warrior-tradition (*bushido*) with which he had been enamoured for many years. This enticement failed to materialize in and through the performance. Skilled as he was, his acting out of the ritual should have enraptured the audience, convincing them of the solemnity of the ritual self-sacrifice itself and thus becoming a collectively acknowledged ritual event, despite the military audience's different view of its role in 'rousing the national spirit.'

According to more recent critical reassessments of the notion of 'ritual' which underplay the intentions of the actor and concentrate on the 'ritual commitment' as the main feature, the performance could have swayed the audience to an awareness that they were attending a ritual act, even if nobody was inclined either to repeat it or to subscribe to the personal intention of the performer (see Humphrey and Laidlaw 1994). This would have been the decisive criterion for effectiveness. For the majority of Japanese, *seppuku* is still identified as an 'authentic' self-sacrifice, typifying their national history and essential character (the *yamato-damashii*), which they locate in the 'heroic past.' Specific historical events of this kind and predecessors are still imbued with cultic reverence inscribed in the consciousness of the populace through school as well as popular tales and festivals. Yet the suicide of Mishima did not lead to an equal reverence of ritual as 'pure act,' which embodies something of the national 'soul' of each Japanese, and Mishima has not been accorded 'divine' status, as were many of those forerunners to whom he actually referred in his action. This failure is due in part to his barnstorming over-acting, which made the solemn performance a shambles and a farce.

I do not deny that Mishima's performance and the reaction can indeed be taken as indicator for a changed perception of reality, even if we can discern this only indirectly. As the event unfolded, it failed to induce in the audience any notion of 'ritual,' and the very fact that one laughed derisorily about it indicates a shift in perception. Such a deed is not longer done, for it has become an anachronism; one remembers, one is enthralled by the nostalgic memory about past deeds of this kind, but the 'ethics of the warrior' (*bushido*) in its concrete forms is perceived as inappropriate. Let me hasten to add that in regard to the effectiveness of ritual performances which by most widely shared consensus in anthropological theorizing is perceived as the constitution or reconstitution of reality or its perception (see, for instance, Kapferer 1979; similarly, Tambiah 1981), where either a reaffirmation of the existing order or its revamping are believed to accrue, this result can be seen to occur, though in a kind of inversion. The ritual itself is not effective in constituting that reality, but the response shows that a shift of the perception about the constituting markers of society has occurred: through the denial of the ritual as concrete act—and the denial of its intended purpose—society has affirmed its divergence from its own dreams of the heroism of warriors, or at least from the notion that the dream should inspire concrete life to imitate mimetically the past in such a concrete and final event.

The event itself remains of utmost importance for locating a break in the modern consciousness of the Japanese majority, a hiatus that also may have shocked the Japanese themselves into actually having to express their disagreement with the event as meaningful in its original intentions and symbolic ramifications. The event forced the onlookers to face up to the fact of their own dichotomization of real life and theatrical re-enactment: but theater is not supposed to invade real life, and the violence of the actor performing the unexpected forced the audience also to face up to their self-deception about the silently held belief that their innermost essence was that of a warrior character.

The derisory laughter may thus also have been the result of shame, of loosing face in the world and among themselves, therefore laced with anger at being publicly exposed to the truth behind the adulation of theatrical heroism, and the laughter may finally indicate a form of defiance against the derision with which the actor actually tainted their real life and their perception of their role as inadequate, effeminate, degenerated from a more virtuous past. To exhaust the metaphor of the belly: through cutting his belly in order to save the face of the nation, Mishima instead exposed the soft underbelly of the Japanese self-understanding as 'innate warriors,' expounding that their wish-dream about themselves was just that and that made the audience lose face indeed, reason enough to shout angrily back at him and not to forgive him for his performance, thus not divinizing his deed with other events as a 'nobility of failure' (see Morris 1975).[1]

Before returning to this very nub of the issue concerning the relation of belly and face and of the changed context of both between reality and the imaginary as well as between the theatrical and the ritual mode of performing it, I want to pick up on the notion of the 'nobility of failure,' as Ivan Morris aptly summed up the Japanese thinking about their adulation of preceding historical and theatrically embroidered and idealized cases of *seppuku*, which indeed became an almost iconic, certainly a nostalgic, image about heroic self-sacrifices which embody the ideal of personhood or the collectively shared image about individuality, so often denied or negated in the literature about Japan as a 'nation of non-individuality, conformity, and imitation.' The collectively shared cultural notions about the 'nobility of failure' seem to play a paradoxical role in Mishima's own life: did he perceive his life as a failure for which the noble way out was self-sacrifice? If so, why was he not accorded in the modern collective memory that status of a divinity on which he modeled himself? This leads to the second question closely connected with the first: is the failure of his performance due to the changed context of the performance or to the very performative strategy he chose? Or to put it more concretely: did his performative histrionics violate the cultural code that the performance of suicide should indicate the elimination of the individual personality, of the ego, of the self?

Mishima's audience did perceive that his acting took over the ritual frame: instead of annihilating his self he was actually enhancing it, showing it so strongly that the frame of ritual was violated by the 'play,' the 'performing' of ritual in the sense of theatrical pretense so that even this kind of 'end-play' of concrete self-annihilation could not save the ritual as 'sacrifice'? Was Mishima thus also a bad actor who failed to annihilate his self in the process of performing? To put it another way: did he annihilate himself formally and bodily, thus giving ritual its significance of finality, without annihilating his personal self in the role, thus giving the audience the impression of self-aggrandizement and making it too obvious that he accorded himself, or at least craved for himself, that form of divinity which the classical historical heroes had achieved in the collective consciousness? This

[1]   For the complex connection of face and belly see also Doi 1973 and Köpping 2000.

question in turn is closely connected with Mishima's self-understanding as actor and his explicit philosophy of the relation of mask and personality, or more specifically, with the relation he saw between theatrical performance and real life activities. Most basic is here his understanding about the onto-logical status of the 'life-world' and one's actions in it. On this level, his staged ritual suicide may indeed have been successful in terms of his personal worldview, which connected him to some form of shared collective cultural capital. However, if it is the case that he was successful as far as his personal intentions behind the suicide are concerned, can or should such personal intentions be considered in a culturally specific frame of ritual? Can or should the effectiveness of ritual be judged from a subjective angle of the performer's intentions?

In this case it seems rather ineffectual to fall back on the distinction between theater and real life in which, as Bailey inferred, a person who has seen Julius Caesar die on stage would look the next day at the obituaries in the newspaper (see Bailey 1996). Yet, as ritual is a part of real life and affects it profoundly, this distinction does not help us if the actor as performer puts an end to the performance by annihilating himself, thus actually exploding the notion of the frame 'theater.' He does not 'perform' a theater of cruelty, as it were, but makes the theatrical play a real ritual. However, he does not evoke even the minimal definition of 'ritual commitment': this exists only in his part, in his mind, not in the mind of the audience. We seem here to arrive at one of the core paradoxes: Mishima is considered a failure, not even a noble one, in the eyes of his audience because he 'plays' the ritual, but breaks the frame of playing at the same time, as he intends to risk his life as if in a true self-sacrifice, thus breaking the frame of 'theater' in objective performance as well as in personal intentions, as publicly announced. Failure to convince the audience of a true ritual act taking place, and even if that were acceded, failure to obtain the accruing nobility for the deed, seem to increase our conundrum of making sense of the performance, except if we can elucidate Mishima's own notion about acting and its relation to life and his philosophy of life itself.

Some authors like Edward L. Schieffelin (1996) have come to the conclusion that the distinction between theater and ritual is largely irrelevant if we concentrate on the performative aspects, in which the acting skills in the execution and staging are of utmost importance to elicit from an audience the response or rather resonance about the efficacy of the action. The audience's disposition or traditional preconception of what is going to happen allocates the performance to a specific category at the same time as the acting skills of the performers convey the expected message. The effectiveness of the performance of a ritual is thus closely connected with the 'acting' skills of performers who determine the recipient's judgment of quality. The effect of an action is to a large degree an 'emergent' quality, which implies—under specific culturally divergent preconceptions, which, for instance, acknowledge the theatrical qualities of ritual from the start—that the failure of the performative staging due to the ineffectivity of the actor does not necessarily invalidate the act as ritual. The resonance which is supposed to be elicited in the audience is the 'risk' of the performer's skill, or, in Schieffelin's words: "The emergent is what performance brings about in social reality. ... This is true even when what emerges in a given performance is not necessarily predictable or is even the opposite of the performer's intentions" (Schieffelin 1996, 81; see also Rao and Köpping 2000).

But the precondition for such theoretical generosity is what Gregory Bateson long ago labeled the 'frame,' which has to be agreed upon by certain cultural preconceptions on the collective (even if negotiated) level (see Bateson 1956). All must perceive that what is going on in a particular domain of social action is 'ritual,' and thus has the iconic quality of a collectively shared imagery about the frame, notwithstanding the fact that the ritual action is performative in terms of being meticulously staged, prepared, rehearsed, with rules which are followed (and negotiated).

But the performativity lies in the very fact that the staging has to be competent in order to be effective, even if it has that reflexive quality which distinguishes both theater and ritual from unconscious social action. Of tantamount importance in the case of Mishima's suicide therefore becomes the exploration of the Japanese iconic notion about 'ritual suicide,' to cite cases when divinity was accorded, and to describe the performative (theatrical) elements traditionally connected with it as well as the already mentioned contextuality of what is perceived as 'nobility of failure.' This process may show that Mishima's failure may lie on a different plane. We then need to deduce from Mishima's preparations, from his activities prior to the event, as well as from his written work what kind of relation he saw between life and theatrical performance and in what way that may coincide with a general Japanese perception about the nature of reality. If it did, yet did not find resonance on a collective plane, can it still be considered effective as personal quest?[2]

A summary comparison of the classical suicide as reported by an early eyewitness of the nineteenth century and of Mishima's performance may give

---

[2]   For a different but comparable case of a failed performance, see the description about the failure of a young shamaness in Korea to achieve her initiation (Kendall 1996).

some hint at the formal similarities as well as contextual differences between these events. When a Japanese *samurai* was forced to commit honorable self-immolation as punishment for having wounded members of foreign legations in the Meiji-time, the British ambassador Lord Mitford was invited to attend. We have the following description by his aide, Sir Ernest M. Satow, of how the condemned person (in the presence of seven Japanese witnesses and accompanied by his best men, *kaishaku*, who will cut off the head) meets his fate in a Buddhist temple in the morning:

> With the calmest deliberation he took his seat on the red felt, choosing the position which would afford him the greatest convenience for falling forward. A man dressed in black with a light grey hempen mantle then brought in the dirk wrapped in paper on a small unpainted wooden stand, and with a bow place it in front of him. He took it up in both hands, raised it to his forehead and laid it down again with a bow. This is the ordinary Japanese gesture of thankful reception of a gift. Then in a distant voice, very much broken, not by fear or emotion, but as it seemed reluctance to acknowledge an act of which he was ashamed—declared that he alone was the person who had outrageously ... ordered fire to be opened on foreigners.... He next divested himself of his upper garments by withdrawing his arms from the sleeves, the long ends of which he tucked under his legs to prevent his body from falling backward.... He then took the dirk in his right hand, grasping it just close to the point, and after stroking down the front of his chest and belly inserted the point as far down as possible and drew it across to the right side.... Having done this he with great deliberation bent his body forward, throwing the head back so as to render the neck a fair object for the sword.... One kai-shaku had been crouching on his left and a little behind him with drawn sword poised in the air from the moment the operation commenced. He now sprang up suddenly and delivered a blow the sound of which was like thunder. The head dropped down on the matted floor, and the body lurching forward fell prostrate over it, the blood from the arteries pouring out and forming a pool. When the blood vessels had spent themselves all was over. The little wooden stand and the dirk were removed. (Satow 1983, 345–346)

After some more polite bowing acknowledgments and formal interchange of words with the Japanese government representatives, the foreign witnesses left around noon.

When we compare this description with that of Mishima's suicide, the formal criteria are almost all present. Mishima had meticulously prepared his manuscripts at home by giving his publishers advice about their final print, donned the mock-military uniform which he had designed years before for his private 'army,' the Shield-Society (*Tate-no-Kai*), and calmly and deliberately went with his two best men—and two more young members of the Shield-Society—by car to the headquarters of the Self-Defense Force in Tokyo where his consummate acting poise gained him access to the buildings where a senior general had his quarters. The pre-arranged reason for meeting the general was to show him one of the rare *samurai* swords from his private collection. Entering the building, he took the general prisoner, binding him to a chair, then barricaded the doors, opened the windows to the balcony and addressed the assembling military men with the following words (the scenario referred to in the beginning of this essay) in a fanatical high-pitched voice which became shriller by the minute when he realized that people were shouting at him and telling him to go away:

> We see how Japan is getting drunk in consumerism and decays because of its emptiness of spirit.... We shall restore the emperors image and die for it. How can you live in a world empty of spirit? ... The army is supporting the same treaty, which denies the army its right to existence. At that point of time the army should have seized power and have requested the revision of the treaties. [He is referring to the Japanese American Treaty of 1969 and the fact that Japan should only have a Self-Defence Force—a clear euphemism to circumvent the establishing of armed forces, forbidden by the Constitution originally approved and introduced by McArthur after the defeat in World War Two, but convenient for American aspirations in the wake of the Korean War] ... Our basic values which make us Japanese are in danger.... The emperor has lost his place which he should be accorded by Japanese historical tradition.... (cited after Yourcenar 1985, 108; author's translation)

In the following ritual act, Mishima, as recreated for film-audiences, sits down in the correct posture, but the first of his best men, Morita, with tears in his eyes, bungles the cutting off of the head, so the sturdy second lieutenant of the Shield-Society, the young Fugu-Koga cut his head off instead. Morita who follows with his own suicide (the famous double suicide of 'lovers') then bungles his own belly-cutting, so that Fugu-Koga again has to intervene and shorten the agony by cutting off his head. The two heads are then placed on the general's carpet where they are later photographed by the press as the only surviving 'documentary' evidence. The general then admonishes the group (the entourage of Mishima comprised four other young men) which collapses in sorrow and tears by telling them to weep as is appropriate and then to gain composure in order to present a decent 'public face' and to release him. He recites the prayer formula of *Namu Amida Butsu* over the two heads, "the only decent deed in this sordid event," as Marguerite Yourcenar was to call it later (1985, 110; author's translation).

Several points come to the fore when compared to the 'classical' ritual. In a purely formal way, Mishima's suicide is in many ways a 'bungled' ritual: things do not go as planned, the attending best men fail or falter, the speech which should show calm collectedness and abnegation of self degenerates into a harangue of desperate fanaticism. Yet looking at ritual in a comparative perspective, the concrete events get their flavor not by their perfection of execution—an understanding colored by notions about the 'redundancy' and 'repetitiveness' of performance in particular its liturgical forms—but exactly by their performative quality of 'rehearsal.' They are almost always texts or descriptions or rules, which may actually only be nebulously remembered artifacts in the minds of the performers, which have to be negotiated in each actualization anew. One feature does seem to make the performance of Mishima an enterprise fraught with ambiguities: he gains access to the 'stage' by stealth and cunning, by subterfuge, by play-acting in a fantasy uniform, as much by force as by pretence. In other words, he does not perform a public ritual, for there is no endorsement or normative expectation of a collectivity.

This points to the contextual shift, which has occurred from the classical historical suicides of predecessors on the one hand, but it points also to a particular understanding of 'role-playing' on Mishima's part on the other. The contextual shift can easily be discerned from the public response to this event. The prime minister declared Mishima mentally deranged; the conservatives could not rally around the 'nationalistic' aims of the Shield-Society as he was seen as a 'crazy actor' whose morals were questionable; the left-wing political movements were understandably not enamored with a nationalistic revival of militarism, and while they agreed with Mishima's criticism of the Japanese American Security Treaty which they were fighting with utmost vigor and violence, they also wrote anti-Emperor slogans. There was little sympathy among Mishima's closer family members either. The father denounced his son as a *nuisance* for whose pranks one would have to apologize to the authorities, the irony being that the father is obsessed with the Japanese notion of 'face-saving,' which the son tried to achieve for the national honor. In short, nobody would identify Mishima's suicide with a ritual act, which needed to be honored to be effective, and nobody seemed to identify with the aims, which Mishima publicly proclaimed for the deed.

Mishima's performance did not accord with the political context: saving the national honor by restoring the imperial system in a military coup was unacceptable in a democratic environment, where economic success had become the measuring rod for virtue. Mishima was not a *samurai*, a warrior, indeed the warrior ethics were already over by the time of the installation of the Meiji Emperor in the nineteenth century. The very basis of feudal society was eradicated by the new central government, which however skillfully used elements of the warrior ethic in order to modernize for industrial competition, and to forge a commitment to a unified abstract nation-state. In short, none of the reasons with which Mishima tried to underpin his per-

formance in public fitted the historical precedents or the imagined past ethical code. *Seppuku* as ritual suicide had a definite canon when it should be
performed: it always involved the loyalty of retainers of the aristocratic ruling class when a clash of values in terms of irresolvable conflict of loyalties
occurred, when the code of feudal subordination was violated, or when the
lord died. Mishima bought into the fabricated ideology of the Meiji-time
when that system of feudal loyalty was artificially grafted on to the Emperor.

What is more, Mishima seemed to have tried to put into reality the very
system of ethics which played a paramount role in the true nature of 'being
Japanese' only in the imaginary landscape of Japan. And that dreamscape
was, to put it bluntly, only alive on the stage and had become paramount in
the imagination only after the real warrior-class had passed its zenith and
lost its role, at the latest after the unification of the country in the mid-
seventeenth century.

A typical example is the case of the often-repeated favorite among the
Kabuki stage plays, *Chushingura*, which revives the memory of the mass-
suicide of the 47 *ronin*, jobless roaming *samurai*, who during the totalitarian
Tokugawa rule undertook to avenge the insult to their lord by a member of
the Imperial Household, Lord Kira. These *samurai* succeeded in their plan
after many years of dissimulation through evading the suspicion of the totalitarian control by drinking, whoring, and abandoning their families:
'performatively' they gave the impression of having renounced their *samurai*-code of honor by leading a debased life. They fooled the authorities to
such an extent that they were able to assemble in Tokyo and assassinate Lord
Kira in his own mansion. While they thus fulfilled their oath of allegiance to
their own lord, they had committed a heinous crime, which had to be atoned
for by public mass-suicide. Their souls were enshrined in a small sanctuary
in Tokyo, and each December thousands of people still make the pilgrimage
to that sanctuary to pay homage. It seems as if Mishima succumbed to the
fantasies of the stage by imposing the imaginary on the concrete reality, and
while his audience may go into frenzy over a good stage performance, they
balk at the bodily concretization in real life of the ideal, which they nevertheless consider the apogee of their cultural heritage. It is debatable whether
the 47 *ronin* succeeded or failed[3] in their self-set goal: by Japanese standards
they succeeded in wiping the face-insult against their lord, clearing thus the
honor of the fiefdom, and while they failed to 'survive,' they upheld the code
of the warrior who has to die with or for his master. Many other historical

---

[3]   The term *ronin* is nowadays applied to students who have failed their entrance examina-
tions at university.

precedents of *seppuku* are clearly failures of a different kind, namely as a response to the awareness of failure in the person's life-project: all those members of the highest aristocratic clans who became the rulers of Japan, in military as well as political domains, between the tenth and thirteenth centuries seem to have chosen ritual suicide as a way to avoid the shame of ending their lives as failures. Sugawara Michizane, a tremendous military strategist, bold fighter and consummate writer, painter and poet, failed to achieve great political power in the face of his wily relatives. He committed suicide and is nowadays revered as god and invoked for success in the arts (the God *Tenjin*, a highly popular folk-deity). However, historical research seems to indicate that the shape of Japanese history and politics would have been no better off had he succeeded, for the successful politicians and military leaders were indeed the most skilled shapers of the systems of power in their own time.

Yet, in the popular imagination, all those successful rulers are made into villains, while their opponents, using much the same tactics and ruses as their counterparts are accorded the status of naivety, goodness, heroism, and 'innocence of the heart' due to the manner of their death. Their failure in real life made them immortals in the imagination of history and in the imaginary history of Japanese popular consciousness. The belief in the 'nobility of failure' in itself is peculiar to Japan: Europe's Christian saints are not dissimilar, for their pursuit of a concrete realization of their ideal in real life was mostly thwarted, making their death a sign of victory in the imaginary ideal world of values.[4]

However, the connection of Mishima's ritual act with the notion of 'failure' is even more paradoxical. He derived the values that he tried to emulate through his performance from the writings of a *samurai*, Jocho Yamamoto (1659–1719), retainer of the Nabeshima Lords of Northern Kyushu who, while himself denied the honorable suicide at the death of his lord, wrote the book *Hagakure* (Hidden among Leaves) which became a handbook of the art of living as warrior, a book kept secret until the Meiji Restoration of 1868. Mishima based his view of the causes of decline of a modernized economically driven culture on this book and, referring to his obsession for it over a period of 20 years, quotes its central tenet in the following context: "I found that the Way of the Samurai is death.... It was this sentence, however, that gave me the strength to live" (Mishima 1978, 23). The ethical tenets of the

---

[4]   The connection to saints is not completely haphazard as a theoretical category, as Mishima himself confesses in his autobiography how the picture of St. Sebastian fired his imagination, in terms of its eroticism as well as its cruel suffering of torture, both images being clearly closely aligned in life and fantasy by Mishima (see Mishima 1958, 88ff.).

Hagakure also seem to mesh very easily with Mishima's close association with the philosophy of the Noh theater, both the *samurai* code of honor and the principles of acting being closely linked through their derivation from Zen Buddhism. The particular closeness of the two domains, which seem to enmesh if not entrap Mishima, is related to the imagery of the body. The *samurai* code implies that a death at young age is to be favored, a challenge, which must be met unflinchingly and perfectly, in terms of a public performance. The body has to be trained relentlessly, while the mind has to be prepared to achieve stillness at the center, a perception of emptiness. Mishima, who sees himself as a living *samurai* and who often refers to his fear and repulsion at the thought of an aging body, puts this philosophy into praxis by active body building, *kendo* exercises and other martial arts, like sword practice a good decade before his suicide, which suggests that his planning of the event has much deeper personal dimensions than the meticulous preparations on the day of the event itself intimates.

Mishima's action is the result of a very complex intertwining of a philosophy of life with images about a theory of acting, both ultimately derived from Zen precepts. The Zen Buddhist philosophy of life has penetrated deeply into Japanese consciousness as the notion of *mono-no-aware*, the 'fleetingness of the world' (in particular, the world of pleasure), and carries with it the tone of a 'sadness' about existence or of futility and emptiness and the 'pathos of things,' for which the *bushido* ethics of emptying the self from all attachments in order to achieve ultimate annihilation in a perfectly performed act of embracing death (through fighting or suicide) seems the ideal answer, even if it results in the paradox of achieving absolute emptiness through selflessness (love) by denying the power of empty reality over the senses. Mishima is a thorough adherent of this philosophy, as the following commentary on the lines of the *Hagakure* show, where he quotes the lines "When a samurai is constantly prepared for death, he has mastered the Way of the Samurai," and continues:

> [this] is the new philosophy discovered by Jocho. If a man holds death in his heart, thinking that whenever the time comes he will be ready to die, he cannot possibly take mistaken action.... The choice between life and death may come only once in a lifetime. (Mishima 1978, 45)

As if anticipating the criticism of his audience after his own *seppuku*, Mishima asserts: that the death referred to here is a chosen one, not a natural one, and that it is a sign of the free will of humans:

Here is the typical Japanese view that being cut down in battle and committing ritual suicide are equally honorable; the positive form of suicide called hara-kiri is not a sign of defeat, as it is in the West, but the ultimate expression of free will, in order to protect one's honour. (Mishima 1978, 46)

The close connection to theatrical metaphors is indicated in a later reference, when Mishima picks up on the line "Human beings in this life are like marionettes," and explicates his own interpretation:

At the very core of his [Jocho's] personality is a deep, penetrating and yet manly 'nihilism.' He scrutinizes each moment to extract the meaning of life, but at heart he is convinced that life itself is nothing more than a dream. (Mishima 1978, 52)

Mishima, steeped in theatrical tradition, uses the metaphor of the mask in his autobiographical works to elaborate further on the play-acting he performs in life, and comes to the following paradoxical conclusion:

Everyone says that life is a stage. But most people do not seem to become obsessed with the idea, at any rate not as early as I did. By the end of childhood I was already firmly convinced that it was so and that I was to play my part on the stage without once ever revealing my true self. (Mishima 1958, 101)

Yet, of course, he discovers that this performative strategy is another illusion, as he reflexively indicates about his playing of roles:

It was as though I had not yet realized that what I was now disgusted with was my true self, was clearly a part of my true life; it was as though I believed instead that these had been years of dreaming, from which I would now turn to 'real life.' (Mishima 1958, 100–101)

But then he is also aware about his own dissimulation and, in spite of careful planning of his different role-domains, he somehow entangles himself in irresolvable conflicts with his aim of playing on the stage what he really is, while performing in real life a 'role,' inverting the classical paradigmatic difference between theater and life, so that he will find it difficult to disentangle himself again:

I was beginning to understand vaguely the mechanism of the fact that what people regarded as a pose on my part was actually an expression of my need to assert my true nature, and that it was precisely what people regarded as my true self which was a masquerade. (Mishima 1958, 27)

These 'confessions of a mask' become even more troublesome in the light of some theories of acting as developed for the Noh stage and the puppet theater in the Japanese historical stage-tradition, and the paradox of a mask making confessions which would by logic only hide all the more the 'true nature,' except if the mask would know what is hidden, thus becoming the active part in the dichotomy of mask (*persona*) and the actor's personality. What if the mask has taken over the personality? In order not to be carried away by pure deductive logic into too many impasses, a closer look at the theories of stage-performances as developed during the last six-hundred years may be appropriate, as these theories will certainly have influenced Mishima's understanding of masks, roles, play-acting and performing as expression of 'true nature' or essences.

What seems to influence Mishima here are those theories of Noh play, where the mask, which appears in the first part of a play, is replaced by the revelation of the 'true person' in the second part which, however, is only another mask, indicating that underneath is nothing or emptiness. However, the great philosopher and theoretician of the Japanese performing arts, Zeami (1364–1443), postulated in his *Fushi Kaden* (The Teaching about the Flowers of Beautiful Shape) that actors were only good if they could perform a 'thick performance.' A thin performance is one which subjects itself to the real which it wants to represent. A thick performance is one which is full of soul: thus an actor who is young is beautiful through his mere existence, while the skilled older actor must perform in such a way that the beauty of youth is evoked in the audience. Similarly, a later theoretician of marionette theater, Chikamatsu (1653–1724), stated that the marionette-player is a truly great actor when he can fill the cloth of the doll with his flesh and blood, taking the analogy of the skin of the body as the membrane through which the inside can be expressed, or rather as a surface at which the inside and the outside meet (see also Ohashi 1998). The doll's rags are only empty make-believe human figure, but energized through the actor's hands it becomes a truer human being than those living in the flesh. The same applies to the *onna-gata*, the males performing female roles that according to Chikamatsu can perform women's behavior better than real women.

These are the works well known to Mishima whose closest friends were famous *onna-gata* of the Japanese stage. This knowledge and reflexivity put his *seppuku* into a quite different light. He is certainly trying to move the nation through his acting skills, putting his life at risk to achieve this. He hones his body as an actor and body-builder in order to master an instrument, which will unreflexively execute something that expresses more than the self. He explicitly refers to the knowledge of the belly (as opposed to the mind or face-knowledge of decorum and calculation) as superior: "bodily training opens, similarly to the acquisition of erotic knowledge, a flash-like insight into spiritual truth," because he perceives during his harsh training how the body "was being intellectualized to a much higher degree and opens insights and closeness to ideas which surpass the abilities of the mind" (cited after Yourcenar 1985, 77; author's translation). As Yourcenar remarks perceptively on this attitude, it is indeed this notion of the 'passion' of experiencing sensually and sensorily, which makes physiology the center of true wisdom. However, it is a physiology, I would add, which is conditioned by cultural perceptions about it and shaped by this idiom. Japanese public and private behavior is often distinguished by their own reflections as contrast between the 'face' and the 'belly,' whereby the 'true self' rests in the belly. Yet the inside cannot be shaped without the outside form, while the facial outside performance cannot become true (to itself and the on-looking or addressed other) without being informed by the feeling inside which is unconscious, directly accessible, in particular in drunken states of unselfconsciousness, such as possession or trance, and in the performance of a perfect actor.

Mishima is caught in a paradox of the Gordian knot variety—and so are we as the interpreters of the logic of his action in relation to his intentions. As we saw, he hated his dissimulation in life but, when reflecting, knows that in acting out his 'true nature' he is still acting, yet desires also to conform to the outside of the social world to satisfy its demands. Thus the only way out is to mask the self on the stage to truly erase the self and act the part as a perfect performer, the stage being not the illusion machine but that medium through which the illusion machine of reality can be shattered.

This still leaves us with the conundrum of why the ritual performance of *seppuku* did not evoke that resonance which Morris adduced for heroes like Sugawara Michizane or Yoshitsune of the Minamoto clan:

> In a predominantly conformist society, whose members are overawed by authority and precedent, rash, defiant, emotionally honest men like Yoshitsune ... have a particular appeal. The submissive majority, while bearing its discontents in safe silence, can find vicarious satisfaction in identifying itself emotionally with these individuals who waged their forlorn struggle against overwhelming odds, and the fact that all their efforts are crowned with failure lends them a pathos which characterizes the general vanity of human endeavour and makes them the most loved and evocative of heroes. (Morris 1975, xxii)

It should be made clear at this point that the idealization of such heroes took place more than a generation after their death. This has not happened to Mishima's suicidal ritual performance. Before coming back to my initial emphasis on the performing skills and the complex dialectic of the inside view of acting and the outside idolization and adulation of 'acted suicides' which seems to contain the nub of an answer, if only hazily perceived, it is apparent that the very action of Mishima focused the Japanese nation on a quest for its self-understanding, if only for a short period. The funeral was attended by thousands of people, and while most of them were critical of his ritual action, the question of the state of the nation was hotly debated, though no attempts of change were undertaken publicly. That the result of a denial of the appropriateness of the action as ritual is concerned, one may wonder whether what Mishima took to be the fulfillment of a Zen ethical statement about life is again only possible in the modern context in the fine arts of Ikebana or in the domain of the fighting arts as sportive entertainment. One may nowadays still try to learn the principles of Zen, but they only have power in the world of the imagination and are supposed to stay there, even if businessmen consider themselves as modern *samurai*, a notion Mishima would have perceived as the final debasement of Zen living. It may indeed be the case that the former merger of aesthetics and ethics in which the aesthetic expression was the embodiment of an ethical ideal, has been ruptured in Japan in that aesthetics are enacted in a separated domain which one enjoys vicariously but which one does not apply concretely. As a statement about his own inability to bridge the imaginary world and reality, this imaginary, which Mishima embodied and theatricalized in the performance with finality in his suicide, shows that for his audience religious axioms and social customs were separated from the theatrical imaginary. Mishima failed to provoke the expected resonance and—to put it in the words of another Asian ritual as performative tradition—he could not rouse the 'taste' in the audience, the taste in this case for a living presence of divinity.

The anthropologist Frederique A. Marglin who practiced as sacred dancer in South India, remarked that the philosophy behind the rigorous dance training there is the 'refining' of the body so that through repetition, body-training and redundancy of movements, which become automatic, the dancer empties herself of all attachments to the world in order to allow the divinity to enter her and speak through her gestures of the refined body, evoking the feeling of divine grace in the audience. This resonance-perception is called *rasa*, or taste, for one has to taste the divine. The dancer as a medium can transmit this, as can priest-ascetics who refined their bodies through preparations of fasting, prayer, *mantras* and *mudras* (see Marglin 1990).

This description would mesh rather well with the Zen based theater and warrior actions of Japanese performance theories, but nowadays only in the 'performing arts.' As Zen does not operate with the concept of the divine, the taste would have to refer here to the divine as the realization of the emptiness of reality. But then that may indeed only be relevant for and resonant with a lifestyle of a warrior-class where the individual has to prepare for death all the time and at an instant, not in a world focused on economic success.

Thus while Mishima may have admirably succeeded in playing suicides in movies and on stage, he failed utterly in his real-life performance, for he could not give his audience the 'taste' of his ideas; he could not transmit the message of emptiness as its solemn ideal of having achieved self-abnegation. His histrionics may have made the ritual in the eyes of the beholders either—through his haranguing speech—too much of an ideological stance, judged as unfashionable in the modern context and inappropriate for the ritual occasion as imagined from re-inventions of the past on the stage, or the performance was too blatantly imbued with the notion of 'performing' as 'acting out,' thus actually transforming the ritual into a threatricalized spectacle. The only possibility acceptable now is a ritual of this kind played as theater. The intrusion of death as ultimate result destroys the illusionary machine of the theater as much as the collective imaginary of ritual ideally surpassing the contingencies of the real life world. Mishima broke both frames in this passage to his empty self.

Yet only theater can preserve the real ritual as the imaginary in its completeness pristinely and unsullied by contextual contingencies. In that sense, Mishima was successful in his own passage to his theatrical self-understanding of life, but his audience did not share his notion of 'life' as theater.

The last word in this matter should go to Mishima's commentary on the *Hagakure*:

> We tend to suffer from the illusion that we are capable of dying for a belief or a theory. What *Hagakure* is insisting is that even a merciless death, a futile death that bears neither flower nor fruit, has dignity as the death of a human being. If we value so highly the dignity of life, how can we not also value the dignity of death? No death may be called futile. (Mishima 1978, 105)

References

Bailey, Frederick G. 1996: Cultural Performance, Authenticity, and Second Nature. In: *The Politics of Cultural Performance*, ed. David Parkin, Lionel Caplan, and Humphrey Fisher. Oxford: Berghahn Books. 47–69.

Bateson, Gregory. 1956: The Message 'This is Play'. In: *Group Processes: Transactions of the Second Conference October, 1955*, ed. Bertram Schaffner. New York: Josiah Macy Foundation. 145–242.

Doi, Takeo. 1973: *The Anatomy of Dependence*. Tokyo: Kodansha International.

Humphrey, Caroline and James A. Laidlaw. 1994: *The Archetypal Actions of Ritual: A Theory of Ritual Illustrated by the Jain Rite of Worship*. (Oxford Studies in Social and Cultural Anthropology). Oxford: Clarendon Press.

Kapferer, Bruce. 1979: Introduction: Ritual Processes and the Transformation of Context. In: *Social Analysis* 1:3–19.

Kendall, Laurel. 1996: Initiating Performance: The Story of Chini, A Korean Shaman. In: *The Performance of Healing*, ed. Carol Laderman and Marina Roseman. London: Routledge. 153–176.

Köpping, Klaus-Peter. 2000: 'Bauch haben': Die Inszenierung von Gemeinschaftsgefühl in Japan. In: *Emotionalität: Zur Geschichte der Gefühle*, ed. Claudia Benthien, Anne Fleig, and Ingrid Kasten. (Literatur – Kultur – Geschlecht 16). Cologne: Böhlau Verlag. 213–237.

Marglin, Frédérique A. 1990: Refining the Body: Transformative Emotion in Ritual Dance. In: *Divine Passions: The Social Construction of Emotion in India*, ed. Owen M. Lynch. Berkeley and Los Angeles: University of California Press. 212–236.

Mishima, Yukio. 1958: *Confessions of a Mask*, transl. from the Japanese by Meredith Weatherby. New York: New Directions.

———. 1978: *Yukio Mishima on Hagakure: The Samurai Ethic and Modern Japan*, transl from the Japanese by Kathryn Sparling. Tokyo: Tuttle.

Morris, Ivan. 1975: *The Nobility of Failure: Tragic Heros in the History of Japan*. Tokyo: Tuttle.

Ohashi, Ryosuke. 1998: Zum japanischen Kunstweg – Die ästhetische Auffassung der Welt. In: *Das Erbe der Bilder: Kunst und moderne Medien in den Kulturen der Welt*, ed. Hans Belting and Lydia Haustein. Munich: C.H. Beck. 149–162.

Rao, Ursula and Klaus-Peter Köpping. 2000: Die 'performative Wende': Leben – Ritual – Theater. In: *Im Rausch des Rituals: Gestaltung und Transformation der Wirklichkeit in körperlicher Performanz*, ed. Klaus-Peter Köpping and Ursula Rao. (Performanzen: Interkulturelle Studien zu Ritual, Spiel und Theater 1). Hamburg: Lit. 1–32.

Satow, Ernest M. 1983: *A Diplomat in Japan: An Inner History of the Critical Years in the Evolution of Japan*. Tokyo: Tuttle.

Schieffelin, Edward L. 1996: On Failure and Performance: Throwing the Medium out of the Séance. In: *The Performance of Healing*, ed. Carol Laderman and Marina Roseman. London and New York: Routledge. 59–89.

Tambiah, Stanley J. 1981: A Performative Approach to Ritual (1979). In: *Proceedings of the British Academy* 65:113–169.

Yourcenar, Marguerite. 1985: *Mishima oder die Vision der Leere*, transl. from the French by Hans-Horst Henschen. Munich: Carl Hanser Verlag.

Changing Media – Changing Rituals: Media Rituals and the Transformation of Physical Presence

Günter Thomas

Introductory Remarks

During the last 20 years, the field of ritual studies has reached beyond its traditional boundaries both in terms of academic disciplines and of the subject areas and social phenomena under observation. Rituals are analyzed not just in anthropology, sociology of religion, religious studies and theology, but also in the study of literature, philosophy, theater, political science and education. These disciplines do not just work on the arcane religious rituals of archaic societies—they have scrutinized practices in today's society and culture like sport, political performances, building corporate identities, reading newspapers and writing academic footnotes. Mary Douglas' almost 30-year-old observation of a "mysterious ... widespread, explicit rejection of rituals as such" so that "ritual [has] become a bad word signifying empty conformity" (Douglas 1982, 1) is no longer an adequate description of the academic discourse. Even though it might still hold true for a common sense perception, in academic reflection we may speak of an inflation of ritual analysis.

One of the new areas for the study of ritual is the mass media and, in particular, the study of television, an activity that the average German now engages in for almost 3½ hours a day. The research on ritual in the context of television has concentrated on at least three specific areas (for an overview see Rothenbuhler 1998; Thomas 1998; 2000):

First, 'ritual' became a key concept in a very large body of research in the analysis of media events (see Dayan and Katz 1992; Handelman 1998), for example, the funeral of Princess Diana.

Second, reception studies focusing on the place of television in the everyday routines of viewers have found it not only to be part of the routines and rituals of the everyday world, but also to generate specific rituals and corresponding reception patterns (see Hoover and Lundby 1997; Hoover 2000, 77–90).

Third, the analysis of audiovisual genres within the flow of the program discovered the quasi-liturgical character of the television stream and the ritualistic character of the particular genres, for example, television news, talk shows, whodunits, etc. Genres rearrange the combination of invariance and variance that characterizes many rituals and apply various types of frames. In addition, according to this view, television as an institution of modern societies in many respects takes the place of ritual communication in more traditional societies (see Goethals 1981; Silverstone 1981; 1994; Bleicher 1999).

In these three sub-fields we can see both the transposition of traditional rituals into the medium of transmission as well as the emergence of rituals on unfamiliar territory, so to speak. Over against some criticism of such extensions of the classical field into audiovisual communication, I contend that it is an unquestionably worthwhile, meaningful and conceptually justifiable academic endeavor (for such criticism see Grimes 1990, 11). For this reason, I do not intend to elaborate here on the concept of 'ritual' as such or on the meaningfulness of the extension.

Instead, I want to tackle a specific problem that is widely neglected when the study of ritual is applied to the field of modern literature or audiovisual communication. This problem calls for some fine-tuning and repair work. Paradoxically, it might be neglected precisely because it points to a quite self-evident fact in traditional rituals, that is, the bare fact that people participating in ritual are physically co-present and share some physical space. In addition, I would like to strengthen the discussion about dynamic frames by indicating possible links between the two theoretical siblings—Niklas Luhmann's theory of communication[1] and frame theory.[2]

Rituals use bodies as their medium of communication, inscribe their messages in or onto bodies, transform them and—without requiring belief or consensus—operate on the basis of acceptance, which is communicated by the physical presence of the body (see Rappaport 1979). All implicit or explicit heirs to Durkheim's notion of 'effervescence' base the effectiveness of rituals at least to some extent on this physical co-presence of bodies. Now, given that physical presence is an essential part of a ritual event, how can we

---

[1]   Luhmanns complex social theory with his communication theory is best accessible in Luhmann 1989, chap. 6. See also Luhmann 1990; 1995, chap. 4.

[2]   For frames see Don Handelman (1998), especially the new preface; also the classic on *Frame Analysis* by Erving Goffman (1974).

talk about ritual in technologically mediated audiovisual communication, where people are not present, but dispersed over space and time? Can we talk about ritual when people are not co-present? Looking at the types of change discussed in this volume, we face a change that exceeds the change in the performance of a ritual, the change of space and time, also exceeding the change of communication medium such as change from body language to speech. The change we face in the case of television rituals is a change into a new 'medium of transportation.'

Four Strategies for Dealing with the Problem of *a-/presence* in Media Rituals

As far as I can see, there are at least four strategies dealing with the problem, three of which are quite unsatisfactory:

One could start to retreat by saying that the notion of 'ritual' is only ap-lied *metaphorically*. However, as long as one does not differentiate between some rather loose 'metaphorical use' of the term (which is questionnable) and its use as a 'conceptual metaphor' (see Hesse 1966; see also Debatin 1995), this strategy removes the challenge presented by audiovisual commu-nication.

Another way out of the problem could be the reference to the fact that traditional religious rituals, too, involve entities that are not physically pre-sent: ancestors, spirits, divine and semi-divine beings or the worldwide community of believers as symbolized in the Christian notion of the body of Christ. However, these entities are not actively participating performers but are only part of the imagined community to which the physically present par-ticipants relate.

The *third* attempt at solving the problem points to the distinction between audience and participants within many traditional rituals. During the Chris-tian ritual of infant baptism, the congregation is part of the ritual event; it participates in a weak sense while the baby, parents, godfathers and god-mothers participate in a strong sense. However, even the participating observers are physically, that is, bodily present.

The *fourth* and only viable way to deal with the problem of *a/presence* is to accept the claim that ritual requires presence and to ask in what way and by means of which processes, television viewers are 'present' in a shared space?

The Processual Nature of Television Presence:
Oscillation between Communication and Perception

To find the missing piece in the puzzle one has to look very closely at the experience of dynamic audiovisual communication. The twofold thesis I would like to put forward is the following:

First, the experience of audiovisual communication like television or cinema is an experience of an ongoing oscillation between 'perception' and 'communication.'

Second, the perception part of this oscillation leads to a specific type of bodily presence in a 'perceptual space' that is substituting for physical presence.

My theory hinges on the notion of an oscillation between 'perception' and 'communication' as the key concepts. Both terms are central elements in Luhmann's theory of communication, which I would like to briefly outline at the risk of simplification (see Luhmann 1990; 1995; see also Fuchs 1993).

Communication is the emergent unity of three selections that can serve as the basis of further communication. Communication consists inevitably of three elements: (1) information as the selection of meaning out of a range of possibilities, (2) an act of utterance as a selection of this information, and (3) understanding as subsequent selection out of a second range of meaning, which is based on the difference between the information and the utterance. If communication is what comes out of this process, no single consciousness can capture or 'see' all three aspects. If we look at the process from the perspective of individual consciousness, it is important to detect, in the stream of perception, units that carry the difference between information and utterance. If we see someone blink this can be just the perception of a physical behavior, or it may be an act containing information—a hint to me to adjust my tie. Within specific media, the difference between utterance and information is conveyed in 'forms.' Listening to vocal talk, that is, speech, we are fine-tuned to such a difference and expect something other than noise. When we detect the difference between information and utterance, we attribute it to another social or conscious system.

Human consciousness is most of the time a perceiving consciousness. We operate much more in the mode of perception than of communication. Even though perception is composed of multiple types of impressions, normally perception creates a compact unity of perception. Perception—or, in the case of embodied conscious systems, sensory perception—does not imply passivity and is not without the making of distinctions. On the contrary, it implies the recognition of patterns, that is, movements and forms that tend to be generalized. Some forms might be, neurologically speaking, hardwired and some pattern recognition abilities are acquired over time. Consequently, the opposition of activity and passivity is not able to relate perception to communication. The differentiating marker is the recognition of selectivity—that is, the difference between information and utterance—which can be attributed to another self-referential system. Between just enjoying a sunset and seeing in it a message from a communicating god there is only a tiny difference: in the latter case, the sun is an utterance carrying information coming from a self-referential godhead, not just a beautiful natural event. In the first case, the sun is just a beautiful object of perception.

This rather simple theoretical distinction is the basis for far-reaching differences between perception and communication:

First, perception allows a high degree of complexity in the processing of information without a high degree of depth of analysis. It achieves almost simultaneity and a high speed in processing information. Communication is much slower and bound to sequential forms of operation. The emergence of the unity of information, utterance and understanding is—compared to perception—very time-consuming. Every driver can testify this difference.

Second, perception has a specific relation to time. For perception, the perceived is simultaneous; what is perceived exists in reality. Therefore, perception leads to a synchronization of the conscious or social system and its environment. In principle, perception is undeniable or unarguable—only subsequent reflexive forms of self-observations let us question our perceptions. Perception creates a 'here and now,' creates 'presence.' In the mode of perception 'I am a parrot,' even a red one (see Geertz 1973; Smith 1993). In the mode of perception, a 'map is territory' on which we, at least temporarily, dwell. In perception, we 'believe' our own constructions; we seem to be real 'realists.'

Third, synchronization and high speed of perception erode the ability to negate and suspend the need for accounting for the perceived. The cultural distinctions that differentiate reality from deception or fiction are not available in the process of perception. Communication can navigate perception but, at the operational level, consciousness cannot evade the world perceived. As one consequence among many, socially shared perception produces socially shared evidence, something that is not in the same way true for communication.

Fourth, communication is not just more time consuming it is also more strenuous. As a necessary result it is very selective and always presupposes a background of perceptions that are not contingent and selective utterances—otherwise there would be a total blockage.

Given these differences, an observer A of a perceiving or communicating person B might be able to see two possible deviations on B's part: (1) B may treat perceptions as communicative utterances. This phenomenon seems to be the basis of conversations with pets. It is certainly the basis of some mental diseases and the core of theological debates about the notion of 'God speaking to us.' Conversely, (2) communicative utterances may be treated by B as mere perceptions: on the way to a buffet table, taking all warning non-verbal hints from other guests just as mere perceptions of bodily states will give B some advantage in terms of speed and might result in an earlier arrival. However, the culturally dominant practice of taking selectively constructed utterances as mere perception is the reception of audiovisual communication with moving pictures: cinema and television.

Dynamics of Audiovisual Communication

The products of cinema and television are highly 'artificial,' and that means every detail from lightening, to camera angle, pieces of dialogue, not to speak of plot structures, settings and music (see Jensen 1995; Carroll 1996). To make this story short: every single piece represents a costly selection that carries the difference between information and utterance. Semioticians might want to talk about an over-determination of meaning. Any part of the television news, movies-made-for-television, thrillers, or commercials is the result of highly sophisticated, contingent selections. The television program or movie is a complex utterance that has to be attributed to all the people involved in the production process, to all those who used to be listed in the credits. Everything in television and films is the result of conscious and highly selective actions. As a compact utterance it might come with various meta-communicative indexes like 'fiction' or 'television documentary' or 'docudrama.' These frames might not say 'This is real,' but rather 'This is not real'—in order to allow for the perception that 'This is real.' That is the paradox of this frame. It is of utmost importance to ensure that we have normally all seen and can talk *about* this created cultural artifact. However, it seems to me to be rather misleading to conceptualize the whole experience of television and cinema as 'decoding' or 'reading a text.' Even though (for a detached academic observer) it is without any doubt a thoroughly encoded 'text' or utterance, for the overwhelming majority of viewers it is *in the act of reception* largely an object of perception. Only elements like human speech are processed as perceived contingent utterances. But even there, to talk back would obviously be to mistake the category. For this reason, the frame has a double side, an inner and an outer surface: 'This is communication, this is not real' and 'You can permit perception, this is real.'[3]

Yet most viewers more or less manage the difference between what they perceive on television and in 'real life' and they quite rarely call the police when someone is murdered on screen. Viewers neither decode a text nor are they caught up in *mere* perception.

What appears to be a paradox in the theoretical setting of frame theory is a dynamic movement, if we include a *temporal* aspect. The experience of movies and television is an ongoing *oscillation* between perceiving what we see and hear, and taking the same material to be a contingent utterance as part of a communication process. Within this process, perception creates in media rituals a kind of presence that substitute for physical co-presence in classical rituals. The presence created or constructed by perception is a bodily presence in spite of the spatial and temporal separation as seen by another observer. Perception in audiovisual products not only makes 'present,' they also attract bodies—or, to put it another way around, attracted bodies experience presence. While this may vary in respect to genres, we always—even in so-called information programs—have embodied minds. Suspense, excitement, humor and curiosity all derive from perception and all lead to bodily states. Widely discussed phenomena like para-social interaction, television interaction or the many processes of identification with plots, actors, etc. are possible only through perception. Advertising 'works' because we know the frame: 'This is just an advertisement' *and* at the same time opt for the other side of the frame strip: 'Perceive it as real.'

If we look closely at the process of involvement, we see a dynamic process. Before entering the audiovisual ritual one is well aware of the 'artificial' nature of all programs and movies—they are just communicative offers. As soon as we accept them, to use a phrase from Clifford Geertz, we 'slip into the reality' of the ritual event (see Geertz 1973, 122–123). While we do not get lost in perception—no one is glued onto the screen—we nevertheless become immersed into the dynamic oscillation and are simultaneously inside and outside the frame, or the frame is intrinsically double-sided, twisted like a moebius strip. We cannot escape processing the audiovisual stream of pictures in the mode of perception. And even oral speech is taken to be perceived communication—which means it is not taken to be an utterance coming from an author of a screenplay or a news writer, but from the person perceived. As soon as we accept the offer we enter into a willing loss of con-

---

[3]   For this reason Handelman talks about the frame as a moebius strip (1998, xxiii). See also Handelman's contribution to this volume.

trol, because we *want* to perceive and be 'present.' Still, we are able to inter-
rupt, to leave the movie theater, to switch channels or to turn off the
television set—but we barely can stay tuned and not operate in some sense in
the mode of perception. What is required for the ritual event is not consensus
but acceptance by the fact of participation, documented by the positioning of
the perceiving body in front of the screen. The willful creation of suspense is
the willingness to avoid communication—to a certain degree—while at the
same time keeping up the illusion of complete self-control. Only seemingly
paradoxical, we can intensify the impressions of perception because—on the
level of communication and meta-communication—we know it is a ritual of
transportation with a secure round trip ticket. Horror movies are not the only
ones based on this paradox.

However, it is not only during the very act of viewing that perception
cannot be completely transformed into communication. The persistence of
perception has even a temporal dimension: Even afterwards, there is a kind
of emotional 'afterglow' (Rappaport 1992, 19) with a longer or shorter half-
life. In the context of discussing John Elster's considerations of inconsistencies in human rationality, Thomas C. Schelling gave an admittedly stark
example of such an emotional afterglow of audiovisual perception. He wrote
about a memorable visit to a movie theater: "I don't know who I thought was
being stabbed in the shower of *Psycho*, but after the movie my wife and I,
having arrived at the theater in separate cars, left one car behind and drove
home together."[4] In this extreme example the following can be seen: Perception was so strong, that even afterwords when leaving the cinema the
communicative frame ("These have been moving pictures") could not erase
the emotional impact of audiovisual perception. The emotional afterglow
well known from 'real rituals' was so strong that it led to specific actions
and even later on became an object of conscious self-observation—
something quite rare. Nevertheless, the point is that there is a limit to our
ability to consciously manipulate or even completely stop the oscillation and
just look back on the artificially created product of communication. In the
case of the Hitchcock movie, the cinematic ritual of transportation turned out
to contain some little element of transformation (see Schechner 1985). Look-

---

[4]   See Schelling 1986, 177. In a similar vein: "Lassie died one night. Millions of viewers,
      not all of them children, grieved. At least, they shed tears. Except for the youngest, the
      mourners knew that Lassie didn't really exist. Whatever that means. Perhaps with their left
      hemispheres they could articulate that they had been watching a trained dog and that that
      dog was still alive, healthy and rich; meanwhile in their right hemispheres (if these phe-
      nomena have a place), the real Lassie had died" (Schelling 1986, 177).

ing at various genres, one is certainly looking at differing intensities of the afterglow as well as, metaphorically speaking, at different colors. Still, the underlying mechanism seems to me to be the same.[5] When there is an accumulation of such afterglow or if the tiny effects of transformation that come out of repeated transportation add up, we normally speak of a problematic 'media effect.'

The ongoing oscillation makes the ontological space opened up by perception in a double sense inherently unstable. The viewer during the reception is somehow a believer and his or her own critic and after that, much worse, just an atheist who does not believe in this fleeting reality but who cannot get rid of the impression that there is something in the reality of God. Academic common sense tells us that in most societies the religious reality is the most stable, most encompassing and overarching reality. Yet television uses two quite old mechanisms and one new one to provide more stability. First, repetition and, second, duration—remember those almost 3½ hours per day.[6] The third stabilization measure is a remarkable invention: the rituals of these fleeting realities merge to form an ongoing, never-ending stream quite independent of my own stream of consciousness. This endless liturgical stream is always and easily accessible, virtually indestructible; it is always there, 24 hours a day and 7 days a week. And we should be reminded that this reality is at least so stable that television attorneys can successfully advertise stocks and television detectives can successfully advertise security systems—in spite of the fact everyone 'knows' he is *not* a real lawyer and she is *not* a real police commissioner.

Let me add a short remark on the communal aspect of this ritual practice. The oscillation between perception and communication creates a quite specific pattern of community that allows switching between three types of

---

[5] An additional remark: the phenomena of channel surfing and casual television watching during other work seems to stand against the suggestion I have made. But this is not the case. Quite the reverse, because audiovisual communication attracts the embodied mind we are so quickly drawn into the fragments of programs while surfing. For the same reason, we can reduce (divest!) the conscious attention we invest in watching television—and do other things at the same time—because perception is at the same time so powerful and so easy and much less strenuous than communication.

[6] Analysing the relation between time spent in traditional rituals and the intensity of the emotional afterglow, Rappaport observes: "The proportion of time spent in ritual becomes very high and the times between ritual so short that the emotional afterglow of one has not fully faded before another commences. Such liturgical orders seem largely confined to cloistered communities of religious specialists who ... do not attempt to bring the divine into this world, but try to spend their lives partway to heaven" (Rappaport 1992, 19).

community. While the private act of watching television reinforces real solitude or the in-house-community, it at the same time allows switching between the large 'imagined community' of the viewers ('communication') of this program and—through processes of identification—communion with the persons seen or watched.

What are the Mechanisms that Reinforce the Binding of 'Embodied Minds' by means of Perception?

Since perception can process information much faster than communication, *speed* is one of the key features that force us to perceive and not to draw a distinction between information and utterance. This refers to the speed of changing screen shots, the speed of the unfolding story line as well as (in the news) the fast pace of changing topics.

Creation of *multi-sensory experiences*: Most religious rituals are characterized by a thickness of sensorial perceptions in multimedia performances. Sight and sound are the only senses addressed in audiovisual communication, yet within this limitation there is a richness of impressions ranging from visual complexities to soundtracks that provide emotional guidance.

Perception is triggered by several *camera techniques*. The angle 'shot/reverse shot' draws the viewer into an almost intimate proximity to other persons. Camera angles and shot sequences are able to release reflexes of fleeing. Camera work and lighting are governed by insights from the psychology of perception.

Themes and scenes close to the body or bodily reactions, which mean violence, sex and action that potentially or really endangers bodies. Not only do such themes and scenes cut through more elaborate and specific cultural patterns in the interest in making more and more globally acceptable products; as perceived bodily states they call for bodily resonance.

I have to break off at this point. Unfortunately, we do not have the space to go through the dominant television genres and look at their specific features as rituals of order, to figure out the 'models of' and 'models for' (see Geertz 1973, 123f.), to look closely at the rituals of confession and moral indignation and to analyze the soaps as rituals that put together the fragments of personal and social life.

Differences

I have tried to highlight a certain feature of experience of audiovisual products in order to respond to the justified claim that talk about ritual means addressing the problem of the presence of bodies. I have stressed very much the commonalities of classical rituals and audio-visually performed rituals. However, given the broad range of the concept of 'ritual,' it is not surprising to see some deeply rooted difference. The social control of the body has fundamentally changed. Television rituals can only control the body by attraction—a profound difference even compared to cinema. The outcomes of television rituals on the part of the viewers (not of the broadcasted event itself and its effect on other social systems) in terms of the *little* thoroughness, if there are any, are neither socially controlled nor socially stabilized, except in fan clubs. As research on the specific genre of religious television seems to show, even religious television cannot create deep personal change but calls for the planting of local communities (see Bretthauer 1998). Television rituals rearrange the relationship between the public and the private, because they are both: public models for replicable private acts. To borrow a distinction from Geertz: the cultural price paid for the tremendous scope or reach of television symbolism might be their slight effect in terms of the thoroughness with which ritual patterns are internalized in the personalities of individuals (see Geertz 1968, 111). Nevertheless, the realities perceived in and through the audiovisual stream participate in the cultural struggle for the 'really real.'

What are the Prospects for Other Rituals in a Culture Saturated with Television Rituals?

Change triggers more change and we might speculate on some possible changes brought about by television rituals. Television rituals *require* an oscillation between perception and communication, whether this oscillation has a playful character or not. They support the cultural routine of a fast and ongoing switching between differing frames below the level of conscious self-reflection. We have to drop out in order to be in, so to speak. As soon as this cultural technique is widely acquired, it might unfold far-reaching consequences for other highly framed symbolic universes and might fundamentally change the style of participation in these framed realities like religious rituals. When this technique of oscillation becomes a widespread habit it supports a cat-and-mouse game, in which symbolic modes of communication have to be experientially intensified in order to deal with participants that are more and more trained in the simultaneous disentanglement of frames. In order to deal with this technique creatively, other rituals are challenged to constructively include reflexivity and deal with their own contingency. Even though these subtle effects are hardly measurable they are part of an ongoing transformation of culture by the most dominant forms of communication. Whether the oscillation between perception and communication in media rituals will eventually justify the use of the term 'ritual' in its full and rich sense is a question that does not need an immediate answer. It can wait, at least as long as the various concepts of 'ritual' have the power to illuminate our shared practice of audiovisual communication—which we enjoy with all accompanying bodily states and which we want to understand more with our embodied minds.

References

Bleicher, Joan K. 1999: *Fernsehen als Mythos: Poetik eines narrativen Erkenntnissystems.* Opladen: Westdeutscher Verlag.

Bretthauer, Berit. 1998: *Televangelismus in den USA: Religion zwischen Individualisierung und Vergemeinschaftung.* Frankfurt a.M.: Campus.

Carroll, Noël. 1996: *Theorizing the Moving Image.* Cambridge: Cambridge University Press.

Dayan, Daniel and Elihu Katz. 1992: *Media Events: The Live Broadcasting of History.* Cambridge, Mass.: Harvard University Press.

Debatin, Bernhard. 1995: *Die Rationalität der Metapher: Eine sprachphilosophische und kommunikationstheoretische Untersuchung.* Berlin: Walter de Gruyter.

Douglas, Mary. 1982: *Natural Symbols: Explorations in Cosmology.* 2d ed. New York: Pantheon.

Fuchs, Peter. 1993: *Moderne Kommunikation: Zur Theorie des operativen Displacements.* Frankfurt a.M.: Suhrkamp.

Geertz, Clifford. 1968: *Islam Observed.* Chicago: University of Chicago Press.

———. 1973: Religion as a Cultural System. In: *The Interpretation of Cultures: Selected Essays.* New York: Basic Books. 87–125.

Goethals, Gregor T. 1981: *The TV Ritual: Worship at the Video Altar.* Boston: Beacon Press.

Goffman, Erving. 1974: *Frame Analysis: An Essay on the Organization of Experience.* New York: Harper & Row.

Grimes, Ronald L. 1990: *Ritual Criticism: Case Studies in its Practice, Essays on its Theory.* Columbia, S.C.: University of South Carolina Press.

Handelman, Don. 1998: *Models and Mirrors: Towards an Anthropology of Public Events.* 2d ed. New York and Oxford: Berghahn Books.

Hesse, Mary B. 1966: *Models and Analogies in Science.* Notre Dame, Ind.: University of Notre Dame Press.

Hoover, Stewart M. and Knut Lindby (eds.). 1997: *Rethinking Media, Religion and Culture*. Thousand Oaks, Calif.: Sage.

Hoover, Stewart M. 2000: Religion im Fernsehen oder Fernsehreligion? In: *Religiöse Funktionen des Fernsehens? Medien-, kultur- und religionswissenschaftliche Perspektiven*, ed. Günter Thomas. Opladen: Westdeutscher Verlag. 77–90.

Jensen, Klaus B. 1995: *The Social Semiotics of Mass Communication*. London: Sage.

Luhmann, Niklas. 1989: *Ecological Communication*. Chicago: University of Chicago Press.

————. 1990: The Improbability of Communication. In: *Essays on Self-Reference*. New York: Columbia University Press. 86–98.

————. 1995: *Social Systems*. Stanford: Stanford University Press.

Rappaport, Roy A. 1979: The Obvious Aspects of Ritual. In: *Ecology, Meaning, and Religion*. Berkeley: North Atlantic Books. 173–221.

————. 1992. Ritual, Time, and Eternity. In: *Zygon* 27:5–30.

Rothenbuhler, Eric W. 1998: *Ritual Communication: From Everyday Conversation to Mediated Ceremony*. Thousand Oaks, Calif.: Sage.

Schechner, Richard. 1985: Performers and Spectators Transported and Transformed. In: *Between Theatre and Anthropology*. Foreword by Victor Turner. Philadelphia: University of Pennsylvania Press. 117–150.

Schelling, Thomas C. 1986: The Mind as Consuming Organ. In: *The Multiple Self*, ed. John Elster. Cambridge: Cambridge University Press. 177–197.

Silverstone, Roger. 1981: *The Message of Television: Myth and Narrative in Contemporary Culture*. London: Heinemann.

————. 1994: *Television and Everyday Life*. London: Routledge.

Smith, Jonathan Z. 1993: I am a Parrot (Red). In: *Map Is Not Territory: Studies in the History of Religion*. Chicago: University of Chicago Press. 265–288.

Thomas, Günter (ed.). 2000: *Religiöse Funktionen des Fernsehens? Medien-, kultur- und religionswissenschaftliche Perspektiven*. Opladen: Westdeutscher Verlag.

————. 1998: *Medien – Ritual – Religion: Zur religiösen Funktion des Fernsehens*. Frankfurt a.M.: Suhrkamp.

The Incorporation of Portraits into Chinese Ancestral Rites

Patricia B. Ebrey

Among the objects for sale in Chinese antique stores today one often finds ancestral portraits, full-length paintings of stern-looking, frontally-posed men and women, seated on chairs and dressed in official robes. These ancestral portraits were a common material component of ancestral rites in the nineteenth and early twentieth century, though they now have largely been supplanted by photographs. They would be hung for major ceremonies when offerings of incense, food, and drink were placed on the altar for the ancestors. The descendants may have also had wooden spirit tablets inscribed with the names of the dead, or they could have used the portraits as the sole representation of their ancestors.

Portraits were not a part of ancestral rites in ancient China, which means that they have a history—they are not simply part of the inherited package of immemorial custom. It is of course not unusual for things we now class as art objects to have been produced for use in religious rituals. In the Chinese case, we have the splendid bronze ritual vessels of the Shang and Zhou as evidence of the extent to which Chinese were willing to devote resources to the material elements of ancestral rites. But portraits differ from vessels in significant ways. Because they evoke the physical body of the ancestor, they have the power to move people (Freedberg 1989; Belting 1994). Thus, this change in the material trappings of ancestral rites would seem to mark a major change in how people experienced the rites.

Most of our evidence of ancestral rites in ancient times shows their close connections to political rank and power. Early ritual experts viewed ancestral rites as a privilege of rank. Practice consisted in offerings of food, drink, prayers, songs, and dances made before symbolic objects and a man or boy, preferably a grandson of the deceased, who stood in for him as an impersonator of the dead. Sanctity was required, and those performing the rites first had to undergo purification. By the third century B.C.E. there were rules governing the number of generations a person could make offerings to, the variety and quality of the food that could be offered, the location where rites could be offered, all with gradation according to rank. Thus, lower officers (*shi*) and commoners were supposed to offer only vegetables to only two generations of ancestors and only in their homes, while those of higher ranks could make more elaborate offerings of meat to more generations in ancestral halls (Ebrey 1991, 14–31).

When visual representations of the dead appear in early sources, they are associated with funerals and burial, not the ancestral rites performed decades or centuries after death. The famous banner in Lady Dai's tomb (second century B.C.E.) and a stone relief in the 151 C.E. tomb at Cangshan, for instance, are believed to represent the tomb occupant. The banner may have been carried in the funeral, but it obviously was not used in later ancestral rites, as it was left in the tomb. Moreover, there is little stylistic connection between these types of portrayals and later ancestral portraits.

By the nineteenth and twentieth centuries, ancestral rites were not limited to the political elite, and the use of visual representations of the dead was associated more with shrines than tombs. Domestic and foreign observers alike report that most households maintained some sort of altar, and even the most lowly commoner could have sons, grandsons, and great-grandsons who made offerings to him. Moreover, besides household shrines, larger kinship groups would often perform joint ceremonies at lineage shrines using tablets for all their ancestors. Impersonators played no part in the rites, but portraits often did. At both the household and lineage level, in addition to representing the ancestors by an object inscribed with their names (wooden tablets or strips of paper), people commonly also had painted portraits of them (De Groot 1892–1910; Hsu 1948; Jordan 1972, 93–102; Ahern 1973; Harrell 1982, 194–206).

Some of the changes between ancient and modern times can be dated fairly accurately. Wu Hung has shown that shrines erected at graves became an important site for ancestral rites in the late Warring States and Han period (Wu 1996). In earlier studies, I have demonstrated that the spread of descent group ancestral rites at graves and halls occurred in the tenth to fourteenth centuries (Song-Yuan period), and also that the limitation on the numbers of generations of ancestors commoners could worship came to be rejected by the Confucian elite in the Song and tacitly by the government in the Yuan and Ming (Ebrey 1986; 1991). But what about the introduction and incorporation of portraits? When did it occur? Did it have anything to do with funerary practice? What social groups was it associated with? What processes or agents of change were involved? Was it supported or opposed by the Confucian elite? Does it have anything to do with a changing emotional climate or perhaps changes in art or technology? These are the questions I address here.

Art historians have done most of the research on ancestral portraits, but none of them has attempted to trace their history. Still, their work offers lots of possible leads in that they link ancestral portraits to a wide range of other elements of Chinese art and religion. Mette Siggstedt relates ancestral portraits to physiognomy, the practice of analyzing facial features to predict fate (Siggstedt 1992). Ladislav Kesner, Jr. associates them with effigies in general, such as the terra-cotta soldiers in Qin Shihuang's tomb (Kesner 1993–1994). Wu Hung ties the use of portraits to funerary practice, but also proposes that they were a substitute for impersonators (Wu 1989, 209). Craig Clunas links ancestral portraits to status concerns, pointing to the practice of portraying the dead in official robes (Clunas 1997, 91–94). Outside of art history, we also have some leads. Edward H. Schafer implies a connection between bowing to a portrait of a living emperor and similar use of a portrait of a dead emperor (Schafer 1963). T. Griffith Foulk and Robert H. Sharf show how halls for portraits of deceased abbots at temples evolved from paying obeisance to portraits in small grave-side shrines (*stupas*) (Foulk and Sharf 1993–1994).

One might think from the diverse sorts of links that scholars have proposed that the use of portraits in Chinese ancestral rites was over-determined, that its adoption was all but inevitable, given how well it fit so many other features of Chinese culture. Here I argue just the opposite. I do not see the incorporation of portraits in ancestral rites as inevitable. To the contrary, it was not until Buddhism had penetrated deeply into Chinese culture and images of spirits became ubiquitous that portraits became a common element in ancestral rites.

My argument depends on establishing a chronology for the incorporation of ancestral portraits into ancestral rites. So far, almost no progress has been made in this regard. Jan Stuart, in a recent study, is reluctant to trace the practice back before the mid-Ming (1368–1644) (Stuart 1997, 14; see also Stevens 1987). By contrast, Wu Hung has asserted that portraits were placed in ancestral halls during the Han (206 B.C.E.–C.E. 220). Therefore, I must begin by laying out the evidence of dating. I will start with the better documented periods and proceed in reverse chronological order.

The evidence at our disposal is of two sorts, surviving paintings that appear to be ancestral portraits and surviving texts that seem to refer to the use of portraits in ancestral rites.

To use paintings, one must first distinguish ancestral portraits from other types of portraits. Ancestor portraits are not simply portraits of people already dead. Rather they are portraits used in ancestral rites to represent the dead. Ancestral portraits thus are not the equivalent of old photo-albums, to be viewed when one feels like reminiscing or wants to recall what grandfather looked like; rather they are ritual paraphernalia, to be taken out as the schedule required. Other sorts of portraits, including ones of living people and of imagined long dead people, have a long and relatively autonomous history in China (see Vinograd 1992; Seckel 1993).

Paintings have generally been identified as ancestral portraits because they share certain stylistic features with ancestral portraits used in recent times, such as portraying the ancestor frontally, in official garments, seated but otherwise not doing anything. Whereas informal portraits might depict a man dressed casually in his garden or study, recording a particular occasion, ancestral portraits seek to convey something timeless. For the Ming and Qing (1644–1911) periods, this difference between informal portraits and ancestral portraits can be observed at both the imperial and non-imperial level, and there are clear congruities between the style of ancestral portraits of commoners and those of emperors.

Textual sources for the use of ancestral portraits are also much fuller for Ming and later times. In Ming ritual guides it is not uncommon to find discussion of ancestral portraits, often with respect to whether their use was permissible (e.g., SLY 1.2a–b; JLHT 9.1a–2a). In addition, two Ming novels have scenes in which families bring in painters shortly after a death to view the corpse in order to do a portrait. The ensuing conversations about issues of likeness make it clear that the custom of making ancestral portraits was commonplace among the readers of these novels (see Clunas 1997, 91–94).

For the period before the Ming, the only ancestral portraits we can point to with confidence are portraits of Song (960–1276) and Yuan (1215–1368) emperors and empresses (see Fong 1995; Ebrey 1999). For the Song period, we have substantial evidence of the use of portraits in Song imperial practice. It became customary for emperors to place painted portraits of their ancestors in two halls in the palace, one near the front and one near the rear. Minor offerings were made daily at the one in the rear hall, and more major offerings were made periodically at the ones in the front hall. In addition, statues of emperors and empresses were placed in halls at temple complexes outside the palace, where they received the seasonal offerings as well as special offerings on their birthdays (Ebrey 1997; 1999).

Although there are no extant Song paintings that we can identify as ancestral portraits, there is scattered textual evidence that ancestral portraits were far from rare in Song society. This evidence is worth summarizing.

First, among the literati at least, in the eleventh century a common term for the room in which ancestral rites were held was *yingtang* ('image hall'). Both Sima Guang (1019–1086) and Cheng Yi (1033–1107), for instance, use this terms casually, as though it was a term everyone would recognize (e.g., ECJ yishu 6.90, 22A.286; SMSSY 10.113). In Cheng Yi's case, although he used the term 'image hall,' he made it explicit he did not approve of using images during the sacrifices:

> Someone asked: Today the families of literati and commoners are not allowed to set up ancestral shrines (*miao*), so what should they do? [Cheng Yi] answered: Commoners should make sacrifices in the "retiring hall," which is our current main hall. In general, ritual can be fashioned on the basis of moral principle. For rich families and literati, it is also fine to set up an image hall, but during the rites they should not use images. (ECJ yishu 22A.286)

In other words, it was fine to have a hall dedicated to the ancestors in which one kept portraits of them, so long as these portraits were merely commemorative, and not used to represent the spirits during the ceremonies. This point is made a different way in another brief passage: "Today people use images in making sacrifices, made for them by professional painters. If a strand of hair is not right, then the one receiving the sacrifice will be someone else, which is very wrong" (ECJ yishu 6.90). Clearly Cheng Yi was familiar with the practice of using portraits during sacrifices, and he associated this practice with rooms called 'image halls.'

Second, Song emperors were said to be following popular custom in making offerings to portraits of their ancestors in shrines. In the 1040s an official objected to the fact that the emperor devoted more attention to visits to the temples that held portraits than to the canonical Supreme Shrine, which had only tablets. His charge was that the ruler was "adopting the worst of contemporary customs" (YH 97.46a–b).

Third, the court assumed that the descendants of former officials would own portraits of them, which it borrowed from time to time when it wanted to paint pictures of eminent officials on the walls of halls. In 1064 when a hall was erected at the Temple of Spectacular Numina to house the image of the deceased emperor Renzong, the walls were painted with portraits of 72 leading civil and military officials who had served under him. Messengers were sent to the homes of the officials to get portraits, with the result that the paintings were done so expertly that the faces could be distinguished and "no one who saw them failed to be amazed at the beauty of them" (CB 200.4852; SHY li 13.3b; THJWZ 6.246). Similarly, in the 1130s when similar temples were being established in Hangzhou, the court called for the descendants of leading ministers of the preceding century to submit portraits so that the paintings of them to be done on the walls of the new halls would be accurate (SHY li 11.8a). There is nothing in these texts to prove that the portraits were ritual rather than commemorative portraits, but the assumption that everyone would have them supports such a supposition.

Fourth, regulations for official dress were emended in 1041 to allow people to depict their ancestors as though they held higher rank. Those whose posthumous ranks warranted only red robes were allowed instead to be depicted wearing purple (the color reserved for the very highest rank officials) (SS 154.3561). Portraits of forebears in official dress would most likely have been intended for use on ancestral altars. If making a portrait of a forebear in official dress was a rare occurrence, there would have been little reason for anyone to ask the government to rule that ordinary sumptuary rules did not apply and forebears could be portrayed wearing garments they did not deserve.

Fifth, there were complaints about how portraits of the dead were made. Apparently, as in more recent times, artists were often called in after a death to paint the portrait of the deceased. This led Sima Guang to lament the impropriety of allowing painters to gaze on the faces of women who would never have revealed their faces to strange men while alive. The portrait would play a part in the funeral ceremonies, be carried in the procession, and brought back from the grave along with the spirit tablet (SMSSY 5.54, 8.87, 92).

If I had only one or two indications of the prevalence of portraits of ancestors, I would be more cautious, since no one text can tell us all that much about the extent of the practice. But taken together, I find them compelling evidence that at least among the literati it was not rare for families to have portraits of their ancestors that they used in ancestral rites.

This practice was certainly not new in Song times. The first Song emperor had portraits painted of his parents to be placed in a temple, showing that the practice of using painted portraits to represent the dead was an established practice at the beginning of the Song in some circles. Judging its prevalence before Song times is unfortunately difficult since textual sources of all sorts are less abundant for the period before the introduction of printing, making it unreasonable to expect as many references to a practice for the Tang as for the Song, even if the practice was just as prevalent.

Nevertheless, it is notable that there is little evidence of Tang emperors using portraits in ancestral halls. Schafer, in a study of the subject, first pointed out that most paintings of Tang emperors were done for other purposes. He then gathered together the evidence that "some pictures of the T'ang sovereigns were indeed worshipped, serving as surrogates for their illustrious originals, just like images of the gods" (Schafer 1963, 158). However, almost all of the examples he cites in support of this statement concern portraits of living emperors, not deceased ones. When it was impossible to pay obeisance to the ruler in person, some people did so before a portrait of him. In addition, as Schafer shows, some rulers donated paintings of themselves to Buddhist or Daoist temples. These probably were treated as images of pious patrons, devoted to the main deity, rather than as central images to receive their own offerings. At any rate, these were portraits of living people, and so cannot be considered ancestral portraits.

Buddhist connections to the use of ancestral portraits are suggested by the practices at monasteries. In the mid-ninth century, the Japanese monk Ennin saw portraits enshrined by both Tantric and Tiantai monasteries. As Foulk and Sharf have shown, by this period it was common for Buddhist monasteries to set up images of former abbots and patriarchs in special halls where they were treated as the monks' ancestors. This practice evolved from paying reverence to portraits at the burial site (*stupa*) of a monk. Portraits of monks placed in shrines by their graves are attested as early as the mid- and late-fifth century and continued through the Tang. But the portraits in halls also had ties to the Buddhist cult of relics. The earliest 'portraits' placed in halls were lacquered mummies, or statues that resembled such mummies by incorporating the physical body of the monk in another way, such as having his relics inside or using his ashes in the clay (Foulk and Sharf 1993–1994, 165–169).

Already in the Northern and Southern dynasties (317–589), some rulers kept portraits of their ancestors in shrines. The fourth ruler of the Song dynasty (r. 464–465), ordered paintings of his grandfather and father for the dynastic shrines, which already had one of the founder. When he visited the shrines, he objected that the portrait of his father did not show the spots on his nose (WS 97.2146; Soper 1967, 17–18). The third Liang emperor (r. 551–552) had a statue carved of his father which he installed in the Hall of a Hundred Blessings and which he served devotedly with daily offerings of vegetarian food (NS 8.243; Soper 1967, 23). When the Northern Zhou ruler Wudi (r. 561–576) issued rules against Buddhist images, a monk reminded him of the images of his ancestors in the imperial shrines, and asked whether it was also absurd to worship them (Soper 1967, 30).

These three references are brief and raise questions impossible to answer. Did most Northern and Southern dynasty rulers maintain shrines with portraits? Did the practice originate at court or elsewhere? The halls that housed these portraits are not called the *taimiao* (supreme shrine), the canonical shrine for rites to the imperial ancestors. Are they therefore evidence of a parallel cult at the imperial level, of the sort we find in Song times, with portraits in halls that were distinct from the halls with the tablets?

Some scholars have pointed to evidence that seems to suggest the use of ancestral portraits before the fifth century, but none of it is very convincing. Most frequently cited is the Han story of Ding Lan, a paragon of filial piety who carved a statue of his mother out of wood and treated this statue with the deference he would have paid her (see Wu 1989, 282–285). But this story makes sense only if Ding Lan's action was seen as aberrant, perplexing to neighbors and relatives. Indeed, the story can be read as evidence against the common use of images on ancestral altars.

The strongest assertion that ancestral portraits began in Han times has been made by Wu Hung who in his *Wu Liang Shrine* states that "During the Han, the old religious practice of using the *shi* [impersonator] as the subject of sacrifices was replaced by the custom of placing a sculptured or painted image in the memorial hall" (Wu 1989, 212–213). There is admittedly an attractive plausibility to the idea that portraits came into use to replace impersonators. However, when his sources are checked, his argument seems to be based on two passages in the *Hou Han shu*, neither pointing to ancestral portraits. The first mentions the provision of clothes, hat, shoes, staff, and so on, as well as a headless doll which "sits down and gets up as though living" during the funerary ceremonies for an emperor. This headless figure certainly stood for the dead, but I see no reason to call it a portrait (HHS zhi 6.3148 commentary). The second citation mentions a portrait, but in a tomb, not an ancestral shrine, and the deceased is shown as a host receiving ancient worthies as guests, not in an iconic pose (HHS 64.2124). Many tombs in Han times are decorated with figures, sometimes including famous figures from history, sometimes including figures that scholars speculate represent the deceased. It is a real stretch to see such portraits in tombs as substitutes for impersonators in the rituals performed by descendants outside the tomb for generations to come.

What can we conclude from this review of the evidence? *First*, it seems clear that the spread of ancestral portraits was not rapid, but rather occurred over centuries, beginning by the fifth century and extending into the fifteenth. We have enough texts from the Tang and Song period to be pretty confident that if this change had occurred abruptly—in imitation of the example of an emperor or leading member of society, for instance—someone would have remarked on how much practice had changed since his youth.

Second, the practice certainly did not spread as a result of active efforts to promote it on the part of the intellectual elite or government. The texts issued by the government and elite to influence ritual performance gradually accommodated the practice, but never urged people to make portraits if they did not already have them. This is the case even though imperial practice may very well have preceded practice in other circles.

Third, practice among emperors and monks seems to have preceded more general practice, though it is difficult to decide which of these got established earlier or the interconnection between them.

Fourth, there is no sign the practice was associated with a more personal or individualistic attitude toward ancestors. If that had been the case, I would expect to see it appear first in somewhat avant-garde intellectual circles, or perhaps commoners in a certain region, not among the rulers of the Northern and Southern dynasties or Buddhist clergy.

Fifth, the coincidence in the time of the gradual penetration of the use of ancestral portraits and the tremendous growth of Buddhism is too strong to ignore. Since Buddhist ideas of reincarnation impinged on Chinese understandings of ancestors, one might expect that ancestral portraits came into use in response to a shift in attitudes toward the dead. Buddhists had no objections to ancestral rites, but the rites did not occupy the same centrality in their body of ritual practices as they had in the ancient courts. Treating ancestors more as memories and less as gods would make sense in Buddhist cosmology. But placing portraits of ancestors on the altars dedicated to them, in the post-Buddhist context of Chinese religious culture, was treating them more like deities, not less. Therefore, I tend to put more weight on the simple fact that Buddhism promoted devotion of images to a degree no earlier Chinese religious tradition had.

Even though Buddhism did not originate as a religion of images, by the time it got to China, the use of images was well established as a means of devotion. One of the earliest sutras translated into Chinese was the *Scripture on the Production of Buddha Images*, which describes the merit that can be earned from making and venerating icons (Sharf 1996). Images that had been consecrated were imbued with the potency to assist believers on their way to true salvation. Often objects of magical potency—relics, scriptures, miniature figures, and other implements—would be placed inside a statue to make it more efficacious. A final step in creating an icon was the ritual of adding the pupils to its eyes (see Brinker 1998).

What I would like to argue is not direct borrowing from Buddhist practice, but a much more diffuse and pervasive shift in the visual culture associated with devotional activity, to the point where people felt it was only natural to (1) use a visual representation (a picture or statue) to represent something understood to be immaterial, (2) use such a representation as an aid to focusing on the spirit when serving it; and (3) to imagine spirits of all kinds in human form. This process had already begun in the Northern and Southern dynasties but continued to grow stronger over time. It led to the proliferation of images of Daoist deities, both sculptures and paintings. It led to the use of portraits in Confucian shrines to historical people, including those that had become apotheosized, but also others like Confucius and the emperors of earlier dynasties (see Soper 1967, 20–21, 25, 27, 58–59). And it led, I believe, to ordinary people taking portraits that might have been left in the tomb and bringing them home to place at their ancestral altars. As this practice spread, people who would not have placed portraits in tombs began to have portraits made specifically for their altars. Portraits of ancestors gradually penetrated ordinary ancestral rites in Tang and Song times, growing stronger over time.

References

Primary Sources

CB   *Xu zizhi tongjian changbian*, by Li Tao. Taipei: Shijie shuju, 1961 or Beijing: Zhonghua shuju, 1985.

ECJ   *Er Chengji*, by Cheng Hao (1032–1085) and Cheng Yi (1033–1107). Beijing: Zhonghua shuju, 1981.

HHS   *Hou Han shu,* by Fan Ye. Beijing: Zhonghua shuju, 1962.

JLHT   *Jiali huitong*, by Tang Duo. Ming manuscript copy held by the Naikaku bunko, Tokyo.

NS   *Nanshi*, by Li Yanshou. Beijing: Zhonghua shuju, 1975.

SDZLJ   *Song da zhaoling ji*, anonym. Beijing: Zhonghua shuju, 1962.

SHY   *Song huiyao jigao*, ed. Xu Song. Beijing: Zhonghua shuju, 1957.

SLY   *Sili yi*, by Lü Kun. 1614 ed.

SMSSY   *Sima shi shuyi*, by Sima Guang. Congshu jicheng ed. Shanghai: Commercial Press Congshu jicheng series, 1936.

SS   *Songshi*, ed. Tuo Tuo et al. Beijing: Zhonghua shuju, 1977.

THJWZ   *Tuhua jianwenzhi*, by Guo Ruoxu. In: *Songren huaxue lunzhu*, part of *Yishu congbian*. Taipei: Shijie shuju, 1962.

WS   *Weishu*, by Wei Shou. Beijing: Zhonghua shuju, 1974.

YH   *Yuhai*, by Wang Yinglin. Shanghai: Shanghai guji chuban she reprint of 1883 ed.

ZXJ   *Zhu Xi ji*, by Zhu Xi. Edited by Guo Qi and Yin Bo. 9 vols. Chengdu: sichuan jiaoyu chubanshe, 1996.

Secondary Sources

Ahern, Emily M. 1973: *The Cult of the Dead in a Chinese Village*. Stanford: Stanford University Press.

Belting, Hans. 1994: *Likeness and Presence: A History of the Image before the Era of Art*. Chicago: University of Chicago Press.

Brinker, Helmut. 1998: Transfiguring Divinities: Buddhist Sculpture in China. In: *China: Five Thousand Years*, ed. Howard Rogers. New York: Guggenheim Museum. 144–158.

Clunas, Craig. 1997: *Pictures and Visuality in Early Modern China*. Princeton: Princeton University Press.

De Groot, Jan J. M. 1892–1910: *The Religious System of China*. 6 vols. Leiden: E.J. Brill.

Ebrey, Patricia. 1986: The Early Stages of the Development of Descent Group Organization. In: *Kinship Organization in Imperial China, 1000–1940*, ed. Patricia B. Ebrey and James L. Watson. Berkeley: University of California Press. 16–61.

————. 1991: *Confucianism and Family Rituals in Imperial China: A Social History of Writing about Rites*. Princeton: Princeton University Press.

————. 1997: Portrait Sculptures in Imperial Ancestral Rites in Song China. In: *T'oung Pao* 83:42–92.

————. 1999: The Ritual Context of Song Imperial Portraits. In: *Arts of the Sung and Yuan*, ed. Wen C. Fong. Princeton: Art Museum. 68–93.

Fong, Wen C. 1995: Imperial Portraiture in the Sung, Yuan, and Ming Periods. In: *Ars Orientalis* 25:7–60.

Foulk, T. Griffith and Robert H. Sharf. 1993–1994: On the Ritual Use of Ch'an Portraiture in Medieval China. In: *Cahiers d'Extreme-Asie* 7:149–219.

Freedberg, David. 1989: *The Power of Images: Studies in the History and Theory of Response*. Chicago: University of Chicago Press.

Harrell, Stevan. 1982: *Ploughshare Village: Culture and Context in Taiwan*. Seattle: University of Washington Press.

Hsu, Francis. 1948: *Under the Ancestors' Shadow*. New York: Columbia University Press.

Jordan, David K. 1972: *Gods, Ghosts, and Ancestors*. Berkeley: University of California Press.

Kesner, Ladislav, Jr. 1993–1994: Memory, Likeness and Identity in Chinese Ancestor Portraits. In: *Bulletin of the National Gallery in Prague* 3–4:4–14.

Schafer, Edward H. 1963: The T'ang Imperial Icon. In: *Sinologica* 7:156–160.

Seckel, Dietrich. 1993: The Rise of Portraiture in Chinese Art. In: *Artibus Asiae* 53:7–26.

Sharf, Robert H. 1996: The Scripture on the Production of Buddha Images. In: *Religions of China in Practice*, ed. Donald S. Lopez. Princeton: Princeton University Press. 261–267.

Siggstedt, Mette. 1992: Forms of Fate: An Investigation of the Relationship between Formal Portraiture, Especially Ancestral Portraits, and Physiognomy (*xiangshu*) in China. In: *International Colloquium on Chinese Art History, 1991: Proceedings, Painting and Calligraphy*. Part 2. Taibei: National Palace Museum. 713–748.

Soper, Alexander Coburn. 1967: *Textual Evidence for the Secular Arts of China in the Period from Liu Sung through Sui (A.D. 420–618)*. (Artibus Asiae Supplement 24). Ascona, Switzerland: Artibus Asiae Publishers.

Stevens, Keith G. 1987: Portrait and Ancestral Images on Chinese Altars. In: *Arts of Asia* 19:135–145.

Stuart, Jan. 1997: Calling Back the Ancestor's Shadow: Chinese Ritual and Commemorative Portraits. In: *Oriental Art* 43.3:8–17.

Vinograd, Richard. 1992: *Boundaries of the Self: Chinese Portraits, 1600–1900*. Cambridge: Cambridge University Press.

Wu Hung. 1989: *The Wu Liang Shrine: The Ideology of Early Chinese Pictorial Art*. Stanford: Stanford University Press.

———. 1996: *Monumentality in Early Chinese Art*. Stanford: Stanford University Press.

Transgenerational Change: The Social Process of Transmitting Oral Ritual Texts among the Rai in East Nepal[*]

Martin Gaenszle

It is commonly accepted that a fundamental characteristic of ritual is its stability over time, and thus a kind of inherent immunity to change appears to be essential. Rituals, in short, are conservative, they tend to preserve a cultural memory (see Assmann 1997). While this is true as a general tendency history shows that rituals do change, and so the question is: How does such change of rituals come about? How is it possible that rituals change, even if the change is sometimes ignored by the actors?

One obvious way to tackle this general question is to look at the changes that may occur (or 'creep in') when rituals are being transmitted from one generation to the next. What exactly happens when a novice acquires the knowledge of performing rituals? Is he or she simply learning by repetition, or is it an active appropriation and re-creation of ritual traditions? There is great variation in this field across the globe. In some cultures a verbatim memorization of ritual texts, for example, is a must, while in others it is rather the 'inspiration' of the novice, which is the crucial indicator of an authentic continuation of tradition. So how does the process of transmission affect ritual practice and in which respect is there room for change?

By looking at the social process of transmission it will also be possible to clarify the fundamental difference between traditions, which are transmitted through ritual and those, which are transmitted through writing. Depending on these modes of transmission one can distinguish between two types of continuity, which Jan Assmann has called 'ritual coherence' in the case of the former and 'textual coherence' in the case of the latter (see Assmann 1997, 87–103). As the mode of writing ensures stability in form (written text), so it is argued, this not only allows for but even encourages innovation (Assmann 1997, 97), whereas the oral mode of transmission, where form

[*] I am grateful to the participants of the symposium on the dynamics of changing rituals for their comments and suggestions.

(performance) is always flexible, largely excludes variation in order to ensure the continuity of the sense (or 'meaning') of tradition.

In the following I will take a closer look at an oral ritual tradition from East Nepal in order to clarify the issues raised above. Examining the social process of transmission among the Mewahang Rai, I will try to find out which institutions are there to guarantee the 'sameness,' that is, the coherence (or the 'hermeneutical identity' in Hans-Georg Gadamer's terms) of the tradition, and what exactly is the scope for variation. I will argue that in the case of this oral tradition there is in fact a considerable degree of variation, which is not only accepted but also expected. While this variation does not necessarily mean a long-term change of the tradition as a whole, it nevertheless elucidates the ways in which gradual change is possible and can affect a tradition under certain circumstances.

Oral Tradition among the Mewahang Rai

The Rai are considered to be one of the larger 'tribal' or ethnic groups in Eastern Nepal, and together with the Limbu, Yakha and Sunuwar they belong to the legendary Kiranti, the indigenous inhabitants of this region. Though all the Kiranti groups have a common linguistic background—they all are part of the Kiranti language group within Tibeto-Burman—there is a considerable diversity of linguistic and cultural traditions. The somewhat fluid ethnic category called Rai is made up of well over a dozen different groups, commonly called 'subtribes,' one of which is the Mewahang Rai, who settled in the upper Arun Valley (for ethnographic details see Gaenszle 1991).

Like most Kiranti the Mewahang Rai have a rich and living oral tradition, which is called *muddum*. This concept comprises the narration of myths (dealing with the creation of the world, the origin of man and culture, and the migration of the ancestors), as well as the performance of ancestral rituals, which require the use of a distinct ritual language (oratory, invocations, recitations). The ritual language is used only in interactions with the ancestors or respected elders, whose status is close to that of ancestors. So the *muddum* is basically a tradition of speaking. But more generally the word stands for the ancestral way of life, the way to remain in communication and in harmony with the world of the ancestors. As the emphasis is thus on speaking, and not so much on text, the speech forms are not entirely fixed but relatively variable according to competence and context.

There are four basic speech genres in which the ritual language is used.[1] Though these genres are not all terminologically labeled, they are distinguished according to context, language style and the required speech competence.

Ceremonial Dialogues: These are highly stylized speech interactions between two groups through eloquent representatives, usually respected elders. In the context of marriage intermediaries from the family of the bride and the family of the groom negotiate the transfer of gifts and rights (Gaenszle 1991, 191–192). Other such dialogues are held during the funerary rites between representatives of the bereaved and representatives of the funerary helpers or the elders (see Gaenszle 1999). Moreover, less elaborate ceremonial dialogues are common during other ritual occasions, for example, the house inauguration or harvest rituals, and generally, too, in the context of parting after a ritual gathering. In this genre of ritual speech, which in principle can be used by any adult male person who feels fit to do so, there is a high portion of ordinary language involved. But it is a formalized kind of language, extremely polite—almost to the point of exaggeration—full of metaphors and parallelist constructions, including many terms from the ritual language. In short, it is a 'flowery' kind of speech, which can be seen as part of a certain etiquette, which was established by the ancestors.

Lay Invocations: This form of ritual speech may be used by all adults, including women. It is mainly used in order to call the souls of the dead during the funerary rites or in the annual Calling of the Good Ancestors (*sùkla che:^ma*), when those ancestors in the ascending line whose death is still remembered are invoked. This kind of calling uses a rhythmic form of speech, formalized to a certain degree, but still contains many elements of the ordinary language. As the addressee is somebody one has known personally, the invocation has the character of a direct, often even emotional, interlocution.

Invocations of the Elders: This group contains all the ritual texts used by the 'knowledgeable old men' (*pasuŋ*, Nepali *purkhã*) who have not undergone a phase of initiation. These invocations are addressed to various ancestral beings, as, for instance, the ancestral stone as a representative of the territory (called *ca:ri*), the hearthstones, the household deity (*khamaŋ*), or the ancestral chicken in a particular healing ritual (*saya po:kma*). In these texts the ritual language dominates, as they consist largely of standard formulae.

---

[1]   The following account does not deal with the narrative part of the tradition. The myths, it must be emphasized, are generally told in ordinary language, both Mewahang and Nepali.

All the older men acquire some competence in this form of speech, but the knowledge of texts usually varies considerably between individuals.

Ritual Texts of the Initiated Ritual Specialists: These texts require special competences: performers must be ordinary tribal priests (*ŋo:pa*) or shamans (*makpa*, Nepali *dhāmi*). Clearly this category is the most extensive. It includes the elaborate ancestral cults which involve complex sacrificial offerings, verbal ritual journeys, and/or divination and mild possession, such as the *nāgi* (cult for a snake deity), the *Saraṅdew* (cult for a heavenly deity), or the *Ma:maŋme* (cult for a deity deriving from women who died in pregnancy, Gaenszle 1994). And it also includes the night-long shamanic healing sessions (Nepali *cintā*) or the elaborate rites to escort away the spirits of those who have died an unnatural death (*selewa*). All these texts are characterized by a high degree of formality in the ritual language.

Obviously the latter category is the most restricted one: this part of the tradition can only be performed by persons with special capabilities. In order to gain access to these rituals one has to fulfill certain conditions and pass through a special initiatory experience. Thus initiation can be seen as a process, which guarantees a high degree of competence, which safeguards the continuity of the most complex part of the tradition and protects it from deterioration. In the following I will focus on the institutional aspects of this process.

Initiation and the Transmission of Knowledge

For becoming a *ŋo:pa* or a *makpa* the crucial experience of a novice is the encounter with his *secimaŋ*. This term is possibly related to *semmaŋ*, 'dream,' both terms containing the root *maŋ*, which may be glossed as 'superhuman being.' In Nepali it is usually rendered as *guru deutā* (lit. 'teacher deity'), or simply *guru*, but this should not be confused with the living and human *guru* who may be consulted separately. The special relationship with the *secimaŋ* as it is viewed from the perspective of the novice is expressed in narratives about dreams. Closely linked with the notion of *secimaŋ* is the notion of *sakhau*, which, as will become clear in the following, may be glossed as 'inherited priestly competence.'[2] The possession of latent *sakhau*

---

[2]   It is not entirely clear whether this term is of Nepali origin (<? Nepali *sākh* 'one's own [e.g., kin or lineage]') or a genuine Rai concept. Among the Thulung the corresponding

is the precondition for becoming 'chosen' by a *seciman*: only those persons who have the right ancestral disposition can come under the influence of a *seciman*'s power. This leads to the question what kind of transgenerational affiliation regulates the inheritance of *sakhau*. This section, then, will deal with the kinship aspect of the transmission process.

The ideal case is a direct transmission from father to son. In this case one speaks of the son inheriting his *akpa:-sakhau*, 'own father's *sakhau*' (in the ritual language the form *akpa:-sakhau sekusakhau* occurs, meaning 'own father's *sakhau* received in dreams'). This is illustrated in the following example.

The father of LX[3] (of the Lumluma clan in Bala), called Rasam Rai, was a well-known *nāgire* (a priest of the *nāgi cult*) and *makpa*. LX used to act as *dhole* (drumming assistant) with his father when he was performing shamanic *séances* and assisted him during the *nāgi* rite. His grandfather was also a *ŋo:pa* and is still remembered by the name 'Lama' because he was attracted to Buddhist rituals which he had learned from Sherpa lamas. With this family background it was no surprise when LX began to have dreams of the *nāgi* deity showing him the way to do the proper offering. In his late forties, after the death of his father, he asked the dominant *nāgire* in Bala, KB (of the Temora clan), to be his *guru*. At first LX had only a small clientele (*siŋkhoŋ*) of about a dozen houses, but when KB died in 1987 he inherited his total clientele and now has a *siŋkhoŋ* of close to 60 households in eight villages in which he regularly performs the *Bhārte nāgi*.

So here the new priest clearly derives his competence from the *sakhau* of his father, who in turn has inherited it from his father. In principle the *sakhau* only 'comes out,' that is, becomes active, after the death of the predecessor. If a son should begin to perform when his father is still alive (he is then called *phendakpa*), this is considered inauspicious and dangerous. But not all sons inherit the paternal *sakhau*. In fact, it is even regarded as inauspicious when two brothers become priests. Interestingly these are called *berli mop*, the term *berli* also being used when two (or more) brothers marry two (or more) sisters—which is likewise considered to be inauspicious (see Gaenszle 1991, 224). The reduplication, or fission, of *sakhau* is seen to have a weaken-

---

term is *yayu*, and this occurs in the ritual expression *yayukhom sakhakhom*. Nicolas J. Allen's analysis of this binomial suggests that *sakha* is related to the Nepali word above (Allen 1978, 246). My consultants, however, felt that it is a Rai word.

[3]   In order to protect the identity of living individuals in the fieldwork area, I use acronyms instead of personal names.

ing effect. It is said that one of two *berli mop* is bound to die a premature death.

In the case of LX there was no problem: he was the only brother to have the calling. During our conversation on the issue LX emphasized that in such a constellation, when the father's *sakhau* is clearly established, one can even 'call the *sakhau*' if it 'does not give dreams.' In that case one would risk no harm in performing the rituals, but still dreams usually come in due course.

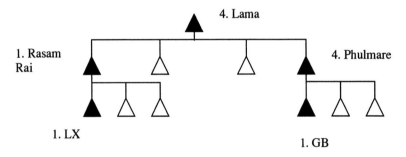

($\triangle$ = male person, $\blacktriangle$ = possessing *sakhau*)
Fig. 1: **Direct patrilineal transmission of *sakhau***

The diagram above gives two patrilines descending from 'Lama': one is that of LX, whose father was the eldest brother; the other is that of Phulmare, Rasam Rai's younger brother, who was also a priest. Thus we have here the constellation of two *berli mop*, but this situation was mitigated by the fact (or some say it was the cause of the fact) that Phulmare, who was a *ŋo:pa* for *Sarandew* and a *makpa*, was only a weak priest who had no *siŋkhoŋ* ('clientele') and performed exclusively in his own household. He died at the age of about fifty.

Phulmare's eldest son GB acted as an assistant (here: *bhägimi*) for *Sarandew* (initially for his father). For many years he assisted the most respected and only active *ŋo:pa* for the *Sarandew* cult, PM, also of the Lumluma clan (but of another lineage). When PM died in 1986 there was no one left to celebrate the cult and eventually GB, after prolonged illness, emerged as his successor. He had had dreams before when he received the calling to be a *bhägimi* but now everybody turned on him to do the rite. His *guru* was BR, a highly knowledgeable *pasuŋ* senior to him, who never did the rite but only acted as *bhägimi*—which he now did for GB. Being the only *ŋo:pa* for the *Sarandew* cult, GB thus had a considerable *siŋkhoŋ* of over 60 households.

This is a typical example of a direct and smooth transmission: inheriting the father's *sakhau* is a first precondition, but for the transmission of ritual knowledge the activity as assistant is particularly helpful: quite often assistants become the successors of their masters.

If *sakhau* is not transmitted directly from father to son, it is also possible and indeed quite frequent that it is transmitted after the lapse of one or more generations. The *sakhau* of one's grandfather is called *akphoba-sakhau*, and that of one's great-grandfather is called *turosakhau*. A greater lapse than this tends to be questionable. Let us consider an example of such a case, which is taken from the politically dominant Temora clan. The apical ancestor Bharte Singh was not only a leading *jimmāwāl* ('headman') but also a *ŋo:pa* who introduced the *nāgi* cult in Bala—hence its name *Bhārte nāgi*.

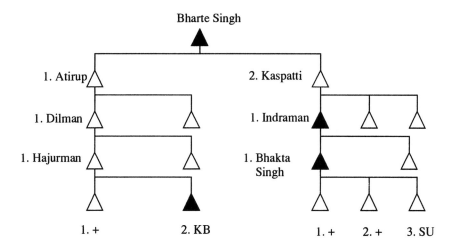

Fig. 2: **Indirect patrilineal transmission of *sakhau* (+ = died in childhood)**

Here we see that at first the priestly competence was transmitted in the junior line descending from Kaspatti. But when SU, whose two elder brothers died at an early age, failed to receive his father's *sakhau*, it was KB who became a *nāgire*. The interesting point is that it is said that KB inherited his *sakhau* from his classificatory uncle Bhakta Singh.

As a member of the senior line in the senior lineage of the dominant clan in Bala KB, whose elder brother died in childhood, became the *jimmāwāl* of the village. During the time when Rasam Rai (see above) was the leading *nāgire*, KB's 'uncle' Bhakta Singh (who was Rasam Rai's disciple) began to perform as a result of increasing social pressure to continue the Temora line. But after Bhakta Singh died, and it was clear that none of his sons would follow, it was KB, at the age of 45, who began to get the calling. As there was no immediate ancestor from whom he could have inherited his *sakhau*, there was some worry that he would risk his life, because if the deity felt offended it could kill the incapable performer. But KB was a *bhuiphuṭṭā* ('self-generated') priest, that is, he had no *guru*. He became a respected *nāgire*, and it was concluded that he must have received his *sakhau* from Bhakta Singh, thus continuing the line. SU became the assistant of KB and remained so until KB's death. After this SU was expected to become his successor but he still failed to get the calling.

This example brings out with particular clarity that beyond a straightforward patrilineal inheritance there are other lines of transmission, and therefore it is more adequate to speak of spiritual descent lines.[4] These are not only patrilineal, as *sakhau* can also be transmitted through uterine descent (then called: *koroyo mimayo*). This allows for diffusion of the priestly competence into clans, which are related through marriage. In fact, the Lumluma line discussed above is said to derive its *sakhau* (for *nāgi*) through an earlier affinal link with the dominant Temora lineage.

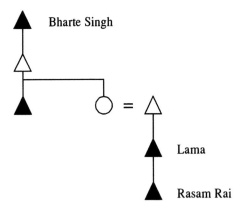

Fig. 3: **Matrilateral transmission of *sakhau***

---

[4] This term is employed by András Höfer in the comparable (but not identical) case of the transmission of shamanic quality—or 'charisma'—among the Tamang, there called *àyo* (Höfer 1994, 21–23). As in Höfer's case a limited number of apical ancestor shamans are distinguished, one can rightly speak of 'spiritual lineages,' which Höfer compares with similar concepts in Tibetan Buddhism as well as Vaishnavism (the term 'segmentary spiritual lineages' has been used in reference to Ramanandi ascetics by Richard Burghart 1983, 650).

Obviously this system of transmission is not 'mechanical' (or 'automatic') but leaves considerable room for individual 'freedom' or manipulation. One could go as far as to say that almost everybody in the village is in a position to trace some sort of *sakhau* in his ancestry and thus claim its inheritance and become a priest. But in the less than straightforward cases such claims may be contested, and here political factors come into play as well. It is likely that under different circumstances KB's claim to possess *sakhau* would have been met with scepticism, but due to the need to continue the Temora line, and also due to his position of power, this did not occur.

The situation was different in the case of JH, who is a *ŋo:pa* for *Waya nāgi* (another ancestral cult) and a *makpa*. He claims to have inherited *sakhau* from his maternal uncle, but several villagers told me that they doubt this. The problem is that JH's father's brother in a neighboring village is also a well-known priest for *Waya nāgi*. Thus there is already *sakhau* in his own patriline, but claiming this affiliation would imply that he could not perform until this senior priest had died. It seems that it is at least partly due to the latent competition with his uncle that JH's priestly competence is contested.

To sum up, it may be said that competence in perpetuating the tradition of the *muddum* is conceived of as an inherent quality—*sakhau*, which is transmitted both through agnatic and uterine descent, and thus constitutes spiritual lines of descent. It is a principle of this kind of lineage that there should be only one descendant at a time (i.e., avoidance of *berli mop*), and that this descendant should only start to become active after the death of his predecessor.

As opposed to this lineal transmission of competence, we need to distinguish the transmission of knowledge through the *guru* to the disciple. Though this may appear in our perspective to be the 'really' significant aspect of the 'process of tradition' (*Überlieferungsgeschehen*), it is for the Rai relatively peripheral. Generally the *guru* remains in the background during the first performances of a novice; even if he assists as a second voice this is more of a safeguard than an actual teaching. In principle the knowledge of the new priest should come by itself—through his *sakhau* and his *seciman*—and therefore it is not only possible for him to make do without a *guru* but particularly prestigious if he can (for example, KB).

Whereas the functioning of spiritual descent lines is organized by the principle of kinship, the *guru*-disciple relationship bypasses such links, as there is no restriction on the choice of a *guru*: there may be more than one and he may even be from a different Rai subtribe. Sometimes there are genuine exchange relationships between clans, as in the case of the Temora and Lumluma lines discussed above: Rasam Rai (Lumluma) was the *guru* of

Bhakta Singh (Temora), whose heir KB (Temora) was the *guru* of Rasam Rai's son LX.[5] One has to be careful, then, to distinguish the two kinds of transmission outlined above, particularly when one speaks of succession. In sociological terms a novice is not necessarily the successor to the person from whom he has inherited his *sakhau*. He may be the successor to his *guru* (like in the case of LX), or else another *ŋo:pa*, for example, the priest for whom he has been an assistant (like in the case of GB). Thus succession in this sense is not defined by the inheritance of ancestral competence (*sakhau*) but by the inheritance of clientele (*siŋkhoŋ*).

Variation and Change

How does all this affect the issue of change in rituals? Whatever may be the case in actual fact, this is clearly an ideology which stresses innate ancestral competence of ritual experts and which downplays any process of repetition and learning that relies on a human teacher (*guru*). Therefore the crucial point is that ritual competence is not seen as something one can consciously acquire but as something, which 'comes by itself,' due to ancestral forces which ultimately come from somewhere else. But a claim to such inherent learning is not enough; it must be continuously validated by a display of competence. And this puts a permanent pressure on the practitioner to show his/her innate powers by a demonstration of personal style and individuality. It is not repetition, which is called for: any obvious copying of a teacher would be seen as a sign of weakness and inauthenticity.

This point may be illustrated by the example of KB and his disciple LX (see above). KB is a typical case of a 'self-generated' priest who claims to have had no teacher. He was highly respected in the village, both as a political leader as well as a priestly figure. Everyone agreed that he had a beautiful voice. His style of incantation was peculiar: he sang in a somewhat slow and melodious manner, with few repetitions and characteristic vibrato at the end of lines. He was clearly in full control of his *séances*. When going on a ritual journey in his chants he would sometimes make little detours in his itinerary,

---

[5] Interestingly, among the Tamang, to the contrary, there tends to be a hereditary relationship between the *guru* line and the line of adepts (Höfer 1994, 24). Thus one could speak here of an asymmetrical relationship, and among the Mewahang Rai of a symmetrical (reciprocal) relationship.

or take short cuts. Suddenly he would stop chanting and switch to ordinary language, perhaps make some jokes, and then, just as abruptly, return to his chants. All this was regarded as an unambiguous sign of authority.

This distinctive individuality obviously affected not only the musical style of his chanting but also the ritual 'texts' which he produced. The first lines of his invocation of *nāgi* have been recorded as follows:

narihoma-ŋo lùplùhoma-ŋo	O *nāgi*
chewatupma-ŋo watupma-ŋo	Deity of the Meeting Rivers
matibu soloma-ŋo thaŋbanam-ye	In the Rising Time
cibhedam-ho o:-robibu sapabupami	With the gift of the *koirala* bird, in the house
khatiru dùŋmarupi-ŋa	of my brother
yamekulo	I make the offering

Also LX, the disciple and successor to KB (but of a different clan), is a respected priest. But though his clientele is equally large, he is more of a modest and humble man, knowledgeable but with little political ambitions. His chanting of the *nāgi* is astonishingly different from that of KB: though the rituals are regarded as the same, there is relatively little congruence in the wording. Moreover, KB sings it rather fast, sometimes to the point of going out of breath, but the speed is made up by using ritual phrases much more repetitively. His initial address looks like this (sung in one breath):

narihomo nucharimo	O *nāgi*
wanaromo waburomo	Deity of the Rising Time
kobusew-ke risisew-ke yamenilo	With speech I make the offering
ennam nu:to mukum nu:to	Take on a pleasant mind!

Of course a more systematic comparison between the two versions would be necessary to draw general conclusions. All I want to show here is that there is a considerable difference in both style and content in the versions of the same ritual presented by different performers, even though—or should one say: precisely because—one is the teacher of the other.

All this, one might argue, is only stylistic variation and not really proof of long-term change. And indeed, a lasting effect is something difficult to demonstrate in the absence of field data that document a longer period of time. What I claim to demonstrate, however, is that there is ample scope for change to 'creep' into such a tradition. For example, in the case of LX there is a considerable degree of Nepali expressions, which are almost absent in KB's version. This seems to indicate that LX is more prone to use this *lingua franca* of the modern state than KB, which is typical of this 'younger' generation in general. Thus history may affect the ritual tradition.

Conclusion

In sociological terms one may characterize this system of transmission, which is rather typical for shamanic traditions,[6] as a kind of compromise between a rigid and mechanical system of succession to office and a system of charismatic leadership (see Weber 1985, 140). The requirement of *sakhau* filiation guarantees that no 'outsiders' (such as members of immigrant Mewahang clans) enter the circle of those who control the *muddum.* And the requirement of an ancestral calling (through a *secimaŋ*) guarantees that only persons with particular spiritual qualities and leanings will acquire this valued ancestral knowledge. Claims to *sakhau* must be validated by the experience of such an ancestral calling,[7] and they must be demonstrated by an authentic and individualized kind of performance.

Thus it is a characteristic of this system that it is open to contesting claims: as ritual experts have to demonstrate their competence this leads to a competitive negotiation of status. Powerful priests and shamans try to outdo 'smaller' ones by showing off their autonomy ('self-generation'). Incompetent practitioners can be recognized by their bad performance, for example, coughing while chanting, forgetting words, inconsistency of texts, mumbling voice. In this case chances are that *sakhau* claims are viewed with skepticism and clients will be reluctant to give an invitation. A competent performer is endowed with a beautiful voice and a personal style that radiates authority.

In consequence novices are not only copying their predecessors but draw on a creative power, which they claim to have received from the ancestral deities. Among other things this allows for the capability to do divinations and diagnose the state and future of clients. Ritual texts are not simply memorized but generated 'in context.' So the authenticity (sameness) of the tradition is here not guaranteed by the stability of texts (through verbatim memorization or in-scription) but by the competence of the performers to

---

[6] For a discussion of the issues of hereditary transmission and 'initiatory illness' in shamanic traditions see Hamayon 1990, 434–435, 439–441 (on Siberia), and in a wider comparative perspective, Eliade 1951, 32–35, 45–47.

[7] In this context, the dreams of the initiates, and especially the telling of dreams, play an important role.

show their link with the ancestral world. It is precisely by re-fashioning the rituals in an idiosyncratic manner that the continuity of tradition is maintained. The ritual tradition has to keep changing, otherwise it is dead.

It may seem that the possibility of sustained change in such a system of transmission is only minimal, the modifications may appear superficial, not having really any long-term effect. But this, I would argue, depends on the social and historical conditions of a time. Minor changes (or apparent 'variations'), which enter a body of knowledge in the course of transgenerational transmission, may under certain circumstances rapidly accumulate and after a few generations something, which is still felt to be the same, may have become something quite different.

References

Allen, Nicholas J. 1978: Sewala puja bintila puja: Notes on Thulung Ritual Language. In: *Kailash* 6:237–256.

Assmann, Jan. 1997: *Das kulturelle Gedächtnis: Schrift, Erinnerung und politische Identität in frühen Hochkulturen.* 2d ed. Munich: C.H. Beck.

Burghart, Richard. 1983: Renunciation in the Religious Traditions of South Asia. In: *Man* (n.s.) 18:635–653.

Eliade, Mircea 1951: *Le chamanisme et les techniques archaiques de l'extase.* Paris: Payot.

Gaenszle, Martin. 1991: *Verwandtschaft und Mythologie bei den Mewahang Rai in Ostnepal: Eine ethnographische Studie zum Problem der 'ethnischen Identität'.* Stuttgart: Franz Steiner Verlag Wiesbaden.

————. 1994: Journey to the Origin: A Root Metaphor in a Mewahang Rai Healing Ritual. In: *The Anthropology of Nepal: Peoples, Problems, Processes,* ed. Michael Allen. Kathmandu: Mandala Book Point. 256–268.

————. 1999: The Making of Good Ancestors: Separation and Exchange in Mewahang Rai Funerary Rites. In: *Ways of Dying: Death and its Meanings in South Asia,* ed. Elisabeth Schömbucher-Kusterer and Claus Peter Zoller. New Delhi: Manohar. 49–67.

Hamayon, Roberte. 1990: *La chasse à l'âme: esquisse d'une théorie du chamanisme sibérien.* Nanterre: Société d'ethnologie.

Höfer, András. 1994: *A Recitation of the Tamang Shaman in Nepal.* Bonn: VGH Wissenschaftsverlag.

Weber, Max. 1985: *Wirtschaft und Gesellschaft: Grundriß der verstehenden Soziologie* (1922), ed. J. Winckelmann. 5th ed. Tübingen: J.C.B. Mohr.

Politics of Acculturation: The Dynamics of Hindu-Christian Ritual in Goa, India

Alexander Henn

Introduction

This article deals with a particular instance of religious acculturation. Geographically the case is located in the small Indian state of Goa. Historically it is situated against the backdrop of 451 years of Portuguese colonialism and Catholic hegemony which left the small tract of land on India's west coast even after its liberation from the foreign rule (1961) and integration into the Indian federation (1987) with a culturally and religiously heterogeneous population. This embraces today little more than 1,100,000 people, of whom 65% are Hindus and 29% Catholics.

What becomes interesting here, is a religious festival which is annually celebrated in a number of Goan villages by former small farmers, land laborers and fishermen, most of whom earn their livelihood today as workers in the private or public sector. The festival is known under the name of *jāgar* or *zāgor*. This name refers to the Sanskrit notion of *jagr*, which means 'to be awake' and which specifies the central purpose and also attraction the festival has for the rural population: to stay awake for a full night and to combine religious rituals with the performance of dance, music and theater in order to honor the ancestors, gods and saints related to the village.

Besides these general features reminiscent of well-known traditions of ludic religiosity and nocturnal ceremonies in India,[1] the festival reflects the interaction between Indian and European, Hindu and Christian traditions

---

[1]   Worthwhile mentioning here are the religious ceremonies, which have been described in particular for North and Northwest India under the names *jāgaraṇa* (Thiel-Horstmann 1985), *jagrātā* (Erndl 1993) and *jāgar* (Leavitt 1985; Gaborieau 1975). Though differing considerably in detail, all these ceremonies share with the Goan *jāgar* or *zāgor* the performance of an all-night vigil in which religious rituals and certain forms of play are combined.

prevailing in Goa today in a distinct way. Hence, the festival has two variants. One is the *jāgar*, which—performed in the context of Hindu temple festivals by members of a particular sub-caste (*jāti*) of temple artists (*kalvantā*)—exclusively honors sacred beings commonly classified within the fold of the universal and local Hindu pantheon. Another variant, central to the discussion here, is the *zāgor*, which—linked with feasts in the Christian calendar and performed by the villagers themselves—pays homage to locally defined groups of divinities, who interestingly, comprise beings from the Hindu and Christian worlds, thus combining, for example: Devu Bappa, Devu Putra, Ispirita Santa, the Christian Trinity, San João, St. John the Baptist, Saibini Mai, the Virgin Mary with Gajānan, the Elephant-headed Hindu God and Hindu village deities like Vetaḷ, Sateri, Bhoomika and others.

The religious invocations and prayers frame an extensive ludic program which—in a series of relatively short, independent narrative-performative plots—presents a multitude of themes and characters in dance, song and play performed by sumptuously costumed men and boys. Following mythical kings and heroes, with allusions to well-known episodes in the Indian epics of *Mahabharata* and *Ramayana*, come members of various occupational groups or castes-bakers, gardeners, soldiers, students, and the 'untouchable' and his family. There come officials, such as the village headman, the town-crier, the tax-collector, the village Brahman, and then kinship-positions: husbands and wives, daughters and sons, sisters and brothers, the maternal uncle and his nephew. Especially interesting are characters representing various sorts of strangers, such as *Firanghi,* the Franconian who became the synonym of the historical European, *Paklo*, the historical Portuguese, *Kapro*, the African, the *Hippie*, the equivalent of the international tourist and, notable for the particular national self-definition of Goans, also *Hindustān Dadlo ānī Hindustān Baiḷ*, the Indian man and the Indian woman. The liturgical and dramatic texts presented in these night-long festivals are composed basically in the local language, Konkani, but with more or less 'creolized' Portuguese and more or less standardized Marathi thrown in, the ceremonial nature of the occasion even providing for occasional insertions of Latin or Sanskrit.

Conversion and Assimilation: The Politics of Acculturation I

To explore how the peculiar blending of Hindu and Christian elements exemplified in the Goan festival came into being, we must examine its broader history. The first textual mention of the festival so far uncovered is in a tax list, or *foral*, from Salcete, Goa's then most southern district. This list was valid for the years 1567 to 1585 and refers to the village of Benaulim by stating:

> Pa[ra] se fazerem dous autos q[ue] se fazem de noite q[ue] se chama zagor en todo o anno pagavã doze t[an]gas br[an]cas. (For the performance of two [theatrical] acts which are performed in the night and are know as zagor twelfe white tangas [a currency then circulating in Goa] have to be paid per year) (Anonymous 1987, 61; additions and translation A.H.)

Interestingly, this official notice comes in the historical text right after a similar tax levy made "por cantarem no pagode q[ue] se chama aoijagar" ('for singing in a temple' with the significant name of 'Aoijagar') (Anonymous 1987, 61). It is interpreted by the Goan historian Panduranga Pissurlenkar as a reference to a historical "Hindu theatre performed during certain religious festivities," something to which he added the interesting, though unfortunately undocumented remark that "already in 1526, the Goan poet Crisnada Xama had talked about the actors, *nattadhara,* of this theatre" (Pissurlenkar 1962, 44). Certainly, the designation of the historical ceremonies mentioned as 'Hindu' is to be qualified in the early modern context in which the notion of 'Hindu' may not have been current yet. There can be no doubt, however, about the date of their documentation coming at a period when the Christianization of Salcete was still in its infancy, and also their relationship to local temples strongly supports the hypothesis that they were not an imported but an indigenous custom.

That there existed a tradition of *zāgores* in Goa before the advent of the Portuguese is also the assumption of the historian Teotonio de Souza. Relying equally on information from a tax list for the village of Karbely (Salcete) in the year 1660, he describes the rural life of medieval Goa as follows:

> It was in the temple premises that children were educated and where the adults organized their cultural activities, particularly their *zagor* or dramatic performances. (Souza 1978, 91)

Zāgores are more frequently mentioned in textual sources, especially in church documents, after the mid-eighteenth century, when the number of Christian converts had considerably increased and formed a clear majority in the territories that had come under Portuguese rule in the sixteenth century. Strikingly, in these documents the village-festivities are now no longer associated with Hindu temples but with Catholic churches and, as a rule, appear in the context of *dias de festas*, that is, Christian feasts. Thus if we accept the hypothesis that *zāgores* existed in 'pre-Portuguese Goa'—whether or not one calls them 'Hindu' ceremonies—we must conclude that, by the mid-eighteenth century at the latest, these were transformed, at least partially, into what now appears to be a Christian observance. Despite this, the references to the village festivities in church documents are anything but favorable, as expressed in this typical pastoral letter, dated from July 18, 1784:

> the way of noisily celebrating the act called *fama* by the Christians and *olly* by the natives is condemned, as also the entertainment called *zagor;* and referring to such means in order to attract people to the church is deplored: and [hence], first, the penalty of excommunication, issued by the arch-episcopal decree of November 17, 1777, against those assisting in the *fama* and the *zagor* is renewed ...; secondly, a priest coming to know that this *fama* is to be celebrated should tell the people that the feast [= *festa*] will not be held which gives the occasion for this *fama* or *zagor*.... (Nazareth 1894, 336; my translation, A.H.)

Despite its unmistakable intention, the pastoral letter strengthens the impression that there was a certain inconsistency in church policy regarding village festivities in 1784. Of course, we know that the *zāgor*—and also the festivities called *fama* or *olly,* to which I will return later—had become a thorn in the church's side and were persecuted by harsh means. A series of decrees renewing the initial ban in the years 1791, 1812, 1897 and 1904 which defamed the festivities as 'immoral,' 'barbarous,' 'superstitious' and ultimately even 'heathen' spectacles (Xavier 1861, 126–127; Albuquerque 1922, 41, 66, 223, 240), gives us an idea of why this was so. However, reading the text carefully, one cannot escape the impression that the *zāgor* and the *fama* were not only quite commonly held by Catholics, but also that they had become quite regular elements of their parochial *festas* and, at times, were even used as a means 'of attracting people to the church.' Thus one might suggest that these festivities were not condemned; rather, they were regarded with certain tolerance, if not strategically used, by some of the clergy.

This inconsistency becomes clearer in the positions held by Catholic priests *vis-à-vis* the festivities called *fama* or *olly* in the 1784 pastoral letter. Without going too much into detail, *fama* was a ludic event, with disguises, songs and music performed by Catholics on various festive occasions in Goa. Obviously, because of its striking similarities with the ludic activities performed during Holi, the Hindu festival celebrated in February or March to which the pastoral letter refers as the '*olly* of the *gentios*' (Dalgado 1988, 2: 121), the *fama* was banned by higher church authorities in 1784 and, thus was mentioned as the 'prohibited *fama*' by Casimiro Christovão de Nazareth, a compiler of Goan church history in 1894. Interestingly, Manuel João Socrates de Albuquerque, another compiler of Goan church history, found it necessary in 1922 to qualify the statement made by his colleague by specifying that there was not only a 'prohibited *fama*' but also a 'legitimate *fama*,' which had nothing 'barbarous' or 'superstitious' about it but was celebrated on the occasion of 'solemn feasts' throughout the Goan archbishopric (Albuquerque 1922, 3, n. 1). This is of interest because it stresses that with respect to the observances mentioned the Catholic church indeed held contrary positions which at times could confuse even the clergy themselves.

In order to account for these inconsistencies and confusions, it is necessary to go back to the earlier period of the Christianization of Goa. It should be recalled that, in the sixteenth and seventeenth century, the Catholic church, in its thrust to establish its regime and to propagate the Catholic faith in Goa, did not simply pursue a policy of suppressing indigenous religious practices, which took the form, above all, of the destruction of Muslim and Hindu places of worship and their replacement by Christian churches, chapels and crosses. As a more subtle means of winning converts, the missionaries also used methods which consciously played on similarities between the religions that had come into contact, emphasizing, for example, on the parallelism between the concept of the Christian Trinity and the Hindu Trimūrti, the ritualistic ablutions of Hindus and the Holy Water in Christian baptism, or Hindu concepts of incarnation and the human embodiment of Christ (Gomes Pereira 1978, 17).

What at times appeared like a sort of strategic syncretism was systematized in the translation of the Christian message into the local languages (Priolkar 1967). In this, the work of the English Jesuit Thomas Stephens (1549–1619) deserves particular attention. Succeeding Etienne de la Croix as Rector of the Catholic College of Rachol in Goa in 1597, Stephens composed a work in a language which he himself called 'Brahman-Mahratta' (analyzed by linguists today as basically Old Marathi with elements of Konkani), which became famous for its excellent linguistic and poetic qualities and became a much-used means of Christian instruction in Goa. Published by the Rachol College in 1619 and reprinted in 1649 and 1654, Stephens' work had the significant title *Kristapurāna* and narrated in two parts all the major contents of the Old and New Testament in metrical form. In doing this Stephens adapted the messages of the Holy Books of Christianity to the stylistic devices of the Hindu *bhakti* literature, and in particular to the works of his contemporary Śrī Sant Ekanāth (1533–1609), to such perfection, that Hugh van Skyhawk notes:

> Only with regard to its specially Christian contents and intention does the Purāṇa from the feather of the first Englishmen in Goa differ from the works of Ekanāth or Śrī Jñāneśvar (died circa 1294) not, however in its literary form and composition. (Skyhawk 1999, 366)

In addition, Skyhawk shows that, even with respect to theological concepts, Stephens consciously alluded to Hindu traditions through, for example, using epithets such as *vaikuṇṭha-nāyaka* or *vaikuṇṭha-pūtra* for Jesus, and *vaikuṇṭha-rāṇī* or *vaikuṇṭha-maulī* for Mary, which for Hindus are common designations for Vishnu and Lakshmi respectively.

It is against this background that I would like to expand on the allusion made earlier, that the *zāgor* too, despite its transformation into a Catholic observance, has retained a remarkable resemblance to the Hindu *bhakti* tradition, something that may well have been mediated by works like Stephens' *Kristapurāna*. Significantly, the *zāgor* hymn retains the structure of many *bhakti* songs by opening with the *namana* or homage. In doing this, it corresponds, if not in the same words, to the praise of the Christian Trinity, of Jesus, Mary and the *bhaktas* which Stephens had also placed at the opening of his work (see Saldanha 1907; Skyhawk 1999). Also noteworthy is the fact that the *zāgor* performers refer to their song lines as *ovīs,* which means 'quatrain' and actually marks the metre of Stephens' *namana,* though this metre is not entirely maintained in the *zāgor* hymn today. Finally, there can be no doubt that the language of the *zāgor namana* is based on a poetic fusion of Old Marathi and Konkani which Stephens had also used in his *Kristapurāna,* notwithstanding the fact that from a purist's point of view much of the antiquated language is not properly pronounced in today's *zāgores.*

We are therefore justified to conclude at this stage that the *zāgor* tradition had originated in some sort of ludic ceremony performed in the vicinity of 'Hindu' temples in medieval times. In the course of the earlier period of the Christianization of Goa, in the sixteenth and seventeenth centuries, it most likely became part of a more or less conscious policy of Catholic missionaries, at least partially, to maintain indigenous traditions as a means of facilitating the propagation of the 'new faith.' More precisely, the transformation of the *zāgor* into a Catholic observance either preserved or consciously introduced some of the stylistic devices of the *bhakti* tradition, and it is the explicit artistic modeling of the Christian message upon poetic devices of the *bhakti* literature that indicates that erudite Christian scholars and priests had played a part in this.

Against this background, the ecclesiastical campaign against the village festivities launched after the mid-eighteenth century marks a shift in clerical policy, which it is not easy to assess. Certainly, assimilative strategies in the propagation of the Christian faith in Goa were practiced above all by Jesuit missionaries in the sixteenth and seventeenth century and had been abandoned in official church policy well before the mid-eighteenth century. Thus it is probably more appropriate to look at the prohibition of the village festivities as the removal of the last piece of toleration towards indigenous customs among Goan Catholics than as a shift in clerical strategies of proselytization. However, even in this sense, the drive against the village festivities does not really seem to fit the historical context, taking into account precisely the fact that historians have described the eighteenth century as the beginning of a considerable religious liberalization in Goa. This assessment relies on a number of changes in the Indian colony, of which the gradual deprivation of the power of the religious orders (the expulsion of the Jesuits in 1761, the dissolution of the other orders in 1834), the abolition of the Holy Office of Inquisition (which was at work with a short interruption from 1560 till 1812) and the lifting of restrictions against non-Christian rituals were the most important (Thomaz 1981; Pearson 1987).

Certainly all these changes were effected only gradually and the judicial assimilation of Hindus especially was fully effected only in 1910, when Portugal became a republic. Yet it is puzzling to note that in the same period the persecution of the *zāgor* and of other religious observances of the Catholics were continuously intensified. Since this is not the place to discuss the problem in the fullness it deserves, I will make just one suggestion for consideration. The guarantee of freedom of worship and the recognition of customary law was first granted only to Hindus living in those territories, which came under Portuguese rule in 1763 and 1788, hitherto known as the *Novas Conquistas* (Thomaz 1981, 25). Later, in 1834, the year a constitutional monarchy was established in Portugal, the same rights were, at least *de jure,* also granted to Hindus living in the territories that had been under Portuguese rule ever since 1510 and 1543, known after the acquisition of the new territories as the *Velhas Conquistas* (Pearson 1987, 148). These changes in religious policies led, among other things, to a steadily growing number of Hindus whose ancestors had fled the heartland of Portuguese domination in the sixteenth and seventeenth century to return to their former homes, thus effecting a gradual '(re-)Hinduization' of the *Velhas Conquistas*. Hence, it is my suggestion that the suppression of the Catholic *zāgor* and *fama* was a reaction by the Catholic church to communication and interaction between the two religious communities, which occurred in the demographically and politically changing situation.

But there were other motives underlying the campaign against the village festivities. There are indications that, in reaction to its prohibition, the *zāgor* increasingly became a hidden and to some extent subversive practice. Thus we read in church documents of 'concealed' *zāgores* held in "hidden and almost dark places" (Albuquerque 1922, 66, 240), and of the recitation of "ridiculous verses" and the presentation of images of "non-canonized saints" (Xavier 1861, 127, 128). Interestingly, old people also remember that the village festivities became occasions for people to raise societal and political grievances at the time of the rise of the nationalist movement in British India and the emerging freedom struggle in Goa. At this time at the latest, surveillance of village festivities also became a matter of government authorities and police forces, and people recall that a special office was set up in Panjim to censor all texts that were to be sung in the *zāgor*. All allusions made in the *zāgor* to the anti-colonial activities going on in the country were removed, and it was forbidden to mention any of the leaders of the nationalist movement, especially Mahatma Gandhi and Jawaharlal Nehru. However, people still recall today with a certain satisfaction that the *zāgor* performers had ways of circumventing the censorship and dealing with prohibited themes by, for example, using for the actual performances a specially camouflaged Konkani, which the villagers could understand but the police could not.

(Re-)Conversion and Purification: The Politics of Acculturation II

It was only in the decade between 1930 and 1940 that the combined efforts of the colonial state and the Catholic church eventually succeeded in suppressing the *zāgores* in most Catholic communities. However, another chapter in the history of the Goan *zāgor* tradition was opening precisely at this time, driven now from within not Catholic but Hindu circles. In order to account for this new development, we must first mention that in the late nineteenth century the Arya Samaj, one of the principal contemporary socio-religious Hindu reform movements, had initiated a proselytizing campaign in North India aimed at bringing people who—or whose ancestors—had once converted to Islam or Christianity (back) into the fold of Hinduism. By calling it *śuddhi,* a term that literally signifies 'state of purity,' the religious re-

formers claimed that their campaign was grounded in ancient rituals performed in order to purify members of high castes from the polluting contacts
they had fallen victim to. However, as both Christophe Jaffrelot (1994) and
Catherine Clementin-Ojha (1994) make clear, in the late nineteenth and early
twentieth century, the notion and practice of *suddhi* became subject to a thorough reinterpretation. Conceptualized by the Arya Samajists as a reaction to
what they considered a dangerously growing number of conversions to Islam
and Christianity in India, the *suddhi* was now used either as a means of ritually uplifting the status of 'untouchables' in order to prevent their conversion
to Islam or Christianity for social reasons, or as an active campaign for conversion to Hinduism. In this, the re-invented *suddhi* not only diverted fundamentally from ancient practice and was criticized for it by orthodox Hindus,
but also copied the proselytizing strategies and techniques of the 'Semitic
religions' in what Jaffrelot calls a "véritable mimétisme stratégique" (Jaffrelot 1994, 76).

The idea to launch a *suddhi* campaign in Goa was first raised in about
1917 in Pune and Bombay in a journal, called *Kesari*, edited by Lokmanya
Tilak, a prominent spokesman of the *Prāthanā Samāj* (Prayer Society) itself
an offshoot of the *Brahmo Samāj* (Society of God), another influential Hindu
reform movement of the time (Kamat 1957). Due to internal controversies
among the Pune and Bombay Brahmans, however, the issue was dropped
again, and only taken up in the late 1920s, when prominent members of Goan
Hindu society invited Vinayak Maharaj Masurkar, the prelate of a Vaishna-
vite *ashram* in Masur (Satari), to campaign actively for Hindu (re-)conver-
sion among the Catholic Gaudas of Goa. The Hindu monk accepted and,
together with some of his disciples, subsequently toured Gauda villages singing devotional *bhakti* songs, performing *pujās,* that is, vegetarian offerings,
and delivering speeches on ancient Hindu texts in a simple language (Kakodkar 1988, 250). In addition to the religious instruction, a series of promises
were made to the Gaudas. If they would undergo the *suddhi* ritual, it was
said, they would become part of the *Hindu Samāj* (Society of Hindus); *puro-
hits* (Hindu priests) would take care of their spiritual needs; they would gain
permission to enter Hindu temples; registers of births, deaths and marriages
would be established for them; and they would be protected against possible
harassment by the colonial government (Kamat 1957).

Having by these means gained a declaration of willingness to be (re-)con-
verted to Hinduism from a considerable number of the Catholic Gaudas, a
ceremony was carefully prepared. In Calapur a *suddhi* center was set up, lawyers were engaged to issue affidavits in which individuals officially declared

their consent to the (re-)conversion, and Hindu members of the legislative councils of Bombay and Delhi and leaders of the Hindu Mahasabha, the Great Hindu Society, in Bombay were asked for their support. On February 25, 1928, *śuddhi* ceremonies were begun in the village of Chimbel in Tiswadi under the guidance of two prominent Hindu Brahmans from Margao (Salcete). In the presence of a large gathering of Hindus, 350 Catholic Gaudas were requested to join in taking the historic oath: "We were in the Christian religion and we are entering Hindu faith again. Kindly accept us." The entire Hindu assembly granted acceptance uttering: "As you wish." Similar ceremonies were held in more than 50 villages and, by the end of May 1928, approximately 7815 Gauda had been (re-)converted to Hinduism (Kakodkar 1988, 253, 261). The Portuguese government, let alone the Catholic church in Goa, were, of course, anything but excited by the movement, and there were some attempts to interfere with it, during which it is reported that, curiously, some people who had undergone the *śuddhi* were immediately baptized again, only to (re-)convert to Hinduism once again (Kakodkar 1988, 265). Yet, given the powerful support, which the movement had received not only from the Hindu reform movements but also from Hindu members of various governmental, legislative and municipal councils in Bombay and Delhi, there was not much the Portuguese government in Goa dared to do about it.

For the *zāgor*, the curious effect of the *śuddhi* movement was that, having been practically eradicated among the Catholic Gauda, the village festival now survived among the (re-)converted Nava Hindu Gauda. This was possible because the Catholic church had lost its power to sanction the festival directly, which was now carried on by people no longer subject to its jurisdiction. Under these new circumstances the festival experienced a kind of renaissance by increasingly becoming a matter of prestige for the Nava Hindu village communities, who started to compete among themselves in celebrating it ever more sumptuously. In addition, it also became a forum for the Nava Hindu Gauda to demonstrate their 'new' religious identity consciously by, for example, changing the date of the festival so that it coincided with a Hindu rather than a Catholic feast, or changing the place of its performance from the vicinity of a cross to a place near a temple, and ultimately even by canceling the invocation of the Christian God and saints in their *namana* hymn. Thus, there are quite a number of village communities today who have decided to substitute the prominent initial homage to "Devu Bappa, Putrā ānī Ispirita Santa" with an invocation to "Brahma, Vishnu and Mahadev." A few other villages have gone even further in this kind of Hinduization of the *zāgor* and replaced all references to the Christian God and saints with homage to Hindu deities.

References

Albuquerque, Manuel J.S. de. 1922: *Sumario cronologico de cecretos Diocesanos do Arcebispado: Desde 1775 até 1922*. Rachol: Paroco de Rachol

Clémentin-Ojha, Catherine. 1994: La Suddhi de l'Arya Samaj ou l'invention d'un rituel de (re-)conversion a l'Hinduisme. In: *Archives de Sciences Sociales des Religions* 87:99–114.

Dalgado, Sebastiao Rudolpho. 1988: *Glossário Luso-Asiatico* (1918). 2 vols. New Delhi: Asian Educational Services.

Erndl, Kathleen M. 1993: *Victory to the Mother: The Hindu Goddess of Northwest India in Myth, Ritual, and Symbol*. New York: Oxford University Press.

Anonymous, 1987: Foral de Salcete 1567–1585. In: *Purabhilekh Puratatva* 7:69–84.

Gaborieau, Marc. 1975: La transe rituelle dans L'Himalaya Central: folie, avatar, meditation. In: *Purusartha* 2:147–172.

Gomes Pereira, Rui. 1978: *Goa: Hindu Temples and Deities*. Panaji Goa: Printwell Press Goa.

Government of Goa; Directorate of Planning and Statistics and Evaluation. 1996: *Statistical Pocket Book of Goa 1993–1994*. Panaji: Government Printing Press.

Henn, Alexander. 2000 The Becoming of Goa: Space and Culture in the Emergence of a Multicultural Lifeworld. In: *Lusotopie: Lusophonies asiatiques, Asiatiques en lusophonies* 1:333–339.

―――. 2003: *Wachheit der Wesen: Politik, Ritual und Kunst der Akkulturation in Goa*. Münster: LIT.

Jaffrelot, Christophe. 1994: Les (re)conversions a l'Hinduisme (1885–1990): politisation et diffusion d'une 'invention de la tradition. In: *Archives de Sciences Sociales des Religions* 87:73–98.

Kakodkar, Archana. 1988: Shuddhi: Reconversion to Hinduism in Goa. In: *Goa: Cultural Trends*, ed. Prakashchandra Pandurong Shirodkar. Panjim: Directorate of Archives, Archaeology, and Museum. 242–263.

Kamat, Jevi. 1957: Dada Vaidya ani Shuddhi Karan. In: *Memoriam Dada Vaidy*, ed. Vaidya Amriti Grantha. Poona: S.M. Joshi. 90–100.

Leavitt, John H. 1985: *The Language of the Gods: Discourse and Experience in a Central Himalayan Ritual*. Chicago: UMI Dissertation Services.

Nazareth, Casimiro Christovão de. 1894: *Mitras Lusitanas no oriente: Catalogo dos Prelados da Egreja Metropolitana E Primacial de Goa e das Dioceses Suffraganeas com a Recopilação por elles Emittidas de Goa*. Lisbon: Imprensa Nacional.

Pearson, Michael Naylor. 1987: *The Portuguese in India*. Cambridge: Cambridge University Press.

Pissurlenkar, Panduranga S.S. 1962: *Goa Pre-Portuguesa atraves dos Escritores Lusitanos dos Seculos XVI e XVII*. Bastora: Tip. Rangel.

Priolkar, Anant Kakbar. 1967: *Goa Re-Discovered*. Bombay: A.K. Priolkar.

Saldanha, Jerome A. 1907: *The Christian Puranna of Father Thomas Stephens: A Work of the Seventeenth Century*. Mangalore: Simon Alvares.

Skyhawk, Hugh van. 1999: "...in this bushy land of Salsette...": Father Thomas Stephens and the Kristapurāna. In: *Studies in Early Modern Indo-Aryan Languages and Culture*, ed. Alan W. Entwistle and Carol Salomon. Delhi: Manohar. 362–378.

Souza, Teotonio de. 1978: *Medieval Goa: Amic Socio-Econo History*. Delhi: Concept Publishing Company.

Thiel-Horstmann, Monika. 1985: *Nächtliches Wachen: Eine Form indischen Gottesdienstes*. Bonn: Indica & Tibetica.

Thomaz, Luis Filipe. 1981–1982: Goa – une societé Luso-Indienne. In: *Bulletin des Etudes Portuaises et Bresiliennes*. 42–43:15–44.

Xavier, Felippe Nery. 1861: *Resumo Historico da Maravilhosa Vida, Conversões, e Milagres de S. Francisco Xavier, Apostolo, Defensor, e Patrono das Indias*. Nova Goa: Na Imprensa National.

Shifts in Place and Meaning: The History of Two Cult Centers in Pre-Colonial Tanzania

Peter Weber

Situation: Cults and Places

The Lubaga cult center is situated beneath the crater of Mount Kiejo, a volcano north of Lake Nyasa overlooking a section of the Central African rift valley. Whereas people came and still come from quite a distance in order to bring sacrificial offerings to Lubaga, the inhabitants of the valley themselves, who came to be known as Nyakyusa during colonial times, adopted a somewhat reserved stance towards this cult center. Local informants, however, insist that in the distant past the Nyakyusa, too, looked very much towards Lubaga, expecting from rituals conducted there gentle rains at the right time and, on the whole, fertility for their land. These are the virtues which, being mainly agriculturalists, they depend on to this day. Obviously, something must have happened with or at Lubaga in the past which had far reaching effects on its meaning to the Nyakyusa.

About fourty miles eastwards, in the adjacent Livingstone Mountains, another important cult center can be found, called Ukwama. The Livingstone Mountains are inhabited by the Kinga. They differ significantly from the Nyakyusa in many cultural and linguistic respects. More importantly, they were originally iron smelters who provided all of their neighbors with hoes. Because in pre-colonial times iron was a scarce and expensive commodity, and at the same time an essential one, the Kinga enjoyed much prestige throughout the region. Their cult center Ukwama is linked with the Lubaga cult center through the story of Lwembe, a mythical hero, who is said to have grown up at Ukwama but who later, for reasons which will soon become apparent, chose to settle at Lubaga among the Nyakyusa.

The cults enacted at Lubaga and Ukwama are known as territorial cults throughout eastern and southern Africa. By definition, their constituency is "a territorial group identified by a common occupation of a particular land area, so that membership of the cult is in the final instance a consequence of residence and not kinship or ethnic designation" (Schoffeleers 1979, 1). Accordingly, if somebody settles in the sphere of influence of a cult center and his destiny is dependent on the success of rituals conducted there, he shares with the local people a sense of belonging to this cult center, regardless of his origin. From then on, they will regard him as a 'man of Lubaga' (*umundu gwa Lubaga*), which makes up part of his identity.

These cult centers consist of sacred groves upon which any disturbance is strictly forbidden. The only people permitted to enter them are the priests, the chiefs, and their headmen. The last are chosen from among the population and then initiated into the cult. These participants may have nothing more in common than that they meet on the occasion of a ritual. It is explicitly stated that every incumbent of a specific ritual office must be present. Their agreement is said to be a further prerequisite for the performance of any ritual. During the author's two-year stay in Tanzania, rituals actually had to be postponed because of an apparent disagreement among those involved. It appeared that the participants inscribed different meanings in their acts. As Howe points out, "inscription is a process, and its importance lies in the fact that it is continuous" (Howe 2000, 63–79). Rituals therefore provide opportunities for reflection. This also implies that power relationships are created and negotiated at the same time. However, when the participants were asked to be specific about the nature of the problem, the flow of information stopped abruptly: the rituals are esoteric and very secretive. On the other hand, everyone in the villages knows when a sacrifice is going to take place.

Cult centers such as Ukwama or Lubaga do not operate to the exclusion of local cults rather they are recognized as the apex of a ritual network. Each chiefdom is equipped with its own sacred groves, but if the rituals directed to the ancestors of the chiefs failed to accomplish their ends, additional cattle would be sent to be sacrificed at Lubaga or Ukwama, respectively. The picture one gets is that of a hierarchy with its divisibility, whereby every part is made up of smaller parts and is itself a component of a larger whole. Therefore, any event occurring, for example, at Ukwama is bound to have effects at a local level and vice versa. This is of course an ideal model, but it is significant that precisely this was suggested by informants from quite different chiefdoms. However, as the anthropologist Henrietta Moore reminds us, "the organization of space has no meaning outside practice" (Moore 1999, 15). In fact, the actual meaning of a cult center can change considerably from one chiefdom to the next. For historical reasons, the respective chiefdoms developed their own perspectives towards a territorial cult center.

Oral Traditions: Myths and Heros

The country of the Kinga and the Nyakyusa must have witnessed a considerable influx of people since the beginning of the seventeenth century. There
are many lively traditions among people who trace their origins back to Central Tanzania. This migration has been named the Ngulube migration by the
historian Kalinga and was probably triggered by several successive droughts
(see Kalinga 1985, 35).[1] It is conceivable that people set off in search of better living conditions. They could certainly find them in the settlement area of
the Nyakyusa and the Kinga, where fertile soils and higher rainfalls prevail.
Throughout Southwest Tanzania the formation of many chiefdoms and even
kingdoms is attributed to this migration. In the oral traditions, the migrants
are portrayed as being state-builders. It is said that they brought fire. In eastern Africa, this is considered to be a basic metaphor for social transformation. Hence, in most areas, this migration involved the establishment of a
new political order.

Oral traditions usually only describe the sequence of events. The following tradition is common throughout the region and summarizes a development which possibly lasted a century. According to this tradition, Ngulube
entered the mountains of the Kinga from the North East and married a
woman there named Mkinga. She gave birth to two sons, Lwembe and Kyabala, who both moved into the Nyakyusa valley. While Lwembe managed to
settle at Lubaga, Kyabala died among the Nyakyusa. Thereafter only his
children continued the journey. They subsequently founded kingdoms, whose
rulers to this day consider Ngulube to be their ancestor or even god.[2]

It appears after analysis that the whole process was set in motion by the
Kinga. When asked about their history, the Kinga relate that these immigrants first came to power at Ukwama. The then ruler sent his three sons to
establish their own courts in the countryside. Thus, the pre-eminence of Ukwama as a ritual center and the authority of its chief in ritual matters is continuously reasserted by the use of genealogical idiom. The foundation of two
chiefdoms was largely accomplished by a peaceful process. The third, however, the chiefdom of Kyelelo, waged at least two wars on the autochthonous
population. In addition, Kyelelo is frequently depicted in the oral traditions

---

[1]   The level of Lake Nyasa is sensitive to climate changes and reached an all-time low
around 1500.

[2]   A detailed version of this tradition can be found in Kalinga 1985, 53–55 and in Tew 1950,
73–74.

of the Kinga as having committed patricide, indicating that he either disregarded Ukwama as the ritual center of the country or that his intention was to usurp the chief's position.

The people on whom Kyelelo waged these wars were the Mahanji. They settled in the Livingstone Mountains long before these immigrants arrived. For this reason, they are considered to be the owners of the land. As such, they are conceded to have a special relationship to its ancestral spirits who are believed to exercise control over natural forces. In contrast to other autochthonous groups, still today the Mahanji emphasize their own identity. They also speak of Ukwama as their original home and still call it Luhenje. The Mahanji even claim that they held ritual offices in Ukwama, from which they were removed when the Ngulube-migrants came into power. They recall that they were constantly at war with Kyelelo who wanted to subjugate them. Eventually, however, the immigrants had to acknowledge the ritual authority of the Mahanji. Still today the Kinga depend on the cooperation of the Mahanji within the realm of ritual, due to the key role the Mahanji played in the cult of Lwembe.

Lwembe is a mythical hero who is said to have grown up near Ukwama, the residence of the principal Kinga chief Mwemusi. When he was young, Lwembe performed miracles, therefore raising suspicion among the ruling elite. As a result, Mwemusi sent orders to persecute and kill him. Lwembe, however, managed to escape because he was protected by leopards who accompanied him on his flight until he reached safe territory on the border of the country of the Nyakyusa. After Lwembe had settled at Lubaga, the country of the Kinga was affected by a severe drought, which was attributed to his rage. Lwembe informed Mwemusi in Ukwama that if he were not placated by offerings, the drought would go on.

Lwembe resembles the archetypal hero found in many myths from all over the world. In his well-known book, Joseph Campbell demonstrates that the story usually begins with a general crisis and the hero's call (see Campbell 1973). The hero starts out and has to overcome many obstacles on his journey, but he is always aided by some supernatural assistants, as with Lwembe who had leopards as escorts. In the end, the hero undergoes a transformation into a deity. In the Livingstone Mountains the situation doubtless came to a crisis when the Kinga waged war on the autochthonous population. Most importantly, in pre-colonial times bloodshed was considered a breach of the existing cosmological order, and would invoke retribution in the form of natural disasters.

Since that time, Mwemusi would send his messengers, who were special priests instructed for this duty, to Lubaga. The offerings they bring include cattle and hoes. The latter were collected the year before from every chiefdom in the country and then placed in the sacred grove of Ukwama before being sent to Lubaga. The path to Lubaga was laid down in the myth: the Kinga priests were to follow the same route Lwembe is supposed to have taken on his flight. The priests have to gather at the place of the Mahanji chief Mwakalukwa, whose home is situated exactly on the border of the Kinga's territory and marks the starting point of the 'way of Lwembe.' According to the myth, this was the place where Lwembe rested three days, until his anger subsided. Shortly after setting out for Lubaga from Mwakalukwa's place, the priests meet the so-called keeper of the Mahanji drum who guides them through the country of the Mahanji. The drum is a symbol of the sovereignty of the Mahanji. Also, the beating of the drum is supposed to warn the people in advance of the coming of these priests. Throughout their travels to Lubaga, they are not to be met by anyone. If they do encounter someone, that person is fined heavily. The whole journey, therefore, must be understood as a coherent ritual, which is just as secretive as a ritual in a sacred grove.

Before they cross the border to Nyakyusa country, the drum has to be exchanged for a Kinga drum. From now on, the Lwembe route stipulates the visit of the homesteads of certain priests. The ancestors of these priests came from the Kinga mountains, probably as refugees like many other people who were expelled during the wars. The Kinga messengers have to pause at each of them and cannot go on until the ancestors of these priests are propitiated. The last homestead, which they are obliged to visit, is located at Lubaga itself. On their arrival, the Kinga messengers enter without even greeting the owners. For the Kinga there is no point in greeting anybody since they have arrived at the source of their country's fertility, and thus they arrived at home.

Moral Community and Identity

At Lubaga all priests assert that the Kinga come regularly every year in order to sacrifice to Lwembe. However, when the author followed the Lwembe path back to its origin and eventually had the opportunity to ask the Kinga priests themselves, he was told that the time of the journey is impossible to predict; they could not tell when they would set out for Lubaga again. At first, the author became worried about his research if even such simple matters are kept secret. It was only much later that he was informed that female spirit mediums act as the mouthpiece for Lwembe. The Kinga priests are sent to Lubaga when these mediums prophesy that misfortune will befall the country. Therefore, the priests could not answer the question, because they may not anticipate the messages of the mediums. These women are considered to be the wives of the deity, a concept, which is widespread in eastern Africa. They practice celibacy and live alone. The people listen to them. Their power is believed to be very potent and dangerous and nobody, including their relatives, will consult them without sound reasons. The author, too, was afraid that his scientific interests alone would not be enough to convince them, so he did not try to contact them either. After all, the implication of their prophecies is clear enough: they create a new spatial orientation by sending the priests to sacrifice at Lubaga. To paraphrase Humphrey and Laidlaw, the priests are committed and necessarily adopt the ritual stance during their journey, whereby the author of their acts is someone else, as in this case, the mediums (see Humphrey and Laidlaw 1994, 98). In their view, Ukwama is no longer the proper cult center, but rather Lubaga. Lwembe's mythical journey accomplished a spatial separation between the political centers and the cult center, in which the rituals for the well-being of the land are conducted. Its yearly re-enactment is a statement which does not require further interpretation: it is the medium's interpretation of the situation itself: Kinga chiefs lack legitimacy. As Janice Boddy noted: a medium "does not extricate herself from relationships with spirits and other humans, she contextualizes them and thus implicitly, herself" (Boddy 1998, 258).

Because every chiefdom contributes to the offerings, the cult of Lwembe has turned the inhabitants of the Livingstone Mountains into a moral community, while at the same time their internal divisions have remained pronounced. For example, the war between the chiefdom of Kyelelo and the Mahanji did not come to an end until a cease-fire was imposed and maintained by the Germans, who established themselves as a colonial power in this region in 1893. Ultimately, the status and the ownership of Ukwama must have been an issue in these armed struggles. Certainly, the Mahanji did not regain their former territory there, but at some stage their priests were called back to Ukwama. Absence had obviously enhanced their reputation. The return of the Mahanji priests could be read as an acknowledgment, albeit belated, that the so-called owners of the land cannot easily be removed from their ritual offices. In addition, a number of people from other Kinga chiefdoms even joined the Mahanji in fighting against Kyelelo, who, according to oral traditions, had twice tried to kill Mwemusi, the chief of Ukwama.

This is especially noteworthy, for the Kinga and the Mahanji gradually diverged into different ethnic groups, each with its own distinctive cultural features and even language. Indeed, the very ideologies on which their respective chiefdoms rest are irreconcilable. Kinga politics centered on a capital village, in which in pre-colonial times the chief had to live in seclusion at his court. He was obliged to take strong and dangerous medicines and therefore had a reputation of being magically empowered. It was assumed that a correlation exists between his healthy body and a prosperous country.[3] In this sense, a Kinga chief embodied his domain, while a Mahanji chief still only headed his people. Just as constitutional of a Kinga chiefdom is the provision of a medicine, which is kept in a particular grove as well. According to the prevailing local discourse, this medicine is gained by the capture of a divine snake, which lives in sacred pools and is usually thought of as being male. The medicine is said to convey this snake's power, a power which is inherently ambivalent, however. Within a chiefdom, it makes everything grow and prosper, but it can also cause misfortune if the medicine is not safeguarded well enough by the local priests. Once a year, and in times of trouble, sacrifices have to be made in the grove in order to appease the spirits which are evoked by it. Because the medicine is seen both as the source of afflictions and at the same time the remedy to alleviate them, the identity of the people focuses on this cult. It is important to note that although this medicine is provided by the local priests, it is said that it only works within the political order of a chiefdom which claims its own cosmological foundation. The medicine therefore underscores local autonomy, once a chiefdom is equipped with it. Provided that it is working adequately, there is no need to propitiate distant ancestors or gods either in Ukwama or in Lubaga. In this way, a new "agency by default," as Parkin once put it, is established (Parkin 1992, 12). Consequently, without the medicine the authority of a Kinga's court would be lost.

To be sure, the Kinga identity was also fostered by other more profane means. For example, all young men from the surrounding villages were obliged to spend some years at the chiefs's court in order to become loyal citizens. They grew up together and formed a standing military force, which

---

[3] For a description of the Kinga see Park 1966, 229–237. I am grateful to Prof. Park for providing me with his manuscript *Four Realms*.

could be put into action against the Mahanji but also if there was a matter of raiding another Kinga chiefdom. Likewise, hostels were built at the court for the young girls of the chiefdom. Age and gender therefore became the structuring principles of the Kinga society. In this way, new social identities have been created which cut across previous divisions. By contrast, the Mahanji retained their descent group organization. However, this certainly does not imply that they disliked change and innovation. Rather, it seems to be the case that the Mahanji deliberately selected certain social and cultural features and emphasized them in order to highlight the difference between them and the Kinga. The Mahanji's sense of identity evolved through their interaction with Kyelelo, the Kinga. Their appearance and ethnic commitment therefore must be understood as a consequence of their confrontation with Kyelelo, rather than its cause.

Dissociation and Authority

It is telling that those people, whose ancestors came either as refugees or merely as settlers from the Livingstone Mountains to the country of the Nyakyusa, at least nowadays do not distinguish at all between Kinga and Mahanji. Once they crossed the border, it seems that they were no longer entangled in the ritual and political affairs of Ukwama. This applies also to the chief of Lubaga, who acts as the living embodiment of the mythical Lwembe. The chief of Lubaga, too, claims that his chiefdom was founded by his forefathers, who were Kinga. This is exactly why other Nyakyusa are suspicious of him and his office. As already mentioned at the beginning of this paper, centralized politics emerged in the entire region, whose founders are all said to have come from the country of the Kinga. This must not be taken literally. It is more likely that the Kinga achieved fame for their smelting skills and that the prestige of their political system spread to other people, albeit not to the Nyakyusa, who are the most notable exception. In the course of interviews, the Nyakyusa never tire of emphasizing that their chiefs have local origins. Far from being considered outsiders who once established their rule, Nyakyusa chiefs are best understood as figureheads who represent their people. In addition, they possess a long history, stretching back to at least the fifteenth century. This continuity is necessarily an important facet of their political identity and the reason why the Nyakyusa have never submitted to the influence of the Kinga.

Because of his putative Kinga origin, the chief of Lubaga and his people are labelled as 'Kinga' by the Nyakyusa, although they display all common features of the Nyakyusa culture and speak the same language. Thus, the term has no cultural implications at all. The Nyakyusa refer to all politics which emerged in the course of the Ngulube migration and which adhere to its ideologies as Kinga. Lubaga was reorganized in a way suitable to the political needs of the Kinga. New offices were founded, but it appears that this was a matter of co-optation by the local people and of ideological innovations, rather than one of conquest. For example, it has been a precondition since this time, for a candidate to become a chief in Lubaga that he conducts a ritual, which had previously been the privilege of a female spirit medium. In the course of this ritual, the chief has to survive an encounter with the divine snake. By passing the test, the chief is endowed with legitimacy.

Formerly, only the Kinga were entitled to nominate a candidate for a priestly office at Lubaga. Nowadays, at least, they still have to be kept informed of a succession to office. Above all, the Kinga placed medicines at Lubaga, probably in order to strengthen the position of the chief. The Nyakyusa doubtless disapproved of the appropriation of the Lubaga cult center for political purposes. The legitimacy of their own chiefs is not related to Lubaga but rather to Kabale, which is a cult center in the north of their country.[4] When the Kinga took control of Lubaga, the Nyakyusa dissociated themselves from the cult. There is evidence that the Nyakyusa formerly adhered to an identity, which clearly extended to or perhaps even focused on the cult center of Lubaga. At that time, they called themselves Walissera (see Weber 1998, 144). However, the taking over of this cult center by a chief who declared himself to be a descendant of Ngulube entailed a reorganization of space and ultimately a change of identity. A symbol of unity became a source of division. As a result, the former Walissera became divided into different groups.

The dissociation of the Nyakyusa from Lubaga is well documented in the writings of the anthropologist Monica Wilson, who conducted research among the Nyakyusa in the 1930s, at a time when the control of rituals was still high on the political agenda. According to her, the chief of Lubaga claimed a 'mystical supremacy' over the whole country. Clearly, he was aware of the meaning which Lubaga had previously held for the Nyakyusa

---

[4] Kabale is perceived by the Nyakyusa as the oldest evidence of their culture and its founding myth serves as a social charter for them.

and consciously invoked it in order to exalt his position. However, as Monica Wilson remarked, it was often a matter of dispute "just what this mystical supremacy implied" (Wilson 1959, 19). Their reaction to the taking over of Lubaga by somebody whom they considered a 'Kinga' varied. Some Nyakyusa took one tree out of the sacred grove of Lubaga and founded their own grove with it. This act created a lasting reminder of one's roots, and a relationship was consciously maintained in this way. Other Nyakyusa tried, possibly for the first time, to install a paramount chief, whose authority would have counteracted any political ambitions of the Lubaga chief. They equipped themselves with a medicine, much like the Kinga chiefs did, but without their chief being secluded away. The Nyakyusa call this medicine the 'spear of chieftainship.' They state that they obtained the snake from the huge nearby Lake Nyasa. Thus, they constructed their identity by making use of a simple analogy: the more prominent the pool, the more powerful the snake. Other Nyakyusa, again, could not accept the fact that they all were to be ruled by a single chief. They rejected the idea of a paramount chief and preferred to choose their own chiefs instead, continuing the traditions of Kabale. They drew a clear dividing line between themselves and the new paramount chief and defined themselves collectively against him. Faced with the alternative of either accepting a paramount chief or resigning themselves to the presence of the Kinga at Lubaga, they decided to retain their relationship with Lubaga and continued to send cattle to sacrifice at Lubaga. It has been reported that they even considered themselves to be the 'sons of Lwembe,' although this description certainly had a religious connotation for them, not a political one. People imputed different meanings to the hero or emphasized certain features of the heroic narrative, corresponding to their needs.

In view of the splitting up of the Nyakyusa on account of their different interpretations of the developments which had taken place at Lubaga, one could be concerned about what was happening to their moral unity. However, as Wendy James pointed out, there is not necessarily a conjunction of morality and religion, which is too often taken for granted (see James 1988, 153). The Nyakyusa only once gathered again at Lubaga in order to conduct rituals together: this was in 1897, when they sought the blessings of all their ancestors for their uprising against the German occupation. It is worth mentioning that the chiefs were urged to do so by Nyakyusa mediums (see Wright 1972, 153–170).

Conclusions

In the foregoing, it should have become evident that the mere existence of cult centers such as Ukwama does not imply the existence of a prior, fixed concept, the meaning and significance of which can easily be imposed on the people. They only have meaning within a context. Various groups of people are likely to interpret them differently, according to their self-image and their historically derived identity. Meanings usually have to be negotiated, but these negotiations obviously failed both in the Kinga mountains and in the Nyakyusa valley. Instead, chiefdoms emerged, which, while pursuing their own political objectives, denied the existence of a more inclusive Ukwama or Lubaga order respectively. The situation in which they found themselves, however, called for medicinal sources of significance. Much like in other African regions, especially during times of social and political change, medicines have gained in importance, whereas central shrines may have declined. These medicines are designed to tap into supernatural resources, which are necessary for the development and maturation of life. As much as the transmission of these powers is normally regulated by the priests of the territorial cult centers, reverting back to medicines can only be understood within the framework of these cults.

References

Boddy, Janice. 1998: Afterword: Embodying Ethnography. In: *Bodies and Persons: Comparative Perspectives from Africa and Melanesia*, ed. Michael J. Lambek and Andrew Strathern. Cambridge: Cambridge University Press. 252–273.

Campbell, Joseph. 1973: *The Hero with a Thousand Faces*. Princeton: Princeton University Press.

Howe, Leo. 2000: Risk, Ritual, and Performance. In: *Journal of the Royal Anthropological Institute* 6:63–79.

Humphrey, Caroline and James A. Laidlaw. 1994: *The Archetypal Actions of Ritual: A Theory of Ritual Illustrated by the Jain Rite of Worship*. (Oxford Studies in Social and Cultural Anthropology). Oxford: Clarendon Press.

James, Wendy. 1988: *The Listening Ebony: Moral Knowledge, Religion, and Power among the Uduk of Sudan*. Oxford: Clarendon Press.

Kalinga, Owen J.M. 1985: *A History of the Ngonde Kingdom of Malawi*. New York and Berlin: Mouton.

Moore, Henrietta L. 1999: Gender, Symbolism and Praxis: Theoretical Approaches. In: *Those who Play with Fire: Gender, Fertility and Transformation in East and Southern Africa,* ed. Henrietta L. Moore, Todd Sanders, and Bwire Kaare. (London School of Economics Monographs on Social Anthropology 69). London and New Brunswick, N.J.: Athlone Press. 3–37.

Park, George K. 1966: Kinga Priests: The Politics of Pestilence. In: *Political Anthropology,* ed. Marc J. Swartz, Victor W. Turner, and Arthur Tuden. Chicago: Aldine. 229–237.

Parkin, David. 1992: Ritual as Spatial Direction and Bodily Division. In: *Understanding Rituals,* ed. Daniel de Coppet. (European Association of Social Anthropologists). London and New York: Routledge. 11–25.

Schoffeleers, J. Matthew. 1979: Introduction. In: *Guardians of the Land: Essays on the Central African Territorial Cults,* ed. J. Matthew Schoffeleers. Gwelo: Mambo Press. 1–46.

Tew, Mary. 1950: *Peoples of the Lake Nyasa Region.* (Ethnographic Survey of Africa. East Central Africa 1). London: Oxford University Press.

Weber, Peter. 1998: *Ritual und Identität.* (Studien zur Afrikanischen Geschichte 21). Hamburg: LIT.

Wilson, Monica. 1959: *Communal Rituals of the Nyakyusa.* London: Oxford University Press.

Wright, Marcia. 1972: Nyakyusa Cults and Politics in the Later Nineteenth Century. In: *The Historical Study of African Religion,* ed. Terence O. Ranger and Isaria N. Kimambo. London: Heinemann. 153–170.

Athens and Delos in the Fifth Century B.C.E.: Ritual in a World of Shifting Allegiances

William D. Furley

In this paper I wish to concentrate on one of the most important pan-Hellenic cult centers in ancient Greece, the one situated on the tiny Aegean island of Delos, in order to show how major political powers in the course of the sixth and fifth centuries B.C.E. tried to exert an influence over the form and conduct of ritual at the site and over the formulation and interpretation of its mythical tradition. In particular Athens will be seen to be the 'guilty party' here: it tried to annex Delos in the course of the fifth century in an overt manner. What was to be gained was clear: on the one hand domination of this major cult of Apollo gave a city-state the impression that they were getting Apollo 'on their side'; on the other, political control of a religious center was a way of demonstrating to other participants in that cult—in this case all the Ionian Greeks of the Aegean islands and coast of Asia Minor—who was pre-eminent.

There were many gods and cults on Delos, but I wish to concentrate only on the main one, that of Apollo, celebrated at the spring festival called Apollonia or alternatively Delia. In fact, like the sanctuary of Delos itself, it concentrated not solely on Apollo but on this male god embedded in what one might call his 'native constellation': together with Leto, his mother, and Artemis, his sister. These three—mother and twin children—formed what has often been termed the Apolline or Delian triad, *triade apollinienne* (see de Santerre 1958, 127–148). The cult record shows that all these divinities had temples from the eighth century B.C.E., whereby that of Artemis may well be the oldest and original center of worship, and that of Leto, the *Letoon*, was important in the late Geometric and archaic period, but declined in the course of time (see Bethe 1936, 351–362; 1937, 190–201; Bruneau 1970).

The chief event celebrated in the cult of these gods was the birth of Apollo and Artemis on Delos. It was a divine nativity which introduced two of Zeus' most important children into the world; from his island birth-place Apollo traveled to mainland Greece where he founded the Delphic oracle, his other pre-eminent cult center. Artemis resided on Delos, but her cult became one of the most widespread in Greece. The birth myth was a saga of difficulties and deprivation, which has some points in common with Jesus' nativity. Sources tell of a long and arduous period of wandering by the pregnant Leto,[1] no place wished to let her give birth on their territory as they feared the wrath of Hera, Zeus' wife but conspicuously not the mother of these babies. Leto was rejected by place after place before finally coming to the rocky and impoverished island of Delos; according to one hymnic source (*Homeric Hymn to Apollo* 66–78), it too feared to harbor the pregnant Leto, this time for a different reason: the island feared that Apollo, having seen the light of day, would kick Delos underwater for being such a humble and squalid rock. Finally, however, persuaded by the promise of the wealth which would accrue from future celebrations of the gods' birth on its soil, Delos agreed to harbor Leto's travail. Still the goddess could not give birth; the jealous Hera kept the goddess of childbirth Eileithyia from traveling to the island. Without her the birth-pains found no end. Finally Zeus intervened, sent Eileithyia to the spot and promptly, according to the earliest account, the *Homeric Hymn to Apollo*, Leto crouched down holding onto the trunk of a palm tree, the "ground smiled under her, and the god leapt forth into daylight" (118–119).

Now Herodotus, the fifth-century Ionian historian, tells an interesting story in connection with this birth (4.32–35). He explains how each year offerings are sent from the very Northernmost people of the inhabited world, the Hyperboreans, via a tortuous route which encompasses most of the northern Greek states, to Apollo on Delos for his birthday (the Apollonia). Originally, says Herodotus, these gifts had been conveyed by two Hyperborean maidens who had traveled, with an escort, to Delos; they had, however, died on delivering their missive and been buried on Delos, in a grave which the historian had clearly seen, 'behind the Artemision.' Now even before these girls had arrived from the far North and died, two other Hyperborean maidens, Herodotus adds, had arrived on the island "at the very same time as the gods themselves," that is, when Leto and Eileithyia had arrived on Delos for the delivery. They, too, had died, been buried and subsequently received tribute from young Delian men and women. Now the offerings reputedly sent by the Hyperboreans were a form of annual tribute to Apollo. Hence we have

---

[1]   The main sources are the *Homeric Hymn to Apollo* (no. 3 in the collection; seventh–sixth century B.C.E.) and Callimachus' fourth hymn *To Delos* (third century B.C.E.).

here one of those typical Greek constellations: a myth telling of an original occasion (birth of Apollo) serving to justify or explain a repeated ritual (annual offerings of the Hyperboreans to Apollo). One more link in the chain: myth also told how Apollo himself came each year *with* the Hyperboreans. The god arrived with the ceremonial tribute-bearers from the North. He spent the cold winter months—parodoxically, it might seem—in the far North with the Hyperboreans, who, however, reputedly enjoyed ideal climatic conditions the whole year round (see Pindar *Pythian* 10.22–23), and then 'arrived' in state with the Hyperborean escort in spring. The annual divine advent corresponded, or ritually re-enacted, the original advent, that is, the god's birth, at which two Hyperborean girls had been present.

An archaic *kratēr* from one of Delos' island neighbors, Melos, shows the arrival of Apollo on Delos, escorted by two Hyperborean maidens, and being greeted by his sister Artemis who stands holding an antlered stag in her right hand (Simon 1985, pl. 120; ca. 640 B.C.E.). The scene clearly depicts the central moment of the Apollonia: Apollo's arrival at Delos accompanied by gifts from the Hyperboreans. The festival celebrates his coming.

Now let us consider a description of the Ionian festival celebrating that happy event. The source is the *Homeric Hymn to Apollo*:

> Phoibos Apollo, you favor Delos most highly, where the long-robed Ionians meet with their children and modest wives. They entertain themselves by holding competitions in wrestling, dancing and song in your honor. One might think them immortal and ageless to see them assembled there for their festival. For one can observe the beauty of everything and take delight in the sight of the men and the well-dressed women, the swift ships and the abundant possessions.

Odysseus knew of this festival. When he was inventing an identity for himself in conversation with Nausikaa, he said "I once saw a beautiful young palm-tree growing by Apollo's altar in Delos. I went there accompanied by a large group" (*Odyssey* 6.162–165; see Harder 1988). Clearly Odysseus is referring to the palm-tree which Leto gripped, according to myth, while she bore Apollo, and the 'large group' Odysseus refers to is precisely one of those delegations, Greek *theōria*, which Greek city-states dispatched to take part in the Apollonia.

Leto's wanderings—a gathering of Ionians from all over the Aegean—Odysseus' pilgrimage—a semi-mythical procession of Hyperboreans from the northernmost extremity of the earth to Delos: in these accounts Delos emerges as a magnetic pole toward which errant gods and later their worshippers congregate. It was a focal point of religion, cult and cultural identity: the festival was a pan-Ionian event (Thucydides 3.104), a ritual demonstration of ethnic unity from disparate origins. This focusing, stabilizing function of Delian cult finds its most extreme expression in another aspect of the birth myth, which justifies Delos' claim to be the birthplace of Apollo. Before Leto's delivery of Apollo and Artemis on Delos, the story went, the very island of Delos itself had no fixed abode but floated over the surface of the sea, pushed by the winds and currents (Moret 1997, 25–56; Barchiesi 1994, 438–443). Pindar explains in a surviving fragment of one his hymns that at the moment when Apollo and Artemis were born, "four straight pillars grew from the seabed and held Delos firmly on their capitals" (Fragment 33d Snell-Maehler of his Hymn to Zeus for the Thebans, lines 5–10). The image is that of a temple being constructed in which pillars support the roof on capitals. Pindar's myth openly links the 'anchoring' of Delos to the birth of the divine twins and implies through this image the construction of the first temple: island and cult derive their origin from the divine birth. Before, everything was in flux, undefined and unstable; after Leto's miraculous birth, Delos finds its fixed place on the map and worship of the twins is permanently localized. It is hardly fanciful to see in this myth of the Ionian Greeks of wandering, homelessness, followed by permanence and structure a mirror image of their own wanderings from the Greek mainland in the so-called Ionian migration.[2]

When history begins to become tangible in the sixth century, we find Delos strongly under the influence of Naxos, a not so distant island.[3] The Naxians erected a colossal marble statue of Apollo there (Pfeiffer 1952), of which the unsightly base survives, and constructed the famous Lion Terrace, along which the state *theōriai* would process toward the temple.[4] In the third quarter of the sixth century, the dictator of Athens, Peisistratos, also turned—possibly highly unwelcome—attention on Delos (Herodotus 1.64). First he conquered Naxos and parceled out its land among Athenian colonists, then undertook what one might term a '*Sanierung*' of Delos. Herodotus records

---

[2]   One may compare another poem by Pindar: *Paian* 5? *For the Athenians*; the song described how Ionians from Athens had colonized the scattered Aegean islands, including "famous Delos," which Apollo gave them as their right. In Euripides' *Ion* 1581–1588, Athena proclaims that Ion's descendants will spread from Athens over the Cyclades and the 'Ionian' coast of Asia Minor.

[3]   For the historical and archaeological connections between Naxos and Delos from the archaic period, see Gruben 1997.

[4]   For a good general introduction to the topography and temples of the ancient site see Bruneau et al. 1996.

how Peisistratos dug up all the bodies of those buried within sight of the Delian sanctuary and moved them to a different part of the island. The verb used, *kathairō* (clean, purify), indicates that the presence of these graves close to Apollo's temple could be construed as a polluting influence on the purity of the god's sanctuary. When we hear later from Thucydides (1.8), however, how more than half the graves turned out to belong to non-Greek Carians, to judge by the offerings buried with the corpses and the manner of burial, one wonders whether there was not an element of 'ethnic cleansing' in this move by Peisistratos. Apollo, god of the Ionian Greeks, of whom Athens increasingly claimed leadership, should not be offended by graves of non-Ionians within sight of his temple.

After Peisistratos' demise we hear of Polykrates, the famous tyrant of Samos, making his influence felt at Delos (Parke 1946). According to Thucydides (3.104), Polykrates captured Delos and proceeded to 'chain' the little islet Rheneia to Delos in order to give Apollo the present of this rock in the sea. The gift, a demonstration of Polykrates' technical prowess in constructing this pontoon bridge, presumably aimed at inclining Apollo's heart in favor of the island dictator. The action of linking Rheneia with Delos inspired a later ritual innovation by an Athenian politician, as we shall see shortly.

In the period 490–480 B.C.E. the Greeks succeeded, largely under the leadership of Athens, in warding off two major invasions by the neighboring Persian empire. Following this a military alliance of Greek states was formed (in 478 B.C.E.), under the leadership of Athens, to prevent a recurrence of hostilities. It was called the Delian League because Delos formed a symbolic cult center uniting the Ionian Greeks under Athenian hegemony. Revenue levied from member states to pay for the military *force de frappe* was paid into Apollo's temple on Delos as the central bank. Athenian officials (*amphiktyons*) were instated to organize the cult and, no doubt, to guard the treasure.[5] The administrative structure rested on the mythical claim of an Athenian—Ion—to be the eponymous forefather of all Ionian Greeks (see the Aristotelian *Constitution of the Athenians* 41 and 55 with commentary by Rhodes 1981, and Euripides, *Ion* 1571ff.). As early as Solon's time (early sixth century B.C.E.) myth told how Ion was Apollo's son, then king of Attica, and hence father of all Ionians.

---

[5] Other officials, known as 'Hellenotamiai,' 'Treasurers of Greece,' were also appointed by Athens to collect revenue from subject states (Thuc. 1.96). See generally Roussel et al. 1987.

It is from this period that we possess a number of fragments of the texts of cult songs performed at the Apollonia festival. In particular one by the Kean poet Bacchylides (*dithyramb* no. 17) is instructive, and has been studied in this connection by van Oeveren (1999).[6] Although there is uncertainty as to whether the poem, preserved in its entirety, is a paian or a dithyramb—two types of cult song—this is a technical question, which need not concern us here. What is certain is that this poem was performed by a chorus of young *Keans* at Delos for Apollo at the Apollonia. All the more surprising, then, that it celebrates the exploits of an *Athenian* hero, Theseus, *en route* from Athens to Crete. According to myth, the Athenians had to send an annual tribute of seven male and seven female youths to the king of Crete, Minos, who fed them to the Minotaur. Theseus saved Athens from this unsavory duty when he killed the Minotaur with the help of Ariadne and sailed back to Athens triumphant. We know that the Athenians continued to celebrate this heroic deed by sending an annual *theōria* to Delos.[7] So when Bacchylides had his Kean chorus sing of Theseus' heroism on his way to Crete on that momentous occasion, we are entitled to see, with van Oeveren, a deliberate attempt by the poet to find subject matter which would please the administrators of the Delian cult in this period, Athens, and leaders of the Delian league.

It is a fine poem: Minos challenges Theseus to prove his descent from Poseidon while they are on board ship bound for Crete by recovering the gold ring which Minos proceeds to throw into the sea. Theseus promptly dives overboard and swims down to the bottom of the sea where he encounters Amphitrite who gives him a number of impressive gifts (but curiously enough not Minos' ring). Theseus surfaces beside the ship, which had sailed on in the meantime—another miracle—and Minos is suitably shamefaced. The theme of the poem seems designed to reflect the experience of those attending the Apollonia, as they too had traveled a considerable distance over water to worship at Delos.

Another poem, this time by the Theban poet Pindar written for an Athenian chorus performing at the Delian festival, appears—although things are not quite certain as the papyrus bearing the text is torn off at the crucial point—to substantiate Athens' claim to be the motherland of Ionians. Where the poem becomes readable it says "they captured Euboea and they settled

---

[6] For text and commentary see Maehler 1997; further, Maehler 1991.

[7] See Plato, *Phaido* 58a8–c5; [Aristotle] *Constitution of the Athenians*, chap. 56. See further Dina 1988

the sheep-bearing Aegean islands and they took famous Delos since Apollo of the golden hair had granted that they live on the body of Asteria" (= Delos; Paian no. 5.36–42 Snell-Maehler). The subject of this sentence can only be the Ionian Greeks expanding from Attica to Euboea, the Aegean islands and Delos.[8] Sung by an Athenian chorus at Apollo's festival there, the message is clear: "we are the founders of this cult and the forefathers of all Ionians." Cult song becomes the vehicle of religious propaganda, whereby the mood in this period among the majority of Greek states is likely to have been enthusiastically pro-Athenian. The Persian invasions had been a real trauma and Greece was grateful to Athens for the lead it had given in repelling the invaders.

However, this early mood of optimism and relief soured in the course of the fifth century as Athens turned what had begun as a defensive alliance for the mutual benefit of the Greek states into an Athenian empire existing fairly blatantly for the greater good of Athens alone. The finances of the League were transferred from Delos to Athens (454 B.C.E.); there Pallas Athena became the tutelary goddess instead of Apollo, and the member states who paid tribute to Athens became increasingly like vassals to a tyrant.[9] Thucydides says that this was the real cause of the Peloponnesian War (430–404 B.C.E.): Athens' power had become too great and the other Greek states had become increasingly resentful.

The first years of the Peloponnesian War went surprisingly badly for the Athenians, mainly because their city was afflicted repeatedly by a dreadful plague, which caused a complete breakdown of civilization as the cultivated, artistically hyper-active Athenians knew it. Apollo was the god thought responsible for plague and, sure enough, the Athenians became nervous that it was Apollo's wrath which was causing their misery (Thucydides 2.54). The measures they took to try to appease this wrath were fairly drastic. In the first place they undertook in 426–425 B.C.E. a radical purge of the graves on Delos, following up what Peisistratos had begun (Thuc. 3.104); this time all the graves on Delos were dug up and reburied in a mass grave on the little islet of Rheneia (which has, incidentally, been discovered during excavations). And a law was passed prohibiting burials and births on the whole island. One may wonder whether the local community of Delians was entirely happy with this relocation of their ancestors, and this awkward restric-

---

[8]   The ancient scholion on line 35 says "the Ionians from Athens."
[9]   Inscriptions recording the tribute paid to Athens by subject states have been famously edited by Meritt et al. 1939–1953.

tion on parturition. At the same time the Apollonia festival was re-organized by the Athenians in a manner which we will shortly examine in detail. Before that, however, it is worth following up the Athenians' purge of Delos to the bitter end. For in 422 they decided that the Delians were not 'pure enough' to serve Apollo and they banished the entire island population to a distant corner of Asia Minor, where the majority was massacred in a battle with the Persians (Thuc. 5.1). Later the Athenians repented of their harsh treatment of the Delians and reinstated the survivors on their home island (Thuc. 5.32), but the damage had been done. The story illustrates in miniature what the Peloponnesian War was about: Athens' ruthless treatment of subject states.

But the idea behind the purge of Delos was to improve relations with Apollo. Thucydides tells us that the Athenians, having cleaned up the island, reorganized the Apollonia festival, renaming it Delia, on the following lines (3.104): it was to be quadrennial instead of annual, and the musical and athletic competitions documented for the early period by the *Homeric Hymn to Apollo*, which had fallen into disuse owing to certain unspecified 'disasters,' were to be resumed with the addition of a new event, horse-racing. Thucydides quotes from the *Homeric Hymn to Apollo* in this passage to show that the early pan-Ionian festival had included musical and athletic competitions and had featured a remarkable performance of singing by a local chorus of Delian women (see Lonsdale 1995). It is likely that the Athenian politicians used this very document as justification for their reform. In it we see a perhaps not un-typical combination of overt good intentions—to restore Apollo's festival to its former glory—and the covert aim of bringing the religious service firmly under Athenian control. None could object to the goal of honoring Delian Apollo, and if the local population and the autonomy of the cult were sacrificed in the process, that was an unfortunate necessity. We can witness one Athenian politician's attempt to flatter Delian Apollo through the detailed account given by Plutarch. In his *Life of Nikias* (3.4–6) Plutarch describes how the Athenian statesman and general Nikias—a key figure in the Peloponnesian War—probably around 417 B.C.E., conducted his own private *theōria* to the Delian festival (see Furley 1995, 32–33). According to this account Nikias had a pontoon bridge constructed in Athens, which he then transported to Delos for the purpose of setting it between Rheneia and Delos as a dramatic walk-way for the chorus which he brought with him. Plutarch describes how Nikias installed the bridge *in situ*, drew up the chorus lavishly adorned with flowers and expensive dress, and then ordered them to cross the pontoon bridge in procession with the sacrificial animals for Apollo and the other gods, singing hymns to the god as they went. It must have been a fine sight. No doubt some were reminded of Polykrates' earlier 'chaining' of Rheneia to Delos, but the Samian precedent may not have been unwelcome as Samos was (at this time) a staunch ally of Athens. Once he had crossed the bridge and sacrificed to Apollo, Nikias gave the god the present he had brought: a bronze palm-tree in memory of the original palm which Leto had clutched while giving birth to Apollo and Artemis.

These two passages—Thucydides' description of the Athenians' reorganization of the Delia and Plutarch's description of Nikias' lavish display of piety—illustrate very clearly the Athenians' desire at this time to link their fate to the cult of Delian Apollo. The cult of Pythian Apollo at Delphi was largely denied them during the Peloponnesian War as it had expressed its support for the Peloponnesian side at the beginning of the war and travel overland to Delphi was difficult. Hence the Athenians' enthusiasm for and desire to dominate the cult of Delian Apollo (see Furley 1996, 79–82).

The changes and innovations they introduced can be divided into administrative and ideological: on the one hand, as we have seen, the Athenians appointed Athenian magistrates, *amphiktyones* and *hellenotamiai*, to manage the cult. On the other, in religious ceremonial, we may observe an attempt to restore the cult to an original, pristine glory, which represented the ideal of Ionian unity. No doubt the *Homeric Hymn* idealized the pan-Ionian festival on Delos; but Athens appears to have used it as blueprint for the reforms in 426; Nikias' bridging of the strait between Rheneia and Delos on the one hand harked back to Polykrates' gift of Rheneia to Apollo, and on the other to the birth myth of Apollo in that Nikias devoted a palm-tree as votive offering. Religion tends to be conservative; origins are often held to be the purest form of worship. But we may observe in the case of Athens and Delos a deliberate attempt on the part of the Athenians to manipulate Delian ceremonial to their own advantage.

I believe the case of Delos within the rapidly-changing power-structures in Greece in the fifth century illustrates clearly a number of factors which are operative in the transformation of cult and ritual. We need to ask ourselves who the celebrants are, whether they come from one community or many, and whether there are changes within the military and civic administrative structures in a given period. For cult and ritual are, to a certain extent, tools of the administrative powers, and the god or gods honored reflect the ideals of a community's leaders. A community at worship is a community on show—to itself and others. The picture it presents is that which it wants to project inward to its own members and outward to onlookers. There is no need to question the authenticity of the religious devotion displayed by worshippers; it is merely that the channels and forms that devotion takes are, to a considerable extent, the constantly changing result of at least two dominant factors: the given, that is, tradition, and the impetus for change which comes from outside cult. Athens tried to claim Delos for its own in the course of the fifth century; it emphasized its founding hero, Theseus, as founder of certain Delian cults; it claimed to be the ancestor of the Ionian peoples through direct descent from Apollo; according to one authority, it claimed that the Hyperborean Maidens had traveled from Attica as their last station in Greece before sailing to Delos (Pausanias 1.31.2); it ousted the Delians from their own sanctuary and dug up and removed the bones of their ancestors. If asked, the Athenians would have said they were merely augmenting Apollo's glory. In fact they were exploiting an international institution for nationalistic ends.

References

Primary Sources

Aristoteles: *Aristotelis Atheniensium Respublica*, ed. Frederic G. Kenyon. Oxford: Claredon Press 1951.

Bacchylides: *Die Lieder des Bakchylides*. Vol 2: *Die Dithyramben und Fragmente, Text, Übersetzung und Kommentar*, ed. Herwig Maehler. (Mnemosyne Supplementum 1.2). Leiden: Brill 1997.

Callimachus: *Callimachus*. Vol. 2: *Hymni et epigrammata*, ed. Rudolf Pfeiffer. Oxford: Claredon Press 1953.

Euripides: *Evripidis Fabulae*. Vol. 2: *Supplices, Electra, Hercules, Troades, Iphigenia in Tauris, Ion*, ed. Gilbert Murray and James Diggle. 4th ed. Oxford: Claredon Press 1992.

Herodotus: *Herodoti Historiae*, ed. Karl Hude. 2 vols. 3d ed. Oxford: Claredon Press 1957-1958.

Homer: *The Homeric Hymns*, ed. Thomas W. Allen, W.R. Halliday, and Edward E. Sikes. Oxford: Claredon Press 1936 (reprint ed. Amsterdam: Hakkert 1963).

Pindarus: *Carmina cum fragmentis*. Vol. 1: *Epinicia*, after Bruno Snell ed. Herwig Maehler. (Bibliotheca Teubneriana). Leipzig: Teubner 1971.

Pindarus: *Carmina cum fragmentis*. Vol. 2: *Fragmenta. Indices*, after Bruno Snell ed. Herwig Maehler. (Bibliotheca Teubneriana). Leipzig: Teubner 1989.

Thucydides: *Thucydidis Historiae*, ed. Henry Stuart Jones. 2 vols. 2d ed. Oxford 1942.

Secondary Sources

Barchiesi, Alessandro. 1994: Immovable Delos: *Aeneid* 3.73–98 and the Hymns of Callimachus. In: *Classical Quarterly* 44:438–443.

Bruneau, Philippe. 1970: *Recherches sur les cultes de Délos à l'époque hellénistique et à l'époque impériale*. Paris: E.de Boccard.

Bruneau, Philippe, Michèle Brunet, Alexandre Farnoux and Jean-Charles Moretti (eds.). 1996: *Délos:Ile sacrée et ville cosmopolite*. Paris: Paris-Méditerranée, CNRS Editions.

Dina, Peppas Delmousou. 1988: The Theoria of Brauron. In: *Early Greek Cult Practice: Proceedings of the Fifth International Symposion at the Swedish Institute at Athens 26th–29th June 1986*, ed. Robin Hägg, Nanno Marinatos, and Gullög C. Nordquist. Stockholm: Åström. 255–258.

Furley, William D. 1995: Praise and Persuasion in Greek Hymns. In: *Journal of Hellenic Studies* 115:29–46.

———. 1996: *Andokides and the Herms: A Study of Crisis in Fifth-Century Athenian Religion.* (Supplements to the Bulletin of the Institute of Classical Studies 65). London: Institute of Classical Studies.

Gruben, Gottfried 1997: Naxos und Delos: Studien zur archaischen Architektur der Kykladen. In: *Jahrbuch des deutschen archäologischen Instituts* 110:261–416.

Harder, Ruth E. 1988: Nausikaa und die Palme von Delos. In: *Gymnasium* 95:505–514.

Lonsdale, Steven H. 1995: Homeric Hymn to Apollo: Prototype and Paradigm of Choral Performance. In: *Arion: A Journal of Humanities and the Classics* 3:25–40.

Maehler, Herwig. 1991: Theseus' Kreuzfahrt und Bakchylides 17. In: *Museum Helveticum* 48: 114–126.

Meritt, Benjamin D., H.T. Wade-Gery, and Malcolm F. McGregor (eds.). 1949–1953: *The Athenian Tribute Lists.* Vols. 2-4. (American School of Classical Studies at Athens). Princeton.

Moret, Pierre. 1997: Planesiai, îles erratiques de l'occient grec. In: *Revue des Études Grecques* 110:25–56.

Oeveren, C.D.P. van. 1999: Bacchylides Ode 17: Theseus and the Delian League. In: *One Hundred Years of Bacchylides: Proceedings of a Colloquium at the Vrije Universiteit Amsterdam*, ed. Ilja Leonard Pfeijffer and Simon R. Slings. Amsterdam: VU University Press. 31–42.

Parke, H.W. 1946: Polycrates and Delos. In: *Classical Quarterly* 40:105–108.

Pfeiffer, Rudolf. 1952: The Image of the Delian Apollo and Apolline Ethics. In: *Journal of the Warburg and Courtauld Institute* 25:20–32.

Rhodes, Peter J. 1981: *A Commentary on the Aristotelian* Athenaion Politeia. Oxford: Clarendon Press.

Roussel, Pierre. 1987: *Délos, colonie athénienne* (1916). Réimpression augmentée de compléments bibliographiques et de concordances épigraphiques par Philippe Bruneau, Marie-Thérèse Coulloud-Ledinahet et Roland Étienne. Paris: E. de Boccard.

Santerre, Hubert Gallet de. 1958: *Délos primitive et archaïque.* Paris: E. de Boccard.

Simon, Erika. 1985: *Die Götter der Griechen.* 3d ed. Munich: Hirmer.

Considerations when Killing a Witch: Developments in Exorcistic Attitudes to Witchcraft in Mesopotamia

Tzvi Abusch

Mesopotamian ideas about witches and witchcraft underwent change over time. Many witchcraft ideas and practices originated in the popular sphere and then entered into the mainstream of urban religion and culture. There, they were re-shaped, in part by their new environment and their increasing importance. In this essay, I shall describe one aspect of this development. More precisely, I shall point to some developments in the interaction of witchcraft and general exorcism (*āšipūtu*) and shall exemplify the interaction by noticing the changing treatments of the witch. By 'changing treatments' I have in mind the different styles of ritual (that is, symbolic) killing or execution by which the witch was destroyed or eliminated, that is, the different modes of death to which she was subjected.

Introduction: Witchcraft and Exorcism

The witch originally belonged to the popular level of Mesopotamian culture, and only eventually did s/he become part of the domain of the temple exorcist. To be sure, the witch is usually regarded as an anti-social and illegitimate practitioner of destructive magic, a practitioner whose activities were motivated by malice and evil intent and who was opposed by the *āšipu*, an exorcist or incantation-priest. But, earlier, the witch had a different form, and witchcraft and *āšipūtu* belonged to different social or cultural worlds.

Several stages can be identified in the development of Mesopotamian witchcraft; the developmental scheme is similar to one discernible also in Europe. The development in Mesopotamia begins with an early stage of 'popular' witchcraft comparable to the archaic shamanistic stage of European witchcraft.[1] In this early popular form, the 'witch' probably belonged to a rural, non-urban world. S/he was not of necessity an evil being and took the form of both a 'white' and 'black' witch. Not infrequently, she helped her fellows by means of magical abilities and medical knowledge; in this popular form, she occasionally exhibited behavior otherwise associated with ecstatic types of practitioners.

For his part, the exorcist (*āšipu*) is well known as a practitioner who confronted the evil forces that threatened human well-being. He was expert at dealing with supernatural forces or beings such as demons. He was a legitimate practitioner of magic, a mainstream 'white magician' whose material reflected a belief system bound up with such major gods as Enki/Ea and Asalluḫi.

Originally, then, the witch was not primarily a doer of evil, and thus there often was no need for anyone to fight against her; in any case, the *āšipu* would not have been the main personage to play that role, for he dealt primarily with supernatural opponents (rather than with human ones). Thus, at first, the witch and her activities belonged not to the main stream of exorcism but rather to other more popular circles. But, eventually, the *āšipu* became the primary opponent of witches. In this context, we should note that whereas there is no mention of a female *āšipu* in our sources, the witch is usually represented as a female when the witch's behavior or appearance is described in any detail. Perhaps, because the witch was often a woman who possessed knowledge and power, the female witch eventually became a focus of interest and even a threat to the prerogatives of the male exorcist. This antagonism may have been a function or result of increasing centralization and stratification of state, temple, and economy. For, as part of such developments, exorcism (*āšipūtu*), especially as a healing profession, expanded its role at the expense of other cultic and healing specialties. In any case, as the *āšipu* became gender-specific, his role more institutionalized, and his *persona* more sharply defined, whatever gray or black sides he may likely have originally possessed (in principle, he was good and these negative features would have been only minor aspects) were sloughed off and projected onto a human counterpart who was made into his opposite: whereas he is a male who is good and helps other humans, she is a female who is evil and harms other humans.

At some point, then, the witch, whether real or imagined, became an important part of the urban landscape, and witchcraft became a growing concern of the exorcist. The *āšipu* now became not only the major legitimate

---

[1]   See Abusch, 1989, 31–39; 1995, 31–32, 38–39, nn. 39–44.

agent of magic but, in the nature of the case, also the primary institutional opponent of witches and witchcraft.

But by its inclusion among the activities of the exorcist, the task of combatting witchcraft became susceptible to influence from the exorcist's other functions. Actually, the influence was not one way; the very contact of beliefs about and practices against witchcraft with the exorcist's other beliefs and activities resulted in mutual interference, and transformed his approach to the various supernatural phenomena with which he was engaged as well as his approach to combatting witchcraft. One set of beliefs and practices assimilated to the other, perhaps as part of a broad set of levelling tendencies.

Thus, the inclusion of witchcraft in the exorcist's corpus both affected his general understanding of the supernatural and transformed the manner in which witchcraft was viewed and combatted. Accordingly, we occasionally observe the reshaping or elaboration of earlier, popular conceptions of the witch and witchcraft and of anti-witchcraft rituals and incantations as well as the creation of new witchcraft beliefs and new anti-witchcraft ceremonies. These changes were effected by the exorcists in line with their own understanding of the supernatural world and of their own place in the world. I would here exemplify this observation by taking up the killing of the witch, a topic which bears witness to the influence of *āšipūtu* on witchcraft beliefs.[2]

Eliminating the Witch

There are a number of ways to counteract a witch. An old form of treatment is the destruction of the witch in such a way so as to both kill her and also keep her out of the netherworld. This approach is already documented in the Old Babylonian period. Reflecting this approach to the witch is the statement in a Sumerian incantation known already from the Old Babylonian period and preserved in both uni-lingual Sumerian and bi-lingual versions.[3] Here the speaker asks that Gilgameš not integrate the witch into the netherworld, that

---

[2] Elsewhere, I have discussed examples where the influence seems to have been in the opposite direction and where witchcraft beliefs affected the *āšipu*'s understanding of the supernatural. See, for example, Abusch 1999.

[3] This incantation was first edited by Adam Falkenstein 1939, 8–41 (the incantation is edited there on pp. 12–15). It has been re-edited, with the addition of new material, first by Claus Wilcke (1973, 10–13) and more recently by Markham J. Geller (1989); see Wilcke's edition, lines 29–39 // Geller's edition, lines 30–40, and Geller's edition, lines 41'ff, there.

Nergal, lord of the netherworld, not reckon her ghost to those of the ghosts of the dead, and that Ningišida deny her water. It is significant that in contrast to ghosts, for example, Mesopotamian witches were often not consigned to the netherworld for purposes of punishment, riddance, or expulsion.

But slowly a different mode or treatment developed: witches were now occasionally sent to the netherworld. Of course, this also constitutes a form of (ritual) execution and death, but while it emphasizes the expulsion or elimination of the witch from the domain of the living, it also allows the now dead witch to take her place among the dead and to remain part of the cosmic community. In this development, the witch has been transformed into a demonic member of the divine world. In one sense, she thus becomes more dangerous; in another less, for she has been brought into and made subject to a circle of power that the exorcist knows and controls. She is now part of his world, a world wherein he has an assured place and role, and he thus gains power over her. For the exorcist can now call upon the divine forces that support order and rule supreme in his world, and can use his traditional weapons against her.[4]

Thus, in cases involving the ritual killing of the witch, we can in fact document two major types of execution: in the one, she is killed, her body destroyed, and she is thus kept out of the netherworld; in the other, she is killed, buried, and consigned to the netherworld. The former is the more original treatment, the latter a later development. It was under the influence of *āšipūtu* that the witch was sent to the netherworld. This is a major example of the formation of a new mode. Here then I shall take up instances that exemplify two ways in which this new mode was brought into being. In the first, we witness the *transformation of old* witchcraft material—the burning of the witch—into a new form—the sending of the witch to the netherworld subsequent to (or, perhaps, by means of) her burning. In the second, we witness the full-blown application of standard forms of *āšipūtu* to the task of combatting witches and the *creation of a wholly new* form of witchcraft ritual—the sending of the witch to the netherworld together with a ghost.

Transformation of the Old
Burning and Destruction. Because of its importance and primacy, we should begin our examination by first looking at the execution of the witch by burning, especially since burning is perhaps the most characteristic Mesopotamian way of punishing the witch and its elaboration exemplifies the transformation of old witchcraft material into a new form.

---

[4]   See Abusch 1989, 39ff.

Good examples of the older approach are to be found in *Maqlû*, the most important Mesopotamian anti-witchcraft text that we possess. Although *Maqlû* was probably composed in its present form during the first millennium and surely reveals many first millennium features, the modes found in the text are old, though perhaps their prominence there owes much to the Neo-Assyrian ambiance of the compilation (or, if you insist, of the final redaction) of our present text.

The several methods of killing the witch that are central to the *Maqlû* text involve the disposal of the witch's body so as to make it impossible for her to enter the netherworld. Among other treatments, the text of *Maqlû* prescribes that the witch is to be burnt. By burning the witch, she is executed, her body is destroyed, and therefore she cannot be buried. She is thus deprived of a burial and a grave and therewith of a resting place in the netherworld.

The purpose of burning is even spelled out by our texts. Thus, in response to Gilgameš's question "Did you see him who was set on fire?" in *Gilgameš, Enkidu, and the Netherworld*, Enkidu answers, "I did not see him. His smoke went up to the sky and his ghost does not live in the netherworld."[5] And this answer is similar in meaning and intent to the formulation in *Maqlû* I 140–143 // V 152–155, where alongside the burning of the statues, the witch is enjoined:

Dissolve, melt, drip ever away!
May your smoke rise ever heavenward,
May the sun extinguish your embers,
May the son of Ea (Asalluḫi), the exorcist, cut off your emanations.[6]

Thus, the witch's being rises up as smoke into the sky and is there scattered; her ghost does not enter the netherworld.[7]

The social and ideological milieu and the divine imagery of this form of treatment are nicely preserved in *Maqlû* I 73–121, the original opening incantation of *Maqlû*. This incantation centers on the judgment and burning of

---

[5] Shaffer 1963, 121: 3–4 (variant from Ur).

[6] *ḫūlā zūbā u itattukā*
quturkunu lītelli šamê
la'mīkunu liballi ᵈ*Šamši*
liprus ḫayyattakunu mār ᵈ*Ea mašmāšu*

[7] See, e.g., the discussion of I 135–143 in Abusch 1990, 19–20, 40, 53. For V 152–155, see Abusch 1990, 44–47.

the witch. In the original textual form of this incantation,[8] the plaintiff raises up statues to the sun and identifies those that he holds as representations of witches that have performed acts of witchcraft against him and have harmed him unjustly. He then appeals to Šamaš, the sun-god, to find and overwhelm these culprits, for here Šamaš, the judge, is the brilliant desert sun who punishes the criminals found wandering in the steppe, outside the bounds of the settled community. Šamaš, the illuminating and killing sun, is asked to pronounce a sentence of death by fire, and the fire-god, Girra, Šamaš's arm, is asked to execute the sentence, for Girra here is the hypostasis of the destructive heat rays of the sun and thus the executioner. This address reflects the primitive situation where a member of society who did not conform to its norms and was seen as a threat would have been expelled or forced to flee and would have been expected to die alone in the wild. (One is reminded of Hebrew *kārēt*, a form of divine punishment that must originally have referred to exclusion and expulsion.[9]) The ritual expression of this form of expulsion and exposure is most naturally that of burning. And, accordingly, the statues of the witch are set on fire.

---

[8]   For a reconstruction of the original textual form of *Maqlû* I 73-121, see Abusch 1990, 26–39. For a somewhat more detailed discussion of the incantation, see Abusch 1990, 15–17 and Abusch 1987, 143–146.

[9]   Biblical *kārēt*, excision, must originally have referred to banishment, being cut off from and expelled by one's community; it is a form of divine punishment, both because the deity is an objectification of society and its values and because without social protection, one is isolated and at the mercy of the wilderness, the non-social side of the divine, the divine in its chaotic and destructive form—and is thus brought to ruin and extinction, for one so punished is not only cut off from his human community but also dies from exposure; furthermore, in death, he does not join his family in the netherworld and is thus effectively cut off from or deprived of family in the present and the future, in this world and the next. Even though the deity is the agent of the curse, the act of banishment is a social phenomenon effected by the force or pressure of the community that ejects one of its members because he has committed an act that endangers the public. (For rabbinic and possibly biblical meanings of *kārēt*, see, e.g., Milgrom 1991, 457–460. Note also Levine 1989, 242: "It has also been suggested that at times *karet* took the form of banishment or ostracism. In the ancient Near East, especially in sparsely inhabited areas, banishment would often have resulted in death, or at least in the extinction of a family or clan as a social unit.") It is interesting to notice that *kārēt* has been regarded as "providing a sanction for acts which violate these boundaries [scil. between sacred and profane] but which are not normally provided with legal sanctions" (Frymer-Kensky 1983, 405). For anti-witchcraft rituals, which serve to destroy and/or cut off the witch from the human community, similarly, provide a sanction or outlet against a 'criminal' who cannot be apprehended and/or punished by normal legal sanctions.

The exposure and/or destruction of the corpse of a hated enemy or an executed criminal as part of a punishment is well known in Israel (e.g., 2 Samuel 21: 7ff.) and the ancient Near East and is part of the same pattern of behavior as the destruction of the body of the witch. To point up the significance of the execution and destruction of the body of the witch, I need only recall, in addition, the concern and fear of the early Christians that martyrs who were consumed by fire or devoured might not be resurrected.[10]

Expulsion and killing (especially burning) then would have been the way a culprit was treated in early periods and primitive forms of Near Eastern society, the way the 'evil' witch was treated in the popular mode before the integration of anti-witchcraft activities into *āšipūtu*, and the way *āšipūtu* treated the witch initially (when it began to deal with witchcraft).

Burning and Conveyance to the Netherworld. But as noted earlier, occasionally the witch was not (expelled and) destroyed, but rather (expelled and) sent to the netherworld. Let us begin our examination of this form of punishment by again focussing on the use of burning but now as a means of execution and conveyance to the netherworld. Examples of this use of burning occur in such compositions as (1) *LKA* 154 (+) 155 (and duplicates), a long ceremony that includes three incantations to Šamaš and a short utterance to the fire-god Girra as its oral rites[11] and (2) *AfO* 18 (1957–1958), 288–298, a ceremony that centers on the recital of a rather long and composite incantation to Šamaš accompanied by a ritual destruction by fire of representations of the witch.[12]

---

[10] On this last point, see, e.g., Lieberman 1965, 527f. (for the larger issue see pages 513–530) and, more recently, Russell 1997, 64–90, esp. 68, 79, 87.

[11] I have reconstructed this composition on the basis of *LKA* 154 (+) 155 // *LKA* 157, i, l–iv, 5' // K 3394 + 9866. (See already Abusch 1987, 72–73, n. 117, 120, n. 70; note that my joins of *LKA* 154 (+) 155 and K 3399 + 9866 are confirmed.) The composition is still somewhat fragmentary and has not yet been published in an edited form (an edition will eventually appear among my editions of Mesopotamian witchcraft texts). The composition opens with a detailed description of the patient's symptoms, a diagnosis, and a statement of the purpose of the ritual; following these, the text prescribes detailed ritual instructions and records the text of three incantations to Šamaš and a short one-line utterance to the fire-god Girra.

[12] W.G. Lambert has edited this composition in Lambert 1957–1958, 288ff. The manuscripts are listed on p. 298; for additional joins and duplicates, see Abusch 1990, 33, n. 60 (and note that von Weiher 1983, 2: no. 19, obv. 1–8 duplicates K 14734: 1'–6'). Note that Bu 91–5–9, 143 + 176 does not contain the Šamaš incantation under study, but begins with the ritual instructions for the ceremony and then provides a new ritual unit (Lambert

In these texts, the fire-god Girra is asked to burn the witches and to convey them to the netherworld; yet even a cursory examination indicates that the form of the burning theme found in these texts is not original and points up the secondary nature of sending the witch to the netherworld by means of burning.

Thus, in the third Šamaš incantation in *LKA* 154 (+) 155 (and duplicates),[13] we read:

... ᵈ*Girra qāmû liqmešunūti*
ana erṣet lā târi lišērissunūti
ana eṭem arallê līrušunūti ....[14]

... May Girra, the burner, burn them,
May he take them down to the land-of-no-return, (and)
May he lead them to the ghost of the netherworld....

And similarly in *AfO 18* (1957–1958), 293:59ff.:

ᵈ*Šamaš* ᵈ*Girra qāmû liqmišunūti* ....
ᵈ*Girra ana erṣet lā târi lišērissunūti* ...
ᵈ*Girra ana* ᵈ*Namtar sukkal erṣeti lipqissunūti*

O Šamaš, may Girra, the burner, burn them....
May Girra take them down to the land-of-no-return....
May Girra hand them over to Namtar, vizier of the netherworld.

The secondary nature of sending the witch to the netherworld by means of burning is evident immediately from the fact that in Mesopotamia asking the fire-god to burn the witch and (thereby/then) to take her, or hand her over, to

---

1957–1958, 298–299); either the Šamaš incantation is on a preceding tablet of the sequence of tablets to which Bu 91–5–9, 143 + 176 belongs or Bu 91–5–9, 143 + 176 has excerpted the ritual instructions, perhaps for performance purposes. For a discussion of some rather rare aspects of the ritual, see Abusch 1990, 44–46.

[13] The text of this incantation is preserved on *LKA* 154, rev. 7'–16', *LKA* 157, rev. iii, 12'–17', and K 3394 + 9866, rev. 23–26.

[14] *LKA* 154, rev. 11'–13': ... ᵈGIŠ.ʿBARʾ *qa-mu-u liq-me-šú-nu-*ʿ*ti*ʾ / *a-na* KUR.NU.GI₄.A *li-še-ri-is-su-nu-ti a-na* GIDIM *a-ra-le-e* / *li-ru-šú-nu-ti* .... The text of these lines as well as that of *LKA* 154, rev. 9'–16' given below are preserved only in *LKA* 154, reverse (with the possible exception of the first two broken signs in the last line of *LKA* 157, rev. iii, and of K 3394 + 9866, reverse, which might be read *ina d*[*i-* and thus correspond to *ina dīnika* of *LKA* 154, rev., 9'; *LKA* 157, rev. iii, breaks off immediately before *LKA* 154, rev. 10', as does K 3394 + 9866, reverse).

the netherworld is, in and of itself, a mixed metaphor, a conflation, as it were, of two ideas that are mutually exclusive. Note, by contrast, that in rituals intended to return troublesome ghosts to the netherworld, their representations are virtually never burnt.[15]

This conclusion regarding the secondary nature of sending the witch to the netherworld by means of burning is supported by a close examination of these texts. First of all, *LKA* 154, rev. 9'b–16', the segment of the Šamaš incantation in which the request to the fire-god to burn the witch and thereby take her to the netherworld (rev. 11'b–13'a) appears, provides typological support for our assessment that the aforementioned conjunction is a secondary construction.[16] I note that the incantation *Maqlû* II 76–102, a judgment and destruction incantation addressed to Girra, is derived typologically from the same incantation type

---

[15] For the absence of burning in these rituals, see Scurlock 1988, 56–57.

[16] *LKA* 154, rev. 9'b–16' read:

9'b .... ᵈUTU *ina di-ni-ka* GAL-*e di-na-ni-ma* UGU-*šú-nu lu-ziz*
10' [*šu*]-*nu li-mu-tu-ma ana-ku lu-ub-luṭ šu-nu* ⸢*li*⸣-*ṭap-pi-ru-ma*ᵃ *ana-ku lu-šir*
11' ⸢*šu*⸣-*nu li-iq-tu-ma ana-ku lu-um-id* ᵈGIŠ.⸢BAR⸣ *qa-mu-u liq-me-šú-nu*-⸢*ti*⸣
12' *a-na* KUR.NU.GI₄.*A li-še-ri-is-su-nu-ti a-na* GIDIM *a-ra-le-e*
13' *li-ru-šú-nu-ti um-mu mu-un-gu* ⸢*zu*⸣-*tú*ᵃ *si-li-i'-tú ši-ḫat* UZU.MEŠ
14' *pa-gar-šú-nu lil-qi ana-ku* ARAD-*ka lu-ub-luṭ lu-uš-lim-ma nar-bi-ka*
15' *lu-šá-pi* ⸢*dà*⸣-*lí-lí-ka lud-*⸢*lul*⸣ *kiš-pi-šú-nu* [*ina*] ⸢SU⸣-*šú-nu li-kil-lu*
16' ⸢ḪUL⸣-⸢*šú*⸣-*nu* EGIR-*šú-nu* ⸢*lit*⸣-*tal-lak*

Šamaš, take up my case in your great judgment so that I may be victorious over them.
May they die but I live, may they be driven away (perhaps bound, i.e., found guilty)
   but I be acquitted (lit., be/go straight),
May they come to an end but I increase. May Girra, the burner, burn them,
May he take them down to the land-of-no-return, (and) may he lead them to the ghost
   of the Netherworld.
May fever, stiffness (?), debility (text: sweat), sickness, (and) wasting away
Consume their bodies. May I, your servant, live and be well so that
I may declare your greatness and praise your heroic deeds. May their witchcraft take
   hold in their bodies.
May their evil constantly pursue them.

Line 10ᵃ: For the reading ⸢*li*⸣-*ṭap-pi-ru-ma*, see my comment to *Maqlû* II 94, below.
Line 13ᵃ: ⸢*zu*⸣-*tú* has been emended by *CAD*, vol. Z, 169 (s. *zu'tu*) to *lu!-tú*; see vol. L, 257 (s. *lu'tu*). The emendation seems reasonable, but if it turns out to be wrong, then read ⸢*zu*⸣-*tú :zu'tu*. The sequence of illnesses in line 13' repeats an identical sequence found in the first Šamaš prayer of our composition: see *LKA* 155, obv. 17'–18' // *LKA* 157, obv. ii, 4'–5'.

found here in *LKA* 154 (+) 155; more specifically, lines 89–102[17] of the *Maqlû* incantation are similar to the aforementioned *LKA* 154 (+) 155 segment.[18] Yet,

[17]   *Maqlû* II 89–102 (Meier's line count) read:

ᵈ*Girra šurbû ilu ellu*
enenna ina maḫar ilūtika rabīti
2 *ṣalmī kaššāpi u kaššapti ša siparri ēpuš qātukka*
maḫarka uggiršunūtima kâša apqidka
šunu limūtūma anāku lubluṭ
*šunu liṭṭappirūma*ᵃ *anāku lūšir*
šunu liqtûma anāku lumīd
šunu līnišūma anāku ludnin
ᵈ*Girra šarḫu ṣīru ša ilī*
kāšid lemni u ayyābi kušussunūtima anāku lā aḫḫabbil
anāku aradka lubluṭ lušlimma maḫarka luzziz
attāma ilī attāma bēlī
attāma dayyānī attāma rēṣu'a
attāma mutirru ša gimilliya TU₆ ÉN

O most great Girra, pure god,
Now in the presence of your great godhead
Two images of the warlock and witch (made) of bronze I have fashioned by your
          power/authority (?).
In your presence I have crossed them and given them over to you yourself.
May they die but I live,
May they be driven away (or perhaps bound) but I be acquitted (lit., be/go straight),
May they come to an end but I increase,
May they weaken but I become strong.
O stately Girra, eminent one of the gods,
Conqueror of the wicked and the enemy, overwhelm them so I not be wronged.
May I, your servant, live and be well so that I may serve you (lit., stand before you).
You alone are my god, you alone are my lord,
You alone are my judge, you alone are my aid,
You alone are my avenger!

Line 94ᵃ: Both here and in *LKA* 154, rev. 10', I have followed, for the time being, *AHw*, 1380, s. *ṭapāru*, Dt. But given the occurence of *kasû* and *egēru* (N) as the contrast to *ešēru* in two other occurrences of this topos—Laessøe 1955, 40: 45 (as corrected by Lambert 1957, 229) and Lambert 1957–1958, 294: 79—I would have preferred a reading which could yield the meaning 'bound' or the like (e.g., a form of *ubburu*, especially apt because it means both bound and accused)—see Lambert's translation of the occurrence in *LKA* 154, rev. 10' as "may they be caught" (Lambert 1957, 229) and *CAD*'s translation of the occurrence in *Maqlû* II 94 as "let them be slandered and let me become acquited" (vol. E, 355a). But if a meaning 'be driven away' is finally required, the verb should then be construed as a form of *dapāru* and read here as *liddappirūma* rather than *liṭṭappirūma* in light in spite of the similarity of the two passages, the *Maqlû* passage, in contrast to *LKA* 154 (+) 155, makes no mention whatsoever of the netherworld when Girra is asked to destroy the witch by burning her.[19] It thus appears that while the *Maqlû* passage preserves a more original formulation of the type, that form has been further developed in *LKA* 154 (+) 155 by the introduction of the request that the fire-god convey the witch to the netherworld.

This impression of secondary development is also supported by *AfO* 18 (1957–1958), 288ff. Unlike *LKA* 154 (+) 155 (and duplicates), that text is well preserved, and perhaps for that reason, it is readily apparent that the lines in which Girra is asked to convey the witch to the netherworld (63–65) are situated in a segment of the incantation (54–65) that may be deemed secondary on the basis of both structural and thematic considerations. Lines 51b–79 read:[20]

51   [...] *dayyān* [*a*]*ttā*
52   *bēl kittu u mīšari muštēšir* ^d[*Igigī*] *attāma*
53   *dayyān* ^d*anunnaki* [*mušt*]*ālu*
54   ^d*Šamaš ša kaššāpiya u kaššaptiya*

---

of William L. Moran's study (1981, 44–47) and conclusion that *ṭuppuru* does not exist in the meaning 'to drive away,' but that there is "only one verb, *duppuru*, transitive and intransitive" (Moran 1981, 47) in the meanings 'to drive away' and 'to go away.'

[18]   For specific examples, compare *LKA* 154, rev. 10'–11'a with *Maqlû* II 93–96 (the 'may she die, but I live, etc.' theme); note also that *narbîka lušāpi dalīlīka ludlul* of *LKA* 154, rev. 14'–15' is the equivalent of *Maqlû* II 100–102 (I shall elaborate upon this latter point elsewhere).

[19]   Further support for my interpretation of the conjunction of burning and conveyance to the netherworld as a secondary construction may be provided by the ritual itself. Note that immediately following the text of the third Šamaš incantation, the text first prescribes its three fold recitation, the burning of the representations of the witches, and the pronouncement of a short utterance to the fire-god asking him to burn them (*LKA* 154, rev. 17'–18': III-*š*[*ú* Š]ID-*tú an-ni-tú* ŠID-*ma* A.ÉSIR ŠE₆ SUD-*šú-nu-ti ina* GI.IZI.LÁ *ta-qàl-lu-šú-nu-te* / ^dBIL.GI *qu-mu-šú-nu-ti* ^dBIL.GI *qu*-⌈*lu-šú*⌉-[*nu*]-⌈*ti*⌉ III-*šú an-na-a* DUG₄.GA-*ma*; "You recite this incantation three times, and then you sprinkle them with hot bitumen and set fire to them with a torch. 'Girra burn them, Girra scorch them,' you say this three times."), and then apparently (given the broken state of the text here, our interpretation is perforce tentative) gives instructions to bury the representation (*LKA* 154, rev. 20'–21': NU IM *ina* É *te-qé-bir* ... [... *ana ereb* ^d]UTU PÚ BAD-*te-ma* / *te-qé-bir* ...; "You bury a statue of clay ... at sunset you dig a well and bury...."). Thus both the third Šamaš incantation and the ritual reflect the conjunction of burning and burial. But it does seem that the basic or central ritual here is burning on to which has been grafted or added a burial.

[20]   Lambert's edition is invaluable. I have, of course, made use of Lambert's translation in preparing my own.

55   *ēpišiya u muštēpištiya rāḫī[ya u rā]ḫītiya*
56   *kišpīšunu ruḫêšunu rusêšunu lēmnūti lā ṭābūti*
57   *libbalkit(ū)šunūti ana muḫḫišunu u lānišunu lil[l]ikū*
58   ^{d}*Šamaš* ^{d}*Girra tappûka lītallil idā[y]a*
59   ^{d}*Šamaš* ^{d}*Girra qāmû liqmišunūti* ^{d}*Girra likkilmešunūti*
60   ^{d}*Girra lišrupšunūti* ^{d}*Girra lišḫarmissunūti* ^{d}*Girra li[ṣ]arripšu[nūt]i*
61   ^{d}*Girra likabbibšunūti* ^{d}*Girra aggiš elišu[nu x x] x^{21}*
62   ^{d}*Girra napištašunu kīma mê lit[bu]k*
63   ^{d}*Girra ana erṣet lā târi lišēriss[unūt]i*
64   ^{d}*Girra munammir ukli ekleti pānīšu[nu ...] x*
65   ^{d}*Girra ana* ^{d}*Namtar sukkal erṣeti lipqi[ssunūt]i*
66   ^{d}*Šamaš ša kišpī ruḫê rusê upšāšê lemn[ūti...]*
67   *ilu šarru kabtu u rubû nekelmû[ᵓ inn]i*
68   *itti ili u* ^{d}*ištari uzennûᵓinni ulammenûᵓinni*
69   *ina bīti ṣaltu ina sūqi puḫpuḫḫû iškunūnimma*
70   *ilūtka rabīti īdu/û*^{22} *ilu ayyumma lā īdu/û*
71   *attāma tīdu/û anāku lā īdu/û:*
      ^{d}*Šamaš ša kaššāpiya u kaššaptiya*
72   *ēpišiya u muštēpištiya rāḫīya u rāḫītiya*
73   *kišpīšunu ina šaplānika kīma gišparri libbalkit(ū)[šunūti]*
74   *šâšunu libārūšunūti* ^{d}*Šamaš ūmka ezzu likšu[ssunūti]*
75   *kīma diqāri ḫubussunūti kīma tinūri qutur(ū)šunu līrimū [šamê]*
76   *liḫīlū lizūbū littattu[kū]*
77   *[n]apištašunu kīma mê nādi liq[tî]*
78   *šunu limūtūma anāku lubluṭ šunu līnišūma anāku lu[dnin]*
79   *šunu liktasûma anāku lūšir šunu liṣṣabtūma anāku lu-[xx]*

51   [...] the judge are you.
52   Lord of truth and equity, organizer of the Igigi are you alone.
53   Deliberate judge of the Anunnaki,
54   Šamaš, regarding my warlock and my witch,
55   My sorcerer and my sorceress, my male poisoner and female poisoner,[23]
56   May their witchcraft, poisons, and charms that are not good, but rather evil,
57   Turn upon them and attack their heads and their faces.
58   O Šamaš, may Girra your companion be bound to my side.
59   O Šamaš, may Girra, the burner, burn them, may Girra glare at them,
60   May Girra scorch them, may Girra melt them, may Girra fire them,
61   May Girra char them, may Girra (shout?) angrily at them,
62   May Girra pour out their life-force like water,

[21] Perhaps the verb *šašû* should be restored here.
[22] *īdû* and *tīdû* are included in my transcription along side *īdu* and *tīdu* in lines 70–71 on the off chance that the verb is in the subjunctive and governed perhaps by *ša kišpī* etc. of line 66; see Abusch 1990, 35.
[23] Originally, the poisoner (here and in line 72) was also or only the giver of drugs; see Abusch 2002.

63 May Girra take them down to the land-of-no-return,
64 May Girra who lights up the darkness and gloom ... the(ir?) face.[24]
65 May Girra hand them over to Namtar, vizier of the Netherworld.
66 Šamaš, those who have (performed) witchcraft, poisoning, charms, and evil
      machinations
67 (so that) god, king, noble, and prince glower at me;
68 They have caused god and goddess to be angry with me and to regard me as bad.[25]
69 They have caused me to be beset with strife at home and conflict in public places,
70 Your great godhead knows but no other god knows,
71 You alone know but (?) I do not know. Šamaš, regarding my warlock and my witch,
72 My sorcerer and my sorceress, my male poisoner and female poisoner,
73 May their witchcraft clamp down upon them like the trap that is beneath you
74 And capture them. Šamaš, may your fiery red light overwhelm them.
75 Smash them like a pot and like a furnace may their smoke cover the heavens,
76 May they dissolve, melt, drip ever away,
77 May their life-force come to an end like water from a water skin,
78 May they die but I live, may they weaken but I become strong,
79 May they be bound but I be acquitted (lit., be/go straight), may they be seized but I
      [...].

Structurally, we notice that the aforementioned segment—lines 54–65—parallels lines 71bff. (When not citing the text by line numbers, I will refer to lines 54–65 as the first section and to lines 71bff. as the second one.): Lines 54–57 and 71b–74a are in large measure identical; in any case, they are parallel and effectively say the same thing (may Šamaš overwhelm the witches). Lines 58–65 // 74b–77 continue along the same sort of parallel path. Thus while line 58 explicitly introduces Girra as the companion of Šamaš, the sun, line 74b also introduces him in the same role by referring to him in his natural form *ūmu ezzu*, "brilliant red light," and placing him in relationship to Šamaš (*ūmka* your [=Šamaš] *ūmu*),[26] as well; moreover, both lines 58 and 74b are then followed in lines 59–65 and 75–77, respectively, by an enu-

---

[24] A verb describing an act that took place prior to handing the witches over to Namtar should probably be restored here. Lambert 1957–1958, 293: 64 and *CAD* N/1, 214 treat the line as if there were no finite verb in the break.

[25] According to Lambert 1957–1958, 293, note to line 68, variant texts have *usaḫḫirū k[i-šad-sun]* as either an alternative reading or an addition to *ulammenū'inni*. This restoration is probably wrong, for although one might think that *kišāda suḫḫuru* should mean 'to turn away,' it apparently means 'to turn back (towards)' (so *CAD* s. *kišādu* and *saḫāru*; according to von Soden 1971, 70 ad 188.190, "*kišāda(m) suḫḫuru(m)* 'den Hals umwenden' steht m. W. immer in Sinn des freundlichen Sich-Zuwendens.") The variant reading in our text must have a negative meaning, and therefore a different restoration is required.

[26] For *ūmka ezzu*, see Abusch 1990, 16, 31.

meration of the acts of destruction that the fire is asked to commit. The parallelism of the burning theme extends thus from 58–65 // 74b–77—note, moreover, *napištašunu kīma mê* in lines 62 and 77 and thus the verbal similarity of these lines. Thus, one or the other of these two sections is redundant and superfluous.

When we examine the text from a thematic point of view, we notice some discordance or incongruity between the two sections. For while the first section asks Girra to burn her and convey her to the netherworld, the second section (specifically, lines 74ff.) would have him burn the witch and thereby transform her, destroy her identity, and bring her to a complete end. Lines 75b–76 provide a powerful expression of this kind of destruction, for they exemplify the theme of destruction of the witch by turning her into smoke. They explicitly contradict the request in the first section that Girra convey the witch to the netherworld and provide a particularly good example of the kind of discordance that exists between the sections.

The redundance and discordance that we have observed indicate that the two sections of the text are not of a piece. Which is the earlier and which the later?

It is particularly significant that while the first section contains the theme of burning and conveyance of the witch to the netherworld, the second section articulates in lines 74–77 some of the destructive themes previously encountered in *Maqlû* I 73–121. Most notable in this regard is the fact that the latter part of the incantation expresses in lines 75b–76 the very same theme and even uses the same words as *Maqlû* I 140–143 and its parallel V 152–155, lines that we quoted earlier to exemplify the early form of destruction of the witch:

> *qutur(ū)šunu līrimū šamê liḫūlū lizūbū littattukū.*
> May their smoke cover the heaven, May they dissolve, melt, drip ever away!

This certainly suggests that the second section (lines 71bff.) represents an earlier stage of conceptual development.

When, then, we take account of the several textual features and related issues that we have noticed in our examination of *AfO* 18 (1957–1958), 293–294:51b–79, especially of the incongruity or discordance between the sections, it becomes difficult to regard the request in the first section that Girra convey the witch to the netherworld as anything but secondary and to come to any conclusion other than that the first section with its request that Girra convey the witch to the netherworld is a later development.

Given the similarities, moreover, between the latter part of the incantation and *Maqlû* II 76–103 / *LKA* 154 (+) 155 (and duplicates),[27] the fact that the second section (lines 71bff.) emphasizes burning but does not contain the very theme that characterized *LKA* 154 (+) 155 (and duplicates) as a later stage of development than the *Maqlû* incantation (but the first section does contain it) suggests that the relationship between the two sections of *AfO* 18 (1957–1958), 293–294:51b–79 is not unlike that between *Maqlû* II 76–103 and *LKA* 154 (+) 155 (and duplicates), and thus supports the primacy of the second section over the first.

Other considerations and textual details support our claim. The composite nature of this incantation finds support also in the generally repetitive nature of the incantation as a whole and in the fact that its complex ritual contains a repetitive second burning, which in itself is a secondary development within the ritual.[28] Moreover, there are additional special points of contact between *LKA* 154 (+) 155 (and duplicates) and *AfO* 18 (1957–1958), 288ff., thus providing some further support to the observation that these texts manifest a certain common tendency or type of reworking and development. Among these points of contact, note particularly the text of the rubric of the Šamaš incantation in *AfO* 18 (1957–1958), 288ff. and of the first Šamaš incantation in *LKA* 154 (+) 155 (and duplicates); this form of rubric is quite rare.[29]

Let us now sum up this part of our analysis. We have observed thus far that where conveyance to the netherworld is mixed with burning, a new mode—conveying the witch to the netherworld—is built or superimposed upon an older one—burning the witch. It suffices to note that were the theme of conveyance to the netherworld not a secondary imposition here, we would expect to find, for example, not Girra, but another more appropriate god functioning as conveyer.

Thus sending the witch to the netherworld is not the usual or original treatment and is a new form that emerged as a consequence of the incorporation of anti-witchcraft responsibilities into the duties of the exorcist.

---

[27] Compare, e.g., *AfO* 18 (1957–1958), 294: 78–79 with *Maqlû* II 93–96 and *LKA* 154, rev. 10'–11'a.

[28] For this double burning and its secondary nature, see Abusch 1990, 44–46.

[29] For these rubrics, see Abusch 1987, 120, n. 70.

Creation of New Forms

Expelling the Witch to the Netherworld. Thus far, we have seen two examples of the reshaping of an older more original form of anti-witchcraft ritual.
But also new forms for combatting witchcraft were created, and it is not unexpected that some of the finest examples of the witch being sent to the netherworld make use of ritual structures and materials that were originally
unrelated to witches and witchcraft but derive instead from rituals that dealt
with ghosts and demonic personifications of evil, usually entailing their exorcism and relegation to the netherworld.

An excellent example of this sort of development is provided by the well
known ritual *KAR* 227 and duplicates (// *LKA* 89 + 90 // K 9860 + K 13272 +
K 13796 // K 6793 + Sm 41 + Sm 617 + Sm 717 + Sm 1371 + Sm 1877 //
Sm 38 // Si 747 // BM 98638).[30] The text records the instructions of a complex ceremonial ritual together with the wording of the incantations that were
recited.[31] This ritual contains a number of anomalies; thus our comments will
also serve to explain some of the difficulties in this ritual.

This ritual makes use of the ghost festival at the end of the month of Abu,
a time when ghosts ascend to the world of the living alongside such netherworld deities as Gilgameš and the Anunnaki and then return to the netherworld. Its goal is to free the patient of witches and of the evil (*mimma
lemnu*) that the witches had presumably brought upon the patient. This riddance is accomplished by having the witches and the evil conveyed to the
netherworld by means of an *eṭem lā mammanama*, an unidentified ghost that
had previously not received the rites of the dead but who is now given these
rites and instructed to take the evils with him to the netherworld. To accomplish this end, a series of incantations are recited, and offerings presented, to
Šamaš, Gilgameš, the Anunnaki, the ghosts of the family, and a skull representing the dead man (= *eṭem lā mammanama*); this last incantation ends in a
series of adjurations by various gods; here follows an exorcistic address to
the evils themselves followed by their adjuration by the great gods. In these
addresses, the approval and support of Šamaš, Gilgameš, the Anunnaki and

---

[30] I am preparing a new edition of this text. For the time being, see Ebeling 1931, 125ff. and
      Abusch 1986, 150–151, nn. 13–14. Henceforth, I will refer to this text simply as *KAR* 227.
[31] More specifically, a dead person (=? *eṭem lā mammanama*) is clothed and outfitted; the
      river is given a payment of money for the use of its clay and asked to take something away
      (the identity of which I have not yet ascertained; there are various possibilities—two of
      which are: the wandering ghost, perhaps together with the several statues of the witch and
      mimma lemnu; a substitute for the sick person); clay is pinched off and statues of
      ᵈNam.tar, *mimma lemnu,* and male and female witches are made and outfitted; various in-
      cantations are recited and offerings presented (see below).

the family ghosts are secured; the ghost in the form of a skull is accorded the rites of the dead and adjured to carry off the witches and *mimma lemnu* to the netherworld; finally, the witches and the evil are themselves adjured to depart.[32]

For our present purposes, it is significant that close genetic parallels to the incantations here addressed to the Anunnaki, the gods of the netherworld, and to the family ghosts show up in another ritual, K 2001 + and duplicates.[33] This latter ritual shows marked similarities to *KAR* 227 but has as its purpose not the elimination of witchcraft but the healing of a sick man by sending off to the netherworld the evil spirits and ghosts that plague him. This ritual, too, makes use of a ceremonial occasion, for it is set in the period of mourning for the god Tammuz at the end of the month of that same name and takes advantage of the presence of the god on earth. In K 2001 +, the evils are taken down to the netherworld by the family ghosts and Tammuz, who here performs the same function as the unidentified ghost of *KAR* 227.

Still we must wonder why the ritual architects and composers have used almost identical materials in the two ceremonies. Here, then, by way of answer, I note the increasing similarity between incantations and rituals directed against witches and those addressed to specters and demonic evils, and observe, on a cosmological level, the changing conception of the netherworld (as a place not only for ghosts but also for forces of evil) and the growing relationship of witches and ghosts. The materials are original to the exorcism of ghosts and demons, and only carried over secondarily to witches. Hence, the conjunction, on occasion, of concepts and genres which originally were independent.[34] Undoubtedly, the *Vorlage* of *KAR* 227 was reworked and applied to the witch—this adaptation would also explain the occasional ap-

---

[32] Nowhere in the preserved sections of the ritual instructions are there explicit instructions regarding what was to be done with the witches and the evil in order to transfer them to the netherworld. Is it possible that these instructions are given or assumed in the opening ritual instructions, especially the part dealing with the river?

[33] The close relationship between these incantations was already noted by Ebeling and von Soden in the early 1930s; see now Farber 1977, 101–206 for an important treatment and edition of K 2001 +, its duplicates and versions (*Tafel* IIa/b); Farber discusses the literary connections between the incantations on pages 116–118.

[34] The phenomenon of contact and influence between ideas and materials concerning witchcraft and those related to other forms of evil is not limited to ghosts; it is observable elsewhere (e.g., in the realm of omens: note the relationship of *namburbi* and *zikurrudâ* materials [a topic to which I shall return elsewhere]).

parent confusion between *kaššāpu/kaššaptu* ('warlock'/'witch') and *mimma lemnu* near the end of the text (e.g., Ebeling 1931, 133: 64–65).

In the present context, moreover, I would ascribe particular significance to the fact that also the Tammuz ritual seems to represent a secondary development. Making use, in part, of an analytic model that I had created in my dissertation in the study of the Marduk witchcraft rituals *KAR* 26 and *BMS* 12,[35] Walter Farber has argued convincingly that in the Tammuz ritual, too, the original goal of the ritual had been changed from that of eliminating a demonic form of illness by casting it out to that of sending a ghost back to the netherworld.[36] The illness was seen as having been caused by a ghost rather than a demon, and the ritual material then adapted to the notion of ridding oneself of ghosts by linking these evils/ghosts up with gods and family ghosts who were to return to the netherworld and then sending the evils/ghosts off together with the latter.

We are witness in both texts to an identification of demons and witches with ghosts and a change of their treatment: (1) the earlier killing of witches and destruction of their bodies and (2) the expulsion of demons to the steppe, are both now transformed into the relegation to and imprisonment in the netherworld of the newly conceived spectral form of both witch and demon.

Thus, the transformation and new treatment of the witch would seem to be part of a general tendency involving the incorporation and assimilation of diverse materials into the corpus of the *āšipu*.

Conclusion

By way of conclusion we note that as regards killing a witch, we have here traced three actually attested stages: (1) burning and destruction; (2) burning and sending to the netherworld; and (3) the use of other kinds of rituals as the means and framework for conveying the witch to the netherworld. Overall, we have suggested that the sending of the witch to the netherworld is one further consequence and indication of the incorporation of anti-witchcraft responsibilities into the duties of the exorcist. At the very least, it reflects the assimilation of anti-witchcraft materials to the other materials of his craft. Concern with witchcraft begins to affect the exorcist's work and to enter into texts originally unconcerned with combatting witchcraft (e.g., *namburbi,*

---

[35] See Abusch 1972, 55–82 and 102–125 (later published as Abusch 1987, 45–75).

[36] See Farber 1977, 102, 110, and 118–121. This point has been ignored by Scurlock 1988 in her later discussions of the text in her dissertation.

anger of gods); but at the same time, the witchcraft materials themselves are re-shaped by and assimilated to the exorcist's standard treatments of and attitudes toward demons, ghosts, and other non-human supernatural powers. These developments are not so very different from changes observable in early modern Europe, where the involvement of the church with witchcraft led to the imposition of the church's attitudes and institutions upon an earlier understanding of and mode of dealing with 'witches' and to a reshaping of the approach to 'witches.'

References

Abbreviations are those of *The Assyrian Dictionary of the University of Chicago*. 1956–. Chicago and Glückstadt.

Abusch, Tzvi. 1972: Studies in the History and Interpretation of some Akkadian Incantations and Prayers against Witchcraft. Ph.D. diss., Harvard University. [Later published as *Babylonian Witchcraft Literature*].
———. 1986: Ishtar's Proposal and Gilgamesh's Refusal: An Interpretation of the Gilgamesh Epic, Tablet 6, Lines 1–79. In: *History of Religions* 26:143–187.
———. 1987: *Babylonian Witchcraft Literature: Case Studies*. (Brown Judaic Studies 132). Atlanta, Ga.: Scholar Press.
———. 1989: The Demonic Image of the Witch in Standard Babylonian Literature: The Re-working of Popular Conceptions by Learned Exorcists. In: *Religion, Science, and Magic: In Concert and in Conflict*, ed. Jacob Neusner, Ernest S. Frerichs, and Paul V. McCracken Flesher. New York and Oxford: Oxford University Press. 27–58.
———. 1990: An Early Form of the Witchcraft Ritual *Maqlû* and the Origin of a Babylonian Magical Ceremony. In: *Lingering over Words: Studies in Ancient Near Eastern Literature in Honor of William L. Moran*, ed. Tzvi Abusch, John Huehnergard, and Piotr Steinkeller. (Harvard Semitic Studies 37). Atlanta, Ga.: Scholar Press. 1–57.
———. 1995: Ascent to the Stars in Mesopotamian Ritual: Social Metaphor and Religious Experience. In: *Death, Ecstasy and Other-Wordly Journeys*, ed. John J. Collins and Michael Fishbone. Albany, N.Y.: State University of New York. 15–39.
———. 1999: Witchcraft and the Anger of the Personal God. In: *Mesopotamian Magic: Textual, Historical and Interpretative Perspectives*, ed. Tzvi Abusch and Karel van der Toorn. (Ancient Magic and Divination 1). Groningen: Styx. 83–121.
———. 2002: Witchcraft, Impotence, and Indigestion. In: *Mesopotamian Witchcraft: Towards a History and Understanding of Babylonian Witchcraft Beliefs and Literature*. (Ancient Magic and Divination 5). Leiden and Groningen: Brill, Styx. 79–88.
Ebeling, Erich. 1931: *Tod und Leben nach den Vorstellungen der Babylonier*. Berlin and Leipzig: Walter de Gruyter & Co.
Falkenstein, Adam. 1939: Sumerische Beschwörungen aus Bogazköy. In: *Zeitschrift für Assyriologie* 45:8–41.

Farber, Walter. 1977: *Beschwörungsrituale an Ištar und Dumuzi – Attī Ištar ša ūharmaša Dumuzi.* (Veröffentlichungen der Orientalischen Kommission 30). Wiesbaden: Steiner.

Frymer-Kensky, Tikva. 1983: Pollution, Purification, and Purgation in Biblical Israel. In: *The Word of the Lord Shall Go Forth: Essays in Honor of David Noel Freedman*, ed. Carol L. Meyers and Michael O'Conner. (American School of Oriental Research 1). Winona Lake, Ind.: Eisenbrauns. 399–414.

Geller, Markham J. 1989: A New Piece of Witchcraft. In: *DUMU-E₂-DUB-BA-A: Studies in Honor of Åke W. Sjöberg*, ed. Hermann Behrens, Darlene Loding, and Martha T. Roth. (Occasional Publications of the Samuel Noah Kramer Fund 9). Philadelphia: University Museum. 193–205.

Laessøe, Jørgen. 1955: *Studies on the Assyrian Ritual and Series bît rimki.* Copenhagen: Munksgaard.

Lambert, Wilfred G. 1957: Review of Laessøe, *bît rimki.* In: *Bibliotheca Orientalis* 14:227–230.

———. 1957–1958: An Incantation of the *Maqlû* Type. In: *Archiv für Orientforschung* 18: 288–298.

Levine, Baruch A. 1989: *The JPS Torah Commentary: Leviticus.* Philadelphia: The Jewish Publication Society.

Lieberman, Saul. 1965: Some Aspects of After Life in Early Rabbinic Literature. In: *Harry Austryn Wolfson Jubilee Volume: On the Occasion of his Seventy-fifth Birthday.* Vol. 2. Jerusalem: American Academy for Jewish Research. 513–530.

Milgrom, Jacob. 1991: *Leviticus 1–16.* (Anchor Bible 3). New York: Doubleday.

Moran, William L. 1981: *duppuru (dubburu) – ṭuppuru*, too? In: *Journal of Cuneiform Studies* 33:44–47.

Russell, Jeffrey Burton. 1997: *A History of Heaven: The Singing Silence.* Princeton: Princeton University Press.

Scurlock, Jo Ann. 1988: Magical Means of Dealing with Ghosts in Ancient Mesopotamia. Ph.D. diss., University of Chicago.

Shaffer, Aaron. 1963: *Sumerian Sources of Tablet XII of the Epic of Gilgames.* Ann Arbor, Mich.: University Microfims International.

Soden, Wolfram von. 1971: Der grosse Hymnus an Nabû. In: *Zeitschrift für Assyriologie* 61: 44–71.

Weiher, Egbert von. 1983: *Späbabylonische Texte aus Uruk. Teil II.* (Ausgrabungen der deutschen Forschungsgemeinschaft in Uruk-Warka 10). Berlin: Gebr. Mann Verlag.

Wilcke, Claus. 1973: Sumerische literarische Texte in Manchester und Liverpool. In: *Archiv für Orientforschung* 24:1–17.

Ritual between Tradition and Change: The Paradigm Shift of the Second Vatican Council's Liturgical Reform[*]

Andreas Odenthal

Liturgical Reforms in the History of the Catholic Church

A consideration of the liturgical history of the Roman branch of tradition shows that in the Catholic Church ritual has undergone change time after time, and will continue to change. We can distinguish two epochal church-wide changes in Roman liturgy after the emergence of the classical liturgy of the patristic period (and its change to Latin as the cult language): the Frankish liturgical reform before the turn of the first millennium and the liturgical reform in the wake of the Council of Trent. Further 'liturgical reforms' are to be mentioned here, namely the changes under Pius X which concerned the hours liturgy of the clergy and the communion piety of the faithful who were now to participate regularly in the eucharistic meal once again. Finally, Pius XII reorganized Holy Week and by shifting the Easter celebration from Saturday morning into the actual Easter night gave the most important liturgical celebration in the church year a firm place in the life of the parish.

Inquiring into the interests and objectives behind these liturgical reforms will help us to define the following axioms. The Frankish liturgical reform was sustained by the objective of uniting the Kingdom of the Franks in respect of liturgy, and thus of integrating worship into the grand design of *renovatio imperii romanorum*, which is why they obtained Roman liturgical books for the land of the Franks and attempted to base their worship on this model. The Council of Trent held up the example of the church fathers. Seeing that the Reformers were attacking the many high and late medieval distortions it had to revert to pre-medieval times and make them the norm. Finally, the reforms of Pius X and Pius XII in the twentieth century were motivated by the 'active participation' of the faithful. In other words, the

---

[*] The manuscript was completed in 1999 and translated by Elaine Griffiths. See also Odenthal 2002.

changes in society and the world were so great that the focus now shifted more to the individual believers. The reforms of these popes were important in paving the way for the great paradigm shift of the last liturgical reform.

This briefest of surveys of liturgical reforms in the whole church—including reforms of particular churches and individual orders—shows: *liturgia semper reformanda et reformata.* The liturgy has always been renewed and always will be.

Yet the problem needs to be defined more accurately by our concentrating here on the latest liturgical reform. My contention is that this one is, more than all other forms, characterized by the fact that it entailed a paradigm shift, brought about by the highest ecclesiastical level, that of an ecumenical council. And this paradigm shift is of special interest here as critics of the liturgical reform accuse it of destroying the ritual side of worship.

The Paradigm Shift of the Liturgical Reform
in the Wake of the Second Vatican Council

The Pre-Conciliar Liturgical Paradigm: The Cult

With Angelus Häussling I define 'cult' in general as that "original behavior of people by means of which they forever and ever (sense) and safeguard in symbolic actions the meaning of their life in the world together with its pre-conditions in time and space which are not at their disposal and are largely felt to be overwhelming" (Häussling 1989, 21). Put in religious terms, cult means that the human act of honoring and worshipping God was always preceded by God's turning to them. The believing person is convinced that he or she is called, gifted and empowered by the celebration of worship. By defining 'liturgy' as a 'public cult' and declaring the salvation of human beings to be the consequence of this cult, earlier liturgical studies occasionally ran the risk of construing liturgical action as magic.

The basic line of pre-conciliar understanding of worship went from the worshipping church to God who worked his salvation in the sacramental action of the people. This was reflected in the very shape of the churches: the congregation gathered facing east (traditionally the direction of the Lord returning at the end of time), the priest also looking east, his back to the congregation. The participation of the faithful at mass was reduced to the act of worshipping God since all liturgical functions (including the preaching of the Word) had been transferred to the clergy alone.

The Post-Conciliar Paradigm: The Congregation Gathered
to Celebrate the Paschal Mystery

The liturgical constitution of Vatican II abandoned the equation of liturgy and cult and developed a more comprehensive liturgical concept; it placed the worship of God by human beings (the cultic or *anabatic* dimension) side by side with God's serving human beings (salvific or *katabatic* dimension), stressing the importance of gathering together. Under No. 6b of the liturgical constitution we find the following definition of 'liturgy': "Since then the church has never ceased to gather to celebrate the paschal mystery." Echoing the Council of Trent the liturgy is described as the celebration of the paschal mystery.[1] This focuses on the Exodus story of the People of Israel with the paschal meal (Exodus 12–15) and the death and resurrection of Jesus with the Last Supper (e.g., Mark 14–16), on which every celebration is based (Pahl 1996). The Council then speaks of 'gathering.' Liturgy is no longer a cult removed from time but has as its criterion the participation, described in No. 14 as full, conscious and active. With this demand the liturgical constitution takes a significant step. In order for the person to fully, consciously and actively participate in the liturgy, every condition for doing this has to be found. And human beings of today, in all their conditions of life, hereby move into view, indeed are made into a paradigm themselves. The liturgy is to be continually renewed so that the persons living at a particular time can participate actively, consciously and fully. The medieval cosmic dimension, which stressed the cardinal point of the East as the way of interpreting the world, has been exchanged for a socially constructed reality, the present way of perceiving the world (see Häussling 1983). Re-emphasis on the human being introduced the 'anthropological revolution' of twentieth century theology into liturgy. Liturgical studies tend to describe this phenomenon as a 'paradigm shift.' This epistemological concept, originating with Thomas S. Kuhn, a scholar specializing in the history of the sciences, means a shift in the worldview undergirding a group with its 'symbolic generalizations' (see Hahne 1990, 363). Every liturgical reform is also connected with a paradigm shift in society or the church to which it responds either by accepting changes or precisely by rejecting the changes necessitated by a paradigm shift, and thus by affirming the past. In this sense the liturgical reforms before that of

---

[1] DH 1741: "Nam celebrato veteri Pascha, quod in memoriam exitus de Aegypto multitudo filiorum Israel immolabat (Ex 12, 1ss), novum instituit Pascha, se ipsum ab Ecclesia per sacerdotes sub signis visibilibus immolandum in memoriam transitus sui ex hoc mundo ad Patrem, quando per sui sanguinis effusionem nos redemit 'eripuitque de potestate tenebrarum et in regnum suum transtulit' (Col 1, 13)."

the last Council probably responded to paradigm shifts but did not implement one for the liturgy itself. Emil J. Lengeling here made use of the concept of the 'Copernican revolution' of liturgical reform (see Lengeling 1964, 112). The celebration of worship is no longer a 'one-way street,' with the priest performing the mysteries on his own and merely distributing the gracious gifts of God to the assembled people. In post-conciliar liturgy the whole gathered, hierarchically structured congregation is meant to experience itself as the actor and bearer of the liturgy. Unlike the congregation of the middle ages, however, this one is not just a group of clerics. Having been baptized, every Christian is a 'liturgist.' This means that the renewed liturgy is redis-covering the plethora of liturgical roles lost over time and placing the liturgi-cal ministries of the lay people beside those of ordained ministers presiding at the mass. Of course, such a paradigm shift and its effects creates problems: that of the often inadequate preparation of the faithful, too many changes made too fast, and finally the uncertainties arising through the redefinition of the relationship between clergy and laity.

The Liturgy Reform – End of Ritual?
Two queries have been levelled at the liturgical reform from outside, one from the sociological angle by Peter Fuchs, and the other from the cultural analytical angle by Alfred Lorenzer.

Following Niklas Luhmann's system theory, Fuchs defines 'ritual' as a communication process since "that unity by which society is constituted" is communication (Fuchs 1992, 2). He then describes the specific aspect of rituals as a form of communication with the special characteristic of restric-tiveness. With this concept substantiated by ethnological research, Fuchs de-scribes a situation that Luhmann calls "prohibition of negation" (Luhmann 1992, 87). By this Luhmann means the exclusion of possibilities of negation: in ritual, debate is excluded for the protection of the content of faith. The in-dividual participant may only identify partially with the content of ritual but this fact must not be expressed in ritual. A further, related characteristic is that of invariance, or the prohibition of variation. Ritual lives from repetition. According to Fuchs, the reason for these two bans is the aporia detected by Luhmann, that of having to symbolize in ritual the "unsymbolizable founda-tions" of a religion (Fuchs 1992, 2; see also Luhmann 1992, 56–57). Fuchs applies these phrases to the liturgical reforms and formulates the proposition that liturgical reform, especially that of the rite of the mass, has created a communication structure that is no longer protected by restrictiveness and invariance. The abandoning of Latin as the liturgical language has, in his view, led to a bridging of the communication gap between clergy and people.

Thus, according to Fuchs, ritual has undermined itself since the reform and is becoming a 'dangerous modernity.' By contrast, he characterizes the medieval mass as a "restriction of specific communication possibilities," in sociological terms a "functionally oriented communication based on barriers" (Fuchs 1992, 4, 6).

A further query about the liturgical reform comes from the Frankfurt psychoanalyst and sociologist Lorenzer, who has drawn attention to the fundamental significance of ritual (see Lorenzer 1981; 1983; 1991). His findings were gained from his own method of 'cultural analysis,' a combination of sociology and psychoanalysis. With Lorenzer ritual has the function of allowing the unconscious-sensual to come to the fore. It hereby makes an indispensable contribution to human freedom and individuation (see Funke 1984; Wilhelms 1991). His criticism of the post-conciliar liturgy is that it has destroyed such a sensual-aesthetic dimension and manipulated liturgy for educational and disciplinary purposes. He may give an accurate account of specific extremes but his criticism hardly applies to post-conciliar liturgy as a whole.

The two examples show how difficult it will be to apply a concept of 'ritual' to liturgy without seeking contact with the theological discipline responsible for this—liturgical studies. For a concept of 'ritual' appearing in theology, more exactly in liturgical studies, three comments seem essential by way of criticism of Lorenzer's and Fuchs' ideas.

Western theology basically starts from the incarnation paradigm; the fact that God became a human being in Jesus. From here the mere coding of the imminent and the transcendent as a description of religious communication becomes just as questionable as the description of ritual as the symbolization of unsymbolizable foundations of religion (= God) (see Dallmann 1994, 202–204, 210). At least it is justifiable to ask questions about the notion of 'symbol' on which this is based.

The concept of 'religion' must not, as appears to be the case with Fuchs and Lorenzer, be restricted to ritual. If religion and ritual are equated then the 'modernization' of ritual naturally endangers the existence of religion itself. Luhmann fundamentally holds to the possibility of carrying out a "certain deritualization of religion" (Luhmann 1992, 86–87). He does this because he places dogmatics at the side of ritual. His concept of 'religion' thus embraces both ritual and dogmatics, the latter understood as the whole of the interpretation of faith and not as a subsection of theology. Here religion is recognized as having reflexive and interpretative functions—and not just a restrictive ritual.

A religion unalterable in its ritual is ultimately stripped of its historicity. Religion becomes the immutable myth so that the historical conditionality of rituals is left out of account. This is totally incompatible with the fact that Christianity is in root and branch a deeply historical religion.

The Concept of 'Ritual' in Dialogue with Psychoanalysis and Psychoanalytical Pastoral Psychology

The 'anthropological revolution' in theology turns our attention to the human sciences. I want to confine myself to dealing with just one of them, psychoanalysis, mediated through psychoanalytical pastoral psychology.

The approach of Dieter Funke presented here is an "explicitly Catholic response to the argument about the meaning of symbol and ritual in the practice of Christian life" (Wahl 1994, 531). Funke is rooted in a current of pastoral psychology that has decided to link up with depth psychology, or rather psychoanalysis. The dialogue between pastoral theology and depth psychology takes place on the basis of their converging options with the goal of the person becoming a protagonist (see Mette and Steinkamp 1983, 170–172; Steinkamp 1983, 382–384; Wahl 1994, 83).

Funke develops his position by assimilating various elaborations of Freud's psychoanalysis (see Funke 1986a, 31–41). Developmental psychology, represented by Margret Mahler, describes the psychological development of the child as a highly dramatic process of identity formation and letting go of its mother. Within this separation process symbols play a great role. In this connection Funke adopts Donald W. Winnicott's concept of 'transition objects.' These are things that become transitory objects for infants, thus acquiring a symbolical quality, by representing the bond between the mother and the separation from her, in other words a relational event (see Funke 1986b, 31–32). For the infant the symbol has a double dimension, that of separation and that of bonding, that of protection and that of encouragement to depart. The human desires for security and autonomy expressed here are rooted in earliest childhood. Funke uses the concept of a person's 'bipolar self.' The transitory objects symbolizing wishes for security and autonomy occur according to Winnicott in their own sphere of reality, the 'intermediary sphere,' located between inside and outside, the psychic inner world and external reality. The area of culture and religion as a non-rational one can emerge due to the infant's ability to develop such an intermediary sphere and its transitory objects (see Funke 1993, 87–90; 1995, 58–60).

Funke then develops his understanding of symbol in grappling with Loren-zer. Lorenzer expands the concept of 'symbol' arising from psychoanalysis into a cultural theory. Accordingly symbols function as "objectivations of human practice functioning as signifiers, and thus meaningful" (Lorenzer 1981, 23). A theory of ritual deriving from this notion of 'symbol' will no longer only rate ritual as something external. In conjunction with the human needs for security and departure, it has the attribute of substantivity. Wher-ever ritual is performed these basic human needs come into play—first spar-ked by the (secondary) substance of a certain religion. Ritual—understood as a symbolic self-emptying of the person—communicates models of successful living. Funke defines 'religious symbols' as "congealed experiences that people have gained in history with their God" (Funke 1987, 380). Precisely here they are "the outcome of human communication and interaction" (Funke 1984, 182). Decisive for Funke's approach is that he draws attention to the structural equality of the primary substantivity (protection and departure) of ritual and the substantivity (then secondary for ritual) of the Judeo-Christian religion. Inspired by the theology of Johann B. Metz, Funke describes the two functions of Judeo-Christian religion: inducing to depart, emancipating, and comforting and protecting (see Funke 1986a, 99–105). On the one hand, religion seeks to give consolation and security, while on the other it exhorts people to depart ('following Christ'). This politically critical dimension of religion is in fact readily overlooked in favor of the sociologically more sta-bilizing approach. The Christian-Jewish tradition is rich in experience of the two dimensions. The search for protection is expressed in the Christian talk of salvation (Christ's death on the cross), the search to become oneself and the departure in the Exodus story. But these are the very poles of the paschal mystery, which the liturgy constitution says is celebrated with every liturgi-cal celebration. Funke sees the double function symbolized in the paschal meal: before setting off to wander through the desert the people of Israel reassures itself again in ritual of the nearness of the protective God (see Funke 1986a, 113).

Funke's recourse to Winnicott and the concept of 'transitory object' is of particular interest for our question. The whole area of the object that can be seen, felt, and tasted hereby gains in significance. This 'intermediary' sym-bolical sphere forms its own reality, in which the utterances of faith, includ-ing rituals, are also to be located. Knowledge of life, "models of other, better lives (Kingdom of God on the horizon)" are communicated precisely in sub-stantive symbols (Funke 1989, 274). Ritual must here also be accorded a bipolarity: the communicated models of a better life challenge us not to identify with this world too quickly (Exodus), and its roots in traditional human knowledge of life and faith offers comfort and security.

Such an understanding of ritual building on symbol theory integrates ritual into the psychic development of people, and thus into their own historicity, establishing it in the historical dimension of Judeo-Christian religion. The bipolarity (protection and departure) prevents ritual from deteriorating into ritualism. At the same time a possible change in the person and the ritual, the further development of both, becomes the subject of (historically grounded) religion. Not least of all, it embraces the sensory and sensual nature of human ritual action.

Result

From the history of ritual of the Catholic Church the following emerges. Changes have always been part of liturgical history. Liturgical reforms always respond to a paradigm shift; to new challenges and changes in society and the church. The liturgical reform in the wake of Vatican II even involved a paradigm shift of liturgy. It thereby reacted to numerous extra- and intra-church changes brought by the twentieth century and which theology can attribute to the anthropological revolution. As has been pointed out, by developing a concept of 'ritual' suitable for Catholic tradition, such major changes do not destroy ritual; they are part of the nature of Judeo-Christian religion, just as change is part of the nature of human beings. It must be admitted, however, that such reforms often conceal difficulties and do not immediately enjoy general approval. Yet accepting new challenges is part of the nature of Christianity if it wants to be true to its own history and faith.

References

Dallmann, Hans-Ulrich. 1994: *Die Systemtheorie Niklas Luhmanns und ihre theologische Rezeption.* Stuttgart: Kohlhammer.

DH = Denziger, Henricus. 1991: *Enchiridion symbolorum, definitionum et declarationum de rebus fidei et morum: Kompendium der Glaubensbekenntnisse und kirchlichen Lehrentscheidungen.* Lateinisch-Deutsch, transl. and ed. Peter Hünermann. 37th ed. Freiburg i.Br.: Herder.

Fuchs, Peter. 1992: Gefährliche Modernität. Das zweite vatikanische Konzil und die Veränderung des Messeritus. In: *Kölner Zeitschrift für Soziologie und Sozialpsychologie* 44:1–11.

Funke, Dieter. 1984: Religion als Ritual? Praktisch-theologische Anmerkungen zur Bedeutung der Symbole und zur Religionskritik A. Lorenzers im „Konzil der Buchhalter". In: *Diakonia* 15:176–183.

———. 1986a: *Im Glauben erwachsen werden: Psychische Voraussetzungen der religiösen Reifung.* Munich: Pfeiffer.

———. 1986b: Vom 'Ding' zum Symbol. Religionspsychologische Aspekte zur Bedeutung vorsprachlicher Symbole für die frühe Identitätsentwicklung. In: *Wege zum Menschen* 38:29–44.

———. 1987: Symbol/Ritual. In: *Gemeindepraxis in Grundbegriffen: Ökumenische Orientierungen und Perspektiven*, ed. Christof Bäumler and Norbert Mette. Munich and Düsseldorf: Patmos. 379–388.

———. 1989: Sehen oder Hören? Zum Verhältnis von Sinnlichkeit und Objekt in der religiösen Erfahrung. In: *Wege zum Menschen* 41:269–276.

———. 1993: *Der halbierte Gott: Die Folgen der Spaltung und die Sehnsucht nach Ganzheit.* Munich: Kösel.

———. 1995: *Gott und das Unbewußte: Glaube und Tiefenpsychologie.* Munich: Kösel.

Hahne, Werner. 1990: *De arte celebrandi oder von der Kunst, Gottesdienst zu feiern: Entwurf einer Fundamentalliturgik.* Freiburg i.Br.: Herder.

Häussling, Angelus A. 1983: Kosmische Dimension und gesellschaftliche Wirklichkeit: Zu einem Erfahrungswandel in der Liturgie. In: *Archiv für Liturgiewissenschaft* 25:1–8.

———. 1989: Liturgiereform: Materialien zu einem neuen Thema der Liturgiewissenschaft. In: *Archiv für Liturgiewissenschaft* 31:1–32.

Lengeling, Emil Joseph. 1964: Die Liturgiekonstitution des II. Vatikanischen Konzils: I. Grundlinien und kirchengeschichtliche Bedeutung. In: *Liturgisches Jahrbuch* 14:107–121.

Lorenzer, Alfred. 1981: *Das Konzil der Buchhalter: Die Zerstörung der Sinnlichkeit: Eine Religionskritik.* Frankfurt a.M.: Europäische Verlagsanstalt.

———. 1983: Erweiterte Fassung meines Vortrags über „Das Konzil der Buchhalter". In: *Pastoraltheologische Informationen* 2:145–178.

———. 1991: Sacrosanctum Concilium: Der Anfang der Buchhalterei. Betrachtungen aus psychoanalytisch-kulturkritischer Perspektive. In: *Gottesdienst – Kirche – Gesellschaft. Interdisziplinäre und ökumenische Standortbestimmung nach 25 Jahren Liturgiereform. St. Ottilien,* ed. Hansjakob Becker, Bernd Jochen Hilberath, and Willers Ulrich. (Pietas Liturgica 5). Sankt Ottilien: EOS Verlag. 153–161.

Luhmann, Niklas. 1992: *Funktion der Religion.* 3d ed. Frankfurt a.M.: Suhrkamp.

Mette, Norbert and Hermann Steinkamp. 1983: *Sozialwissenschaften und Praktische Theologie.* (Leitfaden Theologie 11). Düsseldorf: Patmos.

Odenthal, Andreas. 2002: *Liturgie als Ritual: Theologische und psychoanalytische Überlegungen zu einer praktisch-theologischen Theorie des Gottesdienstes als Symbolgeschehen.* (Praktische Theologie heute 60). Stuttgart: Kohlhammer.

Pahl, Irmgard. 1996: Das Paschamysterium in seiner zentralen Bedeutung für die Gestalt christlicher Liturgie. In: *Liturgisches Jahrbuch* 46:71–93.

Steinkamp, Hermann. 1983: Zum Verhältnis von Praktischer Theologie und Humanwissenschaft. In: *Diakonia* 14:378–387.

Wahl, Heribert. 1994: *Glaube und symbolische Erfahrung: Eine praktisch-theologische Symboltheorie.* Freiburg i.Br.: Herder.

Wilhelms, Günter. 1991: *Sinnlichkeit und Rationalität: Der Beitrag Alfred Lorenzers zu einer Theorie religiöser Sozialisation.* Stuttgart: Kohlhammer.

Expressive Appropriateness and Pluralism: The Example of Catholic Liturgy after Vatican II

Matthias Jung

The growth of religious pluralism in our century, brilliantly captured in William James's book on the *Varieties of Religious Experience* back in 1902, obviously gives rise to tricky questions concerning the dynamics of change within traditional institutions. One such institution, and a prominent one too, is the Catholic Church. Here one might expect to encounter some especially difficult problems concerning changes and the acceptance of their inevitability. This is partly due to the fact that Catholicism must be regarded as a self-contained institution with an hierarchical structure and a long tradition of self-affirmation as a *societas perfecta*, governed by eternal rules and so exhibiting some kind of built-in inertia. Hostility to changes—which in the light of eternal truths are destined to be changes for the worse—is the necessary result of such preconditions. Rituals are the pre-eminent means of symbolic reproduction for any given religion and therefore office-bearers are likely to adopt an extremely conservative attitude towards even minute changes. But this inherent conservatism of the clergy is only one part of the story. We do not need a 'thick description' in Clifford Geertz's sense to see that any closed system containing a class of people responsible for the system's reproduction will try to externalize changes and thereby keep the system going.

The other part of the story is more interesting, and it calls for a thick description in the sense of dealing with the system's self-representation. On this level, just coping with changes coming from outside, cautiously suggesting internal changes and maybe even embracing some changes will not do. Some conceptual reflection has to accompany the changes to justify them in order to keep the self-representation intact. Vatican II can be regarded as Catholicism's attempt to understand the ongoing changes in modern societies, to develop some appropriate theological framework, and to promote some changes in liturgy in order to meet the changing demands. Now in the following I will try to do three things: *first,* I will roughly sketch my conceptual equipment for understanding the profound changes in the way religious attitudes and rituals are enacted in our pluralistic time. *Second,* I will take a look at the conceptual means for coping with these changes developed at the Council and afterwards. And, *finally,* using data taken from liturgical manuals, I will try to show how the dynamics of change are guided by some inevitable tensions rendered intelligible by my conceptual proposals.

A Conceptual Framework for Understanding Religious Changes

In my view, the first and most important step in this direction consists in regarding the whole field of religious attitudes, institutions, rituals, etc. as an expression of life-worldly experience. Religious habits share the fundamental features of such experience and should therefore not be analyzed in terms of metaphysical or scientific attitudes. This conceptual decision is not meant to exclude more external modes of explanation such as system theory, which I have used myself in the above for a first glance at the problem. But it underlines that any explanation in this field will be insufficient as long as it does not pay attention to the way in which religion is performed from the perspective of the first persons singular and plural. This attention should result in a hermeneutical attitude focused on the *structural* features of this life-worldly experience. I underline this structural aspect strongly because any hermeneutics without it is easily prone to a naive reduplication of what is going on in the life world anyway. Explanatory power stems only from a clear insight into the relevant relations and mutual dependencies guiding the process of life-worldly experience.

As the first important feature in this regard I would like to stress the *internal holism* of such experience. The mode of experience relevant in ordinary life—in contrast to scientific research—is holistic in the strong sense that it usually incorporates all typical human relations to the world in an undivided unity. Among the several attempts to conceptualize these relations I choose the model that Jürgen Habermas develops in his *Theory of Communicative Action* (see Habermas 1981, 413, 415, passim). Habermas distinguishes between three 'worlds,' namely the objective world, the totality of truth-claims about reality, the social world, which is the totality of inter-subjective relations, and the subjective world, comprising the personal feelings and attitudes, to which a given human being has privileged access. Internally connected with these world relations are three different validity claims, which derive from speech act theory: the claim for propositional truth, referring to the objective world; the claim for normative correctness in the world of social relations; and finally the claim for expressive authenticity with regard to the subjective reality. As Wilhelm Dilthey puts it in the nineteenth century: "Acts of representation, will, feeling, are contained in every *status conscientiae* and are, at every instant, the manifestations of psychic life in its interaction with the external world" (Dilthey 1989, 494). The specific holism of life-worldly experience—a feature explicitly rejected in science—is the interdependence of these world relations together with their corresponding validity claims. Holistic interdependence implies that it is entirely impossible to separate, for example, truth claims from the normative and expressive features of experience. In life-worldly experience, the rational acceptability of truth claims is due not to their isolated epistemic qualities, but to the network of interdependent validity claims of a given articulation. This general aspect is strongly underlined in religious contexts, and even more so concerning religious rituals. In rituals, at least as far as language is involved, truth claims and ontological commitments are always present. For example, addressing God as 'our father in heaven' trivially implies the existence of such a being. But these cognitive aspects are never dominant, for the acceptability of rituals is a function not of their dogmatic consistency, but of their holistic appeal to their performers, among which expressive qualities are especially important.

Having pointed out the holism of life-worldly religious experience, I want to take a closer look at the aspect of expressiveness. Each symbol used to articulate the meaning of life from the first-person standpoint, which is constitutive for ordinary experience, includes this aspect of necessity. In order to become a part of a person's guiding orientations, it is not enough that a given symbol is regarded as true and/or normatively correct. It must assert itself as appropriate for the expression of this person's individual standpoint. Expressive appropriateness is a decisive factor in the acceptance of religious convictions, in the participation in rituals, in the internalization of institutional bindings, and it works, as I will show later on, as the most important catalyst of religious change and the growth of pluralism. What does it mean exactly to regard some religious symbol as appropriate in an expressive sense? It means that some person realizes it as the most suitable one for bringing to the fore those aspects of personal experience that she/he regards as the most important ones. The most significant token of this suitability will often be a certain emotional appeal, not something merely cognitive. And the only way in which the normative und cognitive components of religious symbols may be embedded into the very core of a person's being leads through their aptness for articulating und structuring first-person experience. Hence the eminent importance of rituals: they enact and perform the non-cognitive dimensions of a given religion in order to give them emotional coloring and credibility.

The aspect of expressive appropriateness can be regarded as a fundamental feature of all natural symbol systems. It has always been there, albeit in very different ways. Therefore, in order to back up my thesis about the pluralistic drive of expressive validity claims, I have to combine it with one from cultural anthropology. This thesis, the last piece of my conceptual puzzle, is taken from Charles Taylor's investigation of modern identity called *Sources of the Self* (1989) and comes under the heading 'expressive individuation.' According to Taylor, one of the main features of the modern self-conception, as developed within European culture in the last two centuries, consists in the demand for finding personal and cultural identity by means of attempting to articulate individual perspectives: "This has been a tremendously influential idea. Expressive individuation has become one of the cornerstones of modern culture. So much that we barely notice it, and we find it hard to accept that it is such a recent idea in human history and would have been incomprehensible in earlier times" (Taylor 1989, 376). It is easy to see that expressive individuation, as far as it gains access to the religious realm, will represent an extremely hard challenge to any institutionalized religion, especially to the Catholic Church, which developed its rituals long before expressiveness was infused with individualistic connotations. As Taylor puts it, the "notion of originality as a vocation," embedded in the self-conception of real human beings, will tend to multiply expressive articulations (Taylor 1989, 375f.). When the criteria somebody uses for selecting the symbols to which they attach themselves are less and less guided by the normative force of traditions and more and more the subject of personal choice, the here and now of individualized first-person experience will play an eminent role regarding this attachment.

Towards the end of the twentieth century expressive individuation, albeit in a paradoxically stereotyped manner, became a predominant feature of mass culture. Much earlier, in the middle of the nineteenth century, it was already claimed philosophically as the most important source of personal religious attitudes. Of all his essays, Ralph Waldo Emerson chose the one on spiritual laws, where one might expect reflection on something entirely trans-personal, to articulate his creed in expressive individuation: "A man's genius, the quality that differences him from every other, the susceptibility to one class of influences, the selection of what is fit for him, the rejection of what is unfit, *determines for him the character of the universe.* ... A man is a method, a progressive arrangement, a selecting principle, gathering his like to him, wherever he goes. He takes only his own, out of the mulitiplicity that sweeps and circles round him" (Emerson 1996, 71). Emerson underlines the inseparability of expressive individuation and comprehensive worldviews. Expressive appropriateness serves as the selecting principle, but its influence stretches beyond the language of inwardness to normative conviction, social rituals and propositional claims about the 'character of the universe.'

In traditional, non-pluralistic cultures religious rituals and dogmatic conceptions could function as principles of subsumption of individual first-person experience and of personal emotions and desires. Sexuality, for example, could in some monastic traditions be regarded as the devil's strongest weapon (see Brown 1988). Individual desires would then be subsumed under this concept and never be allowed to articulate themselves along their own lines. In such a case the pre-given religious forms work to keep the first-person desires at bay rather than to articulate them. But in a pluralistic setting the subsumption model collapses and the gravity center is reversed: the acceptability of convictions, attitudes, and rituals depends more and more on their ability to express those aspects of life that come to the fore from a first-person stance. Hence the career of the Emersonian advice 'Do your own thing,' which could easily be transformed into the 'imperative of expressiveness': Accept only such rituals and attitudes that allow for the expression of what you feel is important about your personal feelings and desires! In the field of religion, this imperative has two consequences, but before pointing them out, I would like to underline that speaking about real consequences of—mostly implicit—self-conceptions is just a short-hand way of talking about complex interactions between social and political changes, on the one hand, and cultural self-representations, on the other.

Though I focus my paper on the latter level entirely, it is obvious that a comprehensive picture would have to include the other dimensions as well. Now back to my two consequences: the first consists in the multiplication of choice even between several religions, leading to syncretistic, overlapping piece-meal attitudes, which are no longer controlled by institutions designed for preserving dogmatic consistency. The strongest empirical support for this development can be taken from the fact, demonstrated, for example, in many studies on youth and religion in Germany, that the belief in the resurrection is declining whereas reincarnation is a living option for many people (see Barz 1992, 125f.). On the level of institutional self-reflection Vatican II has tried to cope with the predecessors of this development by means of a theology of religious plurality as outlined in the dogmatic constitution on the church entitled *Lumen gentium*. But what if the expressive demand asserts itself within the limits of institutionalized religion and calls for changes of the unchangeable rituals? This second consequence of expressive pluralization has challenged Catholicism and promoted changes both at the level of self-reflection and of ritual practices.

The Council on Religious Pluralism and Liturgical Changes

Two important documents of Vatican II are relevant concerning questions of plurality and expressivity: *Lumen gentium*, dealing with the self-conception of the institution, including its relation to other religions and comprehensive worldviews, and *Sacrosanctum concilium* about liturgy and its renewal (see Flannery 1975). I will take a brief glimpse at the former and then go straight to the constitution on liturgy. *Lumen gentium* is an important document insofar as it officially acknowledges for the first time the participation of other religions in religious truth and salvation. The underlying conceptual scheme is that of an inner core, containing and preserving both truth and salvation, surrounded by multiple shells, containing glimpses of this innermost religious reality in proportion to their distance from the core. This core is not simply taken to be identical with the Catholic Church, but the institutional church is regarded as its *realization*: "This church, constituted and organized as a society in the present world, subsists in the Catholic Church. ... Nevertheless, many elements of sanctification and of truth are found outside its visible confines. Since these are gifts belonging to the Church of Christ, they are forces impelling towards Catholic unity" (Flannery 1975, 357). This very moderate conception of religious pluralism presupposes full possession of the truth for the privileged Catholic standpoint and is inherently paternalistic. Deviating convictions and rituals are tolerated at the price of being taken to be crypto-Catholic. The inclination towards Catholic unity is imputed, not taken from the self-interpretation of the divergent standpoint. Throughout the text of *Lumen gentium* one can find cautious acknowledgments of what is called "legitimate variety" (Flannery 1975, 365), but their justification comes from an imputed centripetal force, which is no part of the divergent position's self-ascription. *Lumen gentium* conceptualizes pluralism as a phenomenon that is partly transitory insofar as different positions are regarded as veiled forms of inherent Catholic standards, and partly reducible to a harmless multitude of expressive differences demonstrating that unity and uniformity are not the same thing.

Sacrosanctum concilium stays within these limits. Dogmatic and institutional unity is the limiting principle for ritual plurality. Renewal and conservation of liturgy are seen as complementary, not as mutually excluding aspects, following the scheme of various shells for one eternal core. Under the surface of this harmonious picture profound tensions are visible; tensions between a monistic concept of institutional and ritual unity, on the one hand, and the search for rituals corresponding to the rapidly changing expressive demands of Catholic believers with a wide variety of experiences, on the other. Right at the beginning the text emphasizes that the liturgical performances are meant to reproduce the distinction between those who participate in them and the rest, combining a descriptive dualism with a normative monism. "The liturgy daily builds up those who are in the Church, making of them a holy temple of the Lord…. At the same time it marvelously increases their power to preach Christ and thus show forth the Church, a sign lifted up among the nations, to those who are outside, a sign under which the scattered children of God may be gathered together until there is one fold and one shepherd" (Flannery 1975, 1f.). Along with these proclamations the utmost importance of liturgical performances is underlined: "every liturgical celebration … is a sacred action surpassing all others. No other action of the church can equal its efficacy by the same title and to the same degree" (Flannery 1975, 5). We are left in the dark about what exactly 'efficacy' (*Wirksamkeit*) is supposed to mean here, but there can be no doubt about the importance of the holy rituals for the church's self-representation. Now, in the next chapter, the Council fathers develop the concept of 'participation' in these rituals and develop a certain phrasing which is repeated throughout the rest of the document: "Mother church earnestly desires that all the faithful should be led to that full, conscious and active participation in liturgical celebrations" (Flannery 1975, 7). And this threefold participation is regarded as the guiding principle for the renewal und promotion of the liturgical rituals.

This amounts to conceding by implication that the older rituals, especially the *Ordo Missae* in the form dating back to the Council of Trent, no longer meet the demands of this participation. Hence the necessity of ritual certainly changes. In the next step, the well-known scheme of core and changing shells is applied to those changes: "For the liturgy is made up of unchangeable elements divinely instituted, and of elements subject to change. These latter not only may be changed but ought to be changed with the passage of time, if they have suffered from the intrusion of anything out of harmony with the inner nature of the liturgy or have become less suitable. In this restoration both texts and rites should be drawn up so as to express more clearly the holy things, which they signify. The Christian people, as far as it is possible, should be able to understand them with ease and take part in them fully, actively and as a community" (Flannery 1975, 9). To put it in my own terminology: the expressive values of the rituals should allow expressive participation. Implicitly it is taken for granted that modifications in the alterable parts of the rituals towards greater expressive appropriateness will do. But what if an entire sacrament finds no corresponding expressive demand? Any statistic on the frequency of confession—if only such were available—would show that in a pluralistic society numbness as an expressive option means the institutional decline of that ritual as well. So the Council's emphasis on full participation in the rituals entails implications in an inevitable tension to the emphasis on unity. This tension does not come to the fore because the manner in which the document is written suggests the church is in full charge of the changes to come. This is true concerning the *de facto* performance of the rituals, which is restricted to the office-bearers. Yet this assumption of being in charge is obviously wrong in regard to the first-person participation of the believers, who are, at least in the Western world, objectively living in pluralistic societies with no social constraints for religious choice.

Institutional unification and expressive participation can coexist only if the individuals demand for expression is subsumed under the unifying ritual. But if individuals are free to participate in the ritual in proportion to its expressive appeal, such a subsumption is no longer possible. The liturgical reformation taking place in post-conciliar Catholicism is an attempt to acknowledge expressiveness within the realm of an essentially monistic conception of liturgy.

Ritual Changes in the Liturgy of the Mass

From 1570, when the *Missale Romanum* initiated by the Council of Trent replaced older versions, to Vatican II in the early 1960s, Catholic liturgy remained essentially unchanged. The mass was said in Latin, a fact that excluded most Catholics from any deeper comprehension and restricted them to expressive participation in the nonsemantic parts of the ritual. Furthermore, the priest celebrated with his face turned to the high altar and his back to the laity, thereby creating a hiatus between the holy procedures going on upstage and the congregation. The entire performance was structured by hierarchical patterns, following a scheme of subordination: the priest was subordinated to Christ, the congregation subordinated to the priest. In Anselm Schott's pre-council *Römisches Meßbuch* from 1951, the widespread liturgical manual for the German-speaking countries, there is an introductory part dealing with the 'holy mass-offering,' in which neither individuality nor inter-subjective communication play any role (see Schott 1951, [1]–[7]). The church, represented by the celebrating priest, appears as a quasi-subject, participation is conceptualized as the subordination of single persons to the self-performing ritual, that was taken as something objective. During the high prayer, admitted only in the canonical Roman form and performed in silence by the priest, it was common that the community started praying the rosary, and therefore had to be reminded of the ongoing transsubstantiation by means of little bells designed for that purpose. After the high prayer was finished, the people made a short active appearance, which in Schott's *Meßbuch* is phrased in a fluctuation between description and prescription: "Full of faith the people announce consent by means of a loud and cheerful 'amen'" (Schott 1951, 478).

Vatican II opened the door for what it called *active participation* and the following reforms of liturgy allowed for some significant modifications, which changed the face of the Catholic mass. Aiming at greater transparency, better inculturation, and expressive variety, the reforms replaced Latin as the official language for the celebration, making room for the vernaculars. The high-prayer was no longer performed mute, the priest usually facing his audience, and the canonic unity of the Roman ritual was undermined by the introduction of four main high-prayers. Most importantly, the rigid objectivism of the earlier rituals was replaced by a new emphasis on the subjectivity of the believers. For a pre-council priest, the very idea of having to put creative energies into liturgy in order to keep it expressively alive would have been completely alien. After the Council, ritual changes towards expressive plurality were observable at two different levels. On one hand, there have been alterations promoted by the ecclesiastical institutions, which are incorporated into the liturgical manuals. Even here, on the official branch, cautious attempts towards greater consideration of life-worldly experiences are obvious. On the other hand, on the fringes of the institution, we have a more radical shift towards expressive appropriateness. The gap between these branches is growing, for the institutionalized means for the containment of expressive demands, namely dogmatic consistency, is proving ineffective against the rituals developed within smaller groups, which are held together by corresponding expressive needs of their members. In my concluding remarks, I will first highlight some aspects of the official development and then have a last look at the fringe groups.

As an example, let us take a look at the ritual changes in the canon, the innermost part of the eucharistic liturgy. In pre-council times, the *praefatio* was dominated by invocations of a tremendously mighty, majestic and holy god and the subordinate devotion to his holiness. There were no references to human experience; the emphasis was put on predicates like *omnipotentia*, *aeternitas* and *maiestas*.[1] The *praefatio* of the fourth high-prayer in German

---

[1] See Schott 1951, 470: "Vere dignum et justum est, aequum et salutare, nos tibi semper et ubique gratias agere: Domine sancte, Pater omnnipotens, aeterne Deus: per Christum, Dominum nostrum. Per quem majestatem tuam laudant Angeli, adorant Dominatones, tremunt Potestates. Caeli caelorumque Virtutes as beate Seraphim socia exultatione concelebrant. Cum quibus et nostras voces ut admitti jubeas, deprecamur, supplicid confessione dicentes: Sanctus, Sanctus Sanctus."

has eliminated them all, preserving only the holiness, and favors another predicate that is repeated throughout the canon: *liveliness* (Lebendigkeit). God is praised no longer for his sheer holiness, but for his friendliness to human life. "You have created everything, for you are the love and the source of life. You fulfill your creations with blessings and delight them all with the brightness of your light" (Gotteslob 1975, 400, translated by the author, M.J.). The latter phrase comes as a surprise: it praises the aesthetic qualities of God and his creation from the perspective of the believers. This is an astonishing development towards expressiveness. The new high prayer at least partly replaces the top-down language of the Roman ritual with a bottom-up-approach that looks for more life-worldliness.

Another example within the canon can be taken from the formula used for the transsubstantiation. In the *Ordo Missae*, the chalice is "pro vobis et pro multis effundetur in remissionem peccatorum" (Schott 1951, 476). The new German-language liturgy preserves this meaning, but translates *pro multis* as 'for all' (*für alle*) (Gotteslob 1975, 384), an alteration that immediately caused protest by conservative clergy, who saw the sharp inside/outside distinction endangered. And in the following decades, once the doors were opened towards greater expressiveness, a multitude of different high-prayers emerged, some even with unveiled allusions to hedonistic demands. In a high-prayer coming from the Netherlands the eucharistic sacrifice comes as a kind of a liberal-hedonistic *symposium*: "drink this cup with me all of you, for this is my convenant of love with you, my blood, which is shed for reconciliation, the chalice of liberation and happiness" (Unidentified source (photocopied eucharistic prayer), presumably from the Netherlands, translated by the author, M.J.).

Moving from the core to the fringes, expressive demands become even more important, dogmatic constraints loosen their grip. Progressive Catholic youth movements in Germany are developing rituals to replace the eucharistic celebration with 'celebrations of life'; gender-conscious women explore the bounds of Christianity by ritual adaptations of pagan traditions connected with fertility and feminine goddesses; and there are all kinds of fusions between the Christian heritage and esoteric ideas. Chosen for their expressive appropriateness, new rituals and religious attitudes are only loosely tied to institutionalized religion, but due to the holistic character of religious experience they will have normative and cognitive implications potentially causing conflicts with different positions. Inside and outside the church, expressive pluralism deserves to be taken seriously.

References

Barz, Heiner. 1992: *Postmoderne Religion*. (Jugend und Religion 2). Opladen: Westdeutscher Verlag.

Brown, Peter. 1988: *The Body and Society: Men, Women and Sexual Renunciation in Early Christianity*. (Lectures on the History of Religions 13). New York: Columbia University Press.

Dilthey, Wilhelm. 1989: *Selected Works*. Vol. 1: *Introduction to the Human Sciences*, ed. Rudolf A. Makkreel and Frithjof Rodi. Princeton: Princeton University Press.

Emerson, Ralph Waldo. 1995: Spiritual Laws. In: *Essays and Poems*, ed. Tony Tanner. London: J.M. Dent, Everyman Library.

Flannery, Austin (ed.). 1975: *Vatican Council II: The Conciliar and Post-Conciliar Documents*. Wilmington, Del.: Scholarly Resources.

Gotteslob. 1975: *Gotteslob: Katholisches Gebet- und Gesangbuch für das Bistum Mainz*. 7th ed. Mainz: Matthias-Grünewald-Verlag.

Habermas, Jürgen. 1981: *Theorie des kommunikativen Handelns*. Vol. 1: Handlungsrationalität und gesellschaftliche Rationalisierung. Frankfurt a.M.: Suhrkamp.

James, William. 1902: *Varieties of Religious Experience: A Study in Human Nature*. New York and London: Longmans Green & Co.

Schott, Anselm (ed.). 1951: *Das vollständige Römische Meßbuch [lateinisch und deutsch]: mit allgemeinen und besonderen Einführungen im Anschluß an das Meßbuch von Anselm Schott herausgegeben von Mönchen der Erzabtei Beuron*. 11th ed. Freiburg i.Br.: Herder.

Taylor, Charles. 1989: *Sources of the Self: The Making of the Modern Identity*. Cambridge, Mass.: Harvard University Press.

Patterns of Ritual Change among Parsi-Zoroastrians in Recent Times[*]

Michael Stausberg

Rituals, many are agreed, have an inherent transformative dynamics. The most obvious examples are the rites of passage. In consecration rituals, too, quite ordinary things are transformed into something more significant. On the other hand, there are other types of ritual activities, which obviously serve a different purpose in that they are meant to maintain the existing status quo.

Invariance and Change in Rituals

Be that as it may, one of the characteristics mentioned in most definitions and theories of rituals is the presumed formalistic invariance of their performance. According to a renowned authority, the anthropologist Roy A. Rappaport, for instance, invariance is at the heart of ritual as such, and the invariant sequence of formal acts is a "re-enactment of that which in its very essence is invariant" (Rappaport 1999, 187). Also in one of the very few recent books on Zoroastrian rituals, entitled *Ritual Art and Knowledge: Aesthetic Theory and Zoroastrian Ritual*, 'invariance' serves as a key concept. The authors, the American philosophers Ron G. Williams and James W. Boyd, try "to expose the transformative potential of even the most structured and repetitive ritual practice" (Williams and Boyd 1993, 143). In their aesthetic-cognitive view they try to show that invariant ritual practice can be "an effective means for generating new knowledge" (Williams and Boyd 1993, 143). This hypothesis is strongly supported by their main informant, Dastur Kotwal, a conservative Zoroastrian high priest from India, is directed against the theologian Theodore W. Jennings, who had tried to undermine the supposition "that it is essential to ritual that it be utterly unvarying in its performance" (Jennings 1982, 126). According to Jennings the unchanging character

---

[*]   This paper was written in 1999–2000. Reluctantly, I have agreed to publish it in its original form. While retaining the text, I have added some notes in order to refer to some relevant recent publications. On Zoroastrian rituals see also Stausberg 2003a.

of rituals is merely an illusion. They are adaptive, varying in space and changing in time, and it is precisely their adaptive and varying character, which makes them a mode of inquiry and discovery, in that way establishing their noetic function.

Ritual studies seem to have become quite a dogmatic affair caught in the same trap as some other fields of study. 'Ritual' or, as many authors nowadays seem to prefer, 'ritual practice,' is seen as a substantive phenomenon *sui generis*. It is reified. As usual, behind the controversy between the philosophers and the theologian on the nature of the noetic function of rituals there seems to be a different set of problems, transcending the purely theoretical discourse of the social sciences: that of the ritual changes and variants in the modern Christian churches and some other religions. That may seem far-fetched. However, from a common-sense perspective it should not at all come as a surprise that rituals do vary and change. On the other hand, it is undeniable that change and variance are not exactly the war cry of many a conservative ritualist. However, even a conservative ritualist usually would not hesitate to admit that changes in rituals do occur. The problem for these ritualists rather is how to judge these changes and variations. They can be seen either as a decline or as an improvement in ritual standards.

Ritual Studies and Ritual Experts

This brief excursion into one basic feature of the study of rituals may even serve to illustrate the tendency among scholars of religion and students of rituals in the academy to substitute for indigenous ritualists. Quite often studies of 'ritual,' intentionally or unintentionally, turn out to be a kind of apologetics for ritual practice, and, as a matter of fact, the works of some well-known anthropologists, Clifford Geertz and, even more so, Victor W. Turner, seem to be an important aspect in the recent history and the renewed popularity both of rituals and ritual studies in Britain and the United States. The 'ritual process' and 'betwixt and between' are key concepts in many a ritual innovation, and some scholars have been active as consultants to churches that were considering ritual reforms (see Bell 1997, 218–223, 263–264). Concerned about their epistemological claims and status, liturgical studies have appropriated a good deal of anthropological theorizing on 'ritual.' Reading anthropological accounts of the almost 'magic' effects of rituals, for instance, in creating communities and healing, easily seems to create some sort of a nostalgia and stimulate a *bricolage* of ritual practices. Whereas a couple of decades ago, contrary to much empirical evidence, but in line with general assumptions on the future or rather the non-future of religion, the decline of ritual patterns seemed to be an inevitable effect of modernization and secularization. 'Ritual' nowadays seems to have been rediscovered as a basic dimension of human life.

It is becoming increasingly clear that the academic study of rituals in the West is intimately linked to modern or, perhaps more appropriately, postmodern Western religious history. However, since much of the empirical material, which has generated theories, or, to be more modest, hypotheses on the nature and function of 'ritual,' or rather 'rituals,' it is not surprising that it has had effects on non-Western cultures and religions as well. The aforementioned approach of the American philosophers Williams and Boyd represents only one, albeit a rather far-reaching, model of that form of intercultural feedback: in a certain way, they write the philosophy of the ritual practice they are presented with by their main informant, the Zoroastrian high-priest Dastur Kotwal. It is safe to assume that the sophisticated reasoning and jargon of the American philosophers would exceed the intellectual capacities of the majority of Zoroastrians, even of most of the intellectuals, and certainly of most of the ritual practitioners, the priests in particular, even if the Zoroastrians had easy access to their book. Nevertheless, the very fact that Dastur Kotwal, an exponent of a rather conservative religious policy, gets academic backing from the West to a certain extent increases his status inside the Zoroastrian community.

Zoroastrian Studies and Zoroastrian Rituals

Rituals have always been an important part of Zoroastrian studies. As usual, the exception proves the rule. The study of Zoroastrian rituals, if done seriously, requires the participation of Zoroastrian ritual practitioners and ritual experts. This is a marked difference to studies in Zoroastrian theology, mythology, apocalypticism, or cosmology. Whereas a philologist might elaborate a new interpretation of Zoroastrian theology at his desk by consulting scriptures easily available in all major libraries without ever getting in touch with a single living Zoroastrian, a certain amount of field-work is indispensable for the study of Zoroastrian rituals.

Most handbooks on Zoroastrianism draw a rather normative picture of their object in that they try to define what Zoroastrianism is all about.[1] Usually,

---

[1]   In the meantime, an interesting attempt to go beyond that state of affairs has been published: Philip K. Kreyenbroek 2001.

the handbooks stipulate a rather rigid classificatory system and mostly hypostatize one type of certain rituals as being the so-and-so ritual, hardly mentioning different versions or ritual traditions and ignoring different sets of indigenous interpretations.[2] Moreover, this perspective is mostly restricted to the ritual performers, usually not taking the audience and the sponsors into account.

In another sense, however, Western research has provided the means of disrupting and de-legitimizing indigenous ritual traditions. Back in the second half of the nineteenth century, philological studies established that the ancient ritual texts used by the Zoroastrian priests could not possibly have been composed by the same person or have emerged from the same group of people. One usually assumes that a brief section of these ritual texts, the *Gathas*, five hymns in a very difficult language, were the most ancient part of the Zoroastrian literature. Moreover, the *Gathas* are commonly ascribed to Zarathushtra, who is revered as the founder, prophet or ultimate role model of the religion. According to much received wisdom, in his *Gathas* Zarathushtra had preached a philosophical monotheism, playing down the role of rituals in favor of ethics. These interpretations have become quite popular among Zoroastrians in India and later even in Iran.

Probably more than most other Indian communities, the Zoroastrians, commonly called the Parsis, were early on strongly affected by British colonial rule in India. Their self-perception turned out to be determined by their interaction with the British. In language and cultural tastes—food, dress, music, sports, literature, etc.—the Parsis to a considerable extent adopted British or, in a broader sense, Western patterns. It is a common misconception that westernization has stopped short of the religious sphere, being restricted to changes in social habits. Clearly, this is not the case, and religious changes do not only bear upon the discursive level of religious beliefs but also on the sphere of ritual practices.

The Rise and Design of New Rituals

The intense contact with the West could lead to a shifting in the emphasis in ritual practice. A key figure in this regard is Dastur Dhalla, the most important liberal theologian of twentieth century Zoroastrianism who at the same time, and this is more than a mere accident, was the first Zoroastrian ever to

---

[2]   The most recent example for this approach is Peter Clark 1998, esp. chap. VI, 99-123.

obtain a doctorate in Iranian studies at a Western university.[3] Protestant Christian ritual with its emphasis on preaching and its weekly time-structure made a strong impression on the Zoroastrian priest during his stay in New York from 1905 to 1909. After his return to India Dhalla was appointed to the office of head priest of the Zoroastrians community at the port city of Karachi (now in Pakistan). Dastur Dhalla tried to introduce something similar to Protestant worship in the Zoroastrian context. These prayer and sermon meetings, however, proved quite unsuccessful.

Passing this experience in review, Dastur Dhalla states:

> For seven years we continued these ... meetings, despite the very poor participation. But when it became impossible to attract people to those meetings despite all our varied efforts, and in the absence of enthusiastic co-operation of the community, we had to end with a heavy heart this religious movement meant to foster a feeling of devotion. (Dhalla 1975, 313)

Dhalla tries to explain this failure through the absence of a well-fostered tradition of congregational service among Zoroastrians. The question arises: can one, in a community rich in ritual traditions, simply invent new rituals? It would be very interesting to do a comparative analysis of ritual reforms organized 'from above.' Under which conditions do they fail, and when do they succeed?

As a matter of fact, in recent years in Bombay a new form of congregational prayer has been introduced in a weekly pattern at an old fire-temple in Bombay. True, this development has been initiated by a priest working at that temple. Nevertheless, he has not invented the rather vague story initially surrounding these prayer meetings, which are looked down upon by the leading members of the religious establishment. Dastur Dhalla's invention was aimed at deepening devotion. Many, if not most people attending the prayer meetings at Bombay's Banaji fire-temple on Monday nights, however, come for different reasons. It was said that wishes made during this ceremony in the name of a certain figure will come true, and many still come in order to gain divine support, help, or to experience 'peace of mind.'[4]

All the same, even planned innovations in the organization of rituals may succeed. Here one could refer to the Zarathushtrian Assembly, based in California, which has established new rituals that are exclusively based on what they consider to be the most authentic and normative Zoroastrian texts, the

---

[3] On Dhalla see now Stausberg 2002, 108–111.
[4] For a more extensive study of this ritual innovation, see Stausberg 2003b.

Gathas. This organization, however, is a thing apart: it moves outside of the established religio-ritual institutions, and many of its adherents are converts who were not socialized in Zoroastrian ritual praxis.[5]

Purity Rituals and the Boundaries of Communities

As in many religions, one of the most obvious changes in modern Zoroastrianism, both in India and in Iran, is a large-scale de-ritualization of everyday life. This does not so much concern prayer as the purity rules. Previously, these had, at least in theory, permeated much of daily life. Drinking, eating, sneezing, yawning, urinating, having a motion, the cutting of hair and nails, sexual intercourse and many other aspects of life were surrounded by rules and regulations. Behavior during menstruation was another highly focused part of women's life.[6] Obviously it is difficult to know how far these regulations were observed, but anyway it seems pretty safe to assume that they were enforced more strictly than they are nowadays.

In India, the decline seems to have set in since the early twentieth century. Moreover, in spite of their being incompatible with the system of purity rules, certain modern cultural techniques were eagerly adapted by the Parsis. The very idea of steam engines and water closets, for example, are just the opposite of some fundamentals of the purity system in that they seem to disregard the sanctity of fire and water. Apparently, the Parsis consciously decided to soften their strictness in such matters in order to participate in the colonial project of economic and cultural progress. With many members of the community becoming anglicized and better educated and with the introduction of modern institutions like hospitals the non-observance of certain purity rules seems to have lost much of its threatening dimension. Wrong acts no longer create demons to be scared of.[7]

The systems of purity rules kept members of different communities aloof from each other. Since the identity of social communities is largely a matter of the definition of their boundaries, the purity rules were an important means of the construction of communities. Just as Shia Muslims considered Zoroastrians to be unclean (*najes*), Zoroastrians had to avoid the contact with members of other religions (*juddin*). Since the later half of the nineteenth

---

[5]   On this organization see now Stausberg 2002, 366–372.
[6]   In general see Choksy 1989.
[7]   In passing, Kreyenbroek also mentions that "a strong sense of the menacing reality of the powers of evil disappeared" (Kreyenbroek 2001, 294).

century, however, these barriers have been largely removed. On the other hand, during colonial times the boundaries of the Parsi-Zoroastrian community were raised in a different way. In 1773 a letter written by some Indian Zoroastrians to their Iranian counterparts states that rich Zoroastrians in India "acquire large numbers of Indian young boys and girls as slaves, and then use them for household chores" (see Vitalone 1996, 161–163). Subsequently these slaves were initiated into the Zoroastrian religion and performed duties, which are restricted to ritually competent members of the religion. However, the slave-owners did not allow the bodies of their slaves to be buried in the Zoroastrian burial-places, the *daxme* or 'towers of silence.' This practice is criticized by the Iranians who at the same time insist on the merits of admitting converts, provided they have no scars on their bodies (see Vitalone 1996, 161–163, 193). Instead of following the advice of the Iranians, the Indians seem to have stopped the practice of initiating their servants. Still, the boundaries were not altogether impermeable for certain categories of outsiders. Thus, there were some cases of conversions resulting of mixed-marriages, but even they came under attack. In 1908 the Bombay High Court opined that any such conversions were illegitimate:[8] whereas the Zoroastrian religion enjoyed conversion, the Parsis were seen as a genetically closed ethnic community. Thus, roughly at the same time when the system of the purity rules was relaxed, the community emphatically closed its gates to outsiders.

The Establishment of a Temple Culture

The considerable economic improvement of the Parsi community since the late eighteenth century and the fact that the servants no longer were important factors with regard to another aspect of religious change and modernization led to the establishment of a temple culture. From a methodological point of view, the problem of changing rituals cannot be separated from the religious infrastructure. It is not sufficient to investigate changes in the texture of a ritual alone. One also has to consider its context, which may easily change the character of the ritual(s).

In Parsi-Zoroastrianism nowadays most rituals are performed in temples. This, however, is a recent phenomenon. There were few Zoroastrian temples in India before the nineteenth century. Contrary to the situation in Iran,

---

[8]   On this court case see Stausberg 2002, 54–57 and Palsetia 2001, 226–251.

where every significant community had its high-grade consecrated fire-sanc-
tuary, Indian Zoroastrians had one main temple commemorating their emi-
gration from Iran. The local communities did not have any fixed structure at
their disposal. That was to change since the late seventeenth century. More
and more communities started to consecrate local fire-temples. In Bombay,
the modern center of the Parsi-Zoroastrian community, the first temple was
consecrated in 1709. A second one followed in 1733, and a third one in 1783.
Nowadays, in Bombay alone, there are more than 50 temples of different
categories. In the whole of the Indian subcontinent, between 1783 and the
World War II, over a hundred Zoroastrian temples were consecrated (see also
Hinnells 1985, 266–267, 290–294 [= appendix A]).

The rituals as such, however, do not have to be performed in a temple. All
they require is an environment that meets certain standards of ritual purity.
One of these requirements is the absence of non-Zoroastrians. Now, since the
community was getting richer, fewer Zoroastrians would work as servants to
their richer co-religionists, and, as we have seen, the Zoroastrians stopped to
perform the initiation-rituals of their non-Zoroastrian servants. Therefore, the
requirements of ritual purity in the homes were no longer safe-guarded. Thus,
the daily performance of the rituals was displaced to separate, well-demar-
cated ritual areas, that is, temples to which non-Zoroastrians have no access.
Obviously other factors, such as changes in the architecture of the houses and
urban space, contributed to that shifting of the ritual sphere. Moreover, in an
urban and colonial context, the display of spacious temples obviously became a matter of prestige for a wealthy and successful community. Besides,
the funding of temples was seen as a means of obtaining a high status inside
the community.

Professionalization

Roughly the same clusters of factors contributed to a professionalization of
the ritual practitioners. The *Karachi Zoroastrian Calendar*, published in
1919, gives a good example of that process:

> In the old days when there was a death, Parsi servants who used to be in the service of the
> Seths [rich traders—M.St.] helped out. Later, our people's lifestyle improved, and they
> started employing non-Parsi servants. Even in other ways there was an improvement in our
> living standards and because of this we faced 'difficulties' when a death occurred.... There-
> fore, it was finally decided to start a fund for Khandiyas and Nasarsalars [pall-bearers and
> undertakers—M.St.].... From this fund, one Mobed [priest—M.St.], two Nasarsalars and
> four Khandiyas are kept on the regular payroll. (Punthakey 1996, 77)

Thus, the handling of a death which had previously been taken care of by the Zoroastrian servants or other Zoroastrians who were recruited by the relatives of the deceased as the occasion required, was shifted to a professional team which was funded by the community.

A similar process of professionalization can be discerned with regard to the priesthood. The priests' main place of work was shifted to the temples, and their education to a large extent changed from learning their profession from their forefathers or from serving their apprenticeship with some experienced priest to priestly schools. These schools, which, following the Islamic pattern, are called *madressa* and are nowadays run as boarding-schools. Moreover, to a certain extent, the priests' field of work seems to have narrowed down to the performance of the rituals as such.

An example is the priests' role in weddings. Some descriptions from the nineteenth century suggest a rather extensive involvement of Zoroastrian priests in the process eventually leading to a marriage. It all started with the match-making for which astrological calculations were required. These calculations were based on the horoscope of the bride and the groom, which had been issued by a Zoroastrian priest (or by a Brahmin) at birth. Now, if the priest in his capacity of astrologer came to the conclusion that the horoscopes matched, it was a priest who established the first contacts between the families, and he used to attend the whole procedure eventually leading to the marriage ritual as such. In the course of events the priest would, for instance, serve as an errand-boy, personally inviting the guests to attend the marriage in question, and as a contractor who would take care of supplying all the necessary items such as the formalized gifts or the food. Nowadays, however, the role of the Zoroastrian priests is restricted to the 'liturgical' functions: they give a 'purification bath' to the couple, have them sign the contract, verify their consent and recite the blessings. In all, that may take one hour. The rest is taken care of by caterers and relatives.

Conclusion

One could cite more examples. However, the main points should by now have become clear. Obviously, there were some changes in the performance of the older rituals. Moreover, some rituals have been discarded and new rituals have been introduced, in different forms and with varying success. Finally, due to changing socio-economic circumstances, the religio-ritual field has been restructured on the organizational level.

242   MICHAEL STAUSBERG

References

Bell, Catherine. 1997: *Ritual: Perspectives and Dimensions*. New York and Oxford: Oxford University Press.

Choksy, Jamsheed K. 1989: *Triumph over Evil: Purity and Pollution in Zoroastrianism*. Austin: University of Texas Press.

Clark, Peter. 1998: *Zoroastrianism: An Introduction to an Ancient Faith*. Brighton, Portland: Sussex Academic Press.

Dhalla, Dastur. 1975: *The Autobiography of a Soul: An Autobiography of Shams-ul-ulama Dastur Dr. Maneckji Nusserwanji Dhalla*, transl. Gool and Behram Sohrab H. Rustomji. Karachi: Dastur Dr. Dhalla Memorial Institute.

Hinnells, John R. 1985: The Flowering of Zoroastrian Benevolence: Parsi Charities in the Nineteenth and Twentieth Centuries. In: *Papers in Honour of Professor Mary Boyce*, ed. Adrian D.H. Bivar and John R. Hinnells. Vol. 1. (Acta Iranica 24). Leiden: Brill. 261–326.

Jennings, Theodore W. 1982: On Ritual Knowledge. In: *Journal of Religion* 62:111–127.

Kreyenbroek Philip K. (in collaboration with Shehnaz Neville Munshi). 2001: *Living Zoroastrianism: Urban Parsis Speak about their Religion*. Richmond, Surrey: Curzon.

Palsetia, Jesse S. 2001: *The Parsis of India: Preservation of Identity in Bombay City*. Leiden: Brill.

Punthakey, Jehangir F. (comp.). 1996: *The Karachi Zoroastrian Calendar....* 2d ed. Karachi: n.p.

Rappaport, Roy A. 1999: *Ritual in the Making of Humanity*. Cambridge: Cambridge University Press.

Stausberg, Michael. 2002: *Die Religion Zarathushtras: Geschichte – Gegenwart – Rituale*. Vol. 2. Stuttgart: Kohlhammer.

———. (ed.). 2003a: *Zoroastrian Rituals in Context*. (Studies in the History of Religions). Leiden: Brill.

———. 2003b: Monday-Nights at the Banaji, Fridays at the Aslaji: Ritual Efficacy and Transformation in Bombay City. In: *Zoroastrian Rituals in Context*, ed. Michael Stausberg. (Studies in the History of Religions). Leiden: Brill. 653–718.

Vitalone, Mario. 1996: *The Persian Revayat 'Ithoter': Zoroastrian Rituals in the Eighteenth Century*. Naples: Istituto Universitario Orientale.

Williams, Ron G. and James W. Boyd. 1993: *Ritual Art and Knowledge: Aesthetic Theory and Zoroastrian Religion*. Columbia, S.C.: University of South Carolina Press.

Ritual as War: On the Need to De-Westernize the Concept[*]

Jan G. Platvoet

Ritual is habitually seen as repetitive religious behavior solidifying the society or congregation in which it is celebrated. These qualifications are valid for most, but not for all, rituals. Rituals may also be secular events. They may also be constructed for one particular occasion and purpose only. And they may be a way of exploding a society and of waging war upon one's enemies. It has taken Western scholars of religions a long time to discover these secular, non-repetitive, explosive rituals, for the modern Western Christian notion of 'ritual' as religious cult solidifying society has thoroughly constrained the perspectives of Western scholars on, and approaches to, the religious rituals of humankind. As an analytical category in 'Science of Religions,'[1] it must, therefore, be 'de-Westernized,' if it is serve as an adequate tool for research into the generality of the ritual behavior of humankind, both religious and secular.

The structure of this contribution is as follows. I first discuss the root cause of why we need to de-westernize ritual and the other core concepts of *Religionswissenschaft*. I introduce my argument with an example from the study of the indigenous religions of Africa. Secondly, I suggest that we need to develop an ethological science of religions with ritual as its pivotal notion. Thirdly, I survey three shifts in ritual theory. The first is that from an 'exclusive' definition—ritual being tied exclusively to religion—to an inclusive one: the category of 'ritual' comprising 'ritualizing' communicative behavior of both religious and secular kinds. The second shift is that from Émile Durkheim's theory of ritual as solidifying society to that of Catherine Bell of ritual

---

[*] An earlier version of this article was delivered as a lecture in the University of Heidelberg, Germany, on 25 January 2001. That version was published as Platvoet 2001. I am grateful to Professors Gregor Ahn, Michael Stausberg and Jan Snoek of the *Seminar für Religionswissenschaft* of Heidelberg University for inviting me to deliver this lecture and for the discussions I had with them and the other members of their research group.

[1] In Dutch: *godsdienstwetenschap* (Science of Religion[s]), in English: 'the [academic] Study of Religion[s].' I am using *Religionswissenschaft* throughout this article, because I delivered this address in a German university.

as 'redemptive hegemony,' that is, as maintaining its 'order' by being full of well-hidden violence. And the third is from noting that ritual may solidify society not only by hiding its violent face, but also by being openly violent, aggressive and destructive of society. I demonstrate the latter from a series of politico-religious rituals in India between 1984 and 1992, which all aimed at liberating the god Rama from his Muslim jail. Their apotheosis was the destruction of the Babri mosque in Ayodhya on December 6, 1992. I conclude my contribution with the suggestion that violent rituals may be detected in all religions as a perennial and endemic part of them.

Why De-Westernize?

'Immortality' as Death Briefly Delayed

On being invited to lecture in Heidelberg University, I was thrilled to find that some of my articles on 'ritual'[2] were being studied in this university. It made me briefly feel as if I had attained a measure of academic immortality. However, my study of the indigenous religions of Africa quickly deflated this feeling, for in the religion of the Akan of Ghana—the one I know best[3]—'immortality' is merely attenuated mortality, death briefly delayed. Mbiti correctly termed the ancestors the 'living dead' (Mbiti 1969, 25–27, passim). In many African traditional religions, ancestors are objects of frequent cult, because they are believed to play a prominent role in the lives of their descendants. However, they are not 'immortal' in a Western-Christian meaning of the concept, for African traditional religions know no steady states in afterlife, such as heaven and hell. In Akan traditional religion—and I suggest, pace Mbiti, in African indigenous religions generally—ancestors do not individually occupy a permanent 'ontological state between God and men' (Mbiti 1969, 27). They survive death for a few generations only, as long as they are ritually remembered by name by their descendants. After that, they slip into the nameless collective of 'the ancestors' (the nananom of Akan prayers), and thence into total oblivion. Thus die immortals, quietly, without anyone mourning them. African ancestors are, therefore, not 'immortal.' Their occupying a permanent "ontological state between God and men" (Mbiti 1969, 27) is a Christian theo-

---

[2] Platvoet 1983a; 1985; 1995a; 1995b; 1995c; 1996a; 1999a; 2000a; 2000b; 2001.
[3] See Platvoet 1973; 1979; 1982a: 39–44, 56–68, 84–120, 175–219; 1982b; 1983a; 1984; 1985a; 1985b; 1991; 2000a; 2001.

logical construct, one of the several 'Hellenizations,' against which Okot p'Bitek directed his furious protests.[4]

The Root Cause

This brings me to the subject of this essay, as it is phrased in its subtitle: 'the need to de-westernize the concept' of 'ritual,' as well as all other core concepts of *Religionswissenschaft*. It brings me to the root cause of the problem confronting us. It is the gap between the aims of *Religionswissenschaft*, and the methods scholars have at their disposal to achieve them. That aim is the 'cool, sober, and methodical'[5] comparative study of the religions of humankind in order to gain 'objective' knowledge of them, that is, representations that are not only unbiased, non-normative, and neutral, but also accurate and empirical, that is, testable. The latter requires that these representations be presented in such way that fellow scholars may verify or falsify them by reexamining them in a critical spirit of 'organized scepticism.'[6]

The means are the research methods we use in the study of religions, as they are informed by our analytical concepts and theories. They are far too weak to achieve fully neutral knowledge about religions and what is worse they are inherently too weak. That is why critical testing by fellow scholars is absolutely necessary. But even with the aid of the critical community of the scholars of religions, it cannot be achieved in full. Why not?

Anthropologists, who mainly study other societies and religions synchronically, by participant observation, term their analytical tools the *etic* categories. They are the Western concepts which anthropologists, as observers and outsiders, use, first, for understanding 'the native's point of view' (see Geertz 1999), and then for ordering their data into a description of another culture, for analyzing it, comparing it with other cultures, and developing theory about them. They term the cultures they study the *emic* meaning systems of the particular actors whose behavior they observe. As insiders,

---

[4]   The other is that of dressing up God and the gods of African indigenous religions in 'Hellenic robes,' i.e., presenting them as eternal, omniscient and omnipotent. See p'Bitek 1971, 28, 40, 46–47, 49–50, 58–69, 75–76, 80, 85–88, 91, 102, 105, 107–108, 110; see also Westerlund 1985; Hackett 1990; Shaw 1990.

[5]   Originally, the phrase appeared in p'Bitek's critical review of Placide Tempels' *Bantu Philosophy* (p'Bitek 1964a) when he admonished scholars of African religions to 'prefer a cool, sober, methodical and comparative approach' to the unifying, mystifying, and metaphysical one of Tempels. As 'cool, sober and methodical' it became the title of a critical response to that review by Harris (1964), and of p'Bitek's reply (1964b).

[6]   See the definition of a social-scientific academic discipline as a 'democratic community of organised scepticism' by Köbben (1974, 88).

these actors express their views through the symbol and meaning systems of their own cultures.[7]

We may transpose this *etic-emic*/observer-actor/outsider-insider distinction[8] from anthropology to *Religionswissenschaft*, because both have in common that they are immense enterprises in transcultural hermeneutics. Both aim to represent objectively and neutrally the symbol and meaning systems, cultic behavior, cosmologies, and the social and religious institutions of other societies and/or other periods. That task requires that we use neutral, unbiased, purely technical categories in their analysis, which do not impose upon them, or secretly import into them, our own, culturally specific notions, attitudes, sentiments, values, ideals, cosmology, etc. Nor should they constrain our grasp of the non-Western meaning systems we study, and cause us to fail to perceive their full historical, idiosyncratic particularities.

But this is precisely what our *etic*, Western-analytical concepts do. The reason of this state of affairs is, of course, that our *etic* concepts are our own *emic* concepts. They are the historically contingent and culturally particular concepts of modern Western society as shaped by its peculiar Christian history. They are not at all the empty, unbiased, non-directive, purely technical concepts, fit for the neutral comparative study of religions. On the contrary, they are culturally conditioned ones, and thus eminently subjective, and defective, and inherently flawed, for the neutral analysis and comparison of the religions of the world.

Unfortunately, they are the only means at our disposal. They are the only eyes we have for looking at other cultures and religions, and the only spotlights we can direct upon them. Moreover, our minds are so thoroughly steeped in our own culture and its religious traditions, that we take our own perception of other cultures and religions as the perfectly 'natural' one, and our analysis of them as perfectly 'normal.' Our own culture—as the *forma informans* that shaped our minds in even their deepest recesses—is very successful in hiding from us that it imposes constraining and distorting views

---

[7] This 'outsider/insider' distinction is different from that other 'outsider/insider problem' which has been a bone of contention in the history of the methodology of *Religionswissenschaft* since its inception and is hotly debated even now. It respects the debate whether scholars, who are not themselves religious, can produce valid knowledge about religions. Those denying that they can, presume that only 'insiders,' who are religious themselves, can re-experience by empathy accurately and objectively the full depths of meaning which religious beliefs and actions have for the believers of other religions. For a recent survey of this debate, see McCutcheon 1999a.

[8] On *emic-etic* see McCutcheon 1999b; Pike 1999; Geertz 1999.

and analyses of other cultures and religions upon us (see Lincoln 1996, 226 [= Lincoln 1999, 397]).

The root-problem of the methodology of *Religionswissenschaft* is, therefore, that so far, we, as scholars of religions, have achieved little in the way of increasing the neutral, *trans-emic* quality of our *etic* categories of description, comparison, and analysis. Nor have we as yet cultivated a strong sense of the need to achieve a higher degree of neutrality for them. To empty them progressively of their modern Western-Christian peculiarities, we need to engage in a long, painful and never-ending process of self-critical reflection, that is, in reflexivity, in the meaning of 'us bending-back upon ourselves.'

For striving after more neutral concepts, there are two tracks along which we may travel towards a greater *trans-emicity* and neutrality of our *etic* categories. The oldest one is a constant critical attention to the data supplied to us by the historical study of religions. Despite, or better precisely because of, the pervasively Western character of that discipline, we have been aware that we need to examine them constantly and critically for elements that are discordant with our Western concepts. We must investigate them to find out whether they contain elements that require us to revise our analytical categories. My critique of Mbiti's use of the Western-Christian concept of 'immortality' was based on my historical study of Akan traditional religion. Western scholars of other societies, cultures and religions have, therefore, always cultivated a spirit of not only cultural, but also of conceptual, relativism and been aware of the need to keep our analytical categories constantly open and revisable. We must be aware of the myopia that our modern Western-Christian *etic* categories cause in us, and widen them with whatever they unduly exclude or fail to accommodate—'unduly' being of course the crux of the matter, and the bone of contention.

At the heart of this ethic—or myth?—of *Religionswissenschaft* as an academic discipline is the relentless strive after 'objectivity.' It implies that its canon of truth is the object of study, the religions that are being studied, and not the categories and theories of the scholars with which they study them. This ethic requires the scholars to develop a sharp critical self-reflexivity by a constant awareness of the historical contingency of their analytical categories and the inherent limitations they impose upon their academic work.

If the first road starts from research on the historical data of other religions, the complementary road starts from the opposite end. It consists in the critical examination of the *etic* concepts themselves, as they functioned in *Religionswissenschaft* in the past and till this very day. By means of a thorough study of the history of its methodology, of its core concepts, and of the discipline itself, they may be stripped of their taken-for-granted pretence of providing us with valid, and ostensibly with universally valid, truths. They need to be examined as thoroughly particular, and peculiar, modern Western mental constructs; as inspired by very recent Western ideals, interests and conflicts; and as part and parcel of several types of modern Western under-cover strategies and open, or more often subtly hidden, hegemonies.[9] This road requires an even more difficult and painful exercise in critical self-re-flexivity than the first road, and a greater humility.

One useful exercise along this second road is the study of the shifts in the meaning of the core-concepts of *Religionswissenschaft* in the past. It is the ex-amination of the semantical history from, for example, Roman *religio* to modern Western 'religion,' from *secta* to 'sect,' from *cultus* to 'cult,' from *mageia* to 'magic,' from *superstitio* to 'superstition.' They and such other notions as 'idols' and 'idolatry,' 'witchcraft' and 'sorcery,' 'paganism,' 'syncretism,' etc., should be studied for their distorting effects. Among them also such seemingly innocent categories as 'God,' 'soul,' 'prayer,' 'priest,' 'prophet,' 'sacrifice,' and in par-ticular the modern Western-Christian dichotomies of 'sacred' *versus* 'profane,' 'natural' *versus* 'supernatural,' 'spiritual' *versus* 'material,' etc.[10]

It is important, of course, in this historical semantics, to study, on the one hand, the shifts in their meanings as articulated in the contests over their def-inition by scholars in the past two centuries. But it is, on the other hand, even more important that their inarticulate shifts are studied, as they occurred in extra-academic uses and definitions, whether in pious books and fiction, in decisions taken by bureaucrats in government agencies, by judges and lawyers in the courts, by journalists in the media, by teachers in the classroom, or by the general public in its various factions, etc. (see, e.g., Beckford 1999; Intro-vigne 1999).

Moreover, all these shifts need to be contextualized. That is, the various contexts in which they occurred—political, economical, social, cultural, na-tional, judicial, military, etc.—need to be examined in order to try to determine why the meaning of a concept shifted there and then, in that particular way, by those particular formulators, as part of such and such cultural developments, but also of strategies and power games, local or global.

I have reason to believe that these two roads will deliver the best progress in the de-westernization of our *etic* concepts, if they are seen, and walked, as a single, two-track road. Research in the history of religions should interact

---

[9]   See Chidester 1996 on the intimate link between Western colonization of southern Africa and the development of the core-concepts of *Religionswissenschaft*.

[10] For *religio* and 'religion,' and some of the other concepts mentioned, see Platvoet 1999c; Feil 1986; 1997; 1999; Despland 1979; Despland and Vallée 1992.

closely with that of the history and methodology of *Religionswissenschaft*, and of the history of the semantics of its core concepts. This is what I will try to show in the remaining part with respect to the concept of 'ritual.'

Ritual

Towards an Ethological *Religionswissenschaft*

Apart from the need to de-westernize all analytical concepts of *Religionswissenschaft*, there is a special reason why I urge that we revise the concept of 'ritual.' In my view, research on rituals, and reflection on the concepts we need in their analysis, should become the core business of *Religionswissenschaft*. The history of religions has very much been a text-based discipline until now. Its main business has been the examination of the 'sacred' literatures of scriptural religions in order to present their beliefs after the model of Christian theology. So, it is the cognitive element of religions that has held the center of the stage in *Religionswissenschaft* so far.

One witness for this state of affairs is the massive shift, in the twentieth century, in the definition of 'religion,' from the traditional, substantive one of 'religion as communication' [with the invisible] to the modern, functional one of 'religion as orientation.' One finds the latter as the interpretation of religion as cosmology in anthropology (see, e.g., Forde 1954), and as systems of ultimate meaning in philosophy of religion and *Religionswissenschaft* (see Platvoet 1990, 189–191; 1994, 704–707). Another witness is 'the axial age syndrome': most *Religionswissenschaftler* have viewed the scriptural, or world, religions with their canons, literatures, doctrines and theologies as the proper object of the History of Religions theoretically—without texts, no history—, and as virtually its sole object institutionally. Because the preliterate religions[11] have no texts, most scholars of religions regarded them as an uninteresting fringe to be left to anthropologists. As a result, they have remained virtually unstudied in *Religionswissenschaft*. So have the most recent religions, such as the numerous New Religious Movements and New Age, because they have no doctrines.

---

[11] They are actually the oldest type of religions of humankind. Their 'histories' recede into the mists of the palaeolithicum. Their earliest documentary evidence so far are the remains of a young *homo sapiens sapiens* girl, buried in the 'Border Cave' in KwaZulu-Natal, South Africa. That grave has been dated at 103.000 years BP ('Before Present'). See Platvoet 1996b, 49, n. 15. This kind of religion is also the largest one in number and in terms of diversity of content and form.

I do concede that beliefs are an intrinsic part of religions. So, their study will remain indispensable. Yet, I argue that beliefs should cede their place of primacy in *Religionswissenschaft* to the study of rituals, or at least that we need to complement the traditional philological History of Religions with an ethological *Religionswissenschaft* focusing on religion as behavior, as *cultus*. It will study beliefs indirectly, by examining their role in religious rituals.

I define 'cult' as postulated social interaction between believers and a-empirical addressees. Cult is non-verifiable/non-falsifiable religious communication, because its addressees are invisible beings, realms, powers and qualities, that do not belong to our empirical world in such a way that their existence and activity can be verified or falsified in a testable way before a neutral court of competent scholars (see Platvoet 1990, 192–196; 1994, 708–711; 1999b, 262–263). Cult of the a-empirical, however, also constitutes empirical communication, and community, to wit between those attending the ritual.

By studying beliefs in the context of cult, an ethological *Religionswissenschaft* will modify our views of belief. Beliefs are mental constructs in the minds of the believers that govern their putative interaction with 'the transcendent.' Ethological research into them will show that beliefs are normally not at all exclusively cognitive, and are only rarely reflectively articulated. It will demonstrate that beliefs are more often loosely clustered conglomerates of subliminal, dense and diffuse notions, sentiments, attitudes, and values in respect of the meta- and infra-empirical realms, persons, or powers that are thought to exist by believers, and to affect them and their empirical worlds. It is, therefore, a huge distortion to articulate the beliefs of these religions and present them in a systematic way, for example, top-down, from the Creator God to the 'medicines' made from plants, after the model of doctrinal religions.[12]

In addition, it will prove that these beliefs are most often expressed in ritual communication by means of pregnant symbols, that are opaque, multivocal, and polysemous, and hardly ever by precise ones with an unambiguous, well-articulated meaning. By means of these pregnant symbols[13], believers send a

---

[12] I have been guilty of this distortion myself, when I taught introductory courses on Akan traditional religion. But I was aware of this distortion, and I made my students aware of it, and compensated by presenting them with historical case studies of Akan religious behavior. See Platvoet 1982a, 84–120; 1982b; 1983a; 1984; 1985a; 1985b; 1991; 2000a; 2001 on Akan ritual behavior, and Platvoet 1995b; 1999a; 2000b; 2001 on that of the San (or Bushmen).

[13] Victor W. Turner termed them focal, key, dominant, or 'condensation' symbols. He discerned two clusters of referents in them. One fan of meanings sits on the 'orectic' or sensory pole. It expresses, subliminally, desires and feelings of the ritual participants. The other spectrum of *significata* belongs to its ideological or normative pole and represents

host of polyphonic phatic messages about their relationships and attitudes to the a-empirical, and to their fellow believers and other empirical addressees. In addition, they may express an emphatic message, for example, in words, about the business they wish to transact with the 'transcendent' referents, and/or among themselves.[14]

Therefore, I regard 'religion,' 'ritual,' and 'symbol' as the most important concepts in an ethological *Religionswissenschaft*. It will incorporate the pre-literate and newest religions as fully equal objects of study.[15] We need to include them, because this 'fringe' is of the greatest importance, comparatively and theoretically, for these two kinds of religions are very different in form, content and contexts from the scriptural ones. Both the preliterate and newest religions excel in vague, inarticulate, and confused beliefs, to which no explicit truth claims are attached. In addition, they have a very low visibility, and a near complete lack of institutionalization. Ethological analysis will uncover also unsuspected dimensions of important unarticulated religiosity in the scriptural religions, such as folk piety, folk religious pragmatics, lay devotion, religious enthusiasm, ritual healing, the exorcism of demons, pilgrimage, etc.

The definition of 'religion' has been fiercely contested throughout the history of *Religionswissenschaft*. Recently, publications have begun to appear on the history of its semantics also (see Despland 1979; Despland and Vallée 1992; Feil 1986; 1997; 1999; Platvoet 1990; 1994; 1999b; 1999c; Platvoet and Molendijk 1999). There is, however, virtually no fight as yet over the definition of 'ritual' and 'symbol' in *Religionswissenschaft*, and the study of their semantic histories are as yet fairly virgin fields of research.[16] In anthropology of religions, however, certain developments are under way. Two major shifts in approaches to 'ritual' may be indicated. One is the shift from an exclusive to an inclusive definition of 'ritual.' The other is the development from the Durk-

---

the norms and values inherent in the social structure of their society. See Turner 1967, 19–32, 50–58; 1968, 1–8, 16–21, 43–44, 80–83, 183–185, 207, 213; 1974, 48–49; Turner and Turner 1978, 243–249; Morris 1987, 241–242.

[14] A ritual needs to be examined by three separate analyses: a network, process and context analysis. In the network analysis, the pre-existing relationships between the participants in the ritual (empirical and a-empirical) are examined to determine the structure of the community in which their communication takes place. The process analysis examines the flow and the content of ritual. In the context analysis, the several relevant contexts of both the network and the ritual are examined. See Platvoet 1982, 29–34, passim.

[15] For my draft of a General History of Religions 'from Neanderthaler to New Age,' see Platvoet 1993a; 1993b; 1996b; 1998.

[16] See however Bell 1997, 1–89, for a history of the interpretation of ritual.

heimian notion of 'religion' and 'ritual' as solidifying society, to that of Bell of ritual as 'redemptive hegemony.'

Exclusive Definitions of 'Ritual'

'Ritual' is understood in dictionaries and common parlance as having either a religious denotation, or at least an important religious connotation. In the first case, ritual includes only 'religious rituals,' such as a baptism in church, or a prayer before a meal. In the second case, it refers to public ceremonies with a religious element ranging from minor to major, as, for example, in funerals, marriages, initiations, coronations, etc. In this usage, rituals, as communicative actions,[17] always evince an inner connection with religion and are always defined in religious terms. I term this approach the exclusive definition of 'ritual.' It is standard in *Religionswissenschaft*, witness, for example, the recent (1998) definition of Bernhard Lang in volume 4 of the *Handbuch Religionswissenschaftlicher Grundbegriffe*:

> Ritual ist Oberbegriff für religiöse Handlungen, die zu bestimmten Gelegenheiten in gleicher Weise vollzogen werden, deren Ablauf durch Tradition oder Vorschrift festgelegt ist, und die aus Gesten, Worten und dem Gebrauch von Gegenständen bestehen mögen. (Lang 1998, 442–443)[18]

---

[17] I am concerned here only with those meanings in the semantic cluster of the concept of 'ritual' that relate to 'ritual' as communicative, or social, behaviour. I do not consider here the one other connotative development in that cluster that refers to repetitive, routine but non-communicative behavior, which has become fixed patterns of behavior in individuals of several kinds. One is that of a daily routine (e.g., "My neighbors never skip the ritual of their daily walk along the banks of the river"); another is of a technological kind (e.g., "My mother always goes through the ritual of rinsing the teapot with hot water before she pours the boiling water on the tea"). They may also be of an obsessive kind. See Lang (1998: 453) on the compulsive rituals of persons suffering from a neurosis (e.g., "Before stepping into bed, he must meticulously straighten his pillow many times to forestall bad dreams"). All non-communicative rituals have in common that no message are sent in them to empirical or postulated addressees and that they need not be performed, therefore, in front of a 'public.'

[18] "Ritual is the general notion for religious acts, which are performed in an identical way at specific occasions, their course having been fixed by tradition or prescription, and which may consist in gestures, words and the use of objects" (Lang 1998: 442–443; my translation). Another is by Anonymous (1995: 930): "The term *ritual* needs a precise definition because of the widespread misuse of the word. Ritual is a system of actions and beliefs that has a beginning, a middle and an end, and is directly related to superhuman beings. Superhuman beings are beings who can do things humans cannot do. ... This definition of ritual excludes such things as routines and habits. ... What makes ritual action unique is the relation it has with superhuman beings. This relationship is usually expressed through the language of belief. It

And he continues to quote the Roman Catholic Mass, the Jewish circumcision, the Vedic sacrifice, and the recitation of canonical texts by a Buddhist monk as paradigmatic examples of 'rituals.' The origin of this exclusive definition of 'ritual' lies way back in Roman religion in which *ritus* referred to the proper way, approved by tradition, of bringing sacrifices to the gods. And it was reinforced by the way the Latin, Greek and other churches prescribed the content and form of their liturgies (see Lang 1998, 443, 448). Rituals seem to express, and to presuppose the consensus and the unity of the religious congregation on how to approach the transcendent. In sociological terms, the cohesion of the community is its premise (see Turner 1968, 270).

Among anthropologists, this exclusive definition was standard until the late 1960s. Victor W. Turner (1920–1983) defined 'ritual' in 1968 as "prescribed formal behavior for occasions not given over to technical routine, having reference to beliefs in mystical (or non-empirical) beings and powers" (Turner 1967, 19; 1968, 15). He repeated it in 1978 (Turner and Turner 1978, 243), and did not revoke it before his early death in late 1983,[19] as far as I am aware.

Inclusive Definitions of 'Ritual'
By 1968, when Turner re-affirmed the tradition of defining 'ritual' exclusively in terms of religion, de-colonization and the cold war had already dramatically changed the field of study of anthropologists. Many of them had been forced out of the former colonies and had no choice but to find their own niche in the complex secularizing societies with scriptural traditions, long histories, and doctrinal religions. These new fields of study forced them to interact more closely with historians, political scientists, and sociologists. And also with ethologists of human behavior like Erving Goffman, who published several books in the 1950s and 1960s on how we present ourselves in face-to-face encounters in everyday life and in public places, and termed that our 'interaction rituals' (Goffman 1956; 1961; 1963; 1967).

In Goffman's publications on encounter rituals in the secularizing societies of the West, a paradigm shift set in towards an inclusive definition of 'ritual.' That was one wide enough to embrace all conventional forms of stylized face-to-face communication between any kind of addressable 'persons,'[20] whether

---

is this relationship that constitutes ritual. Thus ritual is made up of act and belief." I am grateful to Michael Stausberg for drawing my attention to this definition of 'ritual.'

[19] On Turner, see, e.g., Manning 1990 and the other contributions to Ashley 1990; and those to Boudewijnse 1994.

[20] 'Person' is taken here, firstly, in the ancient meaning of *persona* in classical theatre, that is as the mask, by means of which a player impersonates a part in a play, and through which

human, meta-empirical, animal, plant, or 'alien.' 'Ritual' then referred not only to the (postulated) communication of believers with God, gods, spirits, and ancestors, etc., in traditional kinds of 'religions,' or—in 'indigenous' and modern 'nature' religions—between humans and, for example, trees, or dolphins, or with aliens from outer space in modern space age religions.[21] It also embraced, in addition, specific forms of secular interaction, social, civil, or national, between humans; and between humans and their pets, and as well as among some animals. That development was completed in 1975 with the publication of *Secular Ritual*, a volume of studies edited by Sally F. Moore and Barbara G. Myerhoff.[22]

The editors discerned the following properties in ritual. It is a collective, repetitive, ordered, and alerting kind of social behavior that aims to create an attentive and focused state of mind in the addressees. It does that by evocative acting (like playing a part on stage in a theater), that is, by stylized behavior, either using extraordinary actions and symbols, or doing the ordinary in an extraordinary way. By these means, ritual provides a frame, a focus, and a structure to a social event. Together these polyphonic means may produce a feeling of 'flow' in the attendants, that is, a mental absorption into the ritual. In addition, ritual is traditionalizing and legitimizing: it dissembles innovation as

---

(*per-*) he/she voices (*sonare*) the verses of his/her role. And secondly, it is taken in the technical meaning of any addressable being, who is capable, or deemed to be capable, to understand a message directed at it, and to respond to it, at once and directly, or indirectly and in a retarded manner.

[21] See my study of the IFO-Sananda space age religion (Platvoet 1982a, 48–55, 74–83, 157–174).

[22] This is true only in retrospect. At the time, the editors were able to bridge the notional 'gap' between an exclusive and an inclusive definition of 'ritual' only through a number of intermediate steps in the definition of 'religion.' Starting from a Tylorian substantive definition of 'religion' as 'invoking spirits,' they shifted first to a Durkheimian functional-exclusive definition of 'religion' as 'the unquestionable sacred,' and then to a Tillichian functional-inclusive one of the 'para-religious' kind, that regards secular ideologies with unquestionable doctrines and imperatives also as 'religion.' These ideologies have 'rituals' too. They "dramatize social/moral imperatives without invoking the spirits at all" (Moore and Myerhoff 1975, 3). They presented the book as a humble attempt to add to established wisdom: "analogous formal procedures are inspected in secular contexts [in order to see] what new material becomes visible if the supernatural element is stripped away" (Moore and Myerhoff 1975, 4). They restricted the subject of the book to "collective ceremonial forms ... in order to make the religious analogy visible throughout," and bring to attention "a previously unobserved dimension." Moore and Myerhoff sounded rather defensive when they stated that they use 'ritual' as "loosely defined" and "in its non-technical sense" (Moore and Myerhoff 1975, 4). This implied that Moore and Myerhoff still viewed 'ritual,' when defined 'strictly,' and in a 'technical' sense, as limited to 'religious ritual.'

tradition, and provides (the semblance of) permanence and legitimacy to what are actually contingent, and often quite recent, and always arbitrary, cultural constructs (Moore and Myerhoff 1975, 7–8).

Rituals as Solidifying Society

Turner's definition of 'ritual' was the paradigmatic product of colonial anthropology, which studied small societies in 'remote' parts of the world. Colonial anthropologists mostly studied these societies in the 'timeless typological mode' of structural functionalism (Moore 1994, 39). At a time when these societies were going through immense changes, anthropologists studied them as if they were self-contained, static social systems uncontaminated by outside contact. They romanticized them as 'traditional societies,' endowed with time-tested institutions for maintaining, or regaining, balance and harmony. They saw them as homeostatic social systems[23] in which the 'laws' governing all human societies might be discovered. A natural science of human social life could be developed from their study, said Alfred R. Radcliffe-Brown.[24]

These societies were all found to be pervasively religious. So, their rituals were found to be always also religious rituals, at least to some significant degree. In addition, they were taken to be their main institution for maintaining harmony, peace, solidarity, or for restoring them. Turner, who studied the notoriously fissiparous Ndembu society of Zambia, wrote: "in many African tribes, rituals are performed most frequently when a small community is in danger of splitting up."[25] He regarded rituals as the social dramas that enabled a society to cope with crises. They were the redressive mechanisms that forestall a Ndembu village falling apart. Even when participants expressed hostility towards each other, as in the 'rituals of rebellion,'[26] they did so, said Turner, 'in obedience to traditional rules' (Turner 1968, 269). That ensured that cleavages were overcome and "the peace and harmony typically promised to ritual participants [were] finally [...] achieved" (Turner 1968, 269, see also 270, 273–274).

---

23 Turner terms them 'cyclical repetitive social systems' (1968, 273–277).
24 The classical text is Radcliffe-Brown (1952), a collection of essays by Alfred R. Radcliffe-Brown (1881–1955) written between 1924 and 1949. On Radcliffe-Brown, see Kuper 1975, 51–88 and passim; Morris 1987, 123–131.
25 Turner 1968: 278; see also 24, 89, and 269-270: "To complete a ritual ... is to overcome cleavages."
25 On Gluckman and 'rituals of rebellion,' see Kuper 1975: 176-185; Morris 1987: 248-252.
26 A category developed by Turner's teacher Max Gluckman; see Kuper 1975, 176–185; Morris 1987, 248–252.

In Turner's view, a society's unity was the product of its (religious) rituals, not their premise (see Turner 1968, 270). Turner's analyses of ritual completed Durkheim's functionalist legacy. Though of Jewish descent, Durkheim was an atheist and a sociologist, and defined 'religion' and its rituals as *the* mechanism indispensable to any and every society. By *his* definition, 'religion,' and especially 'religious cult,' united all those adhering to its beliefs and its practices, "into one single moral community called a Church" (Durkheim 1965, 30).[27] 'Beliefs' is used here metaphorically for the 'collective representations,' of a society and 'Church' for 'society.'[28] For, Durkheim said, it is society that actually inspires feelings of dependency in the believers. When they direct their cult at any emblem of the unseen orders, it actually is society they worship.[29] Durkheim held that (religious) rituals not only curb our destructive drives and foster feelings of dependency on our community in us, but also that they renew those feelings in the members of a society at regular intervals, and whenever society is threatened by a crisis. They may do so by a frenzied dance driven by electrifying drums in an African forest village, or by a soothing singsong session with candlelight in a Christian church in Germany in a mid-winter night.

Ritual as 'Redemptive Hegemony'

In the train of Michel Foucault and Pierre Bourdieu, 'ritual studies' have mainly moved into a praxeological direction in the last two decades, that is, towards the development of a theory of ritual practice (see Bell 1992, 74–117). As legitimating by dissimulation—in Bourdieu's terminology: by *méconnaissance*, 'misrecognition,' failure to apprehend, and even outright denial on the part of the participants[30]—ritual has been shown to be an effective tool of hegemony

---

[27] See Durkheim 1912, 65; 1965, 30: "une religion est un système solidaire de croyances et de pratiques relatives à des choses sacrées qui unissent en une même communauté morale, appelée Eglise, tous ceux qui y adhèrent."

[28] See Moore and Myerhoff 1975, 5–7.

[29] For this reason, Durkheim excluded 'magical ritual' from the category of (religious) ritual. For even though he accepted that 'magical ritual' was a communicative behavior, in which some putative meta-empirical realm was addressed, it did not qualify as (religious) ritual, because it was client-centered instead of community-orientated. It did not express collective feelings and norms, but was meant to be instrumental to the promotion of the 'selfish' interest of individuals. He summarized this dichotomy between 'religion' and 'magic' by saying: "Il n'y a pas d'Église magique" (Durkheim 1965, 30).

[30] On Bourdieu's *méconnaissance*, see Bell 1992, 81, 82–83, 85, 86, 108–110, 114–117, 183–184, 207, 210–211. Bourdieu identifies it also with the symbolic violence and domi-

for the established elite of a society by hiding what it does. For all its alerting, attention captivating qualities, ritual, says Bell, is a "particularly 'mute' form of activity. It is designed to do what it does without bringing what it does across the threshold of discourse or systematic thinking" (Bell 1992, 93).

Ritual is a strategically blind 'poetics of power' (Bell 1992, 85; citing Geertz 1980, 123; see also Platvoet 1995a; 1995c, 40–41). It maintains attitudes and views in the participants that dispose them to accept the quite arbitrary, very unequal division of status, power, and income in society as natural, normal, appropriate and fitting. In Bell's beautifully tragic paradox, ritual is 'redemptive hegemony': inequality and oppression which the oppressed fail to see as such, which they explicitly deny, in which they rejoice, and which they fervently defend as fitting (Bell 1992, 83–85). This approach marries perspectives of Marx and Durkheim. Rituals are both effective instruments of power, distinction, discrimination and inequality, and precisely thereby continue to unify societies. They prevent revolution precisely by hiding their violent face. As a result, theory on ritual has not proceeded beyond unifying rituals, because so far rituals have virtually exclusively been studied in the mono-cultural situations of (seemingly) homogeneous societies.

Ritual as War

Violent Rituals

However, if it makes sense to regard ritual as the ritualization of communicative encounters between humans (and other addressable beings) (see Bell 1992, 219), then it is unlikely that there are no violent rituals, no rituals of war. For violence and war have always been prominent among the dramatic kinds of encounter of humans, especially in the multicultural situations of plural and pluralist societies—ancient and modern—with their huge internal divisions.[31] That war itself is a ritual, Palestinian boys have amply shown in the past few months when they threw stones at Israeli soldiers, got killed, and were paraded through Palestinian towns under green flags as 'martyrs,' in burial processions that were violent political marches.

It is time, therefore, now to walk finally briefly along the other road that of the historical data on specific religions to show that rituals may indeed show a

---

nation a ritual exercises upon the participants (Bourdieu and Wacquant 1992, 167–168, 194–195).

[31] On 'plural' (as distinct from 'pluralist') societies, see Platvoet and Van der Toorn 1995b, 3, n. 1; Platvoet 1995c, 37–38.

face of violence, and may explode a society instead of unite it, or better unite part of it by exploding it. Or better—and this is as tragic as Bell's redemptive hegemony—they are solidifying a section of society by being explosive of larger society. To demonstrate this, I will briefly review the Ayodhya 'rituals of confrontation,' as they were performed in India between 1984 and 1992 (see Platvoet 1995a; 1995c; 1996a). Before I do so, I must make one more methodological point.

The study of ritual so far has virtually exclusively been restricted to what we took to be mono-cultural contexts. It made us take for granted analytically that only one audience is addressed in a ritual, and that that audience takes part in it as a united congregation. That assumption has severely limited the range of communicative events we included in the category 'ritual,' and has unduly constrained our analysis of them. It prevented us from seeing, for instance, that in plural and pluralist societies, rituals may address several audiences at once, and in very different ways, by one and the same message.

This is so in particular in modern societies with 'minorities' and modern media. In these 'plural' societies, ethnic groups, or other political constituencies with conflicting interests, foster the cohesion of their communities by cultivating their identities and guarding their borders by means of segregation. They prohibit, severely limit, or strictly regulate contact with other communities, and sanction any 'unwanted' relations, particularly marriages. They also cultivate generalized pejorative prejudices about them.

In times of hostility, these communities watch each other intently. They become each other's audiences, whenever one of them conducts a public ritual, for the modern media cover all important events, interpret their *double entendres*, and convey the political import of the message of a religious ritual to the audience for whom it is meant.

The Liberation of Rama

One such ominous message, directed in the 1980s in India by militant Hindus to India's large Muslim minority, was that "Rama must be liberated from his jail," the Babri mosque in Ayodhya. The message also said that that mosque, and other mosques alleged to have been built on Hindu 'holy' sites, must be destroyed, and that India must become a de-secularized Hindu nation. We are dealing here with a dense complex of consonant symbols, expressed in several polyphonic forms. I mention only five.

One is the *Ramayana* epic about the seventh *avatara* ('descent,' 'incarnation') of Vishnu, the just ruler Rama, and his faithful wife, Sita. Ayodhya is, by itself, a complex of three symbol systems. It is an iconography in stone by its three thousand temples, most of them devoted to episodes in the story of Rama and

Sita. It is the pilgrimage center for millions of devotees of Rama. And it is the headquarters of three types of monks devoted to Rama. They are, firstly, the naked *nagas* (fighter monks) devoted to Rama, but even more to his monkey-general, Hanuman. Secondly, they are the swooning *rasiks* (temple-servants) who devote their lives to serving *Ramsaguna* (Rama qualified): Rama and Sita in their *murtis* (visible shapes), that is, as statues in their 'living quarters.' And the third are the peripatetic *tyagis* (peripatetic devotees), who direct their devotion to *Ramnirguna* (Rama unqualified) as the expression of the supreme transcendent 'reality.' The fifth form is Rama in his capital of Ayodhya, and later as imprisoned there in a Muslim jail. It served, and serves, as a powerful emblem of the grudges of militant Hindus against Muslims and the Indian adherents of other foreign religions, and of the aspirations of Hindu imperialists.

The Rama/Ayodhya complex has been used on three occasions so far in struggles between Hindus and Muslims. Each occurred in periods of political instability, in which power relationships were being redefined. The first two were local struggles. The third was a national one.

The first occurred in the period 1850–1860, when the British incorporated the Muslim 'kingdom' of Awadth, in which Ayodhya was situated, into their colony. In 1853, Hindus spread the claim that the Babri mosque had been built on top of the ruins of a temple in honor of *Ramjanmabhumi* (Rama's birthplace) in 1528. It was actually a counterclaim to one by the tiny local Sunni minority that a mosque had stood in the precincts of *Hanumangarhi*, the fortress convent of the *nagas*, the naked warrior monks. They entered into a pitched battle with the *nagas* to take their right to pray there by force. The *nagas* drove them back into the nearby Babri *mashid*, killing seventy Muslims. A counter *jihad* of local Muslims in February 1856 was quelled by the British in a three-hour pitched battle at the cost of a heavy loss of lives on both sides (Platvoet 1995a, 194–197; 1996a, 135–136).

The second took place in the period 1947–1950, at the de-colonization of the subcontinent and its traumatic division into the secular state of India and the Islamic state of Pakistan (see Ahmed 1982). Tensions ran high in Ayodhya in December 1949, in the run up to elections, when first the *Ramayana* was recited continuously for nine days in front of the *Babrimashid* (Babri mosque), and then, in the night of December 22–23, 1949 statues of Rama and Sita were smuggled into the mosque. The claim was made then that they had miraculously 'appeared' in the mosque to reclaim that spot for themselves. Riots between Muslims and Hindus followed. When these had been quelled, the Babri mosque was declared out of bounds for both Muslims and Hindus, but the statues of Rama and Sita were not removed from it. Thus Rama got imprisoned into the *Babrimashid*.

The national confrontation was orchestrated between 1984 and 1992 by two RRS-organizations,[32] the VHP,[33] its religious affiliate, and the BJP,[34] its political party. In the run-up to national elections of 1985, 1989 and 1993, they organized nation-wide electoral mass-mobilizations campaigns, by which the tensions between the Hindu majority and large Muslim minority were further incited. The appeal to Hindus to make sacrifices for the liberation of Rama's birthplace, for freeing Rama from his jail, and promoting *Hindutva* (Hindudom), the Hinduization and de-secularization of India, were the focal points in all three campaigns, but more in particular of the first one, in the autumn of 1984.

It consisted of a procession of vans with large statues of Rama and Sita, from *Sitamarhi* (Sita's birthplace) in Bihar, to Ayodhya. It was presented as a *Ramarathayathra* (pilgrimage of war chariots of Rama), for the vans traveled along the road, which Rama was said to have traversed in his war chariot in mythical times in order to collect his bride, Sita. In all the towns and villages along the route, mass rallies were held in which numerous VHP-*sadhus* ('holy men') and militants urged the masses to vote for the BJP and demanded the destruction of mosques on Hindu 'holy' sites. This procession, and later demonstrations of Hindu fervor passed on purpose through districts and regions in which Hindu-Muslim tensions were already running high, and caused them at times to explode. Their coverage by the news media at times set in train more explosions of 'communal violence' in other parts of India. After Ayodhya, the campaign continued towards Delhi, but it fell flat before it reached the capital, when on October 31, 1984 Indira Gandhi was murdered by her Sikh bodyguard.

The next campaign in 1989 was the *Ramshilas* (bricks of Rama) campaign. 300,000 bricks for 'rebuilding' the temple on Rama's birthplace, were sent to Hindu congregations throughout India and the rest of the world. They were solemnly consecrated there in *shilapujas* (brick rituals), and then carried by VHP and BJP activists conspicuously in front of all Hindu households to ask for donations for 'rebuilding' *Ramjanmabhumi*, Rama's birthplace temple. After this they were transported in conspicuous processions from all over India to Ayodhya in early November 1989. The passage of these caravans through Muslim districts again led to violent clashes, particularly in Bihar, with hundreds of dead on both

---

[32] *Rashtriya Swayamsevak Sangh* (National Volunteer Corps), a militant Hindu cultural reform movement founded in 1925; see Platvoet 1995a, 188, n. 9, 188–189; 1996a, 127, n. 1. The RSS is also called the *sangh parivar* (the Family) because it consists of numerous affiliated organizations; see Platvoet 1995a, 188–189.

[33] *Vishva Hindu Parisad* (Hindu World Federation); see Platvoet 1995a, 202, n. 86; 1996a, 127, n. 2.

[34] *Bharatiya Janata* Party (Indian People's Party); see Platvoet 1995, 188, n. 10.

sides. In the 1989 election, the BJP scored its first major electoral success. It rose from 2 to 88 seats in the Parliament of India.

In the period 1990–1992, the BJP leader Advani conducted a 10,000 kilometers long *Ramrathayatra* through India exhorting Hindus to *Rambhakti* (fervent devotion to Rama), *lokshakti* (people's power), and *Ramakarseva* (voluntary service to Rama), for rebuilding his temple in Ayodhya. The procession's war cry was: "we will build the temple there, and only there." Thousands of youths joined him for *karseva*, mainly by swelling the ranks of *Bajrang Dal*, the militant youth association of the RSS.

To cut a long story short, it was this youth movement that supplied the 44,000 *karsevaks* who served as storm troopers on December 6, 1992. They cleared the way to the heavily guarded Babri mosque in Ayodhya for a specially trained force of 1,200 youths who reduced it to rubble in less than six hours, at the cost of several lives. This event was flashed all over the world that very same day. The nationwide violence, which followed took a toll of 1,700 dead and over 5,000 wounded.

These violent rituals have paid off for the RSS. The BJP is now the ruling party of India. In the ongoing confrontation with Pakistan, it has 'tested' its own atomic bomb. India has taken over the production of the sophisticated Mig-fighter planes from ailing Russia. An ICT-revolution is on its way in India, and it is exporting both software and software engineers. Part of the *Hindutva* ideology of the RSS/BJP is a Hindu imperialist aspiration. They aim to regain political, cultural and religious control over not only the whole of the subcontinent, but also over those other parts of South East Asia in which Hindu influence has been strong in those 'glorious' periods when Hindu kingdoms and empires called the tune in that region.

In Conclusion

'Rituals of war' are not limited only to plural societies with histories of 'communal violence.' Rituals expressing hostility are endemic in many religions, and in at least some of them, they have been their most central feature since time immemorial. An example of the latter is the so-called 'curing dances' of the San, or Bushmen, in the Kalahari region of southern Africa. Their tiny bands, or camps, had[35] reciprocity, equality and sharing as their key values (see Guenther 1999,

---

[35] I am using the past tense, because the ethnographic data I use relate to the 2.500 San who still lived mainly as foragers in the 1950s and 1960s (on a total number of 40.000). As

142; Platvoet 1999a, 21–23, 45–46, 49–50; 2000b, 124–125) since time immemorial.[36] They used their one and only religious ritual (see Platvoet 1999a, 33–34; Guenther 1999, 181), the trance dance, for two purposes. One was to share out *n/um* (healing power) among themselves (see Platvoet 1999a, 34–39; 2000b, 127–129; Guenther 1999, 183–184). As such, the curing dance was a powerful rite of solidarity and inclusion. The other was to eject all blame for dissent, disease and death out of the camp by projecting it onto 'god' and the dead. The trance dancer did this in the final dramatic phase of a trance. Having 'pulled out' all evil from the members of the band, the trance dancer either threw it back to 'its origin,' yelling abuse at it and charging towards it with burning sticks. Or he collapsed into a catatonic visionary state in which he sought out and confronted the 'spiritual beings,' that had 'sent' the evil, in a shamanic fashion (see Platvoet 1999a, 34–44; 2000b, 129–132; Guenther 1999, 185–188). As such the trance dance was a dramatic ritual of exclusion, of boundary maintenance with, and war on, god and the dead lurking in the dark, and of chasing them off, time and again (see Platvoet 1999a, 49–53; 2000b, 131f.; Guenther 1999, 188f.).

I suggest that rituals of war, confrontation and exclusion[37] are endemic in all religions. That is certainly the case for traditional orthodox and modern Pentecostal Christianity. Both are predicated doctrinally on an absolute dualism between God and Satan. That enmity is magnificently dramatized in the classical ritual exorcism of the *Rituale Romanum*. Blumhardt rediscovered its ritual practice under the guidance of Gottliebin Dittus (see Blumhardt 1979). The exorcism of devils and demons is practiced presently in rather restrained and subdued ways in charismatic and Pentecostal faith healing in the West, but it is celebrated in florid rituals in much of modern African Christianity (see, e.g., Meyer 1992; 1995).

Discerning that rituals may be openly violent, and integrating that awareness into the analytical notion of 'ritual,' represents, in my view, a significant step in the de-westernization of this *etic* category in *Religionswissenschaft* as an academic discipline for the comparative study of religions and their rituals, as well as in 'ritual studies.'

---

these San too have adopted a sedentary way of life now, foraging as a way of life has virtually disappeared by now among the San (Platvoet 1999a, 13–17). The trance dance, however, has not declined in importance. Sedentary San are practicing it even more frequently, for one reason because it serves as a means of cultural revitalization for them. See Platvoet 1999a, 17–18, n. 77, 56, n. 262; Guenther 1999, 182, 192–196.

[36] Witness their rock paintings; see Platvoet 1999a, 5–11, 44, 46–48; 2000b, 124; Guenther 1999, 181–182; see also the literature referred to in Platvoet 1999a, e.g., Dowson and Lewis-Williams 1994.

[37] For rituals of exclusion, see also Chidester 1988, 12–24.

References

Ahmed, Munir D. 1982: Pakistan: The Dream of an Islamic State. In: *Religions and Societies: Asia and the Middle East*, ed. Carlo Caldarola. (Religion and Society 22). Berlin: Mouton. 261–288.

Anonymous. 1995: Ritual. In: *The HarperCollins Dictionary of Religion*, ed. Jonathan Z. Smith. New York: HarperCollins Publishers. 930–932.

Ashley, Kathleen M. (ed.). 1990: *Victor Turner and the Construction of Cultural Criticism: Between Literature and Anthropology*. Bloomington: Indiana University Press.

Beckford, James, A. 1999: The Politics of Defining Religion in a Secular Society: From a Taken-for-granted Institution to a Contested Resource. In: Platvoet and Molendijk 1999. 23–40.

Blumhardt, Johann C. 1979: Krankheitsgeschichte der G.D. in Möttlingen, mitgetheilt von Pfarrer Blumhardt (1844). In: *Gesammelte Werke*. Vol. 1, ed. Gerhard Schäfer. Göttingen: Vandenhoeck & Ruprecht. 32–78.

Bell, Catherine. 1992: *Ritual Theory, Ritual Praxis*. New York and Oxford: Oxford University Press.

———. 1997: *Ritual: Perspectives and Dimensions*. New York and Oxford: Oxford University Press.

Bitek, Okot p'. 1964a: Fr. Tempels' Bantu Philosophy. In: *Transition* 3 (13):16–17.

———. 1964b: Cool Cool, Sober Sober, Methodical Methodical. In: *Transition* 4 (16):5–6.

———. 1971: *African Religions in Western Scholarship*. Kampala: East African Literature Bureau.

Boudewijnse, Barbara (ed.). 1994: De erfenis van Victor Turner. In: Special issue of *Antropologische Verkenningen* 13 (4):1–69.

Bourdieu, Pierre and Loïc J.D. Wacquant. 1992: *An Invitation to Reflexive Sociology*. Cambridge: Polity Press.

Chidester, David. 1988: *Salvation and Suicide: An Interpretation of Jim Jones, the Peoples Temple, and Jonestown*. Bloomington: Indiana University Press.

———. 1996: *Savage Systems: Colonialism and Comparative Religion in Southern Africa*. Charlottesville: University Press of Virginia.

Despland, Michel. 1979: *La religion en occident: évolution des idées et du vécu*. (Cogitatio fidei 101). Montréal: éditions Fides; Paris: Les éditions du Cerf.

Despland, Michel and Gérard Vallée (eds.). 1992: *Religion in History: The Word, the Idea, the Reality*. Waterloo, Ontario: Wilfried Laurier University Press.

Dowson, Thomas A. and David Lewis-Williams (eds.). 1994: *Contested Images: Diversity in South African Rock Art Research*. Johannesburg: Witwatersrand University Press.

Durkheim, Émile. 1912: *Les formes élémentaires de la vie religieuse: le système totémique en Australie*. Paris: Alcan.

———. 1965: The Elementary Forms of Religious Life. In: *Reader in Comparative Religion: An Anthropological Approach*, ed. William A. Lessa and Evon Z. Vogt. New York: Harper & Row. 28–36.

Feil, Ernst. 1986: *Religio: Die Geschichte eines neuzeitlichen Grundbegriffs vom Frühchristentum bis zur Reformation*. (Forschungen zur Kirchen- und Dogmengeschichte 36). Göttingen: Vandenhoeck & Ruprecht.

———. 1997: *Religio, zweiter Band: die Geschichte eines neuzeitlichen Grundbegriff zwischen Reformation und Rationalismus (ca. 1540–1620)*. (Forschungen zur Kirchen- und Dogmengeschichte 70). Göttingen: Vandenhoeck & Ruprecht.

———. 1999: 'Religio' and 'Religion' in the Eighteenth Century: The Contrasting Views of Wolff and Edelmann. In: Platvoet and Molendijk 1999. 125–148.

Ford, Daryll (ed.). 1954: *African Worlds: Studies in the Cosmological Ideas and Social Values of African Peoples*. London: Oxford University Press.

Geertz, Clifford. 1980: *Negara: The Theatre State in Nineteenth Century Bali*. Princeton: Princeton University Press.

——. 1999: 'From the Native's Point of View': On the Nature of Anthropological Understanding. In: McCutcheon 1999a. 50–63.

Goffman, Erving. 1956: *Presentation of Self in Everyday Life*. Edinburgh: University of Edinburgh.

——. 1961: *Encounters: Two Studies in the Sociology of Interaction*. Indianapolis: Bobbs-Merrill.

——. 1963: *Behaviour in Public Places: Notes on the Social Organisation of Gatherings*. New York: The Free Press.

——. 1967: *Interaction Ritual: Essays on Face-to-Face Behavior*. New York: Doubleday.

Guenther, Mathias. 1999: *Tricksters and Trancers: Bushman Religion and Society*. Bloomington: Indiana University Press.

Harris, R.G. 1964: Cool, Sober and Methodical. In: *Transition* 4 (15):43–45.

Introvigne, Massimo. 1999: Religion as Claim: Social and Legal Controversies. In: Platvoet and Molendijk 1999. 41–72.

Köbben, André J.F. 1974: Sociale wetenschappen en ethiek. In: *Waarden en wetenschap: Polemische opstellen over de plaats van waardeoordelen in de sociale wetenschappen*, ed. Theo de Boer and André J.F. Köbben. Bilthoven: Ambo. 86–104.

Kuper, Adam. 1975: *Anthropologists and Anthropology: The British School, 1922–1972*. 2d ed. Harmondsworth: Penguin Books.

Lang, Bernhard. 1998: Ritual/Ritus. In: *Handbuch religionswissenschaftlicher Grundbegriffe*. Vol. 4, ed. Hubert Cancik, Burkhard Gladigow, and Karl-Heinz Kohl. Stuttgart: Kohlhammer. 442–458.

Lincoln, Bruce. 1996: Theses on Method. In: *Method and Theory in the Study of Religion* 8:225–227 [= Lincoln 1999].

——. 1999: Theses on Method. In: McCutcheon 1999. 395–398 [= Lincoln 1996].

Manning, Frank E. 1990: Victor Turner's Career and Publications. In: *Victor Turner and the Construction of Cultural Criticism: Between Literature and Anthropology*, ed. Kathleen M. Ashley. Bloomington: Indiana University Press. 170–177.

Mbiti, John S. 1969: *African Religions and Philosophy*. London: Heinemann.

McCutcheon, Russell T. (ed.). 1999a: *The Insider/Outsider Problem in the Study of Religion: A Reader*. London and New York: Cassell.

——. 1999b: Introduction [to Part I]. In: McCutcheon 1999a. 15–22.

Meyer, Birgit. 1992: "If you are a Devil, you are a Witch, and if you are a Witch, you are a Devil": The Integration of 'Pagan' Ideas into the Conceptual Universe of Ewe Christians in Southeastern Ghana. In: *Journal of Religion in Africa* 22:98–132.

——. 1995: "Delivered from the Powers of Darkness": Confessions of Satanic Riches in Christian Ghana. In: *Africa* 65:236–255.

Moore, Sally F. 1994: *Anthropology and Africa: Changing Perspectives on a Changing Scene*. Charlottesville: University Press of Virginia.

Moore, Sally F. and Barbara G. Myerhoff (eds.). 1975: *Secular Ritual*. Assen: Van Gorcum.

Morris, Brian. 1987: *Anthropological Studies of Religion: An Introductory Text*. Cambridge: Cambridge University Press.

Pike, Kenneth L. 1999: *Etic* and *Emic* Standpoints for the Description of Behavior (1954). In: McCutcheon 1999a. 28–36.

Platvoet, Jan G. 1973: Verschuivingen in een Afrikaanse godsdienst: Hekserijbekentenissen en de opkomst van de 'beul'-goden in de godsdienst van de Ashanti. In: *Bijdragen: Tijdschrift voor Filosofie en Theologie* 34:15–39.

———. 1979: The Akan Believer and his Religions. In: *Official and Popular Religion: Analysis of a Theme for Religious Studies*, ed. Pieter H. Vrijhof and Jacques Waardenburg. (Religion and Society 19). The Hague, Paris, and New York: Mouton. 544–606.

———. 1982a: *Comparing Religions: A Limitative Approach; An Analysis of Akan, Para-Creole, and IFO-Sananda Rites and Prayers.* (Religion and Reason 24). The Hague: Mouton.

———. 1982b: Commemoration by Communication: Akan Funerary Terracottas. In: *Visible Religion: Annual for Religious Iconography* 1:113–134.

———. 1983a: Verbal Communication in an Akan Possession and Maintenance Rite. In: *Analysis and Interpretation of Rites: Essays presented to D.J. Hoens*, ed. Jan G. Platvoet. The Hague: Boekencentrum. 202–215.

———. 1984: In de koelte van de 'ontvangstboom': De politieke functie van een akan godsdienstig symbool. In: *Van gerechtigheid tot liturgie*, ed. Hans van Reisen. Hilversum: Gooi & Sticht. 61–91.

———. 1985a: Op bezoek bij de god Tano. In: *Inleiding tot de studie van godsdiensten*, ed. Dirk J. Hoens, Jacques H. Kamstra, Dirk C. Mulder. 1985: Kampen: Kok. 140–158.

———. 1985b: Cool Shade, Peace and Power: The *Gyedua* ("Tree of Reception") as an Ideological Instrument of Identity Management Among the Akan Peoples of Southern Ghana. In: *Journal of Religion in Africa* 15:174–200.

———. 1990: The Definers Defined: Traditions in the Definition of Religion. In: *Method and Theory in the Study of Religion* 2:180–212.

———. 1991: 'Renewal' by Retrospection: The Asante Anokye Traditions. In: *Religion, Tradition, and Renewal*, ed. Armin W. Geertz and Jeppe Sinding Jensen. Aarhus: Aarhus University Press. 149–176.

———. 1993a: De wraak van de 'primitieven': Godsdienstgeschiedenis van Neanderthaler tot New Age. In: *Nederlands Theologisch Tijdschrift* 47:227–243.

———. 1993b: African Traditional Religions in the Religious History of Humankind. In: *Journal for the Study of Religion* 6:29–48.

———. 1994: Defining the Definers: Non-Verifiability/Non-Falsifiability as a Definiens in an Operational Definition of Religion. In: *The Notion of 'Religion' in Comparative Research: Selected Proceedings of the XVI IAHR Congress*, ed. Ugo Bianchi. Rome: 'L'Erma' di Bretschneider. 701–711.

———. 1995a: Ritual as Confrontation: The Ayodhya Conflict. In: Platvoet and Van der Toorn 1995a. 187–226.

———. 1995b: God als vijand: De genezingsdansen van de !Kung. In: *Nederlands Theologisch Tijdschrift* 49:89–107.

———. 1995c: Ritual in Plural and Pluralist Societies: Instruments for Analysis. In: Platvoet and Van der Toorn 1995a. 25–51.

———. 1996a: Religions in Contest: The Ayodhya Rituals of Confrontation. In: *Religions in Contact: Selected Proceedings of the Special IAHR Conference held in Brno, August 23–26, 1994*, ed. Eva Dolezalova, Bretislav Horyna, and Dalibor Papousek. Brno: Czech Society for the Study of Religions. 127–144.

———. 1996b: The Religions of Africa in their Historical Order. In: *The Study of Religions in Africa: Past, Present, Prospects*, ed. James L. Cox, Jacob K. Olupona, and Jan G. Platvoet. Cambridge: Roots & Branches. 46–102.

Platvoet, Jan G. 1998: Van vóór tot voorbij de enige maatstaf: Over de canonieke fase in de alge-
mene godsdienstgeschiedenis. In: *Heilig boek en religieus gezag: Ontstaan en functioneren
van canonieke tradities*, ed. Konrad D. Jenner and Gerard A. Wiegers. Kampen: Kok. 93–125.

————. 1999a: At War with God: Ju/'hoan Curing Dances. In: *Journal of Religion in Africa* 29:2–
61.

————. 1999b: To Define or Not to Define: The Problem of the Definition of Religion. In: Platvoet
and Molendijk 1999. 245–265.

————. 1999c: Contexts, Concepts and Contests: Towards a Pragmatics of Defining Religion. In:
Platvoet and Molendijk 1999. 463–516.

————. 2000a: Rattray's Request: Spirit Possession among the Bono of West Africa. In: *Indigenous Religions: A Companion*, ed. Graham Harvey. London: Cassell. 80–96.

————. 2000b: Chasing Off God: Spirit Possession in a Sharing Society. In: *Indigenous Religious
Musics*, ed. Karen Ralls-MacLeod and Graham Harvey. Aldershot : Ashgate. 122–135.

————. 2001: The Rule and its Exceptions: Spirit Possession in Two African Societies. In: *Journal
for the Study of Religion* 13:5-51.

Platvoet, Jan G. and Karel van der Toorn (eds.). 1995a: *Pluralism and Identity: Studies in Ritual
Behaviour*. (Studies in the History of Religions 67). Leiden: E.J. Brill.

————. and Karel van der Toorn 1995b: Ritual Responses to Plurality and Pluralism. In: Platvoet
and Van der Toorn 1995a. 3–21.

Platvoet, Jan G. and Arie L. Molendijk (eds.). 1999: *The Pragmatics of Defining Religion: Contexts, Concepts and Contests*. (Studies in the History of Religions 84). Leiden: E.J. Brill.

Radcliffe-Brown, Alfred R. 1952: *Structure and Function in Primitive Society: Essays and Addresses*. London: Cohen & West.

Shaw, Rosalind. 1990: The Invention of 'African Traditional Religion'. In: *Religion* 20:339–353.

Turner, Victor W. 1967: *The Forest of Symbols: Aspects of Ndembu Ritual*. Ithaca and London:
Cornell University Press.

————. 1968: *The Drums of Affliction: A Study of Religious Processes among the Ndembu of
Zambia*. Oxford: Clarendon Press.

————. 1969: *The Ritual Process: Structure and Anti-Structure*. (Lewis Henry Morgan Lectures
1966). Harmondsworth: Penguin Books.

Turner, Victor W. and Edith Turner. 1978: *Image and Pilgrimage in Christian Culture: Anthropological Perspectives*. Oxford: Basil Blackwell.

Westerlund, David. 1985: *African Religion in African Scholarship: A Preliminary Study of the Religious and Political Background*. Stockholm: Almquist & Wiksell International.

Theoretical Afterthoughts[*]

Jens Kreinath

The aim of these afterthoughts is to outline an analytical matrix of the theoretical issues that were discussed during and after the conference on the dynamics of changing rituals. After first outlining this matrix while primarily taking the theoretical issues into account, these issues are specified subsequently in light of the contributions contained in the present volume.

Distinctions

The topic 'dynamics of changing rituals' may seem paradoxical at first glance since rituals derive much of their authority and power from presenting themselves as unchanging and timeless. Nevertheless, it has become clear that rituals as events in time change constantly in the process of historical time.

This observation gives rise to the general question of how one is to determine the actual degree and modality of ritual change since any modification of a single element or a particular sequence has an effect on the ritual as a whole. Some elements or sequences of rituals apparently may change while the ritual preserves its identity. This means that it is the practitioner or the observer who regards it as remaining the same. On the other hand, a ritual may also change in such a way that it is experienced as being transformed into something else. If rituals change to such an extent, a practitioner or a scholar may ask whether they should still be regarded as the same. One may tentatively distinguish, therefore, between two extreme kinds of ritual change: *modifications* and *transformations*. Modifications are minor changes, which do not affect the identity of the ritual, whereas transformations chal-

[*] I would like to extend my thanks to the participants of this conference for the intensive and fruitful discussions we had. For their lucid critiques and helpful suggestions concerning earlier versions of these afterthoughts, my thanks go to Nils Heeßel, and especially to Jan Snoek and Michael Stausberg. For further comments I would like to thank Don Handelman.

lenge the ritual's identity. To put it differently, a modification is a change *in* ritual, whereas a transformation is a change *of* ritual. There is, however, no sharp boundary between these two kinds; rather, they form the extremes of a wide spectrum of how rituals can possibly change.

Such a distinction between modifications and transformations may only be a first step towards outlining the field of the dynamics of changing rituals, but it already indicates the realm of possibilities within which rituals change. A second step requires that one takes into account the notions of *identity* and *difference* which also form a pair of relative terms that designate two extremes with many shades in between. Because there are no two versions of a ritual or sequences of rituals that are identical without any difference (otherwise, they would not be two versions) and there are no different versions or sequences without any identity as long as the practitioner or observer regard them as part of the same ritual, these terms have to be conceptualized in relation to one another.

This relation between identity and difference should be related to the concept of 'change.' Within the relation of these concepts, change can most likely be specified more precisely as implying a relative position in between, that is,—following the laws of probability—any change in a ritual introduces a difference while maintaining some identity. These modalities of change can be combined with those of modification and transformation. In the case of modification, the practitioner or observer experience the differences as relatively small, while the identity of the ritual is maintained. In the case of ritual transformation, however, they regard its identity as lost and the differences as paramount.

Although the concept of 'change' implies the temporal dimension as an asymmetric relation between at least two events, one also has to consider the velocity of change. The concepts of *continuity* and *discontinuity* may describe this temporal dimension of changing rituals. Continuity occurs when over a long period of time nothing more than slow changes in a ritual take place, whereas discontinuity indicates significant changes of a ritual that take place during a short period of time. The velocity introduces the measurement of ritual change over time. To measure ritual changes by using temporal indices, one must also recognize the frequency with which the ritual in question is actually performed. If one takes these temporal indexes—the frequency of ritual performances as well as the velocity of its change—into account, one can literally talk about the dynamics of changing rituals.

Demarcations

As was already indicated above, rituals might be based on repetition because they present themselves as timeless and unchanging. At first glance, it is plausible to argue that changes in a ritual performance are excluded by means of repetition. But it is likely that the opposite is more often the case, namely, that ritual changes—at least, in the case of the modifications— almost exclusively occur as a result of repetition because changes emerge and may become apparent only on the basis of repetition. One can even argue conversely, though it may be quite difficult to prove, that repetition not only appears on the basis of changes but is also conditioned by it. However, repetition necessarily presupposes the very concept of 'change,' and vice versa. Because of such a correlation between repetition and change at the various levels of ritual, a distinction can be drawn on the basis of the different layers of continuity and discontinuity. Thus repetition refers to the continuity of ritual over time and the various versions of it while also implying a high degree of sameness and a period of time in between. If one speaks about the repetition of a ritual, its identity and continuity are likely to be assumed. By contrast, change refers to the discontinuity and differences in a ritual, which may appear over almost any period of time and may effect the various versions of a ritual. This again implies various degrees of difference that extend from modifications to transformations.

Because slight changes may emerge with every repetition, the question arises of how one is to distinguish between variation and change as asymmetric relations between at least two versions of a ritual. To make such a distinction, these terms have to be defined in relation as well as in contrast to repetition. A variation can be a reversible occurrence, which appears with every repetition without having any further significant consequences for the identity of the ritual. Variations are unavoidable. The differences occurring by variation are not considered as relevant for the identity of a ritual because they are at least to some degree reversible. Such a concept of 'variation' is based on reversibility and identity rather than on irreversibility and difference. Nevertheless, over a long period of time variations may also result unavoidably in ritual changes that might creep in slowly. Change can also be defined conversely. It is an irreversible process that transforms the relevant aspects of a ritual and affects its identity at least to some degree while nevertheless allowing it to be still regarded as the same. In comparison with variation, a changed ritual significantly differs in relation to a former version at earlier points in time. Thus within an asymmetric relation of time between two versions of a ritual, the ritual's change necessarily implies repetition and a lapse of time. This concerns not only the changes *in* rituals but also the changes *of* rituals because transformation necessarily presupposes a previous version. Thus, the notion of 'ritual change' presupposes at least two different versions, which differ significantly and appear as versions of a ritual because of its repetition. Such changes lead to a specific difference that to some degree becomes relevant for the identity of the ritual. If such aspects change, the identity of the ritual is concerned, as it is determined through the differences between the two relevant versions involved.

Specifications

The problem of approaching the dynamics of ritual change can best be specified by means of a distinction between its respective aspects. Ritual change concerns such aspects as function, form, meaning, and performance. Although one aspect may change, other aspects may remain unchanged. Even if the form of ritual remains stable, its meaning may change because of the different interpretations and representations involved. It is likely that some aspects may change over short periods of time, whereas other aspects are more likely to withstand rapid changes. Although the function of a ritual may persist over a long period of time, obvious differences between various performances may already become apparent in quite a short period of time. These aspects of ritual alter or change differently according to the different temporal dimensions of continuity and discontinuity in question. Moreover, they are correlated with the various modalities of ritual change.

As has been seen above, variations and changes are inherent in ritual because they emerge in every performance. Given the fact that every performance is a unique event in itself, changes in rituals can even be produced by different interpretations of the rules concerning how a ritual should be or is actually performed. These changes may again be experienced differently in another performance, resulting in different perceptions and interpretations by the participants. Such different experiences and perceptions may change the ritual by emerging within every performance, or they motivate changes in the prescript for the following performances.

Nevertheless, the notion of 'ritual change' is a question of relevance regarding the various aspects involved, which again depend on the specific genres of ritual action. Some aspects of a ritual may change, but if these aspects are regarded as less relevant for the identity of a ritual, such changes may do not matter from the participant's point of view. In liturgies, for example, with their highly formalized sequences of ritual actions, the meaning for the participants might change without calling into question its identity. The introduction of new forms in healing rituals, which emphasize the performative efficacy of ritual actions, may have almost no effect on the identity of the ritual as long as its efficacy depends on performance and not on form. These examples may again only indicate two extremes of ritual actions.

Over a long period of time, even changes in an irrelevant aspect will have an effect on the ritual as a whole. Because form and meaning are interrelated, changes in form stimulate changes in meaning and conversely, change in meaning will have an effect on change in form as well. Moreover, different performances will have consequences for the function of a ritual, just as by contrast, the change in function will also have an effect on subsequent performances of the ritual. By the shift in or loss of some relevant aspects, the whole ritual transforms radically or may lose its identity as ritual altogether.

Perspectives

Again, to perceive changes and distinguish them from mere variations, one must be familiar with at least more than two versions of the ritual in question. Judgments about the degrees in dynamics of changing rituals take the different viewpoints of participants into account. Practitioners and observers probably perceive and interpret ritual changes differently. A practitioner may see changes that an observer is unlikely to recognize or might interpret them as mere variation, whereas an observer may notice changes a practitioner might overlook. It is even apparent that the perception and interpretation of ritual changes differs to a certain degree between different participants or observers. Here the differentiation and de-differentiation between various emic and etic perspectives come into play.

As regards the plurality of perception and interpretation, a further problem should be mentioned, namely, whether one has to differentiate between changes of which participants are aware or unaware. Actual changes in ritual may take place rapidly or creep in slowly. Practitioners probably recognize rapid changes more easily, whereas slower changes are more likely to be exposed by the analysis of an observer. The recognition of changes in ritual also depends on the relevance of the difference and whether one places more emphasis on the differences than on the similarities between the various performances and versions involved.

Changes are intended or unintended by the practitioner. It is more likely that changes that creep in slowly are unintended, whereas rapid changes are intended. Unintended ritual changes in short periods of time are also possible, though they are less probable. However, changes that take place over a long period of time are unlikely to be intended. The scholarly observer participating in ritual performances may recognize intended rather than unintended changes because the practitioner probably makes intended changes more explicit than unintended changes. In order to distinguish between these changes, one has to consider a practitioner's intentions concerning a particular ritual in relation to the actual changes since unintended changes can only be perceived subsequent to a ritual performance and only in contrast to the changes that formerly were intended. The difference between acceptable and desirable or suitable and tolerable changes must also be taken into account.

Moreover, one may need to distinguish whether specific changes in ritual originate inside or outside the ritual. Even if rituals change as a result of given circumstances—such as, for example, social relations and environments, political coalitions and conditions, or cultural styles and habits—it is still possible for changes to arise inside the ritual due to the very dynamics of its form and performance. Because of its efficacy with regard to function and meaning, a ritual may become an agent for modifying or transforming the ritual's various social, political, and cultural contexts.

Therefore, one has to recognize that some practitioners may consciously and deliberately make use of all these changes for their personal or collective interests in and strategies for transforming or modifying social relations, political coalitions, or cultural styles. Whether or not a change in ritual practice takes place also depends on the specific interests and strategies of varying agents and protagonists in promoting or preventing changes. Although some changes are intended, forced, or required, the recognition of as well as the interest behind them will change inadvertently over time.

Approaches

For the purpose of current scholarly research, it is necessary to distinguish rituals tentatively from other forms of social action. The concept of 'framing' is helpful for making such distinctions more apparent. Setting the ritual apart from its various contexts by means of framing leads to such meta-communicative distinctions for the participants as inside and outside, as well as inclusion and exclusion. These distinctions are useful insofar as they indicate and adduce that a ritual is something different from related forms of social action. Because of their meta-communicative framing, rituals differ to certain degrees, for example, from play, game, sport, fight, rally, rebellion, or war and from opera, dance, ballet, circus, festivals, folklore, celebration, parade, or theater. It is likely that this framing also holds for participants, the practitioner as well as the observer. However, even if rituals as 'texts' are set apart from their related 'contexts' by a dynamic concept of 'framing,' it is by contrast, necessary to place such a text back into its context as far as the question of the dynamics of changing rituals is concerned, because the notion of 'dynamics' has to take the interrelationship between the 'texts' and 'contexts' of changing rituals into account.

Approaches that intend to analyze ritual changes adequately on the basis of the dynamic concept of 'framing' have to take into consideration that changes emerge both from inside and outside the ritual. The origin and emergence as well as the contingency and agency of change in the dynamics of ritual performances cannot exactly be determined or distinguished. Because ritual changes emerge from inside and from outside and the various components necessarily overlap, clear-cut distinctions of commonly used conceptions have to be placed in question. Therefore, the dynamics of changing rituals demonstrate that even such distinctions as 'text' and 'context,' 'inside' and 'outside,' or 'ritual' and 'non-ritual' are relational with regard to the concept of 'framing' one uses and are relative to the concepts in use and the empirical data under consideration.

The empirical basis for the analysis of changing rituals is the perception and interpretation of rituals within their different social, political, and cultural contexts by scholarly observers. Such perceptions and interpretations of ritual also change over time due to the concepts in use and the discourses addressed. Because the rituals themselves as well as their perception and interpretation change, the analytical concepts for describing them and the scholarly discourse change, respectively. Thus, the analysis of the dynamics of changing rituals involves not only a transfer between different texts and contexts, but also a transfer of these events and their changes into the analytical and conceptual framework of the scholarly discourse. Such etic or emic points of view are, of course, not independent of the social and political as well as cultural and historical contexts within which they emerge, persist, and vanish.

In the forgoing it has become clear that the notion of 'dynamics' alludes to such different aspects as ability and power, emergence and agency, as well as capability and strength. Thus the dynamics of changing rituals point to the realm of possibilities within which rituals probably may or actually do change. Because such a realm can be specified only by means of empirical data, the contributors to this volume have tried to specify the possibilities within this realm of changing rituals. This necessarily requires a significant and characteristic selection of case studies for determining the large variety of changing rituals within the spectrum of their dynamics.

Challenging Basic Assumptions

To consider the dynamics of changing rituals, it seems rewarding to open up and specify this field by a diversity of approaches. Moreover, it is worthwhile to take a closer look at particular changes as they appear during different periods of historical time in different societies and cultures as presented by the papers in this volume.

To elaborate a more adequate concept of 'ritual change,' it is necessary to question common theoretical and methodological assumptions of scholarly discourse. For example, universal validity claims for the analysis of ritual change have to be taken into account, as well as the concepts and approaches one uses in order to make such validity claims (see Handelman, Fernandez, Schröter, Stausberg, and Platvoet). Social and cultural background of the basic theoretical assumptions and guiding principles in the analysis of ritual change cannot deny or escape the Western contexts and traditions in which they emerge (see Platvoet). Rituals may change the social, political and cultural reality because of the impact they have, but scholarly research on ritual may also change ritual practice (see Stausberg). This aspect of the dynamics of changing rituals has to be recognized and reconsidered in the analysis and comparison of rituals of different societies (see Schröter). One also must acknowledge the different resonance of ritual practice with Western traditions (see Rein, Henn, and Schröter).

As indicated above, it is important to distinguish rituals from other forms of social action in order to study them as 'rituals.' Although the concept of 'framing' helps to make the first requisite and tentative distinctions, this concept also must account for the fact that rituals—their practice and performance—change all the time. Hierarchical framing by which the form determines the performance is not suitable for the analysis of dynamics of changing rituals because it categorically neglects the emergence of slight changes as they appear and are negotiated within every performance. Such a notion entails or rather implies a dichotomy of static distinctions that cannot aid in the description of minimal variations and slight changes that emerge in every version of a ritual performance (see Handelman, Fernandez, and Köpping). Relational distinctions of asymmetric and dynamic concepts such as 'planfulness' and 'playfulness' or 'moebius framing' can make the concept of 'ritual framing' more precise and—at the same time—Western dichotomies fuzzier (see Fernandez and Handelman). Therefore, besides ritual practice, one also needs to take into account the issues of discourse that arise inside and outside ritual. Moreover, one has to recognize the consequences of discourse for the performance of rituals in promoting or preventing strategies to cope with the dynamics of changing rituals (see Guibbory, Köpping, Henn, Gaenszle, and Weber).

An alternative approach to the same problem would be to analyze rituals as forms of discourse and social action. Actual performances may have such inherent dynamics that they lead to unpredictable and irreversible consequences for the participants involved (see Köpping, Schröter, and Fernandez). Although the actors may have planned a performance otherwise than it turned out, it is possible that they also negotiate their ritual practice before, during or after the ritual performance (see Fernandez, Köpping, Weber, and Platvoet). Ritual performances can be perceived and interpreted as a commentary on social reality by introducing the protagonist or recipient point of view by reconstructing the historical and contextual semantics of the ritual's performative enactment as an inherent dynamic of its performance (see Fernandez, Schröter, Henn, Köpping, Guibbory, and Furley).

Rituals and Social Order
Although the dynamics of changing rituals are inherent in every ritual performance, changes also emerge through their interference with the social environments, political conditions, or cultural habits. Rituals can be perceived as preserving the continuity of social and political order by temporally inverting it and thereby resolving social and political conflicts in rituals of rebellion (see Fernandez and Schröter). They also may undergo abrupt transformations if the social reality changes rapidly. Rituals may change unintentionally because of their inevitable interplay with the social, political, and cultural reality. They may also change radically, even though they were intended to stabilize hierarchical structures or power relations by resolving or suppressing the conflicts of social relations (see Schröter, Guibbory, and Weber). Ritual changes are unavoidable because every form of social action intervenes with its various contexts and leads to unintended consequences. Although the intention for continuity or discontinuity may matter, the dynamics of changing rituals are already given by their interplay with the various contexts of social reality (see Fernandez, Schröter, Guibbory, Henn, Weber, and Furley).

The interplay between rituals and social reality implies that rituals may also be modified or invented because of the changes of social reality (see Odenthal, Jung, and Stausberg). The change in rituals can also induce religious and political changes if the practitioners of a ritual community introduce different interpretations or actually transform the meaning of a particular ritual (see Guibbory, Rein, Henn, Abusch, Odenthal, and Jung). Rituals may radically change because their political and social implications were utilized for the construction of social and political identity (see Guibbory, Weber, Furley, and Platvoet). Because rituals can aid in constructing a community, the connection between ritual and community can become so close that an intended change of ritual form would place the identity not only of the ritual but also of the community in question (see Guibbory and Schröter). The particular purposes that practitioners of a ritual seek to accomplish can correspond to the respective social and political conditions of its practice and thus may change the ritual accordingly (see Köpping, Weber, Stausberg, and Platvoet).

Political Power and Ritual Places
If rituals become the focus of religious or political interests, the ritual practice turns out to be a central issue of negotiation since its meaning shifts significantly. Apart from changes of ritual that are politically or ideologically motivated, rituals can become an instrument for inducing political coalitions by means of its signifying and communicative function (see Guibbory, Henn, Furley, and Platvoet). Rituals can function as political instruments of administration if the practice of worship suits the ideals of the political leader (see Furley). As protagonists or agents of changing rituals, religious and political leaders are capable of projecting suitable images of themselves against others by using rituals as their instruments (see Guibbory, Furley, and Köpping). The demarcations of the political coalitions as signified and communicated by the participation in a particular ritual enable the protagonists to define the identity of a community by means of the prevalent ritual practice. If rituals function to construct political coalitions by raising clear-cut boundaries of insiders and outsiders, the ritual's meaning changes insofar as it then becomes a statement of conviction and loyalty. If rituals were to become an instrument of the ruling class, the participation in such rituals has the connotation of a political statement as well (see Furley, Guibbory, Henn, and Schröter).

A change in the meaning of a ritual occurs when it indicates the demarcation of political interests. The meanings of ritual places in which political interests become manifest may also play an important role in the dynamic change of rituals. Ritual places often become platforms on which competing groups negotiate their power relations by claiming to have a historical privilege in order to legitimize their authority and power (see Weber, Furley, and Platvoet). Ritual places can indicate ritual change insofar as they are places for negotiating power relations, since rituals have to be performed at distinct places. If rituals adduce and signify distinct meanings, the meaning and role of cult-centers change according to the differing interests of competing groups and the legitimization of political power. Moreover, the shifts in meaning of the ritual places may also change the religious identity of the people (see Weber). The question is to what degree the validity claims as negotiated by the various protagonists give rise to intended or unintended changes in ritual practice. A further question is what the role rituals and ritual changes play in the negotiation of power relations (see Schröter, Guibbory, Henn, and Platvoet).

Cultural Attitudes and Religious Worldviews

The validity of a ritual practice can be seen as a process of negotiating different interpretations and modes of perceptions. It is possible that the validity of a ritual's practice may be habitually established in a long-term process of a religious tradition without being intended by a particular group of protagonists. Even though rituals may remain formally the same in their sequence and pattern of performance, different interpretations or modes of perception can emerge or be adapted that change the attitude towards a ritual practice (see Ebrey, Abusch, and Jung). Long-term changes in ritual are likely to appear according to durable and dominant religious worldviews. If a new interpretation of a ritual practice is established, its meaning and validity may bring about changes in ritual practice (see Henn and Odenthal). If different modes of perceiving ritual practice are informed by different worldviews, they can be explained as changes in habit and attitude without being intended by the particular practitioners (see Ebrey). Rituals may also change due to diverging meanings gradually being ascribed to the ritual practice by the practitioner (see Rein and Henn).

Cultural habits as embodied in a ritual practice can change through a shift in the aesthetic attitudes towards a religious tradition or in the modes of perception. Those shifts might emerge through slow or rapid changes in the prevailing religious and cultural conditions and the respective tendency to use different media of representation (see Ebrey and Thomas). Because cultural habits change slowly, they do not necessarily change as a result of active efforts of ritual actions but as a consequence of a long-lasting sedimentation of ritual practices. Moreover, a change in rituals may depend on unconscious changes in the modes of perception. Such changes in ritual practice creep in slowly and are observable only over long periods of time. Because changes in cultural habits are not reflexive and conscious, it is most likely that a scholarly observer who is capable and in the privileged position of using a wide range of historical documents is able to perceive these changes in ritual practices (see Abusch, Ebrey, Guibbory, Köpping, and Henn).

Transmission and Ritual Competence

Apart from the sedimentation of aesthetic attitudes and embodied habits, the transmission of ritual competence is crucial for the persistence of ritual traditions. Within the processes of transmission, ritual traditions may change over a period of time, even if various participants of a particular period of time may seek to maintain the identity of their tradition by interpreting changes that creep in slowly as variation (see Gaenszle, Rein, Stausberg, and Odenthal). Although practitioners may develop their own style of performance in order to emphasize their authority and power, the identity of a ritual tradition might be guaranteed by the religious, social, and cultural norms that minimize or limit the possible changes within the ritual practice (see Gaenszle, Weber and Stausberg).

Ritual practitioner may virtually recite or recreate their ritual texts in every performance by communicating their tradition or interacting with their ancestors (see Gaenszle). Although variations by the practitioner within a series of performances may be acceptable, the process of transmitting ritual competence transforms or modifies rituals due to different modes of ritual transmission. However, religious norms keep the perception of possible changes within limits (see Stausberg and Gaenszle). From the performer's point of view, the changes in ritual practice are likely to be legitimized or even to be suppressed if they guarantee the persistence of a ritual tradition (see Odenthal and Stausberg). Although a scholarly observer might interpret the changes of ritual practice as an unintended outcome of the process of transmitting ritual traditions, such effects might be perceived from the performer's point of view as variations by means of which a ritual performance becomes persuasive (see Gaenszle and Henn).

Cultural Contact and Ritual Infrastructure

Besides the changes in ritual traditions as they appear in the transmission of rituals, the meaning communicated in ritual performances may change by fusing rituals with other religious traditions (see Henn). Because of cultural contact and the shift in the communicative context the meaning of a ritual inevitably changes (see Rein and Stausberg). If, for example, participants have to keep the meaning of some elements or sequences within a ritual performance secret in order to resist the control of religious or political authorities or the process of transformation, the meanings communicated by this ritual are only accessible to the initiated participants (see Henn, Rein, and

Fernandez). The meaning communicated in a ritual undergoes modifications or transformations in accordance with the traditions that are amalgamated or adapted within a ritual performance (see Henn and Stausberg). The meaning ascribed to a ritual performance may even differ according to the various points of view (see Köpping and Rein). A scholarly observer is likely to overlook the fusion in ritual performances by focusing exclusively on different traditions that are undifferentiated within the participants' point of view (see Henn and Gaenszle).

The situation of cultural contact initiates a shift within the meaning of religious tradition. It is possible that the conditions of cultural contact arising through migration and a transfer of ritual traditions to a different context may change ritual practice (Rein and Stausberg). Changes in ritual habits, the invention of new rituals, and change in performance style are not independent of the religious infrastructure as given by the transfer into different contexts (see Stausberg and Henn). Members of a community might be forced to reinterpret their ritual or invent new rituals in order to obey the commandment of ritual purity (see Rein and Stausberg). In the light of contextual demands, a religious community may transform its traditional rituals in order to preserve their religious identity within the process of cultural assimilation (see Henn and Stausberg).

Modernization and Plural Societies
The change in context may have an effect not only on the meaning of a ritual but also on the organization and form of ritual practice. Due to the shift in context, the interplay between ritual actors and their audience may change the ritual practice insofar as the actors organize the performance of a ritual in such a way that they try to fulfill the expectations of an audience (see Rein and Henn). Though forms and gestures may still remain the same, a ritual can change according to new practical, organizational, or strategic demands that arise outside the ritual frame (see Stausberg and Rein). These demands may correspond to the emergence of individualistic lifestyles, tourism, and national identity (see Jung, Rein, Guibbory, and Furley). Though the form and choreography of a ritual performance may be regarded as still the same expression of the ritual meaning at least from the practitioner's point of view, the organizational features, the setting of the audience frame, as well as the individualistic attitudes towards the performance may have changed in such a way that its identity or efficacy must be placed in question (see Rein and Köpping).

The dynamics inherent in plural societies cause unintended and irreversible changes in the meaning and performance of religious rituals. The practitioners can become protagonists of ritual change only insofar as they appropriate and consciously make use of the dynamics of such conditions. The introduction of a new interpretation reflecting the dynamics of pluralism in modern societies may change the form of the ritual script and subsequently change the ritual performance as well (see Jung and Odenthal) or may lead to the invention of new rituals (see Stausberg). Ritual traditions can be maintained or invented although the meaning and function ascribed to it may differ radically. The changes in ritual script may be conceived as threatening the identity of a ritual tradition, but such changes also may simultaneously be regarded as the strength of a ritual tradition that it entails the capacity for change or for remaining constant (see Odenthal and Thomas). The various interpretations of ritual changes and the invention of new rituals practices can be regarded as the result of the different ways of dealing with the plurality of participants' expectations (see Stausberg, Henn, Jung, and Rein). If a community suppresses or neglects the possibility of ritual change in favor of even a long-lived tradition, the ritual can become meaningless for the participants. They are likely to place the meaning of a ritual performance into question if they can no longer relate their religious experience to the meaning attached to a ritual tradition (see Jung and Stausberg).

Media, Meta-Communication, and Performance
Not merely the change in the ritual script or its meaning but also the invention of different media for the communication and perception of a ritual performance can have an effect on the ritual's identity. This also counts for the processes of acquiring ritual competence, as well as for the bodily memory of ritual traditions. The processes of transmitting ritual competence may differ with respect to the media of the respective ritual instructions of a ritual script, regardless of whether they are transmitted in an oral or a written form (see Fernandez, Henn, Weber, and Stausberg). There is also a difference whether the respective traditions are transmitted through the practice of ritual or through writing (see Gaenszle and Harth). Moreover, the modes of perception and communication of ritual practice obviously differ between oral, written, and visual media in the process of transmission. The change of media may even change the performance of a ritual to such an extent that they can transform the ritual practice (see Ebrey and Thomas). Despite the fact that there still exists a difference in terms of agency and reception between actors and audience, similar to participant and observer, within a medium such as television, the mode of participation and reception radically changes since the participants cannot be bodily present with one another (see Thomas). However, in this case bodily presence might not be crucial for the ritual

community insofar as it simulates a type of presence that substitutes the pre-requisite of bodily presence (see Thomas in contrast to Guibbory, Henn, and Furley). Even though the efficacy of the ritual performance may change, the visual media are capable of stimulating a virtual presence by a constant oscil-lation between perception and virtual communication, so that these media can be seen as a seductive play within the various frames of reference (see Thomas).

As mentioned above, the framing of ritual is important for considering ritual as a particular form of social action. This tentative assumption becomes relevant for the comparison of the various genres of social action such as theater, play, dance and ritual as different forms of social action with their respective modalities of framing and reflexivity. The meta-communicative framing might not only count for the meaning communicated in a ritual, thea-ter, or dance, but it is also important for the efficacy of a performance as far as the participants are concerned. This is also valid for the performances of ritual, theater, and dance because actors and their audiences may interact differently inside such meta-communicative frames from outside (see Han-delman, Harth, Rein, Köpping, and Thomas). The theatrical or ritual qualities of performance are fragile and risky because a performance can fail if the audience does not understand the meta-communicative frame intended by the actor or the actor does not recognize the resonance of the audience (regarding the risk of performance and the recognition of the audience, compare Köp-ping, Fernandez, Handelman, and Thomas with Rein, Gaenszle, and Henn). Moreover, the success of an interaction between actors and their audience depends among other things on how a performance is meta-communicatively framed (see Handelman, Harth, Rein, Henn, and Thomas).

Apart from the failure or success of a ritual performance as an emergent and effective interaction among the ritual's participants, one might place the differences between theater and ritual at least from the observer's point of view into question (see Harth, Rein, Köpping, and Henn). An actor, practi-tioner, or scriptwriter might consciously use the similarities between ritual and theater performances and might play with the expectations of the audi-ence by transforming a theater performance into a ritual or a ritual perform-ance into a theater performance while using various forms of communication and meta-communication (see Harth, Köpping, Rein, and Thomas). The staged performance of carnival, theater, or dance might be distinguished from a ritual performance by the different forms of framing (see Fernandez, Harth, Rein, and Köpping). The interaction between actors and audience in the interplay of the frames of ritual and theatrical performances might have the capacity to transform a ritual performance into something else. The interplay of ritual performances and other forms of social action can be regarded as a significant issue of the dynamics of changing rituals. This can even be interpreted from a reflexive perspective as an adventure of the Western scholars approaching the dynamics of changing rituals in different times and places (see Platvoet).

Implications and Consequences

The foregoing theoretical afterthoughts suggest that scholars from different disciplines and academic traditions focus on specific aspects within the dynamics of changing rituals due to the distinct theoretical approaches they use and the respective methods they apply to the empirical material under consideration. Such diversity may challenge the boundaries within the growing field of ritual studies and subsequently set new standards in the research of rituals. Theoretical approaches concerned with issues related to the dynamics of changing rituals should be based on a highly diversified range of case studies in order to grasp the realm of possibilities within which rituals may change. Much of methodological problems addressed in our discussions were initiated and elaborated by the contributions to this volume focusing on the problem how to bridge the boundaries between different disciplinary approaches.

Moreover, an unexpected side-effect of this is that different concepts of 'time' and 'temporality' as well as 'change' and 'dynamics' are used or presupposed with regard to the analysis of the dynamics of changing rituals. Since researchers of ritual investigate various issues based on different material while using different methods, the question is how do different temporal models of time, change, and dynamics impact on the methods used for approaching the dynamics of changing rituals. Different analytical concepts are likely to influence the modalities of how one investigates the empirical material in question. As a result, the exploration of the dynamics of changing rituals raises new questions and may also change the way one looks at rituals themselves constantly change. These issues discussed during and after our conference prove to be quite fruitful because the diversity of contributions provokes and opens up new questions and forces one to develop new perspectives on theoretical issues concerning the dynamics of constantly changing rituals.

Notes on Contributors

Tzvi Abusch is Rose B. and Joseph Cohen Professor of Assyriology and Ancient Near Eastern Religion at Brandeis University. He received his Ph.D. in Assyriology from Harvard University. He has taught at the Jewish Theological Seminary of America and The Hebrew University of Jerusalem and has held a number of awards and fellowships. At present (2003-2004), he is a Member of the Institute for Advanced Study at Princeton. His primary fields of research and publication are Mesopotamian religion, magic, and literature. Most recently, he published a book on *Mesopotamian Witchcraft: Towards a History and Understanding of Babylonian Witchcraft Beliefs and Literature* (2002).
e-mail: abusch@binah.cc.brandeis.edu

Patricia B. Ebrey is Professor of History at the University of Washington. Her research has focused on the social and cultural history of Han through Song period China, especially topics concerning class, family, gender, ritual, and visual culture. Among her books are *Confucianism and Family Rituals in Imperial China: A Social History of Writing About Rites* (1991), *The Inner Quarters: Marriage and the Lives of Chinese Women in the Sung Period* (1993), and *The Cambridge Illustrated History of China* (1996). She is editor or coeditor of several volumes, including *Religion in T'ang and Sung China* (1993) and *Culture and Power in the Reconstitution of the Chinese Realm, 200-600* (2001). She is currently working on the Song emperor Huizong and the cultural politics of his court.
e-mail: aguibbor@uiuc.edu

James W. Fernandez is Professor Emeritus of Anthropology at the University of Chicago. He has conducted field research over many decades in three parts of Africa; Equatorial among Fang, Souteastern among Zulu, and Guinea Coast among Ewe and Fon. In recent years he has been working in Northern Spain among Asturians on Asturian language and culture. Most recently, in company with his long term interest in trope theory, he has edited with Mary T. Huber, *Irony in Action: Anthropology, Practice and the Moral Imagination* (2002).
e-mail: jwfl@midway.uchicago.edu

William D. Furley studied Classics at University College London where he graduated with first class honours in 1975. A year of study abroad at Tübingen University was followed by a Ph.D. in Classics (Ancient Greek) at Trinity College, Cambridge (supervisor Geoffrey S. Kirk). A first appointment as assistant professor at Heidelberg University in 1980 was followed by appointment to a permanent position as Akademischer Rat, also at the dept. of Classics, Heidelberg. He received his Habilitation in 1989, and was awarded the title of Ausserplanmässiger Professor in 2002. His most important publications are *Studies in the Use of Fire in Ancient Greek Religion* (1980); *Andokides and the Herms: a study of crisis in fifth-century Athenian Religion* (1996); and co-edited *Greek Hymns. Selected Cult Songs from the Archaic to the Hellenistic Period* (2001). He has written numerous articles on (mainly) Greek literature and religion.
e-mail: william.furley@urz.uni-heidelberg.de

Martin Gaenszle received his Ph.D. from Heidelberg University (1989) and teaches there in the Department of Anthropology at the South Asia Institute. He has done extensive fieldwork on social processes, ethnic identity, religion, and oral traditions in Eastern Nepal (since 1984), and has recently conducted research on the Nepali community in Benares, India. His latest book publications include *Origins and Migrations: Kinship, Mythology and Ethnic Identity among the Mewahang Rai* (2000), and *Ancestral Voices: Oral Ritual Texts and their Social Contexts among the Mewahang Rai of East Nepal* (2002). He also co-edited *Himalayan Space: Cultural Horizons and Practices* (1999).
e-mail: martin.gaenszle@urz.uni-heidelberg.de

Achsah Guibbory is Professor of English and Religious Studies at the University of Illinois, Urbana-Champaign. She is the author of *The Map of Time* (University of Illinois Press, 1986) and *Ceremony and Community: Literature, Religion, and Cultural Conflict in Seventeenth-Century England* (1998). She has also published numerous scholarly essays on John Donne and other seventeenth-century writers, and is currently writing a book on the uses of Judaism in early modern England.
e-mail: aguibbor@uiuc.edu

Don Handelman is Shaine Professor of Anthropology, in the Department of Sociology and Anthropology, The Hebrew University of Jerusalem. He received his Ph.D. in Social Anthropology from the University of Manchester in 1971. His publications include, *Models and Mirrors: Towards an Anthropology of Public Events* (1998), with David Shulman, *God Inside Out: Siva's Game of Dice* (1997), *Nationalism and the Israeli State: Bureaucratic Logic in Public Events* (forthcoming), with David Shulman, *Siva in the Forest of Pines: An Essay on Sorcery and Self Knowledge* (forthcoming).
e-mail: mshand@mscc.huji.ac.il

Dietrich Harth was educated at universities in Frankfurt am Main and Tübingen studying German Literature, Classics and Sociology. After his Habilitation at the University of Erlangen he was appointed professor of German Literature at Heidelberg University where he, until he retired from teaching in 2000. He is a member of the Executive Committee of the interdisciplinary research project Ritual Dynamics (Sonderforschungsbereich 619) located at Heidelberg University. His main research topics include theory of literature and ritual, cultural anthropology and memory, and the history of European historiography. Among his book publications are *Die Erfindung des Gedächtnisses* (1991), *Gotthold Ephraim Lessing oder Die Paradoxien der Selbsterkenntnis* (1993), *Das Gedächtnis der Kulturwissenschaften* (1998), and *Dimensionen kultureller und ästhetischer Differenz* (2003). He is editor of *Fiktion des Fremden. Erkundung kultureller Grenzen in Literatur und Publizistik* (1994), and co-editor of *Kultur und Konflikt* (1990), *Mnemosyne. Formen und Funktionen der kulturellen Erinnerung* (1991), *Kultur als Lebenswelt und Monument* (1991), and *Revolution und Mythos* (1992).
e-mail: HarthDiet@AOL.COM

Alexander Henn achieved his Ph.D. in anthropology at the University of Mainz in 1987, and completed his habilitation (second degree of higher learning) at the University of Heidelberg in 2000. Among his publications are: *Reisen in vergangene Gegenwart*, a reflexive critique of 19th Century anthropology and philosophy (1988), *Wachheit der Wesen*, a study of the politics, rituals and arts of acculturation in Goa (2003), and numerous articles. After holding

positions as assistant professor at the South Asia Institute in Heidelberg and associate professor at the Institute of Ethnology in Mainz, Henn works at present as a research fellow at the Institute of Ethnology in Heidelberg. Together with Klaus-Peter Koepping he co-ordinates an international research project funded by the German Volkswagen Foundation on processes of identity formation in hybrid spaces in India and Japan.
e-mail: a.Henn@urz.uni-hd.de

Matthias Jung studied philosophy and theology in Frankfurt/Main, where he also finished his dissertation about Heidegger. After his habilitation on "experience and religion", he went to the Technical University of Chemnitz, where he currently teaches philosophy with the focus on ethics. In 2003, he spent the spring term as a visiting professor at Emory University. Atlanta, USA. His main areas of research are: hermeneutics, pragmatism, philosophy of religion and the anthropological foundations of ethics. His major publications are *Das Denken des Seins und der Glaube an Gott. Zum Verhältnis von Philosophie und Theologie im Denken Martin* (1990), *Dilthey zur Einführung* (1997), *Erfahrung und Religion. Grundzüge einer hermeneutisch-pragmatischen Religionsphilosophie* (1999), and *Hermeneutik zur Einführung* (2001).
e-mail: matjung@t-online.de

Klaus-Peter Koepping is currently Professor of Anthropology at the University of Heidelberg (since 1991) and in charge of a project on "ritual and identity" funded by the German Science Foundation as well as a project on "cultural hybridity" funded by the VW Foundation. Previous appointment to the Baldwin Spencer Foundation Chair of Anthropology at the University of Melbourne, Australia (1985-1991), after having taught at the University of Queensland, Brisbane (1972-1984) and at various other universities in Japan, the USA and in the Philippines. His main research focus is on Modernization and Messianic Religious Movements, on Anthropological Theory and most recently on Performance Theory, Embodiment and Ritual with various field studies in Japan (since 1966), the Philippines, Afghanistan and in Australia among Aborigines and German migrants. His main book publications are *Adolf Bastian and the Psychic Unity of Mankind* (1983) and *Shattering Frames: Transgressions and Transformations in Anthropological Discourse and Practice* (2002). He is editor of *The Games of Gods and Man, Essays in Play and Performance* (1997).
e-mail: Klaus.Peter.Koepping@urz.uni-heidelberg.de

Jens Kreinath studied theology, philosophy, *Religionswissenschaft*, and social and cultural anthropology at the University of Heidelberg and at Connecticut College. His doctoral thesis is on *The History and Method of the Phenomenology of Religion*, in which he undertakes a historical discourse analysis of a paradigm in the history of *Religionswissenschaft* exemplified by Pierre Daniël Chantepie de la Saussaye, Willem Brede Kristensen, and Gerardus van der Leeuw. Currently, he is member of a junior research group on 'Ritual Theory and the History of Religions' and is consulting member of the interdisciplinary research project 'Ritual Dynamics' at the University of Heidelberg. He is co-editor (with Jan Snoek and Michael Stausberg) of *Theorizing Rituals: Classical Topics, Theoretical Approaches, Analytical Concepts, Annotated Bibliography* (forthcoming). His main fields of research are metatheory, methodology, history of scholarly research, semiotics, discourse analysis, and performance theory.
e-mail: Jens.Kreinath@urz.uni-heidelberg.de

Andreas Odenthal studied Catholic theology, philosophy, Germanistik and pedagogic at the universities of Freiburg i.Br. and Bonn. After he received his Diploma in 1987 and his civil service he finished his Ph.D. in 1994 with a dissertation in liturgical studies at Bonn university. In 1996 he was ordained as a priest at the Dom zu Köln. During his service as a Kaplan in Ratingen, Düsseldorf, he wrote his habilitation at Bonn university. Since 2002 he is professor for liturgical studies at the Theological Faculty in Fulda. His various publications document his research intersts in the history of liturgy of medieval times as well as his interest in the interdisciplinary dialog between theology and psychoanalysis with a special focus on rituals. Since 1995 he is member of the *Gesellschaft für Psychoanalyse und Psychotherapie*.
e-mail: 113404.636@compuserve.com

Jan G. Platvoet received his Ph.D. at Utrecht University with a thesis on *Comparing Religions: A Limitative Approach; An Analysis od Akan, Para-Creole, and IFO-Sananda Rites and Prayers* (1982). He taught Science of Religions at the Utrecht Roman Catholic College of Divinity and the Faculty of Theology of Utrecht University (1969–1991) and served as Senior Lecturer in the Comparative Study of Religions at the Faculty of Theology of Leiden University (1990–2000). His publications are mainly on indigenous religions of Africa and on the development of the academic study of religions in African Universities, on spirit possession and 'ritual studies', and on the history and methodology of Science of Religions. He was Vice-President of the African Association for the Study of Religions (1995–2000), and is co-editor of the AASR-Newsletter. He co-edited *Pluralism and Identity: Studies in Ritual Behaviour* (1995); *The Study of Religions in Africa: Past, Present and Prospects* (1996); *The Pragmatics of Defining Religion: Contexts, Concepts and Contests* (1999).
e-mail: jgplatvoet@wxs.nl

Anette Rein studied Social Anthropology, Pedagogic, and *Altamerikanistik* at the Freie Universität Berlin (M.A. 1984). She did field research in Bali (Indonesia) on traditional Balinese dances (1985–1987) and worked as an assistant at the *Institut für Ethnologie* und *Afrika-Studien*, University of Mainz (1988–1994) and received her Ph.D. in 1994. She taught as a short time professor at the Universitas Nusa Cendana in Kupang, Timor, Indonesia (1994) and worked as an assistant professor at the *Institut für Ethnologie* in Leipzig (1995–2000). Since April 2000 she is the acting director of the *Museum der Weltkulturen*, Frankfurt a.M. (Museum of World Cultures) and teaches at the universities of Frankfurt and Mainz. Her scientific work is focused on Indonesian traditions esp. on traditional dances, worldviews, religions, gender, ritual theories and material culture. She is author of *Tempeltanz auf Bali: Rejang - der Tanz der Reisseelen* (1994).
e-mail: Anette.Rein@stadt-frankfurt.de

Susanne Schröter completed her Ph.D. at the University of Mainz in 1993 and her Habilitation at the University of Frankfurt in 1999. She taught anthropology and gender studies on various visiting appointments as guest professor in Mainz (1999), Yale (2000), Frankfurt (2001/2002) and Trier (2004). She is doing fieldwork in Indonesia since 1994 and is currently working in a research project on the indigenization of Catholicism in Indonesia. Her research interests cover the complex of religious discourses and practices in the postcolonial era, gender ambivalence and the ritual construction of masculinity.
e-mail: suSchroet@aol.com

Michael Stausberg received his Ph.D. from the University of Bonn in 1995. He is Docent of Religionshistoria at Uppsala University and Privatdozent of Religionswissenschaft at the University of Heidelberg and taught at the universities of Uppsala, Heidelberg, Tübingen, and Bern. Currently, he is acting as the head of a junior research-group at the University of Heidelberg (Institut für Religionswissenschaft). His main fields of interest are European religious history, Zoroastrianism, and (ritual) theory. His books include *Faszination Zarathushtra* (2 vols., 1998), and *Die Religion Zarathushtras* (3 vols., 2002-2003). He is the editor of *Kontinuitäten und Brüche in der Religionsgeschichte* (2001), *Zoroastrian Rituals in Context* (2003), and co-editor of *Studies in Religious Iconography and Iconology* (1998), *Riter och ritteorier* (2002) and *Theorizing Rituals* (2004).
e-mail: Michael.Stausberg@urz.uni-heidelberg.de

Günter Thomas received his Ph.D. in Protestant Theology from the University of Heidelberg in 1996 and his Ph.D. in Sociology from the University of Tübingen in 1999. He teaches at the Faculty of Protestant Theology in Heidelberg. His publications include: *Medien–Ritual–Religion. Zur religiösen Funktion des Fernsehens* (1998) and *Implizite Religion. Theoriegeschichtliche und theoretische Untersuchungen* (2001). He is editor of *Religiöse Funktionen des Fernsehens? Medien-, kultur- und religionswissenschaftliche Perspektiven* (2000). His main fields of research are Systematic Theology of the twentieth Century, Sociology of Religion and the intersection of Media Theory and Ritual Studies.
e-mail: Guenter.Thomas@urz.uni-heidelberg.de

Peter Weber has obtained his Ph.D. in Anthropology from the University of Freiburg, Germany. He has conducted extensive fieldwork among the Nyakyusa in southwestern Tanzania. He is the author of *Ritual und Identität* (1998).
e-mail: pweber-0001@t-online.de

TORONTO STUDIES IN RELIGION

Donald Wiebe, General Editor

This series of monographs is designed as a contribution to the scholarly and academic understanding of religion. Such understanding is taken to involve both a descriptive and an explanatory task. The first task is conceived as one of surface description involving the gathering of information about religions, and depth description that provides, on the basis of the data gathered, a more finely nuanced description of a tradition's self-understanding. The second task concerns the search for explanation and the development of theory to account for religion and for particular historical traditions. The series, furthermore, covers the phenomenon of religion in all its constituent dimensions and geographic diversity. Both established and younger scholars in the field have been and will be included to represent a wide range of viewpoints and positions, producing original work of high order at the monograph and major study level.

Although predominantly empirically oriented, the series encourages theoretical studies and even leaves room for creative and empirically controlled philosophical and speculative approaches in the interpretation of religions and religion. Toronto Studies in Religion is of particular interest to those who study the subject at universities and colleges but is also of value to the general educated reader.

For additional information about this series or for the submission of manuscripts, please contact:

Peter Lang Publishing, Inc.
Acquisitions Department
P.O. Box 1246
Bel Air, Maryland 20104-1246

To order other books in this series, please contact our Customer Service Department:

(800) 770-LANG (within the U.S.)
(212) 647-7706 (outside the U.S.)
(212) 647-7707 FAX

or browse online by series at:

WWW.PETERLANGUSA.COM